Library of Congress Cataloging-in-Publication Data:

LaFantasie, Glenn W.
   Twilight at Little Round Top, July 2, 1863 : the tide turns at Gettysburg / Glenn W. LaFantasie.
     p. cm.
   Includes bibliographical references and index.
   ISBN 0-471-46231-4 (cloth : alk. paper)
1. Gettsyburg, Battle of, Gettysburg, Pa., 1863.   I. Title.
E475.53.L24 2005
973.7'349—dc22   2004011820

In loving memory of my father and mother,
Warren Edward and Edith May

Is war perhaps nothing else but a need to face death,
to conquer and master it, to come out of it alive—
a peculiar form of denial of our mortality?

—*Elisabeth Kübler-Ross*

CONTENTS

PREFACE

During the great national conflagration of the Civil War, the contending armies of North and South often sought a common tactical goal in the bloody battles they fought across America: occupy and hold the high ground. The technological development of firearms—especially long-range rifled artillery—over the first half of the nineteenth century meant that such weapons could potentially be the key to victory when deployed on hills and ridges. Napoleon put the maxim well: "In mountain warfare the assailant has always the disadvantage." Civil War soldiers came to learn that charging uphill was not only exhausting, it was usually deadly.

At Gettysburg, several hills figured prominently in the battle and ultimately determined the outcome of the military contest there—Oak Hill, Blocher's (Barlow) Knoll, Benner's Hill, Cemetery Hill, Culp's Hill, Big Round Top, and Little Round Top. Over the years, Little Round Top has acquired a legendary reputation as the place where the Army of the Potomac averted destruction and ensured that the three-day battle would end in a Union victory. That legend has been enhanced in recent years by the rise in popularity of Joshua Lawrence Chamberlain, who has become known as the savior of Little Round Top, largely as a result of his portrayal in Michael Shaara's novel *The Killer Angels* (1974), which won the Pulitzer Prize; Ken Burns's monumental PBS documentary *The Civil War* (1989); and the theatrical movie *Gettysburg* (1993), based on Shaara's novel. While Chamberlain's fame has tended to overshadow the role that other individuals played in attacking and defending the hill, there is no doubt that his renown has served at the same time to spread an awareness of Little Round Top among Civil War enthusiasts and the general public. Little Round Top is now the most visited spot at Gettysburg National Military

Park, and visitors regularly leave tokens of their affection—poems, votive candles, coins, flags—to Chamberlain and his brave men at the base of the marble monument to the 20th Maine Regiment.

But there is more to the Little Round Top story than fiction and legend, glory and remembrance. In the late afternoon of July 2, 1863, thousands of men struggled over this parcel of terrain, many of them giving their lives as they grappled to capture the hill or defend it. Its significance was real enough for those who fought there. To understand the hill's tactical importance, though, we might consider the words of Lieutenant General Antoine-Henri Baron de Jomini, the great French military theorist: "There is in every battlefield a decisive point [i.e., place], the possession of which, more than any other, helps secure the victory, by enabling its holder to make proper application of the principles of war." At Gettysburg, Little Round Top—the eye in the shank of the Union army's famous fishhook line—was one such place.

As the battle on July 2 roared south of the town, both armies determined that the hill was of vital importance to them and to the cause of victory. In the end, the Union triumph on Little Round Top set the stage for the battle that was to be fought on the following day, July 3, because Federal possession of the hill meant that General Robert E. Lee's options for any further attacks against the defensive line of the Army of the Potomac would be, by necessity, severely limited. Having failed to turn the flanks of the Union army that rested on high ground, Lee chose to attack the Federal center on Cemetery Ridge—a doomed assault that would become forever known in American military annals as "Pickett's Charge." In that sense, I would argue that the victory on Little Round Top augured well for the Union's victory at Gettysburg, and that it was the fighting on the second day, not the third, that sealed the fate of the Army of Northern Virginia in its second invasion of the North.

When it is not singling out Chamberlain for magnified praise, the Little Round Top legend also emphasizes how several key officers on both sides, using their quick wits and their formidable courage, shaped the battle on the hill's slopes that summer afternoon; their various decisions, good and bad, brought the contest to a bloody but firm conclusion. Yet the fight for Little Round Top was ultimately determined by the grim-faced, rock-hard soldiers of the line, North and South, who gritted their teeth, braved thunder and flames, and followed their officers' commands as much as human endurance allowed. All told, Little Round Top was a grinding and mangling soldiers' battle. An enlisted man in the 44th New

York Infantry informed his friends at home that the battle had been a soldiers' fight: "The battle of Gettysburg belongs to the rank and file of the Army of the Potomac. The battle was not won by any superior handling of the troops; after our lines were once formed, they stood so. It was by the stubborn bravery of the men that the battle was won for us."

This book tells their stories, officers and enlisted men alike. I have attempted to render, in as many detailed strokes as I can, a picture of who these men were and what they experienced on Little Round Top as the shadows lengthened and as twilight fell on the evening of the second day at Gettysburg. No one, of course, can recapture all that the soldiers saw and felt, or describe the battle as it actually was, for to do so would constitute something as horrific and terrifying as the original battle encompassed in all its ghastly fury.

Nevertheless, the surviving sources for reconstructing the story of Little Round Top are amazingly plentiful and rich (except for the relative paucity of official Confederate papers), and it is possible from these records to describe what it must have been like to fight on that hillside, even if we can never quite grasp the enormity of the personal trauma, fear, and even courage that individual soldiers—from generals down to privates—experienced that day as they wrestled for control of the hill's rocky slopes and summit. Some of those sources, including documents contained among the Oates Family Papers and untapped accounts found in several repositories or in the hands of private collectors, are being used in this book for the first time. Others have been mined specifically for salient facts, new information, and different perspectives—all in the hope of catching, in military historian John Keegan's words, "a glimpse of the face of battle."

There was, as I hope this book shows, no single Union "savior of Little Round Top," just as there was no particular individual in the Confederate command who deserves the blame for failing to capture the hill. Great achievements and terrible mistakes were made by men on both sides who operated in the fog of war and who, at the time, could not know how the clash on Little Round Top would turn out in the end. In writing this narrative, I have tried to keep in mind what historians today like to call "contingency," but what social scientists as long ago as the 1930s referred to as the unintended consequences of social (or, in the case of this study, military) action. Military thinkers have another name for it. They call it "friction," and they link it directly to chance on the battlefield and to what otherwise might be deemed simply the unpredictability of war.

Nothing was written in the stars that the Union army would successfully occupy and defend Little Round Top at Gettysburg. The result of the contest lay entirely in the hands of the soldiers who stood on the hill that gray and sultry day and who, for good or bad, gave what they could for the sake of their fluttering flags.

Yet the events that occurred at Little Round Top possess an even larger significance beyond the men who fought and died there, or the contingencies of what happened and did not happen on that fateful afternoon. Some historians have argued that the Union was saved at Little Round Top or that the Confederacy was lost there. These claims, truth be told, are pretty much poppycock—romantic and exaggerated notions of the central place Little Round Top played in the drama of Gettysburg or the larger drama of the Civil War. Gettysburg was an important battle that, as many writers have shown, changed the course of the Civil War, and Little Round Top was a significant engagement in the larger battle. But the fight for this little hill in southern Pennsylvania neither won nor lost the war. The war, quite obviously, rolled drearily along for another twenty-two months.

So what importance *does* Little Round Top hold for us today in the twenty-first century? If anything, it reveals the utter sadness, the bitter tragedy, the miserable futility of war. John Wilkerson, a soldier in the 3rd Arkansas who served at Gettysburg, saw the lesson plainly: "War is a terrible thing. It wrecks men's bodies, and sometimes their spiritual values." The fighting soldiers, North and South, who survived the fight for Little Round Top recalled with striking clarity the sadness that gripped them once twilight had passed and night had descended on July 2. Their thoughts and feelings focused on the miracle of their own survival and the sorrow they felt so overwhelmingly for their fallen comrades. Little Round Top was a horrendous American episode of killing and mourning. Not until their later years, when time had helped to heal some of their wounds, did the survivors begin to see any glory or romance in what they had accomplished at Little Round Top. But in the waning hours of July 2, as the peach-colored flush of twilight melted into the blackness of night, they wrestled with anguish and exhaustion, grief and emptiness, sadness and loss.

The men who fought there believed that the struggle for Little Round Top was decisive, even though historians might question that today. Hardened veterans, North and South, remembered this fight as something out of the ordinary, something that made other combat experiences pale in comparison, something that told them they had survived a great ordeal by the blessings of Providence when, in fact, so many of their comrades had not. Some of those conclusions would not dawn on these soldiers until long after the battle was over. But many of the survivors recognized at once that waging war on Little Round Top, and living to tell the tale, was an unparalleled event in their personal histories and in the history of their respective nations. That particular understanding of Little Round Top's importance—the understanding reached by the warriors who fought there—makes examining in detail how these soldiers, Union and Confederate, performed in battle and remembered their role as a worthy undertaking, and it opens the way for modern Americans to comprehend the terrible nature of war and the supreme tragedy of all its costs. Too often we forget that the Civil War transformed America into a bloody carnival of death. This book is offered as a reminder.

It seems to be a convention among authors to thank their families last, but I would like to thank my own family straight off. This book, researched over a considerable number of years, although written over a relatively short period of time, owes its existence to my family and to their wonderful support of my work. My wife, Donna A. LaFantasie, who has stayed by my side for twenty-five years, has been a beacon of love and understanding in my life. I owe her more debts than I can ever repay. She has shown me new worlds. She has helped me dream my dreams. She has helped make those dreams come true. She has taught me the meaning of love. She will always be my best friend.

My children, now all adults, allowed me, while they were growing up, to take the time that every author must spend alone in his study, excusing himself from the lives of those around him. They regularly complained about this, and thus reminded me of what's really important in life. Donna M. Hayes helped in an additional way by researching some facets of Joshua Chamberlain's life while she was vacationing in Maine. Ryan T. Hayes patiently listened to my long lectures about Gettysburg and asked salient questions while visiting our farm and exploring nearby woods and streams. Mary Sarah LaFantasie lived some of the story I tell here by accompanying me on treks over the Gettysburg battlefield, including one very memorable hike over the summit of Big Round Top on a drizzly May day, and on research trips to the Gettysburg National Military Park Library, the Adams County Historical Society, and a good number of other libraries and repositories, where she served as my trusty and very able amanuensis. She also kept me laughing through this project, which in its own way saved my life. William E. Metzger Jr., a close friend of the family, expressed considerable interest in this book and helped the cause by donating, of all things, a comfortable chair for my study.

The book is dedicated to my late father and mother, who first sparked my interest in history and then nurtured it. Both of them were talented writers who never published a word. My sister, Terry Lynne Pezzi, healed some old wounds just in time to be there when things seemed as though they might fall apart. My sister-in-law, Nancy Fulford, fell in love with Gettysburg on her first visit, but the crucial support she and her husband, Robert Fulford, provided had nothing to do with Gettysburg and everything to do with love when the sky started falling. The late Donald A. Dignon, my father-in-law and a retired military man, made this book possible in more ways than one, but it was his faith in me and his love that kept shining through. I'm sorry he did not live to see it published. Surrogate members of our family, Evelyn Furse and Jennifer Farrell, have never talked to me about Gettysburg, which certainly was refreshing and more helpful than they can imagine.

Many friends helped me research and write this book. In New York City and Gettysburg, my closest friends, Ira Meistrich and Barbara Benton, talented historians in their own right, picked me up when I was down, cheered me on until they were hoarse, loved me like a brother, kept me warm and dry on a number of other occasions, fed me when I was hungry, and generally took care of me over the course of many years. I cherish them more than Lee cherished Stonewall Jackson, if such a thing is possible. Oh yes, Ira Meistrich came up with the idea for this book.

I am forever thankful to Amy J. Kinsel, a very gifted historian, for her friendship and for the years we have spent sharing the fruits of our Gettysburg research and the joys and sorrows of writing. She has taught me how to be a better historian, besides showing me how love can prevail in an often loveless world. She has pulled me through some pretty tough times, always treating me gently and with great empathy.

Marion Oates Leiter Charles, known to her friends as Oatsie, allowed me to invade her homes in Georgetown and in Newport and her privacy to consult the Oates Family Papers in her possession. Mrs. Charles is the granddaughter of William C. Oates; she is also a dear and loyal friend, one of the best and wittiest conversationalists I have ever met, and a true lady. I also came to know another grandchild of a Civil War soldier, the late Abbott Spear, grandson of Captain Ellis Spear of the 20th Maine. Before he died, Mr. Spear generously shared with me a multitude of historical documents and records in his collection pertaining to his grandfather.

A dear friend in Rhode Island, Gladys Wyatt, put up with me—and put me up—as I struggled through the final throes of revising the manuscript. Two other Rhode Islanders have helped me over the course of many years: Bruce and Marcia Read are bosom friends whose love never fades, never falters. Pamela Kennedy and Robert McMahon have spent thirty years proving again and again that their friendship is a gift of Providence. A renewed friendship with Nancy J. Lees Rowell has reinforced my own understanding of how the past lives on in the present. In Virginia, Susan Wyatt and Robin Anderson showed mercy when, for a moment, the world had turned upside down.

Amy Kinsel and another good friend and historian, D. Scott Hartwig, read the entire manuscript, made incisive comments, and saved me from a ton of silly errors. Stephen W. Sears, whose book on Gettysburg is a masterpiece, helped me understand the intricacies behind Lee's invasion plans. I thank them all for their enormous help, but needless to say, any deficiencies in this book are my own and not theirs. My best friends know that if I could blame someone else for the mistakes in the book, I would.

I received considerable assistance, and sometimes heroic efforts, from a number of individuals at libraries, archives, and other repositories. At Gettysburg National Military Park, my warm thanks for many favors and the answers to hundreds—if not thousands—of questions go to Scott Hartwig, John Heiser, Eric Campbell, Darrell Smoker, Karlton Smith, Robert Prosperi, Kathleen Georg Harrison, Winona Peterson, and John Latscher, the park's superintendent.

At Fauquier County Public Library in Warrenton, Virginia, the interlibrary staff and other librarians have expeditiously worked miracles to get rare books into my hands over the past decade. My special thanks go to Catharine Ogilvie, Ann Alexander, and Jenny Lyons for all their tremendous efforts and for making it a pleasure to step inside the library's doors. Two librarians at the two different campuses of the Lord Fairfax Community College Library in Virginia deserve my thanks for filling endless interlibrary loan requests: Linda Harper and Vivien DeWitt.

Staff members at the Adams County Historical Society, Gettysburg, made my research go smoothly there. My gratitude goes to Charles H. Glatfelter, Elwood W. Christ, Timothy J. Smith, and Wayne Motts. In

Damariscotta, Maine, Faith Healy and her family took me in for a week while I researched Chamberlain's world, and I appreciate Sean Healy's part in setting up my temporary base of operation. At the Pejepscot Historical Society, Brunswick, Maine, Eric Jorgensen and Julia Oehmig helped me find my way through the Alice Trulock Collection and offered their ideas about sources elsewhere. Susan Ravdin and Dianne M. Gutscher of the Hawthorne-Longfellow Library, Bowdoin College, Brunswick, responded to my many questions about the Chamberlain Papers in their care. In the Manuscript Division, Library of Congress, James H. Hutson, John R. Sellers, and Jeffrey Flannery provided able assistance and good suggestions. Michael Musick and Michael Pilgrim at the National Archives were a godsend. Working in the rich archives of the U.S. Army Military History Institute, Carlisle Barracks, Pennsylvania, is always rewarding, but my research visit there for this book was made all the more enjoyable and profitable by Richard J. Sommers, Michael Monahan, Jay Graybeal, and especially Joanna McDonald. At the Alabama Department of Archives and History, Edwin C. Bridges and Norwood A. Kerr answered my every question and offered valuable information about William C. Oates and the 15th Alabama. B. D. Patterson, Hill College History Center, helped in my search for illustrations. David T. Hedrick of the Musselman Library, Gettysburg College, was efficiently helpful. My thanks also go to John D. Glasscock and Dr. Jack Anderson for letting me use documents in their possession relating to the 15th Alabama. William R. Treichler graciously sent me copies of accounts written by his great-great-grandfather who served in the 96th Pennsylvania.

Thomas A. Desjardin, the undisputed expert on the 20th Maine at Gettysburg, and Jeff Hall, Brandeis University, who teaches a class on the battle of Gettysburg, both helped me clarify my thinking, refine my approach, and pointed me to useful sources. Other friends, writers, colleagues, and scholars also kept trying to point me in the right direction or took good care of me when I needed it, including Steven Bashore, Brian A. Bennett, Frank Black, Stefan Brodsky, Peter Cozzens, Thomas Duggan, Terrence Fullerton, Ernest B. (Pat) Furgurson, Fraser Hubbard, Terry Jackson, Robert K. Krick, Gary Laine, Laura Leftwich, Philip Peacock, John J. Pullen, Kathy Read, Diane Smith, and Joy Tutela. Brenda Bruce Branscome of Warrenton, Virginia, was a pillar of strength and a good listener. John Y. Simon, Lynda L. Crist, Joan Waugh, and Gary W. Gallagher supported my labors with kind words and even kinder encouragement. I am grateful to Gordon S. Wood for all his favors over the years and for demonstrating, by example, what it takes to be a brilliant historian. At Brown University, several faculty members in the Department of History supported my scholarly endeavors, including Michael Vorenberg, Amy Remensnyder, Timothy Harris, and Abbott Gleason.

At Gettysburg College, where I taught for two semesters, three members of the Department of History showed interest in my writing and helped me feel very much at home: Michael Birkner, William Bowman, and Timothy Shannon. To all my good friends, past and present, at Barnes and Noble, Manassas, I thank you for your complete faith in me. I wish particularly to express my gratitude to Marc Cessna, Liz Covey, Madeleine Ellison, Geoffrey Holscher, Dorothy Hudson, Kerri Myers, and Sharon Plummer.

I owe a great deal to three friends, all fine writers and historians, who are now gone: Richard K. Showman, Cranston Jones, and William G. McLoughlin. Three of my professors, Joel A. Cohen, Mario DiNunzio, and Maury Klein, inspired me and cultivated my interest in history.

At John Wiley & Sons, Hana Umlauf Lane has been a superb editor and a guiding light. Thanks to her, this is a better book. Other capable hands at Wiley—namely, Hope Breeman, freelance copy editor Catherine Revland, and Michael Thompson—made sure that the publishing process sailed along through calm waters. George Skoch, who is well known to Civil War enthusiasts, worked through a number of difficulties with grace and style to produce a superb set of maps for this book. My agent, Shelley Roth, came on board late into this project, but her expert guidance has been like a gust of fresh air.

A grant from the National Endowment for the Humanities provided travel money to research in Montgomery, Alabama.

Lastly, I wish to extend my profound thanks to Gabor Boritt, director of the Civil War Institute and professor of history at Gettysburg College, who asked me to write a paper on Joshua Chamberlain, and to Paul A. Hutton, professor of history at the University of New Mexico, who asked me to write something up on William Oates. Those two requests started the whole affair.

Finally, an editorial note: Spelling as found in original documents and printed primary sources has been retained, although I have in some instances silently added capitalization and punctuation to quotations for the sake of clarity.

PROLOGUE

IT IS A SMALL HILL that was probably known by no formal name until a great battle—the Civil War's most costly—made it necessary to give it a name everyone could recognize, a name that had a ring to it and would stand the test of time. Before the titanic clash of Union and Confederate armies at Gettysburg in the summer of 1863, a struggle that would make the hill an American household name, local citizens casually called the place "sugar loaf mountain" or "granite hill" or "rocky ridge"— references to the huge boulders that formed the hill's western face and that prominently marked its jagged crest. Not until after the last shots had been fired at Gettysburg and the smoke had cleared and the dead had been buried did the hill acquire the distinctive name of Little Round Top.[1]

Located about three miles south of Gettysburg, Little Round Top rises to a height of 170 feet above its base, approximately 135 feet lower than its companion hill to the immediate south, Big Round Top.[2] By the summer of 1863, the western face of Little Round Top had been mostly cleared of trees and brush, and the granite boulders and outcroppings up the entire length of the slope were plainly visible. Most of that clearing had been done by woodcutters in 1862, when the rocks and boulders near the summit became the hill's most prominent feature. On the eastern and southern sides of the hill, sparse second-growth trees grew tall and straight and provided only partial shade. Small gullies and swales cut across all the slopes, where heavy rains would drain off the hill in rushing freshets. No road traversed the hill, although an old logging path wound from the northern base, up the slope to the west, until it nearly reached the hilltop.

1

The hill seemed to have little purpose other than as a source for a limited amount of hardwood lumber or, more likely, for firewood. Its rocky surface made it unsuitable for cultivation, and its granite ledges were probably too soft for quarrying. There was nothing about Little Round Top that foretold its great and lasting fame.

IN 1863, death gripped America in its iron hand. While the wildflowers of spring blossomed in colorful splendor from Florida to Maine, the country itself was cloaked in black, and the people could be heard moaning for their many young sons who had been lost in battle. By this spring of 1863, the death toll in America's great Civil War had become staggering; no one could quite believe how efficient Northerners and Southerners had proven themselves to be in the bloody business of slaughtering one another. An anonymous Southern poet tried to ignore the awful truth of death's harvest by declaring: "There's no such thing as death!"[3] But the toll of battle, and the thousands of vacant chairs in homes throughout both sections, revealed otherwise.

That spring the Confederacy's military situation was becoming desperate. Despite a glorious string of victories won by Robert E. Lee's Army of Northern Virginia against Union armies in the east, Federal forces in the west under General Ulysses S. Grant tightened their siege lines around Vicksburg, threatening to open up the entire Mississippi River to Northern control and cut the Confederacy in two. Civilian authorities in Richmond, including President Jefferson Davis and Secretary of War James A. Seddon, wrung their hands and worried that the end of their nation—and the Southern cause of independence—might be in sight. The mood in the Confederacy improved with news of Lee's sparkling victory at Chancellorsville in early May, but delight turned to despair when word spread that Thomas J. "Stonewall" Jackson had been mortally wounded in the battle, accidentally shot by his own troops. While "we mourn his death," wrote Lee, "we feel that his spirit still lives, and will inspire the whole army with his indomitable courage and unshaken confidence in God as our hope and strength."[4]

But hope and strength seemed in particularly short supply that spring. Even before Chancellorsville, Lee pondered the prospects of launching an invasion of the North, believing that such a maneuver would result in something more substantive than had his raid into Maryland in 1862. At least it might allow his men to find forage in Pennsylvania, where the war had not depleted foodstuffs as it had in Virginia. In the most optimistic

General Robert E. Lee, Army of Northern Virginia

scenario, moving the war above the Mason-Dixon line would take pressure off Richmond and its defenses and enable Lee to select a battlefield to his own liking. Any plan that Lee may have contemplated for invading the North in the spring of 1863 had to be postponed, however, when Major General Joseph Hooker, commanding the Union Army of the Potomac, attempted to outflank the Confederate army by crossing the Rappahannock River in late April and the first few days of May. Hooker's advance failed when Lee and Stonewall Jackson effectively outflanked the outflankers. When the Army of the Potomac retreated once more to the northern side of the Rappahannock, Lee resumed his thoughts about a raid into Maryland and Pennsylvania.

Lee was at the peak of his military prowess. His victory at Chancellorsville would come to be regarded as his greatest achievement, although he was less than satisfied with the battle and its outcome. He later confessed that he was "more depressed" after Chancellorsville than he had been after any other battle fought up to that time, for his army was

still facing Hooker's Army of the Potomac, which was superior in numbers and weapons, while other Confederate forces throughout the South
also confronted Union armies of greater size that seemed ready to attack
at any moment.[5] Nevertheless, Lee remained the Confederacy's best
hope for winning the war.

He looked every inch the professional soldier. Despite the fact that
he had suffered earlier that spring from a severe ailment, perhaps the result of coronary artery disease or even a slight heart attack, Lee had recovered well and experienced no adverse medical symptoms during the
battle of Chancellorsville. Then fifty-six years old, tall and straight in his
bearing, he was regarded by the ladies as handsome, charming, and gallant. His full gray beard, ruddy complexion, and thinning gray hair made
him look distinguished and noble. He stood less than six feet tall and
usually wore a white shirt with a drooping black tie, a double-breasted
plain gray officer's coat without adornment (except for three stars on each
collar, the insignia of a Confederate colonel rather than a general), gray
trousers, and highly polished boots.[6] He never wore a sword or sidearms.

Not only did Lee look grand, but his men adored him. "Language is
inadequate to convey an idea of the supreme confidence this army re-
poses in its great and good leader," wrote one soldier in the Army of
Northern Virginia. Even if disaster waited for the Confederates down the
road, "Lee is there, directing with his steady hand, which no crisis can
make tremble." No matter what might happen, said this soldier, "all will
be well" with Lee in command.[7]

The crisis in the West that could cut the Confederacy in two, however, made the hands of President Davis and War Secretary Seddon tremble and consumed their thoughts more than did Lee's intentions to
invade the North. On May 15, Lee traveled to Richmond for a conference to discuss the military situation confronting the Confederacy. Over
several days, from May 15 to May 17, meetings took place behind closed
doors at the War Department in the Mechanics Institute Building. Lee
probably only attended the conference on May 15, although Postmaster
General John H. Reagan later claimed that Lee returned to consult with
the Confederacy's civilian leadership on May 26. In the end, the participants in these meetings remembered differently what had actually been
decided. Despite these discussions and briefings, which probably focused
most fully on how to save Vicksburg from falling into the hands of Grant's
army, Davis wrote to Lee on May 31 and declared that he "had never
fairly comprehended your views and purposes" until receiving a letter

written by Lee the day before. Davis did not make clear whether he was referring to Lee's strategic plans for a raid on Northern soil or to a dispute that had been festering between Lee and Major General D. H. Hill, who commanded Southern troops in North Carolina. The president, however, alluded with more clarity and confidence to "the full execution of your designs," but he did so in such a way that ignored Lee's earlier statement that the time for an advantageous advance had actually passed.[8]

More damaging than any confusion that might have existed in Richmond was the misunderstanding over strategy that beset Lee and his most able commander, Lieutenant General James Longstreet. After missing the battle of Chancellorsville while commanding a foraging expedition for the Army of Northern Virginia in southside Virginia and the northern counties of North Carolina, Longstreet at first proposed that his divisions—along with a portion of the army under the command of General Joseph E. Johnston—be sent to reinforce General Braxton Bragg's forces in central Tennessee; together these troops would attack the Union army led by Major General William S. Rosecrans, who threatened to capture Chattanooga. With this victory, the Confederates would then turn west and strike against Grant's army at Vicksburg. In suggesting this scheme, Longstreet allied himself with other Confederate leaders—including Secretary of War Seddon, Generals Johnston and P. G. T. Beauregard, and Senator Louis T. Wigfall of Texas—who supported the idea of a "western concentration" to relieve the mounting crisis in the Western theater of the war. Despite Lee's opposition to this plan, Longstreet discussed it in person with Seddon and revised his strategy by offering to lead his two divisions against Rosecrans and then on a march through Kentucky, which would draw Union forces from other threatened areas in the Confederacy. But Lee firmly opposed letting Longstreet remove himself from the Army of Northern Virginia.

Just before Lee's conferences in Richmond with Davis and Seddon, however, the commander of the Army of Northern Virginia and Longstreet reached an accord as to the best means of avoiding a catastrophic defeat if their army should become embroiled in another battle with Hooker's larger army, and, at the same time, of taking some of the pressure off the Confederate armies in the West. According to Longstreet, who described his strategy sessions with Lee in a letter to Senator Wigfall, there was now "a fair prospect for forward movement" by the Army of Northern Virginia, and, reflecting his own change of heart, he explained that "we can spare nothing from this army to re-enforce the West." Longstreet told

Lieutenant General James Longstreet, Army of Northern Virginia

Wigfall that if the Confederates could cross the Potomac with a huge army "we could demand Lincoln to declare his purpose."[9]

Long after the war, Longstreet tried self-servingly to free himself of blame for the defeat at Gettysburg and earned instead the vilification of his former Confederate comrades in the Army of Northern Virginia (a group of Lee defenders who have come to be known as the "Lee cult"). Longstreet argued that he had only agreed to an offensive in the spring of 1863 in return for Lee's promise to assume the tactical defensive in the campaign and not to undertake an offensive against Hooker's army. Lee himself later vehemently denied that he had ever made such a promise. "The idea," said Lee in an 1868 interview, "was absurd." Nevertheless, it does seem likely that Lee agreed in 1863 that a defensive posture would give the military advantage to the Army of Northern Virginia while in enemy territory, if such a posture could be assumed under the shifting and unpredictable circumstances that always occurred with the onslaught of combat. Somehow, however, Longstreet came away from his discussions with Lee in early May convinced that "the ruling ideas of the campaign" were to avoid giving battle unless the Army of Northern Virginia could successfully "force the enemy to do so in a position of our own choosing." Lee held to no such understanding, except perhaps in acknowledging that defensive tactics would always be preferable to offensive ones in facing a Union army that invariably outnumbered the troops under his own command.[10]

Longstreet said that Lee wanted to advance to the North "with the expressed hope that he might be successful in Penn. and in that way draw off the Federal army at Vicksburg," but nothing in Lee's surviving papers—or in any other records of the Army of northern Virginia —verifies his lieutenant's assertion. In formulating a northern raid, Lee had several goals in mind, but none of them included the possibility of pulling Grant's forces away from the Mississippi. By moving north, Lee hoped to get the drop on Hooker and ruin his foe's plans for a summer campaign in Virginia by taking the initiative. As he did so, he also wanted to smash some annoying pockets of Union troops in the lower Shenandoah Valley. If he could reach the Potomac, he would cross the river if it seemed "practicable" to do so. Such a move into Yankee territory might prompt the removal of enemy troops from other beleaguered areas of the Confederacy, but Lee did not specify that he hoped Grant's army would be forced away from the siege lines at Vicksburg. A Confederate victory north of the Potomac, Lee believed, would undermine Northern morale, encourage the Peace Democrats in the North, and possibly force political circumstances to such a degree that the Lincoln administration might have to sue for peace. From the available evidence, his design seems to have been aimed at threatening the cities of Washington, Baltimore, and Philadelphia as his army collected foodstuffs and provisions from the rich farms of southern Pennsylvania. He did not want to give general battle, if he could avoid doing so. As he saw things, he had two choices in the late spring of 1863: "Either retire on Richmond and stand a siege, which must ultimately have ended in surrender, or to invade Pennsylvania."[11]

Whether his civilian superiors fully understood his plans, and whether his military subordinates grasped precisely what he had in mind, Lee was determined to seize the initiative, go on the aggressive, and lead his army and the war out of Virginia. On one point, all Confederates were in agreement: something had to be done in the summer of 1863 to avert disaster both in the East and the West. On June 10, Lee sent Lieutenant General Richard S. Ewell's Second Corps from Culpeper toward Front Royal, a march that marked the beginning of his army's summer campaign. He had, as he explained to Seddon, decided between "the positive loss of inactivity and the risk of action."[12] He was moving his army north.

BY THE EARLY SUMMER of 1863, the winds of change blew steadily across America. The war that had begun two years before, with endless parades and bright-eyed young men marching off to find their dreams of glory, had transformed itself into something sinister and unrecognizable to North-

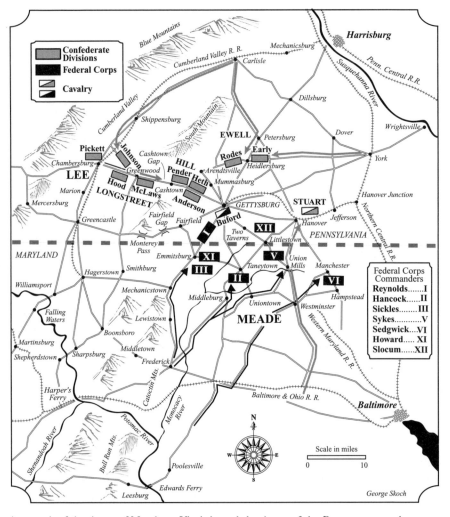

Approach of the Army of Northern Virginia and the Army of the Potomac toward Gettysburg, June 30–July 1, 1863

erners and Southerners alike. Glory was a word that now had a hollow ring to it, and the war itself had produced so much destruction, so much death and suffering, that almost all of the romance had been squeezed out of the combatants' hearts. In every state, in every city and town, in almost every house, the joyless reality of war hung like a dark canopy over the daily lives of Americans. With the prospects of a summer campaign in the Eastern theater of the war, everyone realized that more death and sorrow lay just down the roads along which the armies marched toward their grim destinies.

Other changes floated on the winds. In the North, the war that in the beginning had been fought to save the Union was now changed into something more, something higher in purpose and significance. On January 1, 1863, President Abraham Lincoln had signed the Emancipation Proclamation and with one stroke of the pen altered the very character of the war; what had been a war for the Union now became a crusade for freedom. The document, which Lincoln had issued as a military measure, technically freed not a single slave in the unoccupied Confederate states. But Lincoln knew well what he had actually accomplished. In the proclamation he boldly declared: "And upon this act, sincerely believed to be an act of justice, warranted by the Constitution, upon military necessity, I invoke the considerable judgment of mankind, and the gracious favor of Almighty God." Before signing his name to the document, he said: "I never, in my life, felt more certain that I was doing right than I do in signing this paper."[13]

Even while the proclamation allowed blacks to enter the Northern armed forces and take up arms for the first time against their former masters, it also achieved much more in the minds of African Americans, both free and slave. Blacks came to regard the proclamation as a document of freedom, even though many former slaves had already obtained their own freedom by passing into the Union army's lines throughout the South and becoming "contraband" in the process. For them, the proclamation heralded the end of slavery. With its issuance, slavery could not survive for very long. Each forward step of the Union army carried freedom closer to those still held in bondage and harkened the ultimate destruction of the "peculiar institution." In that respect, the proclamation was like a divine decree. Lincoln had not only signed a military measure; he had signed slavery's death warrant.

As a military measure, though, the Emancipation Proclamation also ushered in another aspect of change in the Civil War. Under the provisions of the proclamation, slavery—the economic bedrock of the

Confederacy—became the target of military annihilation. Slaves through their forced labor had assisted the Confederacy by working to build roads, construct bridges, dig trenches, hammer out iron for cannon in foundries, and lay steel tracks for the railroads. The proclamation potentially removed this labor source from being used by the enemy and thus struck at a crucial component in the Confederate war effort and in the Southern economy. No longer would the Union be fighting a limited war directed only against the Confederacy's armies or its military resources. The Emancipation Proclamation opened the floodgates to the tide of modern war, a war that henceforth would be increasingly waged without discrimination against any target, military or civilian, that kept the Confederate martial machine afloat. Slavery was foremost among those targets.

As the root cause of the war, slavery had always existed at the center of the conflict between North and South, although until the shells began exploding over Fort Sumter in April 1861 the issue of slavery had been effectively swept under the rug of the nation's politics. In those instances when it revealed itself, such as in time of crisis, both sides compromised their principles so the matter could be brushed quickly under the carpet once more. The sectional compromises that had been included in the federal Constitution, the Missouri Compromise of 1820, the compromises that ended the nullification controversy in the early 1830s, and the Compromise of 1850 all worked successfully to defuse the slavery powder keg, at least temporarily. But the Emancipation Proclamation brought the problem of slavery, and its concomitant issue of racism, out into the bright daylight. Any battle that the Confederacy henceforth would wage must be inexorably fought in the name of defending slavery, white supremacy, and a culture that had already died and was simply waiting to be buried. The great American sin had been recast into the great Confederate millstone.

THE STALEMATED WAR, which had gone on for two years, was about to expire, trampled underfoot by fighting generals who would do whatever it took to crush the Confederacy and by determined battle-scarred soldiers who, while expressing no particular affection for African Americans and demonstrating no desire to abandon their racial prejudices, saw that the end of the war might come more quickly with the destruction of slavery. Hard war took the place of stalemate, but the change did not necessarily come quickly or all at once. The Army of the Potomac, for instance, still suffered under the hand of poor leadership and inept generals who, for whatever reason, could not win battles.

Major General Joseph Hooker was one of those generals. After bragging that the Army of the Potomac was "the finest army on the planet," which just possibly might have been true, and quipping that he hoped God would have mercy on General Lee, for he himself would have none, his overconfidence unraveled rapidly at Chancellorsville, where Lee—with a smaller army—outgeneraled Hooker from the first shot of the battle to the last.[14] As May tumbled into June, it was beginning to look like Hooker was not the sort of general who understood the new hard war or how to fight it.

For one thing, he let Lee and his army slip away from Fredericksburg virtually undetected, and then he tried unsuccessfully to find out where Lee was and where he was headed, despite all the clues gathered by the Army of the Potomac's cavalry—which fought a pitched battle against Confederate Major General J. E. B. Stuart's horsemen at Brandy Station on June 9—and the expert gathering of information about enemy movements by a crack unit of military intelligence led by Colonel George H. Sharpe. On June 14, Lincoln stated the obvious to Hooker: "If the head of Lee's army is at Martinsburg and the tail of it on the Plank road between Fredericksburg and Chancellorsville, the animal must be very slim somewhere. Could you not break him?"[15]

For another thing, Hooker could not comprehend what the new war, the hard war, required of him. As he pondered the reality of Lee's advance toward the North, he told Lincoln that the Confederate offensive could be halted by crossing the Rappahannock and striking at the rear of Lee's army that remained entrenched at Fredericksburg. Lincoln, who must have been thunderstruck by the general's suggestion, tried to teach Hooker some strategic lessons of hard war: "In one word, I would not take any risk of being entangled upon the river, like an ox jumped half over a fence, and liable to be torn by dogs, front and rear, without a fair chance to gore one way or kick the other." A few days later, Hooker, who obviously could not grasp Lincoln's point, recommended that he ignore Lee's invasion entirely and march the Army of the Potomac on to Richmond. Lincoln's reply was a model of constraint: "I think *Lee's* army, and not *Richmond*, is your true objective point. If he comes towards the Upper Potomac, follow on his flank, and on the inside track, shortening your lines, whilst he lengthen his. Fight him when oppertunity offers. If he stays where he is, fret him, fret him."[16]

As Lee's army tramped steadily northward without resistance, Hooker focused more of his attention on arguing with Major General Henry W. Halleck, Lincoln's general-in-chief, over various command issues and asserting his authority as general of the Army of the Potomac than he did on the impending arrival of the Confederates north of the Potomac River. He took a fatal misstep, however, on June 27, when he asked Halleck to approve his request to abandon Harper's Ferry and assume command of that garrison's troops. When Halleck refused to give his permission, Hooker erupted in anger and offered his resignation, claiming he could not comply with various orders "to cover Harper's Ferry and Washington" while also trying to figure out just what to do with "an enemy in my front of more than my number"—a statement that exaggerated the size of Lee's army in the same way that a previous commander of the Army of the Potomac, General George B. McClellan, had consistently overestimated enemy numbers.[17]

When Lincoln readily accepted Hooker's offer to resign, so swiftly that it must have surprised even the disgruntled "Fighting Joe," Lee's Army of Northern Virginia had already entered Pennsylvania and his forces, reaching northward nearly to Harrisburg, found comfortable campsites near Chambersburg, and penetrated the countryside as far east as York and Wrightsville on the banks of the Susquehanna. To deal with the alarming presence of Confederate troops spread throughout southern Pennsylvania, Lincoln ordered Major General George Gordon Meade, a Pennsylvanian, to assume command of the Army of the Potomac. Lean and lanky, with a narrow face, huge, bespectacled eyes, and a large, hooked nose, Meade appeared more like a caricature of a gentleman scholar than a bona fide major general. "He was not a soldier by instinct," said one of his fellow officers who simply echoed what Meade himself readily admitted. He lacked flamboyance and luster and often demonstrated a fierce temper, yet he was a loyal soldier and a formidable warrior, as he had already proved in several battles, including Antietam and Fredericksburg. He didn't seem to mind that his men called him "a damned goggle-eyed old snapping turtle," taking the description as a compliment rather than as an insult. In the White House, Lincoln was heard to say: "I tell you I think a great deal of that fine fellow Meade."[18]

Meade received the news of his promotion, at 3:00 A.M. on June 28, with something less than enthusiasm. But he rose immediately to the occasion. He put the seven corps of the Army of the Potomac in motion northward, prepared plans for a defensive line in Maryland, if he should

Major General George Gordon Meade, Army of the Potomac

need to stand his ground, and sent advance units probing into the Pennsylvania countryside to find the enemy. Among those reconnoitering units were two cavalry brigades under the command of Major General John Buford, an experienced officer who had seen action in the old army against Indians in the West and who had fought with distinction at Second Bull Run and Fredericksburg. On June 30, two days after Meade's appointment to command, Buford and his troopers rode in a drizzling rain toward the small crossroads village of Gettysburg, Pennsylvania.

OUT OF THE BLEAK NIGHT DARKNESS on Sunday, June 28, a civilian scout named Harrison brought word to Lee at his headquarters tent, pitched in a grove east of Chambersburg, that the Federal army had crossed the Potomac, advance columns had reached Frederick, Maryland, and Union troops appeared to be headed westward, over South Mountain toward the Cumberland Valley. This was the first inkling Lee had that the enemy was closing in on him. Most of his cavalry, the eyes and ears of his army, was out of contact at the moment, for Lee had given J. E. B. Stuart discretionary orders that resulted in a break in communications between the Army of Northern Virginia's infantry corps and Stuart's marauding horsemen. Lee could not ignore Harrison's news, and he quickly moved to concentrate his scattered army to the vicinity of Cashtown, eight miles west of Gettysburg at the base of South Mountain.

On June 30, Major General Henry Heth, commanding a division of Lieutenant General Ambrose Powell Hill's Third Corps, ordered one of his brigades east from Cashtown toward Gettysburg in search of provisions, including a stockpile of shoes he mistakenly believed to be in the town. As the Confederates approached the town, they spotted a column of Union cavalry and, having no orders to bring on an engagement, pulled back to Cashtown. The following morning, under bright sunshine, Hill sent Heth's division, supported by Major General Dorsey Pender's division, toward Gettysburg to determine the strength of the Union forces there. Lee's army, however, remained scattered, and the commanding general himself set out from Chambersburg that morning in the company of Longstreet knowing that Hill's men were moving forward in a reconnaissance-in-force, but unaware of precisely what they might find waiting for them in Gettysburg.

It was General Buford and his troopers who waited for the Confederates on the ridges west of town. Scouts the night before had reported the concentration of Confederate forces in the direction of Gettysburg. To one of his brigade commanders, who said that he could hold the enemy back for twenty-four hours, if he had to, Buford replied: "No, you won't. They will attack you in the morning and will come 'booming,' skirmishers three deep. You will have to fight like the devil to hold your own until [infantry] supports arrive."[19] The old Indian-fighter's instincts served him well at Gettysburg. He deployed one brigade of his unmounted men—one in four detailed to hold the horses—astride the Chambersburg Pike on McPherson Ridge and the other to the north, toward Oak Ridge, to cover the cavalry's right flank. At about 8:00 o'clock on the morning of July 1, his advance pickets, posted three miles west of the town, opened fire on the approaching Confederate column. The outnumbered troopers fought stubbornly, using their breech-loading carbines with great effectiveness, as they withdrew in orderly fashion across the small stream, Willoughby Run, to the high ground along McPherson's Ridge. There Buford and his men made their stand.

The Union cavalrymen, fighting tenaciously and supported by artillery under the command of Lieutenant John H. Calef, held the Confederates back for about two hours. Calef recalled that the battle rapidly heated up, noting how "the demonic 'whir-r-r' of the rifled shot, the 'ping' of the bursting shell and the wicked 'zip' of the bullet . . . filled the air."[20] Before the struggle reached a fever pitch, Major General John F. Reynolds, a Pennsylvanian and a seasoned officer who commanded the Army of the Potomac's First Corps, arrived on the battlefield with the infantry reinforcements Buford had so desperately been waiting for. When the Confederates again attacked the Union lines, they discovered the famous Iron Brigade, the "Black Hats," in their front, and the clash erupted into a full-scale confrontation between determined infantrymen on both sides. No sooner had Reynolds deployed his troops and ordered his men forward, when he was struck in the back of the neck by an enemy round and fell to the ground, dead. His command was assumed by Major General Abner Doubleday, the man later mistakenly credited with inventing the game of baseball.

From the vicinity of the McPherson farm, south of Chambersburg Pike, the battle swept northward like a meandering tornado, jumping across the road and toward a railroad cut, where the tracks and ties had yet to be laid. There the Confederates, led by Brigadier General Joseph R. Davis, the Confederate president's nephew, turned the Union right flank and sent the bluecoats reeling toward the rear. A brisk Federal counterattack, spearheaded by the 6th Wisconsin, drove the Confederates into the railroad cut, where the bluecoats captured two hundred enemy soldiers, and pushed the remainder of Davis's brigade back beyond Willoughby Run. "Men fell like leaves before the blast," remembered a sergeant in the 6th Wisconsin, "but we never checked up for a moment."[21]

A lull in the fighting allowed both sides to gain strength from reinforcements moving up to the sound of the guns, to consolidate their lines, and to brace themselves for the fighting yet to come. The Union forces received badly needed reinforcements as the Eleventh Corps, led by Major General Oliver O. Howard, came up and formed its lines north and northwest of the town, creating practically a half-circle that eventually linked with Doubleday's First Corps to the southwest. At about the same time, Confederate units from the Army of Northern Virginia's Second Corps, under the overall command of General Richard Ewell, arrived from the vicinity of Carlisle and approached the battlefield from the north. A Confederate division led by Brigadier General Robert E. Rodes came through a huge apple orchard on Oak Hill, north of the railroad cut, soon after 1:00 P.M., and occupied this high ground before Union troops of the Eleventh Corps could reach this strategic spot.

When Ewell saw Federal troops massing for what appeared to be an attack on the Confederate lines, he ordered Rodes to advance his men and hit the Union forces before they could launch their own assault. From a distance, Lee witnessed the flowing waves of Rodes's butternut ranks smashing into the Federal lines north of the railroad cut, and while he had preferred that a general engagement not be brought about at Gettysburg, he realized the battle was now at full tilt, and he told A. P. Hill to send his troops forward to hit the enemy once more from the west. Along the broad crest of McPherson's Ridge, the blue lines withstood for a while the relentless assault of Heth's division, but the Confederates inched forward through the heavy battle smoke and the rolling crash of musket fire. Eventually the left of the Iron Brigade crumpled, and the entire Union line along the ridge, now threatened as well from renewed assaults by Rodes's division to the north, fell back in as orderly a fashion as possible to the Lutheran Seminary located on a long ridge directly overlooking the town. Meanwhile, one of Rodes's brigades, commanded by Brigadier General George P. Doles, plunged into the storm by striking the sparse Union Eleventh Corps line north of town, where Brigadier General Carl Schurz tried to keep his small division from being overrun.

More than half of the Eleventh Corps, including Schurz's brigades, was comprised of German immigrants who had had the bad fortune to have occupied the right of the Federal line at Chancellorsville, where, on May 1, 1863, Stonewall Jackson's surprise flank attack broke these German regiments all to bits. Now, as the German defenders tried to keep their lines from breaking again under the considerable weight of Doles's assault, they discovered that they were also being hit at the same time by the arrival of Major General Jubal A. Early's Confederate division, which attacked from the east in a shattering charge. "I never saw as hopeless a battle as that afternoon's fighting," recalled one soldier in the Eleventh Corps. "There was no alternative for Howard's [Eleventh Corps] men except to break and fly or to throw down their arms and surrender," wrote General John B. Gordon, who commanded one of Early's brigades.[22]

With Reynolds's death, command of the entire wing of the Union army at Gettysburg fell to Major General Howard. From a vantage point on Cemetery Hill, Howard watched the progress of the battle with falling confidence and soon realized that the Confederates, who came in a swarm from the north and the west at once, had successfully enveloped the Union lines. Shortly after 4:00 P.M., Howard decided to pull the First and Eleventh Corps back through the town and take up a defensive position on Cemetery Hill. It was really the only decision he could make, for the Confederates were pressing the Union lines so fiercely and with such a galling fire from artillery and muskets that the Federal forces could no longer stay where they were. A survivor of the 119th New York Infantry remembered: "Back across the field and through the town the broken and scattered battalions flew, the victorious enemy close upon their heels."[23]

The local citizens who remained in the town fled to their cellars. One woman described the "bustle and confusion" that accompanied the Federal withdrawal. "No one," she wrote, "can imagine in what extreme fright we were when our men began to retreat." Another woman recalled the frightening noise out in the street—"the rattling of muskets, the unearthly cries mingled with the sobbing of the children [in our cellar], shook our hearts."[24] Many of the citizens took fleeing Union soldiers into their homes, hiding them in closets and in dark basements—anywhere that would keep them out of the clutches of pursuing Confederates. No African Americans were to be seen in town; most of them had evacuated Gettysburg at the first word of Lee's approach. Indeed, those who did not flee town in time were captured by Confederate soldiers and later forced to accompany Lee's army back to Virginia, where they were placed under the yoke of slavery against their will.

Finally the staggering Union forces clambered up the slopes of Cemetery Hill, to the south of town, reformed their regiments as best they could, and took their places in the battle lines, fully expecting that the Confederates would attempt to dislodge them from the heights. Major General Winfield Scott Hancock of the Second Corps, who had been sent by Meade to Gettysburg that afternoon to take command of all the Union troops there, worked with Howard and Doubleday to throw up entrenchments, place the batteries, and prepare for an enemy assault. Hancock decided to hold this ground at all cost. But no assault came.

ABOUT FOUR HOURS of daylight remained on July 1, when Lee pondered what his next move should be. Doubt plagued him more than indecision. Longstreet's First Corps still had not arrived in Gettysburg, and Lee did not know the whereabouts of Meade's remaining corps. Nevertheless, it did seem obvious, under the circumstances, that his army should make the attempt to push the Federals off the two hills to the south of town. In the end, he suggested—rather than ordered—that Ewell assault

Cemetery Hill "if practicable" but added that he should "avoid a general engagement" until the rest of the army could arrive.[25] But fearing the possibility of a flank attack by fresh Union forces coming in from York, and concerned that his own troops lacked support on their right, Ewell finally decided not to order an assault that evening. So the rest of the night, bathed in moonlight, passed without a Confederate attack against the hills held by the Federals south of town. On the morrow, when the sun rose, it would shine on an entrenched and formidable Federal position that extended from Culp's Hill to the summit of Cemetery Hill and south along a long rise called Cemetery Ridge—the makings of the barb and hook and shank of the Union's famous "fishhook" line at Gettysburg.

THREE MILES SOUTH of town, along the Taneytown Road, the Jacob Weikert family huddled in their small stone house wondering—as so many other Gettysburg citizens did that night—what the following day would have in store for them. So far, their house and farm, nestled beneath the gentle eastern slopes of Little Round Top, had been spared the dangers and penalties of war, but all day long the family had watched Union soldiers stumping along the soggy road on their way north, and even into the night the shambling columns continued to fill the roadway and to block out all other night sounds with their sharp shouts, their low barks and laughter, their clanging equipment, and the steady pounding of their feet. Even with the bright moon, the night seemed dark and foreboding. Up on the crest of Little Round Top, where heaven seemed slightly closer to mortal earth, all was silent, except for the muffled and discordant echoes of war that rose up to the rocks on the crest and soon blended with the almost inaudible sighing of the wind through the trees.

1

Midnight to Morning

U NDER THE PALE WHITE LIGHT of a full moon, Gettysburg looked nothing like its former self. There was a ghoulish quality to the landscape, and eerie shadows fell across the dead and wounded who remained on the trampled fields where the first day's fighting had raged. The pungent aromas of death and burnt powder filled the air, and startling military noises—the rumble of caisson wheels on the hard surfaces of the roads, the sudden human shouts of commands and heralds, and the death cries and moans of the wounded who littered the meadows and clogged the town's alleys and streets—sounded through the night like the jolting peals of a firebell.

At Lee's headquarters in an apple orchard across from Mrs. Mary Thompson's tiny but sturdy stone house on the Chambersburg Pike, the commanding general put together his plans for the following day, having already called in Longstreet to discuss an attack on Meade's left flank "as early . . . as practicable" on the morrow and sent a courier to Ewell with a message not to attack the Union army's right until he could hear the sound of Longstreet's artillery to the south.[1] A short while later Lee went to bed, although it could hardly be said that the details of the impending battle had been worked out to perfection.

Longstreet spent a more worrisome night. Late in the afternoon of July 1, as the Confederates drove the Union forces back through the town toward Cemetery Hill, Longstreet had come upon Lee at Seminary Ridge, near the seminary building perched on the crest. Scanning the horizon with his field glasses, Longstreet observed that the Union army was being pushed back toward the high ground, a position that gave the enemy a defensive advantage. To Longstreet's surprise, Lee said that he intended the following morning to attack Meade's army on the heights. Longstreet boldly suggested that such a course seemed to be at variance with the plan originally designed for the invasion—that the Army of Northern Virginia would fight a defensive campaign, choosing its own ground if the circumstances warranted.

Lee replied: "If the enemy is there to-morrow, we must attack him." Longstreet pointed out, "If he is there, it will be because he is anxious that we should attack him—a good reason in my judgment for not doing so." He urged Lee to move the army around "by our right to the left" of the Army of the Potomac "and put our army between him and Washington, threatening his left and rear, and thus force him to attack us in such position as we might select." Lee, however, believed that the Confederates could dislodge the Union forces from the high ground and "whip them in detail." It appeared to Longstreet that the day's battle had excited Lee and that his desire to strike the enemy "threatened his superb equipoise."[2]

Longstreet had gained a reputation as a general who favored fighting on the defensive, as he and his corps had so successfully done at Fredericksburg in December 1862, though truth be told he was by nature aggressive and tenacious on the battlefield. Subordinates described how Longstreet would ride headlong into battle "amid a perfect shower of balls," encouraging his men forward as he chewed on the stump of a cigar.[3] He was a physically imposing man, standing two inches above six feet, brawny in build, with a huge head, auburn hair receding from his broad forehead, piercing blue eyes, heavy brows, high cheekbones, and a long and thick beard that covered his rather cruel mouth. With the death of Stonewall Jackson after Chancellorsville, Longstreet at age forty-two had assumed the mantle of Lee's most trusted lieutenant, the general whom Lee affectionately called "my old *war-horse*."[4]

On the morning of July 2, Longstreet was up by 3:00, having slept only a few hours. In the early morning darkness, he rode under the sparkling stars to meet with General Lee and argue, one more time, that the commanding general should abandon his plan to assault the Union army's strong defensive line and, instead, move the Army of Northern Virginia to more advantageous ground.

JUST BEFORE MIDNIGHT, while the moon rose steadily higher in the sky, General Meade arrived in Gettysburg with his entourage, which included his son and aide-de-camp, Captain George G. Meade, and Brigadier General Henry J. Hunt, his artillery chief. Meade quickly found General Howard and asked, rather brusquely: "Well, Howard, what do you think, is this the place to fight the battle?" Howard and the other officers assured him that they could hold their position against a Confederate attack. "I am glad to hear you say so, gentlemen," Meade replied. "I have already ordered the other corps to concentrate here and it is too late to change."[5]

Later he looked over the entire length of the Union lines with Howard and Hunt. He may have been relieved to discover that two regiments—the 5th Ohio and the 147th Pennsylvania—from Brigadier General John W. Geary's Second Division of the Twelfth Corps had, sometime just before dark on July 1, occupied the slopes of Little Round Top, the eye of the Union army's fishhook line. Between the hill and the left flank of Major General Daniel E. Sickles's Third Corps, two other brigades from the Twelfth Corps—those commanded by Colonel Charles Candy and Brigadier General George S. Greene—filled the gap in the shank of the Union line, where Cemetery Ridge melted into the lower ridge of Little Round Top. But mostly Meade's attention was fixed on the right of his line, Culp's Hill and Cemetery Hill, where he knew the Confederate forces had been massed in what certainly appeared to be a firm intention of the enemy to storm the Union works on those hills.

After daybreak, Meade established his headquarters on the Taneytown Road in a small white cottage owned by a widow, Mrs. Lydia Leister. Almost at once, the tiny house became a beehive of activity as Meade worked feverishly to ensure the proper placement of his corps; as daylight came over the land, Union troops flowed down the narrow roads and spread like a blue ink stain across the fields and hills and ridges south of Gettysburg.

IT WAS LATE in the afternoon of July 1, while the fighting still raged around Gettysburg, that Major General John Bell Hood, who commanded one of the three divisions in Longstreet's First Corps, received orders to move his men east from their bivouac outside of Chambersburg and on toward Gettysburg. In Hood's division, the Texans in the brigade commanded by Brigadier General Jerome B. Robertson, "lazily and plethorically" moved in column, as one private in the 4th Texas reported. Marching toward the sound of the guns, the Texas brigade—which consisted of the

1st Texas, 4th Texas, 5th Texas, and 3rd Arkansas regiments—passed a field hospital, where the wounded of the first day's fighting were receiving medical treatment. "I saw a great many wounded . . . who were mangled and bruised in every possible way, some with their eyes shot out, some with their arms, or hands, or fingers, or feet or legs shot off, and all seeming to suffer a great deal"—so remembered Private John C. West of Company E ("Lone Star Guards"), 4th Texas Infantry, the only married man to serve in his entire company.[6]

West differed from his comrades in Company E in other respects as well. He was a former schoolteacher who had joined the 4th Texas in May 1863, so he had yet to see action as he marched with the men of his company along the moonlit Chambersburg Pike toward Gettysburg. Nor was he a native Texan, like most of the men in Company E and in the regiment. He was born in Camden, South Carolina, on April 12, 1834, where he demonstrated his ability as an apt student and a quick learner. Twenty years later, he was graduated from the University of South Carolina, and the following year, he moved to Austin, Texas, where his brother Charles, an attorney, resided. While he read law in Charles's office, he also taught school. He returned to South Carolina in 1856 to marry Mary E. Stark of Columbia, and the couple set up their household outside Austin. In 1859, after passing the bar, he moved with his wife to Waco, where he became the headmaster of the Waco and Trinity River Classical School.

When the secession crisis drove Texas out of the Union, West sided with the Confederacy and condemned Governor Sam Houston for taking a stand against disunion. Showing his commitment to the Southern cause, he enlisted in a local militia company, the Lone Star Guards, but he served in the unit only a short time. In May 1861, President Jefferson Davis named him district attorney for the Western District of Texas. Less than a year later, West resigned his position and enlisted in the newly recruited 15th Texas Infantry. But he served with the regiment only a few weeks in March 1862 and transferred to Company K of the First Regiment of Texas Heavy Artillery. In July 1862, he was appointed district attorney again, and he reluctantly accepted the office and left the military. He remained in that position until the following April, when he enlisted in the 4th Texas and managed, as luck would have it, to find a place in his former company, the Lone Star Guards.

Although his friends and neighbors urged him not to go for a soldier, West was determined to "see a fight" and "remain in the ranks, if necessary, until the close of the war."[7] In the early spring of 1863, he left his

Private John C. West, 4th Texas Infantry, late in life

wife and two small children—a boy, Stark, and a girl, Mary—in Waco and set off with a Bible in his carpetbag, an overcoat, and a blanket to join the 4th Texas with Lee's army in Virginia. With his blue eyes, fair complexion, and light hair (already starting to thin on the top), he looked like a robust Viking off to seek adventure and glory. But West was no Scandinavian warrior; he was a sober Christian soldier. He had just turned twenty-nine years old.

It took him nearly a month to catch up with the regiment in May 1863, encamped on the Rapidan after the battle of Chancellorsville. Along the way, traveling through the heart of the Confederacy, he noticed that "more than *two-thirds*" of the women he saw were dressed in black. Although he could not know what combat was really like, he enjoyed the bravado expressed by his comrades: "We can't be whipped, but we may all be killed."[8] But the sight of those women dressed in black was a picture he could not erase from his mind.

Hood's division plodded along the Chambersburg Pike and followed the winding road that led over South Mountain and into Cashtown, a small crossroads about eight miles west of Gettysburg. Although rumors flew about the battle being fought at Gettysburg, the 4th Texas could not know precisely where it was going or what it was expected to do. "We never know anything," West admitted in an earlier letter home.[9] Like his comrades, West carried about twenty or thirty pounds of baggage and equipment on his back. Along with his musket, cartridges, and canteen, he also carried his trusty Bible, an extra pair of underwear, and a daguerreotype of his wife, Mary, which he gazed upon daily without fail. Every time he looked at her picture, he said, he remembered Jeremiah 49:11— "Leave thy fatherless children, I will preserve them alive; and let thy widows trust in me."

Sometime after midnight, Hood's division reached Marsh Creek, only two or three miles west of Gettysburg, but around 3:00 A.M., Hood's gray ranks were back on the Chambersburg Pike, groping forward in the black hours before dawn, until they reached the fields below the western slope of Seminary Ridge, where they halted in the cheerless light of day to receive orders—orders that did not come for several hours. Standing in line, exhausted beyond strength, West fell asleep on his feet and dreamed of his little son, four years old, and his wife and daughter, "and I asked God to take care of you if I am taken away from you."[10]

THE WORD RAN through the blue columns like wildfire: McClellan was back in command of the Army of the Potomac! Major Ellis Spear of the 20th Maine Infantry was less impressed with this news than the men in the ranks seemed to be.[11] As far as Spear was concerned, General George B. McClellan had been a disaster for the Army of the Potomac, and he did not relish the thought of serving in an army under a man who had demonstrated a peculiar inability to win victories. Luckily for Spear, and for the army as a whole, the rumor proved false. So he and his comrades silently trudged forward into the blackness of the night.

Spear's regiment had been marching since the morning of July 1, when it left Union Mills, Maryland, and followed a twisting little road that ran up and over countless swales and ridges to Hanover, Pennsylvania. The 20th Maine was brigaded with the 83rd Pennsylvania, the 44th New York, and the 16th Michigan, in the Army of the Potomac's First Division, Third Brigade, led by a dashing and handsome young officer, Colonel Strong Vincent of Erie, Pennsylvania. Commanding the 20th Maine was another energetic officer, Colonel Joshua Lawrence Chamberlain, a former professor of rhetoric at Bowdoin College in Brunswick, Maine. Spear, in fact, had been his student at the college. Chamberlain received command of the 20th Maine in May, after the regiment's previous commander, Adelbert Ames, accepted a promotion to brigadier general. Spear liked Chamberlain and trusted him. He described him as "a gentleman and a scholar[,] and although he was also without military knowledge or experience[,] he was a man of such intelligence and urbanity and kindliness of feeling that he exerted a useful influence" over the men.[12]

Chamberlain alone did not positively influence the men of the 20th Maine. Major Spear, a former schoolteacher who had been studying law when the war broke out, worked arduously in the summer of 1862 to raise the regiment, in response to Abraham Lincoln's call for three hundred thousand more volunteers in the North and Governor Israel Washburn's decision to authorize the formation of the 20th Maine as one of four new regiments that state would offer up to the nation. Although born in Warren, Maine, Spear recruited men from Wiscasset and its environs, joined forces with other recruiters in the area, and put together an entire company

Acting Major Ellis Spear, 20th Maine

that the governor assigned as Company G, 20th Maine, appointing Spear as its captain.

From the very start of his military experience, Spear viewed war without romance. Ever the realist in his perception of the world around him, he was matter-of-fact in his approach to the military and the sacrifices it demanded on those who served their country, but he also blended this no-nonsense attitude with a healthy dose of down east humor. He admitted that when he joined the army "he scarcely knew a line of battle from a line of rail fence." Recognizing that he and others who helped recruit the 20th Maine shared mixed motives, including the hope of gaining officer commissions, Spear remarked that they "sailed by Deuteronomy, modified by an eye to the main chance." As an officer, Spear proved to be capable and courageous. His military record included numerous occasions when he was praised for "gallant and meritorious services."[13]

In appearance, though, Spear seemed an unlikely soldier. Twenty-eight years old, he was of average height, two inches below six feet, and was thin and frail looking, a lean wisp of a man who looked like a strong wind might blow him over. He had a full head of wavy reddish-brown hair, which he wore stylishly parted on the left side and long enough to cover the tops of his protuberant ears. His pale blue eyes were deep-set and routinely looked drowsy. Like so many other soldiers, he wore a full drooping mustache and a Vandyke beard that, in the field or on the march, sometimes grew fairly bushy and, on occasion, looked unkempt. Yet he carried himself well and demonstrated an ability to give orders and have them obeyed.

So far, Spear and the 20th Maine had not seen much action with the Army of the Potomac. At Antietam, the regiment remained in reserve while the bloodiest day of the Civil War raged on September 17, 1862. In December of that year, at Fredericksburg on the Rappahannock, the 20th Maine went into the battle late, got its first taste of combat, and spent the night huddled close to the ground below Marye's Heights, shivering and listening to bullets whine above their heads or strike already dead and wounded soldiers with a hollow thud. The regiment missed the fight at Chancellorsville, in late April and early May 1863, because an attack of smallpox in its ranks had caused the medical surgeons to quarantine the unit. Then, during the march north in June, the 20th Maine found itself engaged in a hot skirmish outside Middleburg, Virginia, when Vincent's brigade successfully pushed Confederate troopers and horse artillery from Major General J. E. B. Stuart's back toward the

Blue Ridge Mountains. This engagement took the life of one of Spear's men in Company G, and it was Spear's unpleasant duty to bury the man with military honors. Although burning up with malarial fever, Spear saw to it that the man was buried near the impressive stone bridge over Goose Creek, about two miles west of Middleburg.

Despite the relatively few casualties suffered by the 20th Maine at Fredericksburg and Middleburg, the regiment had lost nearly half its strength in its first nine months of service. Sickness, rather than bullets, accounted for most of the deaths. Even the regiment's commander, Colonel Chamberlain, had been stricken with heatstroke during this march north. A corporal in Company H worried about Chamberlain's condition: "Our Colonel is off duty[,] and we dread to go into action without him." Spear's malaria made him feel sick and weak. "But going to the hospital in such an emergency was not to be thought of," he wrote, because the regiment's lieutenant colonel, Charles D. Gilmore, had abused sick call and made it impossible "for a really sick man to go to the hospital without discredit." He felt better on June 28, however, when he received news of his promotion to major (which placed him in an "acting" capacity, for the promotion would not be confirmed until after the battle of Gettysburg) and three letters from his wife, Susie, whom he had married in Maine while on furlough in March 1863. She was, he said, "the dearest, best girl in the world."[14]

At about noon on July 1, the 20th Maine marched in a rhythmic shuffling over the state line between Maryland and Pennsylvania and on to Hanover. Crossing into the Keystone State, the regiment unfurled its colors and gave three cheers. "The people appear delighted to see us," reported one private in the regiment. "They were out all along the road with water and milk for us." Despite the warm welcome, the officers and men knew nothing about where they were headed or what their forced march would lead them to. "It was curious afterwards," Spear remarked years after the war, "to remember how ignorant we were . . . of the position, or movements, of the other corps of the army."[15] All they knew was that Lee's army had crossed the Potomac and swarmed north into the Cumberland Valley, perhaps reaching as far as Harrisburg on the Susquehanna. The 20th Maine arrived in Hanover by about noon, and there the regiment rested for a while, found water, and gathered fence rails for fires to cook their rations.

Two hours later, after sunset, the regiment received orders to resume the march. Colonel Chamberlain recalled the flurry of activity that rippled through the 20th Maine: "Staff officers dashed from corps, to division, to brigade, to regiment, to battery—and the order flew like the hawk, and not the owl. 'To Gettysburg!' it said, a forced march of sixteen miles." The regiment assembled with the noise of clattering equipment, orders barked by officers and sergeants, and the grumbling of the men. Even in the darkness, the men insisted on marching with the colors flying, so all would know that the 20th Maine was moving to the sound of the guns. As the Fifth Corps—and the 20th Maine with it—passed toward Gettysburg, the local residents came out of their houses and broke the stillness with their cheers and shouts of encouragement. "This was a small matter," Spear acknowledged, "but I think it had a great effect in raising the spirits of the men. We were now marching to battle in defence of our own."[16]

After passing through McSherrytown and Bonnaughtown, the brigade cut to the south and, shortly after midnight, finally halted for the night on the Baltimore Pike, one of the main thoroughfares leading into Gettysburg. "The troops," said Spear, "could safely be pushed no further without rest." He himself still felt weak from his fever, and all day and into the night, walking the twenty-five miles that the regiment had covered since the previous morning, he had had a difficult time keeping up with the column. Looking back on that night, all he could remember was "weakness, utter fatigue, [and] no food other except pork & hardbread, which my soul loathed."[17]

Longstreet found lee on Seminary Ridge standing in the fading moonlight. It was still too dark to see the enemy's position, so Lee waited to formulate his plans of battle. Longstreet tried once more to talk Lee out of ordering an offensive against the fortified Union lines and moving instead to Meade's left and rear. The general commanding, according to his staff, considered such a movement as Longstreet proposed, but he decided against it because he did not yet know the enemy strength and he lacked the cavalry to screen such a maneuver. In the end, Lee decided to strike the enemy lines as soon as he could gain a better sense of how the Federals had been deployed and how many of their troops had come up in the night.

To get a clearer idea of what the Federal lines looked like to the south, at the Union army's left flank, Lee sent out a reconnaissance party led by one of the engineers on his staff, Captain Samuel R. Johnston. Longstreet ordered an engineer from his own staff, Major John J. Clarke, to accompany Johnston. Lee's orders to Johnston were simple and to the point: he was "to make a reconnaissance of the enemy's left and report as soon as possible." Johnston was an experienced officer, and while Lee had not told him specifically to determine the best route by which the Confederates could approach the Union left unseen by the enemy, the young engineer knew that such a particular order was unnecessary, for he understood that making such a determination "was a part of my duty as a reconnoitering Officer."[18] In the waning darkness, Johnston and Clarke, joined by two or three others on horseback, rode southward toward the Round Tops.

With the sunrise, Lee could see for himself that the Union army held a strong position on the high ground just south of the town and along the prominent ridge that ran to the base of the two Round Tops. Lee seemed uncharacteristically disquieted. Francis Lawley, a correspondent for the *Times* in London, described him as looking "more anxious and ruffled than I had ever seen him before, though it required close observation to detect it."[19]

Sometime after sunrise, Generals Hood, Heth, and Hill rode up with their staffs and joined Longstreet and Lee near the seminary building as they pondered how to seize the day. In the dim light of morning, the men in gray sat on a fallen tree, Longstreet and Hood both whittling sticks as the discussion proceeded over what should be done that day. High above them, wedged between the branches of an oak tree, were Lieutenant Colonel Fremantle and Captain Justus Scheibert of the Prussian Army, two foreign observers who watched from their precarious perch as American history unfolded before their eyes. Lee paced back and forth, his coat buttoned to his throat and field glasses in his hand at his side. "He seemed full of hope," noted General Hood, "yet at times buried deep in thought." Hood asked about the enemy's deployment, and Lee answered: "The enemy is here, and if we do not whip him, he will whip us."[20]

Around 7:00 A.M., Johnston, who had raced back to headquarters jumping farm fences to make time, returned and reported to Lee, after first experiencing some difficulty finding the commander's headquarters under the trees, north of the seminary building. Lee, Longstreet, and Hill were all sitting on the fallen tree trunk when Johnston galloped up. Although the substance of Johnston's report is not known, he apparently told Lee and the other generals that he and his small party had encountered no Federal troops during their entire reconnaissance, except for four Union troopers they had successfully avoided on their return trip.

When Johnston pointed to the Round Tops, Lee asked him directly with some surprise, "Did you get there?" The engineer assured Lee that he had.[21]

What Lee and Longstreet could not know at that moment, however, is that Johnston's reconnaissance of the Union left was fatally flawed, owing to the fact that Johnston reported achieving the impossible by claiming he had seen no Federal troops—except for the puny cavalry patrol—during his entire ride toward the Round Tops. In fact, had he actually ridden the route he later claimed to have followed, he would have encountered—at the very least—Buford's cavalry patrolling near the Peach Orchard and in the woods near the Round Tops. Plenty of Union infantry also occupied nearby ground, just to the north of Little Round Top. According to one estimate, there were probably eighteen thousand Union troops between the Emmitsburg Road and the Taneytown Road and between Little Round Top and the George Weikert farm when Johnston was reconnoitering the same ground. On the basis of Johnston's erroneous report, Lee assumed that no Federals occupied the ground that Johnston had seen. The die had been cast.

Longstreet, who had lingered after Lee had dismissed Johnston, was still conferring with the commanding general when Major General Lafayette McLaws arrived at headquarters. With McLaws looking over his shoulder as he sat on the fallen tree with a map in his hands, Lee indicated the Emmitsburg Road and a perpendicular line drawn across it. "General," Lee said, "I wish you to place your division across this road, and I wish you to get there if possible without being seen by the enemy. Can you get there?" McLaws, who as yet had not seen the ground in question, replied carefully, "I know of nothing to prevent me," but he asked for permission to conduct his own reconnaissance. Longstreet interrupted and told McLaws that he did not want him leaving his division. Pointing to the map with his finger, Longstreet slid his finger along a parallel—not a perpendicular—line to the Emmitsburg Road and said, "I wish your division placed so." Lee demurred. "No, General," he said, "I wish it placed just perpendicular to that." To McLaws's reckoning, Longstreet seemed "irritated and annoyed," but he could not ascertain the reason.[22] Having heard his orders, McLaws returned to his column, which waited near Herr Ridge, about a mile and a half west of Seminary Ridge.

Already the morning air was filled with confusion, tension, and misunderstood instructions. Lee may have been expressing his acute frustration with Longstreet when he upbraided the lieutenant general in front of McLaws by insisting that he wanted McLaws's troops to be perpendicular to the Emmitsburg Road. As a result, Longstreet turned sullen, McLaws sensed the strain that existed between his two superiors, and only Lee seemed entirely clear about what he expected to be accomplished in the impending battle. Before this day was finished, there would be a good deal more confusion to come.

AT THE LEISTER HOUSE, Meade worked tirelessly with preparations and the placement of his troops along the convex fishhook line, a line that allowed him to move any force from one end to the other—a distance of only about two and a half miles—without exposing the movement to the enemy. Nearly all of the army corps had arrived in Gettysburg, except for the Second Corps, which was close by, and the Sixth Corps, which was pounding its way in an all-night march to the battlefield. Though looking pale and careworn, Meade kept up his frantic pace of issuing orders and studying the placement of his troops. He rode down the lines once more, attentive to details, concentrating on the likelihood of an enemy attack, and glad to see the arrival of Hancock and his Second Corps, which the commanding general immediately deployed on Cemetery Ridge.

After returning to headquarters, Meade told his son, Captain George Meade, to find Sickles and let him know where the command post was located on the Taneytown Road, while also telling Sickles to report in person to the commanding general. The young captain rode along the crest of the ridge until he located the temporary headquarters of the Third Corps in a grove of trees and discovered that Sickles, apparently exhausted from the forced march of his corps to the battlefield, was resting in his tent. When one of Sickles's staff officers carried the message to the fatigued general, Sickles replied that his corps had not been deployed and that he was in "some doubt as to where he should go."[23] With this startling news, Captain Meade returned at once to his father and repeated Sickles's words. The elder Meade flushed with anger and shot an order to his son—ride back to Sickles and instruct him to place his corps on the left of the Second Corps, where General Geary's Twelfth Corps had spent the night.

Meade's exasperation was not without obvious cause. Sickles was his most unreliable—and untrustworthy—corps commander. A political general who lacked any great familiarity with the military or with warfare, but who had obtained his commission by being a powerful player in the

Tammany Hall faction of the Democratic Party in New York City, Sickles had become used to doing what he wanted on and off the battlefield. Lincoln knew he had to court favor among the Democrats to build a successful coalition in Congress, so Sickles profited from this political necessity. Despite his poor performance as an officer and his tendency to be absent from the army whenever it was about to engage the enemy, he managed to win the two gold stars of a major general for his blue blouse. Arrogant and self-assured, he curried favor with no one, except those who he knew could help him advance in the army or in politics. Nothing ever seemed to bother Sickles; no censure, criticism, or complaint could ever touch him.

He had been born with thick skin, made all the tougher by his successful rise in the brawling politics of New York City during the two decades leading up to the Civil War. It is said that he always carried a bowie knife and a loaded pistol to raucous Tammany meetings, where presumably his friends and supporters had all gathered. As a congressman representing New York's Third District during the Buchanan administration, he sided with the slaveholders of the South. He gained his greatest notoriety, however, in February 1859, when he deliberately shot down his wife's lover, Philip Barton Key, the son of the author of the "Star Spangled Banner," in Lafayette Square across from the White House in broad daylight. He fired his pistol not once but several times, until he finally wounded Key fatally and stood over the lifeless form to ask: "Is the damned scoundrel dead yet?"[24] Edwin M. Stanton, the acclaimed Democratic attorney who would later become Lincoln's secretary of war, headed Sickles's defense team and successfully won an acquittal for his client by having him plead "temporary insanity."

On the morning of July 2, as the early haze burned off to reveal a brilliant sun, young Captain Meade returned to Sickles's headquarters and found the general's tent struck. Nearby, Sickles was mounting his horse. When the captain delivered his father's latest message, Sickles replied that his troops were just now moving and would soon be in position. Captain Meade, who must have been tired of being lobbed back and forth like a tennis ball, returned to headquarters and reported that Sickles and the Third Corps were moving at last. Unknown to the captain or his father was the fact that Sickles had failed to anchor his left flank by occupying Little Round Top. Except for a Union signal party up on its summit, the little hill stood empty in the bright morning sunlight.

2

PATCHWORK PLANS

OR MANY MEN serving in the Army of the Potomac, the Emancipation Proclamation, issued in January 1863, did little to improve their negative opinions of African Americans or motivate them to fight any harder for the abolition of slavery than they otherwise had been doing for the cause to restore and preserve the Union. In fact, a good number of Union soldiers regarded the Emancipation Proclamation as a scurrilous document, a presidential action that artificially made black people and their freedom the central issue of the war; for these soldiers, steeped in the racial prejudices of the time, African Americans would never be worth the price of a white man's precious life given in combat on the battlefield. Wrote one Indiana private: "I think the Union is about played out. I use to think that we were fighting for the union and constitution but we are not. We are fighting to free those colored gentlemen. If I had my way about things I would shoot ever[y] niggar I come across."[1]

Not Porter Farley, first lieutenant of Company G, 140th New York Infantry. Farley was a diminutive man of twenty-two who stood five feet, four inches tall, had brown hair, a dark complexion, bluish-gray eyes, and wore a mustache and goatee in the style and manner of George B. McClellan. He had been raised on a farm outside of Rochester by parents who helped to hide fugitive slaves traveling northward by means of the Underground Railroad. His aunt and uncle, Samuel and Susan Porter, were founding members of the Rochester chapter of the American Anti-Slavery Society. Farley's uncle was a close associate of Frederick Douglass, the former slave and abolitionist crusader who made Rochester his home while editing his famous antislavery newspaper, the *North Star*. Unlike some other white abolitionists, who couldn't quite bring themselves to argue in favor of black equality, Porter "cheered on and supported" Douglass's earnest demands for African American equal rights.[2]

As a lad, Porter Farley would sit enraptured outside the lustrous Corinthian Hall in Rochester to hear Jenny Lind perform or to listen to the musical strains of orchestras in concert. When he was older, he attended performances of a different kind during "the days of great political excitement, the very height of the antislavery agitation," when speakers such as Lyman Beecher, Ralph Waldo Emerson, James Russell Lowell, and Dr. Oliver Wendell Holmes filled the hall with eloquent words spoken in favor of social reform and of abolishing the immoral and evil institution of slavery.[3] He also sat in the splendidly decorated and acoustically marvelous hall on October 25, 1858, when William H. Seward, the thumping and ambitious U.S. Senator from New York, who was campaigning for a fellow Republican running for governor in the state, delivered his famous speech on the "irrepressible conflict" between North and South. His words rocked Corinthian Hall, just as they shook the unity of the nation. The conflict between the sections over slavery, said Seward, meant "that the United States must and will, sooner or later, be-

Lieutenant Porter Farley, 140th New York

come either entirely a slaveholding nation, or entirely a free-labor nation."[4] By any measure, Seward seemed to be saying that a war over slavery, fought between the North and the South, was truly inevitable.

How much Farley, a college student at the time, may have applauded Seward's inflammatory address and taken it to heart is not certain, but he avoided enlisting in the Union army with the first call for troops and waited instead until the summer of 1862, when the president called for volunteers and reinforcements to aid in the Union cause. Farley was studying law that August when he decided he could no longer ignore the summons of his country. "The time," he wrote, "seemed to have come when every man who could do so should join the ranks."[5] He left behind his law studies and his childhood sweetheart, Mary Caroline Bates, and enlisted.

Eventually he was appointed a second lieutenant in what became Company G, 140th New York Infantry. The regiment, under the command of the energetic and capable West Pointer Colonel Patrick H. O'Rorke, was placed in the Fifth Corps of the Army of the Potomac and stayed pretty much on the sidelines for the battle of Fredericksburg in December 1862 and at Chancellorsville in the spring of 1863. Attrition among the regiment's officers led to a brief transfer to Company A, but Farley returned to his original company in January 1863, earned a promotion to first lieutenant, and served for a short time as the regiment's acting adjutant. He resumed his duties as first lieutenant of Company G in June, when Brigadier General Stephen H. Weed was given command of the Second Division's Third Brigade, which included the 140th New York, the 146th New York, the 91st Pennsylvania, and the 155th Pennsylvania.

On July 2, 1863, Farley, along with his comrades of the 140th New York, would get an opportunity to prove his commitment to the Union cause and to the goal of emancipating America's slaves by putting his life on the line in battle. At 4:00 A.M., as the sun began to creep over the eastern horizon, Farley's regiment shook off a "terrible drowsiness which oppressed us" and left its bivouac beside the Baltimore Pike, heading westward. The men of the 140th marched for about two hours and were halted for a short time while Colonel O'Rorke handed a circular from General Meade to Farley and told him to read it aloud. From the head of the column, Farley read the directive. It was up to the Army of the Potomac, said Meade, to deliver the whole country "from the presence of the foe." The enemy's invasion of Northern soil, the commanding

Colonel Patrick H. O'Rorke, 140th New York

general pointed out, threatened "homes, firesides, and domestic altars." Then, in closing, Meade gave a stern command: "Corps and other commanders are authorized to order the instant death of any soldier who fails in his duty at this hour."[6]

O'Rorke, dressed in a billowing blue military cape, soft felt hat, and long white leather gloves, sat his horse and said a few words of his own to the regiment, echoing Meade's harsh edict and the seriousness of the army's situation. "I call on file-closers," the colonel said, "to do their duty, and if there is a man this day base enough to leave his company, let him die in his tracks—shoot him down like a dog."[7] Tumbling through the ranks came a low murmur of approval. For the time being, the 140th was held in reserve behind the Union right, near Powell's Hill where Rock Creek crossed the Baltimore Pike. Little could Farley know that he and his regiment spent those slow morning hours only a stone's throw from McAllister's Mill, at one time an active station on the Underground Railroad. Many of his comrades might have argued the point, but the war always seemed to devolve in one way or another down to its core issue, the problem of slavery.

* * *

Private billy jordan of Company B, 15th Alabama Infantry, never gave slavery much thought. It was a social and economic arrangement that he very much took for granted. On the morning of July 2, he and the rest of his regiment—part of Brigadier General Evander M. Law's brigade, Hood's division, of Longstreet's corps—waited for orders under a scorching sun atop Herr's Ridge, one mile east of the seminary in Gettysburg. It's unlikely that slavery weighed on his mind.

In fact, slavery was an institution that had never troubled him. Born William Christopher Jordan in 1834 to enterprising parents who established a small plantation at Jordan's Cross Road, near Midway, Alabama, he was raised in a setting where slavery seemed to be the natural order of things. When he was thirteen or fourteen, Jordan became the overseer on his father's plantation, where fifty-three slaves worked as field hands and domestic servants. The plantation produced a diversified crop of corn, oats, potatoes, peas, and a little cotton. Jordan recalled, rather matter-of-factly, that his father also raised horses, cattle, hogs, sheep, and "negroes."[8]

Private William C. Jordan, 15th Alabama

Before his twenty-first birthday, Jordan received a plantation of his own, the result of his father deciding to divide his property among his children before his death. Billy Jordan thus began running his own plantation of 920 acres, just outside of Midway in what was then Macon (later Bullock) County, and supervising more than twenty slaves. In 1856, he married Fannie A. Thornton, a local girl; that year he raised "the best crop I ever made in my life of all kinds of produce." Over the next few years, his wife gave birth to three children, two girls and a boy. Those years, he said, were "the happiest and most satisfying part of my life."[9]

Jordan was a stern and serious young man who claimed to know how to enjoy "fun and frolic," but who showed more capacity for running his business affairs, living a pious life, and scorning the frivolity of others. He proudly declared that from a young age he "made up my mind that I never would take a drink of ardent spirits as long as I lived"; he never refused spirits, however, for medicinal purposes. He was truer to his word in asserting that he never used profanity and would tell others who cursed in his company that he would understand them better if they tried speaking without the "wicked words."[10] The essence of his temperament could be found in his admission that his firm Baptist beliefs included the principle of predestination, the Calvinistic doctrine that relied on the assurance of God's having elected the faithful for salvation before the creation of the world. Small wonder that Jordan often sounded like a Southern Puritan, born out of time.

But when it came to slaves and slavery, Jordan was very much a man of his age, and he held the same thoughts and assumptions that together defined the slaveholders' worldview in the antebellum South. He considered himself a benevolent master, always treating African Americans "kindly, firmly, and honestly," but he declared that under no circumstances should white people "equalize with them in a social sense." Slaves were both property and persons, a fact that was underscored by Southern paternalism. As a result of these attitudes, shared culturally by so many slaveholders, Jordan praised the hard work (and obedience) of some slaves, including one of his favorites, Big Frank, but he would not—and did not—hesitate if economic necessity required him to break up slave families by selling off some of their members.[11]

Not surprisingly, he regarded Lincoln's Emancipation Proclamation with disgust and scorn. Anything that attempted to elevate blacks to the white man's station was, in his estimation, contemptible. He particularly berated whites who treated blacks as equals, for he believed that these whites only disrupted racial relations by instigating "all the trifleness and unreliabilness" that existed among African Americans.[12] With his firm ideas about black inferiority and the efficacy of the peculiar institution, he relied on slaves for his livelihood and his family's welfare, exploited their labor and their lives as he saw fit, and didn't think twice about the social standing of his slaves or how much he used them for his own gain. Even the war could not interrupt his dependence on slave labor. Like other Southern soldiers (including the commander of Jordan's company, Captain Isaac Feagin), he sometimes had a slave with him on the march or in camp. Big Frank would bring him food and mail from home and stayed with his master so long as a battle did not seem imminent.

Like countless Southerners, Jordan maintained that he was a devoted Unionist and that he had, during the winter's crisis of 1861, opposed secession. Such defensive pronouncements make one wonder how secession was ever accomplished at the time, given its unpopularity among the hundreds of thousands of young men who later rather enthusiastically became loyal Confederates and who later still became diehard unreconstructed Southerners, but Jordan decided after Alabama left the Union to do "his duty" and serve "in the Southern cause as if I had been a secessionist."[13] He helped organize a militia company in Midway and served as a sergeant.

When the governor of Alabama called up the company to service in the spring of 1861, the militia unit voted Jordan, without his consent (or so he claimed), out of its ranks because his responsibilities required him to stay home rather than march off to war. At the time, he was running his own plantation and administering the estates of his father-in-law, brother-in-law, and brother, all of whom had died in the years leading up to Fort Sumter. As Jordan explained the situation: "So I was then guardian or representative of a widowed sister with eight minor children, a widowed sister-in-law with four minor children, a widowed mother-in-law and two minor children, a wife and three children and a dear father; in all, consisting of three widows, a wife, seventeen minors and over one hundred slaves that had to be hired out or otherwise looked after."[14] Jordan was simply too hamstrung by family responsibilities to fight Yankees. The onus of Southern gender relationships and the paternalism that white males imposed on their wives, children, and slaves meant that these dependents required protection, and a good number of men besides Jordan successfully avoided military service because of their pressing responsibilities at home.

At last, in the spring of 1862, he managed to find someone to handle his business affairs and family matters, and he reenlisted during a recruitment drive for his old company, which had become Company B of the 15th Alabama Infantry. He thought of his military service as a great sacrifice. Going off to war required "some nerve, will power[,] and determination."[15] He believed he was well suited to be a soldier. A slim man with a narrow face, prominent chin, large protruding ears, and a firm, determined mouth, Jordan liked the outdoors and reckoned that he would have little difficulty adjusting to army life.

He caught up with his company in Virginia, near Manassas, but he almost immediately contracted "old fashioned dry tongue typhoid fever" and ended up in a military hospital in Charlottesville.[16] He lay recuperating for three months. After trying to return to his company before he was fully recovered, he ended up on sick call again and was sent home. He stayed in Midway until after the battle of Sharpsburg, traveled north to find his company again, and suffered another relapse. He was once more sent home to Alabama. Not until April 1863, when the 15th Alabama— along with two divisions of Longstreet's corps—was sent on detached service to southside Virginia, trying to hem in a Union force in Suffolk and gather forage from the rich farms of upper North Carolina, did Jordan finally link up with Company B and begin his actual field experience as a soldier for the Confederacy.

Jordan saw his first action in May, when, at the conclusion of the Suffolk siege, the 15th Alabama performed rear guard duty to keep the Federals at bay while Longstreet and his corps withdrew with orders to hook up again with the Army of Northern Virginia. He found combat an unsettling experience. "I came very near being shot," he later reported. With wonder and relief, he described his close call: "I was in the corner of the fence behind a sapling. A ball struck so near my face that particles of the bark spattered my face and caused the blood to ooze out, the only blood I lost in the war by the missiles of the enemy."[17]

Shortly before Lee's invasion of Pennsylvania began, Jordan received news from home that his only son had died of measles. He was devastated by the loss. For three days after receiving the letter from his wife, he could not pull himself together. Finally, he mustered the inner strength necessary to fall in with the rest of his comrades, join the column as it marched north, and cross the Potomac and the Mason-Dixon line into Pennsylvania. Despite his personal grief, his spirits were high, as were those of most of the men. "I don't believe that a better army ever trod the earth than the one which followed General Lee to Gettysburg," he declared in his twilight years. It was, he noted without flourish, "the grandest army."[18]

Late on the morning of July 2, after having marched from New Guilford (a small hamlet east of Chambersburg) to Gettysburg, a distance of nineteen miles, Jordan was tired and hungry. The march, he said, "was terrible."[19] Anxious for the generals to make up their minds and get on with the war, the 15th Alabama rested on their arms along the ridgeline from where they could see without obstruction the cupola of the seminary a mile to the west. There was little shade on Herr's Ridge, and the men looked more like wilted wildflowers than warriors.

More unsettling than the exhaustion they felt from their forced march through the morning were the disquieting field hospitals they had passed on their approach to Herr's Ridge. Colonel William C. Oates, commanding the 15th, remembered that "wounded men and thousands of prisoners" stood in full view of the Alabamians—evidence of "the bloody engagement" that had taken place at Gettysburg the day before.[20] Jordan and his fellow Alabamians waited into the early afternoon with the memory of those wounded men fresh in their minds and with the sobering realization that the coming battle that day might deliver them into a similar misery—or worse.

LEE WAS IN A QUANDARY as the morning waned. He wondered mostly what was taking place on his army's left and whether Ewell was about to launch an attack there. As he paced back and forth on the ridge slope near the seminary, where he had established his observation post, he occasionally diverted his path to the tree where British Colonel Fremantle and Prussian Captain Scheibert had spent the better part of the morning. Twice, said Scheibert, Lee called up "to ask about the positions and movements of the enemy."[21] Finally Lee could no longer stand the wait, and he decided to ride to Ewell to find out for himself what was happening on his left.

When Lee arrived at Ewell's headquarters, he abandoned an earlier idea of shifting Ewell's troops to the right to open an attack on the Union lines. Instead, he reiterated his earlier instructions to Ewell, emphasizing that the Second Corps was to demonstrate against the Union right as soon as Ewell heard the sound of Longstreet's guns booming to the south. With this, Lee returned to Seminary Ridge, now overly anxious that Longstreet's movement against the Union left had not begun. "What *can* detain Longstreet?" the general asked Colonel Armistead L. Long, who had returned from a reconnaissance of the Federal lines.[22]

The question was peculiar, for Lee still as yet had not established a full plan for his army that day. In fact, Longstreet—or so he claimed after the war, during the bitter controversy that surrounded his role at Gettysburg—had yet to receive any final orders from Lee about the attack of the First Corps. Longstreet felt unsure about moving forward without all three of his divisions in place. Law's brigade of Hood's division was not yet fully up, and Major General George E. Pickett's entire division was still moving from Chambersburg toward Gettysburg at the time that Lee rode over to see Ewell. To General Hood, Longstreet said: "The General [i.e., Lee] is a little nervous this morning; he wishes me to attack; I do not wish to do so without Pickett. I never like to go into battle with one boot off." According to Longstreet, Lee returned from his visit with Ewell and said that the Second Corps would not be altering its position or opening the attack. Lee ordered Longstreet to "make the attack on the extreme right."[23] It was about 11:00 A.M. Longstreet, finally satisfied that he had been given a direct command, asked Lee if he could wait just a while longer for Law's brigade—the last of Hood's division—to arrive. Lee consented to the delay (another odd bit of behavior by a man who, only minutes before, had articulated frustration with Longstreet's apparent slowness).

Under the blistering noon sun, the Confederates waited uneasily for the next chapter in the Gettysburg saga to unfold. It never seemed to occur to Lee or his subordinates that while the morning hours slowly crept by, the situation over on the opposite heights was changing dramatically. At best, Lee's plan had evolved over the course of the summer's morning in bits and pieces so that by noontime it resembled more a patchwork than a seamless cloth. Throughout those morning hours, Lee appeared to suffer from doubt, indecision, anxiety, confusion, forgetfulness, and lack of resolve. These responses were only exacerbated by his inability to get his generals to act. Lee seemed strangely off his game, out of sorts, disconnected with the events that were shaping the coming engagement. He was not the Lee who had fought so brilliantly in Virginia. On Northern soil, he had—in an almost spiritual sense—lost his inner compass.

* * *

Near daybreak that morning, Ellis Spear awoke to the trill of bugles and the groans and coughs of men who wished they could have gotten a few more hours' sleep. No one in the 20th Maine seemed to feel his best that morning. Spear was still struggling with his fever, aches, and diarrhea. The regiment's commander, Colonel Chamberlain, was suffering from sunstroke. Other soldiers in the regiment also felt the effects of heat and sun and forced marches. Chamberlain formed the regiment, held an inspection of arms, and marched it in a warm mist two miles or so, where it took up a position in line of battle at a peach orchard south of Wolf's Hill and the Hanover Road. In a short while, Chamberlain remembered, "we were moved to the left, across Rock Creek and up the Baltimore Pike to an open field more nearly overlooking the town." To the regiment's right was the Twelfth Corps occupying Culp's Hill. The 20th was told to rest for a while, so the men stretched out on the ground "to make up for lost sleep."[24]

Chamberlain later took note of "the great calm, the uncertainty of overture, and [the] seeming lack of [a] tactical plan for the tremendous

Colonel Joshua Lawrence Chamberlain, 20th Maine, shown here in a photograph taken later in the war, when he was a general.

issue." He and his men realized, he said fifty years later, that the entire army was assembling itself in Gettysburg and that the Confederates were massing their forces as well. "But what we had no means of knowing or judging," he wrote, was "which side would take the offensive and which the defensive, or where the battle would begin." All Chamberlain knew at the time was that he and his regiment had been ordered "to hold ourselves ready to take part in an attack on our right."[25] The men were given an additional twenty rounds of ammunition to augment the sixty rounds already in their cartridge pouches.

Noncombatants were dismissed from the regiment, except for Chamberlain's younger brother, John, a volunteer worker with the Christian Commission, who remained at his brother's side. Chamberlain also had another younger brother with him, Thomas, who held the rank of lieutenant in the 20th Maine and served as the regiment's adjutant. Spear considered Lieutenant Chamberlain "an excellent officer," and the two men had bunked together during the previous winter, when a blizzard once blocked the door of their camp cabin with drifted snow.[26] Spear and the other men of the 20th Maine seemed not to mind that the Chamberlains had taken over the regiment as a family affair; the colonel and the lieutenant had already demonstrated their leadership talents on and off the battlefield.

But Colonel Chamberlain seemed like a fish out of water. As a professor who had earlier attended seminary and earned ordination as a minister, Chamberlain was mild-mannered, soft-spoken, and retiring in his demeanor and manners. There was nothing warlike about him. Born in 1828 in Brewer, Maine, he was the son of a small farmer who worked a hundred-acre farm overlooking the Penobscot River. His father named him Lawrence for the great naval hero of the War of 1812, Commodore James Lawrence, who had proclaimed, "Don't give up the ship!" Chamberlain's father hoped he would pursue a military career.

His mother later added Joshua to the boy's name by asking the local Brewer keeper of records to emend the first name, a Chamberlain family tradition, to the town's books. She hoped her son would fulfill the religious symbolism of his name by becoming a man of the cloth. Torn between these two parental wishes, the young Chamberlain did become a minister but had no desire to make a living as a pastor. In 1856, he married Frances (Fanny) Adams, the adopted daughter of a Congregational minister. The courtship had been tumultuous; so, too, was the marriage. Chamberlain's teaching at Bowdoin, his undergraduate alma mater, became a middle course—that is, a path that was neither military nor ministerial—until the Civil War and the cause of the Union compelled him to take up arms against the South. By doing so, Chamberlain deceptively made the college's administrators believe he was taking a scholarly sabbatical, when in fact he had applied to the governor of Maine for an appointment as an officer in the new 20th Maine Infantry in the late summer of 1862.

As lieutenant colonel of the regiment, Chamberlain revealed that he had found his calling as a soldier in what became an eerie culmination of both of his parents' desires: the Civil War enabled Chamberlain to transform himself into his Old Testament namesake, the hero of Jericho, a soldier who was embarking on a godly military crusade against the Canaanites of the Old South. He found that he enjoyed soldiering, more than he ever could have imagined, and he discovered, too, that he had never felt better in his entire life. In the experience of war, which often revealed the horror and brutality of mankind, he could find something positive, something abidingly noble to savor. "War is for the participants a test of character; it makes bad men worse and good men better."[27] During most of his life, Chamberlain struggled with bouts of deep depression and melancholy. But not during the war years. It was as if the war and soldiering had made a new man of him.

In late May 1863, Chamberlain received a promotion to the colonelcy of the 20th Maine in the wake of a round of smallpox that struck down many in the regiment. At nearly the same moment, rambunctious veterans of the 2nd Maine Infantry, disgruntled with the fact that the rest of their comrades had returned home after serving two-year enlistments, had been reassigned to the 20th and began showing up in camp. Chamberlain treated the grumbling men decently, and almost all of them agreed to take up their muskets again in the service of the 20th Maine. Down with heat prostration, he missed the engagement at Middleburg on June 21, but he moved out with the regiment as it marched north, refusing to ride in a wagon as his brother John wanted him to. "I'll ride like a man," he said, and took his saddle, loping along in the company of Colonel James C. Rice, commander of the 44th New York.[28]

Yet there was something about Chamberlain that didn't quite add up. It was an intangible, whatever it was, yet the man occasionally made others slightly suspicious of him. Even Spear could not quite put his finger on what it was. To be sure, Chamberlain's earnestness put some people off. After the war, however, Spear identified the problem more specifically.

What troubled him about Chamberlain, he said, was the man's "ego-
tism." The colonel often seemed too full of himself, too vainglorious, too
conscious of his own actions and how they would be perceived by others.
Chamberlain possessed, said Spear, an "inordinate vanity."[29]

IN THE LITTLE WHITE COTTAGE on Taneytown Road, General Meade
continued to make his preparations for the day. The house was crammed
with officers whose urgent conversations created a babble of voices; whenever the two small rooms filled up with aides and orderlies, the congrega-
tion of blue overflowed outside onto the narrow porch and into the yard.
Meade seemed oblivious to the chaos around him. Poring over maps
placed on a table, he studied the terrain, received reports about which
units had taken up their positions, and tried to imagine what might be up
Robert E. Lee's sleeve. Meade looked tired and haggard, his brow fur-
rowed and his eyes intently focused. He was the man of the hour in so
many respects, and his performance this day would not only prove his
mettle as a general, it must also somehow save the country.

Like an unwanted and unexpected guest, Sickles appeared suddenly
at headquarters, professing that he still could not understand where
Meade wanted the Third Corps to be placed. Sickles's uncertainty about
what had been direct orders must have further confirmed Meade's already low opinion of the man as a general officer. Meade told Sickles one
more time what he had attempted to communicate earlier through his
son, Captain Meade—that the Third Corps was to occupy the same ground
that General Geary's division of the Twelfth Corps had held the night before. Sickles replied that, in his opinion, he had seen some good ground
for the placement of artillery and would like a staff officer to take a look
at the terrain and assess the situation for the placement of batteries. He
also asked Meade if he was authorized "to post his corps in such a manner as, in his judgment, he should deem the most suitable." Meade answered with caution: "Certainly, within the limits of the general instructions
I have given to you; any ground within those limits you choose to occupy
I leave to you."[30]

Meade told General Hunt, who had just returned from a surveillance
of the army's right wing, to accompany Sickles and examine his line. But
here Meade abandoned his usual caution. For one thing, Hunt knew
nothing of Meade's insistence that the Third Corps should occupy the

ground where Geary's division had been. For another, Meade himself—given all the trouble that Sickles had already caused that morning—should have ridden over and explicitly pointed out the position. Instead, he remained for the moment at headquarters, while Sickles and Hunt cantered off together on a mission that would only add more entanglements to a situation that had become—partly as a result of Sickles's own desire to muddy the waters—an exercise in faulty communications.

But the kind of confusion that breeds mistakes had not finished its work with Meade. Soon after Sickles and Hunt rode south toward the lines of the Third Corps, Major General Alfred Pleasonton, the army's cavalry commander, showed up at headquarters on the Taneytown Road wanting Meade to allow Buford's cavalry brigades, which had been deployed about a half mile west of Little Round Top since the previous night, to withdraw from their position for refitting at the cavalry depot in Westminster, Maryland. Concerned over the condition of his troopers, who had practically been ground to dust in their hard ride throughout the campaign and the pounding they had taken in the previous day's battle, Buford had requested permission to withdraw from Pleasonton, who in turn wanted Meade to give his approval. Meade, who knew that the welfare of his left wing depended on the presence of cavalry there to fend off a flank attack by the enemy, probably also realized that some of Buford's horsemen had been engaged in skirmish fighting near the Emmitsburg Road that morning, and that these men had given all that could be expected of them in this battle.

Meade gave his permission; he had no reason not to, just as he had no reason to assume that Pleasonton would not quickly replace Buford's troopers with some other cavalry brigades. But when Buford and his tired men left the ground beneath Little Round Top sometime before noon, Pleasonton neglected to send urgent orders for replacements to move up and cover the army's flank. That left the entire left wing of the Army of the Potomac "in the air"—a military phrase used at the time to describe an unanchored and unprotected flank. When Meade discovered later that Pleasonton had failed to obey orders, he became "exceedingly annoyed" and sent some bristling dispatches ordering his cavalry commander to rectify the potentially disastrous situation by either recalling Buford or bringing forward other cavalry.[31] But Pleasonton still did not act with alacrity. In the end, no cavalry would move up to cover the army's left until after the fighting on July 2 was finished. As the noon hour approached and the day grew only hotter and the heavy air became suffocating with every breath, Meade had no idea that the left wing of the Army of the Potomac lay vulnerable, inviting an assault.

DURING THE MORNING, while Meade adjusted his lines and tried from a distance to determine what Sickles was up to, Lieutenant Aaron B. Jerome of the army Signal Corps scampered up the northern slope of Little Round Top and decided to establish a signal station where signalmen had maintained a torch post through the previous night. Atop the boulders on the hill, Jerome could see signal parties on Cemetery Hill and at Meade's headquarters even without using field glasses or a telescope. With him was a sergeant who held the signal flag and waited for Jerome to make contact with the army's nearest stations and with more distant stations in Taneytown and on Jack's Mountain in the South Mountain range.

At 11:45, Lieutenant Jerome had his flag sergeant signal a message to General Butterfield, Meade's chief of staff, at army headquarters on the Taneytown Road: "Enemy's skirmishers are advancing from the west, 1 mile from here." What Jerome saw were the lead units of Confederate Brigadier General Cadmus M. Wilcox's brigade of Alabamians getting into position along the southern stretch of Seminary Ridge, near Pitzer's Woods. Ten minutes later, the signal officer watched as Lieutenant Colonel Casper Trepp, commanding one hundred of Colonel Hiram Berdan's famous sharpshooters, dressed in their green uniforms, and supported by another two hundred officers and men of the 3rd Maine Infantry, moved toward the woods to flush out the enemy. After a brisk firefight, the Union troops fell back, and Jerome sent another message to Butterfield: "The rebels are in force, and our skirmishers give way. One mile west of [Little] Round Top signal station, the woods are full of them."[32]

Having sent this intelligence, Jerome packed up his flags and rode down the slopes of Little Round Top to accompany Buford and his brigades on their withdrawal to Maryland. For the time being, no one remained on Little Round Top. The Army of the Potomac's left flank not only fluttered in the air, it was now blind as well.

3

MARCH, COUNTERMARCH

LIEUTENANT GENERAL JAMES LONGSTREET, all surly and bearish to everyone around him as the noon hour passed away on July 2, simply did not want to make the flank attack against the Union left. He had argued vigorously with Lee against the idea and had done everything in his power to convince him that it would be far more prudent to move the Army of Northern Virginia to ground of its own choosing, where it could force the enemy to attack its defensive lines. But Lee would not leave the field to the Federals; his blood was up, and he was determined to attack the Union lines.

Even Longstreet's most loyal followers, who were there with him at Gettysburg, admitted that he was in a sour mood on the afternoon of July 2. Lieutenant Colonel G. Moxley Sorrel of Longstreet's staff observed that the general showed "apparent apathy in his movements" and that his actions "lacked the fire and point of his usual bearing on the battlefield." Longstreet also "failed to conceal some anger." Immediately after Gettysburg, Lafayette McLaws expressed his ire with Longstreet by claiming that the corps commander had issued "contradictory orders to everyone, and was exceedingly overbearing." No longer could McLaws abide Longstreet: "I consider him a humbug—a man of small capacity, very obstinate, not at all chivalrous, exceedingly conceited, and totally selfish."[1]

While McLaws attacked Longstreet's character and dismissed him as a fraud, and while later generations of Southerners took delight in placing the blame for the defeat at Gettysburg entirely on Longstreet's shoulders, the reason for the general's poor performance at Gettysburg was probably far less diabolical than his fellow Confederates assumed. Experience and

Major General Lafayette McLaws, Army of Northern Virginia

instinct told Longstreet that this battle could not be won; the same sensibilities convinced Lee otherwise. As a result, Longstreet found himself caught in an officer's worst dilemma—the necessity of carrying out orders in which one has no faith.

After waiting for Law's brigade to arrive outside Gettysburg, Longstreet finally got his two divisions moving to reach the jumping-off point for the day's assault up the Emmitsburg Road. The approach was made all the more difficult by Lee's admonition that Longstreet should "proceed cautiously upon the forward movement, so to avoid being seen by the enemy."[2] Although Captain Johnston had reported that no Federal troops occupied the Round Tops, Confederate observers could plainly make out the presence of Union Signal Corps flags on Little Round Top. That meant that Longstreet's divisions could not simply march cross-country to the south behind the screen of trees along Seminary Ridge.

Colonel Edward Porter Alexander, whose artillery rolled off ahead of Longstreet's infantry, did manage to find a route south to the Emmitsburg Road that avoided observation by the Federal spotters, detouring an open spot that offered a clear view from Little Round Top of the fields behind Seminary Ridge. Actually, the Confederates need not have worried as much as they did. Although the signal officers on Little Round Top were diligent, they couldn't always discern what it was they were looking at. At one point, after signal officers arrived to occupy the hill after Jerome's departure with Buford's cavalry, the flags sent a misleading signal to headquarters saying that "a heavy column of enemy's infantry, about 10,000 strong, is moving from opposite our extreme left toward our right"—in exactly the opposite direction to which Longstreet's troops were actually moving, although in all fairness to the signalmen, they probably were observing efforts by Longstreet's divisions to double back on their route to avoid being spotted.[3]

It was McLaws's division that the Federals had noticed. In accordance with Lee's orders, which had specified that McLaws would spearhead the attack against the Union left, McLaws had led the column that afternoon, after it had formed up with Hood's division to the rear in the vicinity of Willoughby Run. McLaws stepped off probably between noon and 1:00 P.M. As best as can be determined, McLaws, under Longstreet's apparent approval, followed the many narrow roads and farm lanes that traversed the terrain that Alexander, by cutting across the fields, had successfully avoided, thus effecting a better screen for his limbers and caissons. Why Longstreet and McLaws did not simply trail in the wake of Alexander's wheel tracks remains one of Gettysburg's most tantalizing mysteries.

Captain Samuel Johnston, on Lee's orders, accompanied McLaws, but he later claimed that when he rode at the head of the column he was not acting in the capacity of a guide, which makes little sense, under the circumstances. Johnston had surveyed the ground earlier—no matter how imperfectly—and would afterwards admit that as a good engineer on reconnaissance duty it was his job to determine a favorable approach route for the Confederate assault. After the war, Johnston said that Lee had given him no specific instructions, other than "to join General Longstreet." But surely he must have understood Lee's intentions at the time, even if he claimed not to later on. Johnston also maintained that he had not been told where Longstreet's divisions were going and he assumed that Lee wanted him to ride with the column in order to give Longstreet "the benefit of the information that I had obtained by reconnaissance" earlier that morning—a seeming contradiction. He asserted, rather incredulously, that he "had no idea that I had the confidence of the great Lee to such an extent that he would entrust me with the conduct of an army corps moving within two miles of the enemy's lines."[4]

McLaws and his division marched under the brutally hot sun in open country until they passed from the Fairfield Road to a road running southeast toward the Pitzer Schoolhouse. Suddenly, as they mounted a hill, McLaws realized that his men were in clear view of Little Round Top, so he halted the column and tried to figure out what to do next. McLaws was convinced that they could not proceed without being observed by the Federals. He was furious, and one soldier heard him sputtering obscenities that "I would not like to teach my grandson."[5] Cantering down the line, McLaws found Longstreet, who had been in the rear with Lee and riding with Hood, and reported the problem, but Longstreet made it clear that he was impatient with the halt and with any delays in getting his divisions into position. After the two generals rode back to the crest and McLaws pointed out how they were exposed to Federal observers on Little Round Top, Longstreet agreed that the situation was not good and that an alternative route must be found. McLaws knew another route, one he had discovered while doing his own reconnaissance earlier in the day, but he warned Longstreet that using it would involve a countermarch. By this time, both McLaws and Longstreet showed their "considerable irritation," which became apparent to their subalterns and to the men in the ranks. Finally Longstreet gave the order: "Then countermarch."[6]

It was much easier said than done. The troops could not simply turn around and retrace their steps, for McLaws's division needed to remain in the lead of the column. Before ordering the countermarch, Longstreet's impatience had led him to tell Hood's division to push forward "by the most direct route" to take up a position to the right, but when McLaws attempted to effect his countermarch, his division ran into Hood's maneuvering brigades, which resulted in a tangled traffic jam.[7] Rectifying the jumbled divisions and getting everyone in their proper place in column took time. Longstreet suggested as a practical matter that Hood should lead the countermarch, but McLaws would not hear of it, probably because Lee himself had told him to lead the assault. Longstreet, to his discredit, failed to insist, and so more time was spent waiting while McLaws assumed what he considered to be his rightful place at the head of the column. Although accounts of the countermarch are sketchy at best, it would appear that McLaws returned his division to the place where it had begun its initial march on Herr Ridge, and it was probably this movement, heading toward the Confederate right, that the Federal signalmen spotted from their station on Little Round Top.

From Herr's Ridge, the column moved down into the valley of Willoughby Run and then probably along a farm lane to the Pitzer Schoolhouse. McLaws later wrote that the countermarch was accomplished "with considerable difficulty, owing to the rough character of the country in places and the fences and ditches we had to cross."[8] Longstreet, writing after the war, minimized the effects of the countermarch, making it sound like he personally expedited the movement of his divisions toward the Emmitsburg Road. The soldiers doing the tramping remembered the countermarch as grueling. An Alabamian remembered the ordeal: "The roads were the roughest and the long, sloping hills the steepest. The day was hot, and we were thirsty and had not stopped to rest or drink."[9]

Among the men of the 15th Alabama, Colonel William Oates showed concern not only for his weary and thirsty men, he was also worried about the well-being of his younger brother, John, who was a lieutenant in Company G. John Oates was suffering from severe rheumatism, which had grown worse since the previous April, when his pain had become almost unbearable. Now the long march north to Gettysburg, and especially the endless march of this day, took its toll, and he discovered that he could no longer keep up with the regiment as it wound its way toward the Union army's left flank. Breaking regulations, William gave John a horse to ride, so he would not fall behind with the other stragglers, but staying in the saddle proved to be as much a challenge as walking, for the pain in John's hips and legs simply would not go away.

The two brothers had always been close and had made special efforts to look out for one another. Born in the wiregrass country of southeastern Alabama, the two boys had spent their youth learning how to survive. Not only did Indian raids threaten their early lives, but so too did the demands of a violent frontier, where men used their brute strength to prove their manhood in countless brawls and drunken donnybrooks. Their own father often fell into a drunken stupor after taking his anger out on his wife and children. William, born in 1833, the eldest of eight children, sometimes emptied his father's bottles and jugs, refilling the containers with vinegar; more than once, his father discovered the boy in the act and brutally punished him for tampering with his liquor supplies. Two years younger, John often relied on William for protection from their abusive father.

More than anything, violence shaped the lives of the Oates brothers. William got into frequent fistfights and scuffles with local adversaries, including bullies and ne'er-do-wells he could not abide. When he was seventeen, he attended a seance and imprudently revealed the spiritist to be a fraud. The medium's father went after William with a board, and the two became entangled in a terrific mêlée that ended when young Oates struck the man on the head with a hoe, cracking his skull and rendering him unconscious. In a panic, Oates fled from Alabama, convinced he had killed the man, and soon began a journey of discovery that took him from Pensacola, through the Creole bayous of Louisiana, to the wild country of Texas, where he became a rather unsuccessful gambler and a brawler of considerable skill.

Although he had learned that the man he had bludgeoned in Alabama had not died, Oates remained in Texas avoiding other warrants for his arrest that had been issued in Shreveport, Louisiana, and Marshall, Texas. While walking the streets of Henderson, a small frontier settlement located about forty miles north of Nacogdoches, William unexpectedly looked up to see his brother John coming toward him. Young John

Colonel William C. Oates, 15th Alabama

had been sent by the family to find William and persuade him to come home. "Our joy at the meeting was very great," wrote William many years later.[10] The two brothers traveled back to Alabama, most of the way on foot, and surprised their parents when they came marching down the dusty road that led to the old homestead.

To evade the long arm of the law, William took up residence in a different county from the one in which his family resided, and after teaching school for a while, he settled down to studying law. He passed the bar in 1858 and opened up a practice in Abbeville, the seat of Henry County on the Chattahoochee River. There he became a pillar of society, buying a local newspaper and running it as editor and publisher and involving himself in local politics as a steadfast Breckinridge Democrat. He became so prosperous, he may have even owned a slave or two. John followed in his older brother's footsteps, successfully studied law, and eventually joined William's firm as a partner. The law firm of Oates & Oates thrived in the months before the Civil War, but when Alabama seceded from the Union in January 1861 and cannons forced the surrender of Fort Sumter in Charleston harbor three months later, the Oates brothers quickly and solemnly pledged their lives to the fate of the Confederacy.

John Oates was the first to act by enlisting in the 6th Alabama Infantry during the spring of 1861 and seeing combat on the sidelines of the first battle of Manassas in July. That summer William formed a militia company in Abbeville, the "Henry Pioneers," marched it north to join the 15th Alabama Infantry, and became captain of the regiment's Company G. In November 1861, while the Confederates established their makeshift winter camps in the vicinity of Centreville, John transferred to his brother's company and regiment, accepting a promotion from private to the rank of first lieutenant, an arrangement his brother, no doubt, worked out with the 15th Alabama brigade leadership. Now John was where William could easily keep an eye on him. Both of them saw action with Stonewall Jackson's Army of the Valley in the battles fought in the spring of 1862 at Front Royal, Winchester, and Cross Keys. Later they participated in the Peninsula Campaign, fighting at Gaines's Mill and Malvern Hill. They also fought virtually side by side with Jackson's forces at Cedar Run, Second Manassas, and Chantilly, but just before the fight at Sharpsburg on September 17, 1862, the bloodiest single day of the Civil War, William took ill and fell behind to recuperate.

The toll in lives at Sharpsburg was high for both armies and particularly for the 15th Alabama. When William caught up with the regiment after the battle, he assumed command of the entire 15th Alabama, for he was the only officer above the rank of lieutenant left alive or in good enough condition to lead the shattered companies. John survived the carnage along the Antietam, and in December the two brothers came under fire with their regiment along Lee's left flank at Fredericksburg. They dodged bullets again, after the 15th Alabama was transferred to Law's Alabama Brigade in Longstreet's corps, during the siege at Suffolk. The men in the ranks had mixed feelings about Oates as their commanding officer. Some praised him highly. "There are a great deal of men here," wrote Bud Cody to his sister, "that wants to be under him." Others, however, regarded William Oates "a handsome and brave leader," but believed him to be "too aggressive and ambitious" for his and their own good. Many soldiers, nevertheless, admitted that Oates could usually be observed during battle "well to the front[,] and [he] did not require his men to charge where he was unwilling to share the common danger."[11]

Now, in the company of their thirsty and fatigued comrades, the Oates brothers followed the narrow, winding roads that led them—and the rest of Hood's division of Longstreet's corps—through the tree-lined and shaded valley, where Willoughby Run cut its way down and across the rolling hills that undulated to the south of Gettysburg. With every foot of ground gained, John Oates grimaced in pain, and William Oates knew that his brother was in no condition to be marching into battle.

LEAN AND HANDSOME DAN SICKLES demonstrated no particular aptitude for things military. But that didn't stop him from thinking he did. As he and General Hunt surveyed the lines of the Third Corps and the terrain along the Emmitsburg Road, the two generals rode to a peach orchard (it would later gain fame as *the* Peach Orchard) on an elevated plain, slightly less than a mile west of the ground where Meade had told Sickles to post his Third Corps. Sickles told Hunt that he wanted to advance the Third Corps to this position, for it offered a perfect platform for posting his artillery batteries, whereas the lower elevations of Cemetery Ridge to the rear could not command the expanse of open farmland that stretched from the Peach Orchard to Seminary Ridge to the west. Although Sickles was no military man, Hunt had to concede that this advanced position did have several advantages, not the least of which was the fact that it commanded the ground to its front and rear and thus "constituted a favorable position for *the enemy* to hold." But Hunt also saw immediately that in Union hands the Peach Orchard would require Sickles's corps to form a salient, which would expose "both of its sides to enfilade fires," and would be unconnected to the Second Corps on Cemetery Ridge, about five hundred yards to the rear, unless the left wing of the Second Corps was thrown out to link up with the Third Corps. Even with that, said Hunt, he doubted if Sickles had enough men to defend such a salient.[12]

It was Hunt who suggested that Sickles send forward Berdan's sharpshooters to reconnoiter Pitzer's Woods and determine whether enemy troops were there. If so, the defense of the Peach Orchard salient would become untenable. Hunt did not wait to learn the results of the reconnaissance. Sickles asked him if he should advance the Third Corps, and Hunt prudently answered: "Not on my authority; I will report to General Meade for his instructions."[13] Stopping at headquarters on his way to the Union right, Hunt advised Meade not to allow any troops to move forward toward the Emmitsburg Road without personally inspecting the position himself.

Having learned from Berdan's probe into the woods that Confederates occupied that portion of Seminary Ridge directly in his front and

Major General Daniel E. Sickles, Army of the Potomac

that Buford's cavalry had retired without replacements being deployed, Sickles grew increasingly convinced that he could advance his corps forward, and he worried about how he was supposed to defend his left flank without cavalry. Taking matters into his own hands, he made the decision to move his corps up to the Peach Orchard and put his divisions into position along an extensive line that ran from the Emmitsburg Road to a pile of granite boulders called Devil's Den, more than a thousand yards southeast of the orchard.

Sickles loved the theater and opera, which he often attended in the West End of New York City with his favorite prostitute on his arm, and his advance to the plain of the Peach Orchard on the afternoon of July 2 seemed straight out of Wagner. While he would later maintain that Meade ignored the vital circumstances of the Third Corps because the commanding general wanted to withdraw the Army of the Potomac to a defensive line near Pipe Creek in Maryland (a red herring meant to deflect attention away from Sickles's reckless disobedience of orders), the advance of his corps to the Peach Orchard was predicated almost entirely on Sickles's own anxiety about being the target of a Confederate flank attack, his paltry understanding of infantry tactics, and his lack of experience about how best to use terrain in deploying troops.

So his men moved forward, without Sickles notifying headquarters or General Hancock, whose Second Corps occupied the main Union defensive line to Sickles's right. Later he made no apologies for the unauthorized advance. He boldly admitted to a joint Congressional committee of inquiry in 1864: "It was not through any misinterpretation of orders. It was either a good line or a bad one, and, whichever it was, I took it on my own responsibility . . . I took up that line because it enabled me to hold commanding ground, which, if the enemy had been allowed to take—as they would have taken it if I had not occupied it in force—would have rendered our position on the left untenable; and in my judgment, would have turned the fortunes of the day hopelessly against us."[14]

What Sickles could not know at the time, and which no one within the Union lines knew either, was that Longstreet's corps had begun its approach for an attack that would, by sheer happenstance, collide with the Federal Third Corps along a front Sickles had chosen and where the Confederates least expected to find any enemy forces at all. So by pure luck, and through the fortitude of the troops in blue that would give their blood to hold back Longstreet's onslaught that afternoon, Sickles could later claim to be the hero of the day, the savior of the Union. Skillful lawyer that he was, he presented his own case so effectively that in 1891 he was awarded the Medal of Honor for his actions at Gettysburg—actions that Meade and nearly every other general officer in the Army of the Potomac condemned as insubordinate, irresponsible, and murderous in their effect.

As the blue tide of his corps surged forward, Sickles learned that he had been called to headquarters for a meeting of corps commanders. He rushed a courier to Meade asking to be excused, but the commanding general refused the request. Exasperated by the inconvenience of this meeting, Sickles galloped to the little white cottage on the Taneytown Road. Before he reached headquarters, however, the thunder of cannon sounded along his lines. While Sickles rode quickly toward the cottage, Brigadier General Gouverneur Kemble Warren, the army's chief engineer, was telling Meade and the assembled corps commanders that, based on his own reconnaissance of the Union lines, the Third Corps was out of position and occupied ground well in advance of the terrain selected by Meade for defense. Meade was shocked and angry.

By the time Sickles arrived at headquarters, the meeting had broken up in response to the sharp reports of artillery along the Union left. Meade instructed Sickles not to dismount and to get back to his lines as quickly as he could; he would follow him directly. With that, Meade decisively ordered Major General George Sykes's Fifth Corps to march from the rear in the vicinity of the Baltimore Pike to reinforce the Union left. Then he found a horse and rode with Warren toward Sickles's lines. Warren pointed to Little Round Top as they moved toward the sound of the guns and said: "Here's where the line should be." Meade replied: "It is too late now," for the enemy's attack had already begun. A few moments later, Meade reined in his horse. "Warren!" he exclaimed, "I hear a little peppering going on in the direction of that hill off yonder. I wish you would ride over and if anything serious is going on, attend to it." Warren, followed by an entourage of aides, spurred his horse in the direction of Little Round Top.[15]

With sporadic musket fire having already begun in bursting ripples that cascaded across the Emmitsburg Road, General Meade came upon Sickles and his staff near the Peach Orchard. Although accounts of the conversation between the two generals differ, it seems most likely that Meade informed Sickles that he had overextended his lines "beyond supporting distance of the army."[16] Yet Meade also recognized that the situation, as bad as it was, could not be corrected in time before the enemy's advancing lines would be upon them. At that moment the Confederate batteries opened with a reverberating explosion, a salvo that initiated a tremendous barrage by Longstreet's artillery, and Meade ordered Sickles to hold on as best he could, promising to provide as much support as the army could send up.

LIEUTENANT PORTER FARLEY and his comrades in the 140th New York, Third Brigade, Second Division, of Sykes's Fifth Corps spent the early afternoon gratefully lounging on the southeastern slopes of Power's Hill, just off the Baltimore Pike. While some men napped under shade trees that provided little relief from the day's stifling heat, others dipped into their rations or looked longingly for water. Vague rumors circulated among the men about what was to happen that day, but no one really had any idea if there would be a battle or if they might the spend the rest of the day on this comfortable hillside. The men did not seem terribly excited or unduly agitated about the likelihood of a battle. "With that habitual stoicism with which the soldier ever regards the prospect of an encounter," wrote one veteran of the Fifth Corps after the war, "after listening to a few [distant] discharges we dozed as calmly and chatted as carelessly as if assembled on a festive occasion."[17]

On the hillside, Brigadier General Stephen H. Weed, commander of the 140th New York's brigade, made his headquarters for the afternoon with the regiment, and he and Colonel O'Rorke spent those uneventful hours quietly conversing as they, too, heard the occasional rumbling of artillery and the periodic rattling of muskets. At one point, remembered an officer in the 140th, Weed and O'Rorke could be heard singing the chorus of the sentimental song, "No One to Cherish." The singing became contagious, and the New Yorkers joined in with their officers and soon the hillside was alive with song. When they finished one tune, they moved on to another, and the men filled part of the afternoon lifting their voices to the melodies of "Lorena," "The Virginia Lowlands," and "Listen to the Mockingbird."[18]

If O'Rorke seemed not the type of officer to give speeches to his men, as Farley had believed, he seemed even less the kind who would break out in song. Born in County Cavan, Ireland, in 1836, O'Rorke moved with his parents to America, settling in Rochester, New York, during the great wave of Irish immigration between 1838 and 1844. He was raised in an Irish neighborhood called "Dublin," where he attended St. Bridget's Catholic Church, became a member of the church's "Young Men's Mutual Aid Society," and felt with other immigrants the rebuke of native-born Protestant Americans. The young O'Rorke excelled in school, and after spending two years as a marble cutter, managed to win a coveted appointment to West Point, which he entered in the summer of 1857. Unlike his fellow cadets, O'Rorke was from a struggling urban family, and he was the only foreign-born member of his class.

At West Point, O'Rorke learned not only the substance of the academic subjects he studied, he also gained discipline in his life. One classmate described him as "spare, medium in size, with raven black hair, his face inclined to freckles, but as mild as a May morning, his manner and voice those of a quiet, refined gentleman." General Warren, who taught at the academy from 1859 to 1861, thought O'Rorke "was a man of noble character, and had nothing of the wild Irish in him."[19] He was taciturn, studious, and determined. In 1861, he was graduated first in his class. With the war already begun at Fort Sumter, O'Rorke was immediately ordered with his classmates to Washington, where he joined the staff of Brigadier General Daniel Tyler. The following autumn, he served on the engineering staff of Brigadier General Thomas W. Sherman's Port Royal Expeditionary Corps.

In the summer of 1862, he returned to Rochester to marry Clarissa Wadsworth Bishop, "his fellow parishioner, his fellow schoolmate and his boyhood sweetheart." After the wedding, he accepted the command of the newly raised 140th New York regiment and received a colonel's commission. Proclaimed a local newspaper: "Under Col. O'Rorke our new regiment cannot fail to become one of the most efficient in the service."[20] He was twenty-six years old.

There was enough wild Irish in him, despite General Warren's opinion, to make him an outstanding leader of men and a courageous combat officer. A soldier in the regiment applauded O'Rorke's performance on the battlefield and announced that the colonel had "proved himself all that we supposed him to be—a brave and cool commander." Porter Farley admired O'Rorke for his "soldierly qualities," and it was clear to him that the colonel was "not only scholarly and elegant, but . . . fitted for emergencies."[21] Aggressive and bold, there was also something about O'Rorke that implied gentility and tenderness. So perhaps the singing of songs on a dreadfully hot afternoon on a Pennsylvania hillside was not so very out of character after all. Beneath the mettle of a young professional soldier was a romantic heart that could croon a ballad before wielding the sword.

BEHIND THE THICK COVER of trees along Seminary Ridge, Private John West and his comrades in the 5th Texas stumbled along the shallow valley carved by Willoughby Run and, despite the broken terrain and the merciless heat, made good time. Longstreet, with Lee's assent, had finally overruled McLaws's insistence on leading the assault. With Hood's division now moving across McLaws's rear in order to outflank the Union defenders of the Peach Orchard, Longstreet's men picked up the pace of their laborious trek toward the Emmitsburg Road—the jumping off point for the planned attack on the Union left. Like most soldiers on the march, West could not determine where he and his fellow Texans were headed. "I am unable without a map," he wrote soon after the battle, "to describe the locality of the forces or the face of the country along the entire line."[22] But he was very impressed with the sight of General Hood, who pranced on horseback beside the long column of butternut men and encouraged the troops forward. Hood ordered up an advance force to tear down fences and clear the way.

Hood was beloved by his men. Every inch the fighter, the general stood over six feet tall, had sunken eyes that gleamed a brilliant blue, and an abundant mane and beard of blond. His associates—especially his fellow cadets at West Point—called him Sam. His men held him in high regard for his boldness and bravery on the battlefield. Before the Peninsula campaign in 1862, his men presented him with a fine war horse. "In you we have found a leader whom we are proud to follow—a commander whom it is a pleasure to obey," said a sergeant of the 4th Texas, the regiment that Hood had earlier commanded before being promoted to general, in making the presentation. Private Billy Jordan of the 15th Alabama said he loved Hood's spirit. "He was kind, brave and a patriot," wrote Jordan, "[and] would go where he wanted his men to go."[23]

But Hood was less serene this afternoon. As his division filed out behind the line of trees on Seminary Ridge, expecting to deploy across the Emmitsburg Road in support of McLaws's attack against the Union left, Hood discovered—as did Longstreet and McLaws as well—that the Federals were not where the Confederates had thought they were. All at once it became clear that the Confederates had not known where the enemy left really was located. Initially Lee seems to have assumed, based on Johnston's faulty reconnaissance and his own piecemeal information about the enemy lines, that the Union left rested on Cemetery Ridge, just south of the soon-to-be famous copse of trees on its crest, or possibly in the vicinity of the Rogers farmhouse on the Emmitsburg Road. As such, Lee's battle plan called for McLaws's division, supported by Hood's, to form a battle line out of view of the enemy, behind a swale south of the Peach Orchard, and to drive up the road, in Lee's words, "partially enveloping the enemy's left," which Longstreet's two divisions were "to drive in."[24]

For his part, Longstreet appears to have believed that the Union flank was weakly anchored somewhere near the Peach Orchard—even before Sickles's Third Corps moved forward to occupy that orchard in force. On the countermarch, Longstreet informed McLaws that his division would end up being deployed with no Federals in his front and "entirely on the flank of the enemy." In that case, McLaws said, he would continue marching in columns of companies and, after getting into position on the Federal flank, he would "face to the left and march on the enemy." Longstreet replied: "That suits me," and rode off to the rear.[25] Apparently no one realized before the Confederates emerged down the eastern slope of Seminary Ridge that Sickles had moved his entire corps forward to the Emmitsburg Road and held the Peach Orchard. If nothing else, Sickles had thrown the Confederates off balance, and for that accidental and unanticipated consequence of his forward movement, he would later claim to be the hero of the day.

At once, Hood recognized that he could not place his troops in support of McLaws's division as he had intended to, and by necessity his men were forced to scramble through crop fields and meadows of wilting wildflowers to a point farther south than where he expected to place his division, crossing the Emmitsburg Road more than six hundred yards south of the Peach Orchard. This maneuver stretched the Confederate battle line well south to take into account the reality—which was a surprise to Longstreet and his generals—of a Federal line that reached all the way to Devil's Den. Ever the efficient officer, Hood sent out some of his Texas scouts to find out where the Union flank actually ended.

Leading the scouts was John M. Pinckney of Company G, 4th Texas. With five other men, Pinckney stealthily passed around the Federal flank, climbed to the summit of Big Round Top, and saw below, massed along the Taneytown Road, "the trains of the Union Army, its artillery, and thousands of its troops huddled together, not suspecting the enemy was so near." Pinckney quickly dispatched two of the scouts back to Hood with the information that the Union left flank was exposed. When they reached Hood, the scouts also reported that the Federals occupied Little Round Top, although the Texans may have been misled by seeing

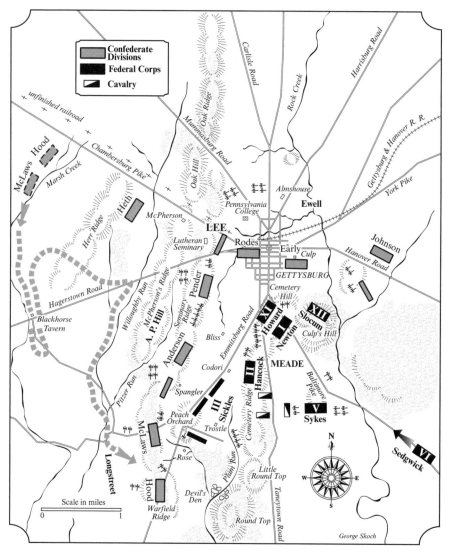

The situation, 4:00 P.M., July 2, 1863

signal flags on the crest of the hill and thinking that they represented more than just a skeleton signal crew. Suggesting a wide flanking movement, not unlike what Longstreet had been recommending to Lee since yesterday, the scouts told Hood he should march his division "through an open woodland pasture around [Big Round Top] and assault the enemy in flank and rear."[26] The general weighed this advice carefully while he ordered one of his batteries to open fire. Without hesitation, enemy guns from Devil's Den—the 4th New York Independent Battery under the command of Captain James Edward Smith—returned the fire with gusto and, to Hood's satisfaction, revealed the full extent of the Federal lines. It was about 4:00 o'clock, and the afternoon's heat sizzled on as both armies readied themselves for the day's bloodletting.

Everything now seemed to happen at once, as if the events of the afternoon had been suddenly transformed into a blurring kaleidoscope of color and smoke and flames. Having arrived at the Emmitsburg Road, Hood determined that he could not make his attack as ordered. Meanwhile, McLaws was astonished by the size of the Federal force forming the salient at the Peach Orchard. The best he could do, given the changed circumstances, was form his battle lines nearly parallel—rather than perpendicular, as Lee had ordered—with the Emmitsburg Road and throw his troops forward. McLaws realized that if he attempted to carry out his original orders, he would bring on disaster.

Amid the cascading noise of cannon fire, Lee and Longstreet met and hammered out a new plan of attack. According to Longstreet's postwar account, Lee gave the order for Longstreet to attack "by my right—following up the direction of the Emmitsburg Road toward the Cemetery Ridge, holding Hood's left as well as could be toward the Emmitsburg Road, McLaws to follow the movements of Hood, attacking at the Peach Orchard." It fell to Longstreet to put this new plan into motion. But he was clearly frustrated and agitated by the circumstances of this assault. One South Carolinian, who watched Longstreet intently, believed the general "had more the look of gloom than I had ever noticed before."[27] Longstreet's frame of mind would only get worse as the afternoon dragged on.

4

ON WARFIELD RIDGE

URROUNDED BY BOUNTIFUL FIELDS of corn and oats, a neat and simple farmhouse stood at the head of a low ridge that began in a small forest called Pitzer's Woods and extended to the south from Seminary Ridge to the Emmitsburg Road, where the ridge took a dog-legged turn and became a natural platform for the roadbed. The ridge was named for James Warfield and his family who lived in the small farmhouse on the Millerstown Road that looked like so many of the humble wood-and-stone residences dotting the rural landscape around Gettysburg. Near the farmhouse was a well-appointed smithy, for Warfield was known to operate "one of the best blacksmith stands" in all of Adams County, and his shop, which consisted of two hearths, attracted "a large and steady run of custom[ers]."[1]

Like other nervous citizens of the region, the Warfields had evacuated their home when word came that the Confederates were moving toward Gettysburg. But the family had a more compelling reason than most Gettysburg residents for fleeing from the tentacles of Lee's uncoiling army. James Warfield, a widower who was forty-four years old, and his four young daughters, who ranged in age from eight to fifteen, were black. They well knew that any African Americans who fell into the hands of the Confederates—whether free blacks born in Pennsylvania or runaway slaves who had established new homes for themselves above the Mason-Dixon line—would be involuntarily transported back to the South and sold into bondage. Untold numbers of blacks from Gettysburg and its environs suffered just such a fate. In the face of this very real threat, the Warfields abandoned their home and farm, only to return after the battle to find their house pillaged, their possessions destroyed or stolen, their livestock gone, and their crops ruined.

Along the ridge named for this respected black family, whose ownership of a farm and property and a prosperous business all signified the profound personal meaning that freedom had in their daily lives, General Hood spread his Confederate division out into line to the east of the Emmitsburg Road. His brigades formed into two lines along the crest of the ridge with two brigades in front and two in support to the rear. Law's exhausted Alabama brigade (comprised of the 4th, 15th, 44th, 47th, and 48th Alabama regiments) took position at the far right of the Confederate line, while Robertson's Texas brigade (made up of the 1st, 4th, and 5th Texas regiments with the added component of the 3rd Arkansas regiment) occupied the left. Behind the double battle lines of these brigades stood the Georgia brigade (2nd, 15th, 17th, and 20th Georgia regiments) under the command of Brigadier General Henry L. Benning, overlapping the Alabamians' left and the Texans' right, while another Georgia brigade (8th, 9th, 11th, and 59th Georgia regiments), commanded by Brigadier General George T. ("Tige") Anderson, formed up on Benning's left. Artillery crews wheeled up two batteries to support the attack of Hood's division.

As his division deployed into battle lines, Hood decided it was time to let Longstreet know what the Alabama, Texas, and Georgia brigades would be up against. Dispatching a staff officer, he told Longstreet that the attack plan should be changed by swinging around the Round Tops and coming up on the Federals from the rear. It did not take long for Longstreet to reply: "Gen'l Lee's orders are to attack up the Emmettsburg road." Hood sent another officer to Longstreet, this time saying that he "feared nothing could be accomplished by such an attack" up the road, and he "renewed the request to turn Round Top." Longstreet answered again: "Gen'l Lee's orders are to attack up the Emmettsburg road."[2]

In the meantime, General Law sent out a reconnaissance party of his own from the Alabama brigade and discovered what Hood's Texas scouts had already learned: that the way around the Union left was clear and that Federal ordnance wagons stood unprotected near the Taneytown Road, beneath the eastern slopes of the Round Tops. On the basis of this intelligence, Law decided that the Confederates' "true *point d'appui* [i.e., pivot point] was [Little] Round Top." A youthful looking general of twenty-seven years, clean-shaven, with jet-black hair, whose men

Major General John Bell Hood, Army of Northern
Virginia

thought of him as "small of stature but brave and alert," Law went looking for Hood and found him near the Texas brigade.[3] Although Hood
wholeheartedly agreed with Law that a movement around the Round
Top would enable the Confederates to outflank the Federals, he told
Law of Longstreet's unbending instructions to proceed with the attack
according to Lee's battle plan. Law protested formally to Hood, citing
the fact that a frontal attack on the enemy "would be purchased at too
great a sacrifice of life."[4]

Yet another appeal to Longstreet that begged for the corps commander to reconsider the assault plan produced the same reply, this time
delivered by one of Longstreet's own staff officers: "Genl Lee's orders
are to attack up the Emmetsburg road." That, at least, is what Hood
thought the officer said. But Law heard Longstreet's response differently.
Law believed the officer told Hood: "General Longstreet orders that you
begin the attack at once." Either way, the message was clear. Hood
turned to Law. "You hear the order?"[5] Law heard it, or said he did, and
understood that it was time to order his troops forward. He rode back to

Brigadier General Evander M. Law, Army of Northern
Virginia

his command, knowing that the ensuing attack was about to cost Lee's
army dearly.

ON THE SUNLIT RIDGE, Hood's men had been taking a steady beating
from the Union battery perched atop the boulders of Devil's Den. In reply, the Confederate batteries began to thunder, and the rows of infantry—some of which stood straight up during the barrage, while others
gratefully hugged the earth as rounds whistled over them or exploded
into deadly metal fragments above their heads—found themselves
caught between a hideous dialogue of flame and smoke and unnerving
noise. Private West stood with his comrades on the open crest of the ridge
and watched in horror as "one poor fellow had his head knocked off in a
few feet of me." West was sure he would never see his wife and children
again. Among the anxious souls in the 15th Alabama, Billy Jordan endured the "heavy shelling" as the regiment formed its lines with the rest
of the Alabama brigade.[6] Gratefully, he heard the order to lay down on

the ground, but the enemy's shot and shells still took a formidable toll while the Alabamians waited to advance in open country, completely exposed and in full view of the Federal gunners.

Standing in the threshold of battle, soldiers rarely contemplate the events that have led them to this decisive moment in their lives. Yet at least one uneasy Confederate waiting on Warfield Ridge, a captain in the 4th Texas with the most unlikely of names, was doing just that. Decimus et Ultimus Barziza, obviously the last of ten children born to his parents, observed that during a severe cannonade, "one had time to reflect upon the danger, and there being no wild excitement as in a charge, he is more reminded of the utter helplessness of his present condition." Around him, Barziza gazed at his fellow soldiers who lay "flat on the ground, keeping their places in the ranks, and as a shell is heard, generally try to sink themselves into the earth."[7]

What had brought Barziza, John West, Billy Jordan, and their fellow Texans and Alabamians to this place, this bare ridge overlooking a gentle farm valley of plowed fields and the two imposing Round Tops in the near distance, this barren rim of earth where the fates were cruelly dealing out death as wild cards? Oddly, almost perversely, the jittery Confederates under Hood's command who waited to go forward as the enemy's artillery shells rained down on them believed—like the Warfields and every other American, North and South—in the twin ideas of freedom and liberty. While many of these Southern soldiers felt the earth tremble beneath them and hoped that the next artillery shell would sail harmlessly on by, they understood that they were about to do battle, and possibly die, in the name of liberty. John West explained, after the war, that most soldiers in the Confederate military seemed perfectly willing to declare, as Patrick Henry had done during the American Revolution, "Give me liberty or give me death." Billy Jordan, although supposedly a reluctant supporter of secession, said he went into battle out of "a sense of duty," but behind that sense was a firm loyalty to the South and a belief that the cause of liberty lay at the very heart of the Confederate war effort.[8]

Northerners and Southerners believed that they fought with the same spirit, the same conviction, that had motivated their ancestors in the American Revolution. But the Confederates seemed to proclaim the cause of liberty the loudest. Early in the war, a captain in the 4th Alabama had declared to his wife, one of Mary Todd Lincoln's half sisters, that he was "willing to fall for the cause of Liberty and Independence."[9] The irony, of course, was that while Southerners convinced themselves they were fighting for freedom and liberty, they had aligned themselves with a cause and a new nation that sought to deprive slaves of the very things that motivated white men to pick up their muskets, persevere through a deadly artillery bombardment, and charge the fortified defenses of the enemy.

At the beginning of the war, Alexander Stephens, the Confederacy's vice president, pronounced openly and without apology: "Our new government is founded upon exactly the opposite idea [that "all men are created equal"]; its foundations are laid, its cornerstone rests, upon the great truth that the negro is not equal to the white man; that slavery . . . is his natural and normal condition." Stephens called this proposition a "great . . . moral truth."[10] How deeply this "moral truth" had taken root in the hearts and minds of white Southerners was revealed in 1862 in a letter written by a North Carolinian to Governor Zebulon Vance: "We are opposed to negro equality. To prevent this[,] we are willing to spare the last man, down to the point where women and children begin to suffer for food and clothing; when these begin to suffer and die, rather than see them equalized with an inferior race[,] we will die with them. Everything, even life itself, stands pledged to the cause; but that our greatest strength may be employed to the best advantage and the struggle prolonged[,] let us not sacrifice at once the object for which we are fighting."[11]

Most Confederates were less forthcoming in their sentiments. They conveniently overlooked the paradox of fighting for white liberty and black slavery at the same time, while freely quoting Jefferson's Declaration of Independence and defining themselves as defenders of liberty, just the Old Revolutionaries had been. Private John West, the erstwhile lawyer and teacher from Texas, saw things differently and expressed his ideas with a commendable honesty. Slavery, he said, was "the real bone of contention" in the war, the proverbial "apple of discord." "The inner and germinal question of slavery," wrote West, "was the real cancer which poisoned the entire blood and circulation of the body politic." With slavery, West concluded, "there could be no permanent and friendly Union."[12]

So Southerners fought for freedom and slavery, for liberty and bondage, for white superiority and black inferiority. Yet, no matter how inspiring Southern rhetoric about liberty might become, it would always sound hollow, like the empty bellow of a boiler drained of water. No matter how often Confederates harkened back to their Revolutionary forefathers, their words would lack luster, meaning, and depth. For the South was trying to perpetuate an anachronism, and in so doing the Confederates dug in their heels and refused to acknowledge that the rest of the world had passed them by. They would hold on to this anachronism to the death, clinging to it as a mother does when she refuses to give up a dead child to the coldness of the earth, and the burning question of slavery, and its equally troubling corollary of race, would become the great and terrible Southern burden. The burden, however, would not remain the South's alone. After the smoke had cleared from Warfield Ridge, after the Warfield family had returned to its home to rebuild its life and to reclaim its freedom, the heavy weight of race would soon rest solidly on the shoulders of the entire nation. It rests there still.

WHEN GENERAL WARREN LEFT MEADE and turned his horse toward Little Round Top, he rode in the company of several aides and orderlies. En route, the party came upon Major General George Sykes, commander of the Fifth Corps, who had received Meade's orders to bring his corps up and deploy it to the left of Sickles's Third Corps. Warren talked briefly with Sykes, then the engineer and his party moved on, stopping next to discuss the situation with General Weed, who was at the head of his brigade. While Warren spoke to Weed, Lieutenant Washington A. Roebling, Warren's aide and brother-in-law (and the future builder of the Brooklyn Bridge), rode to the crest of Little Round Top and spotted Hood's Confederates on Warfield Ridge in the distance. Roebling ran down to Warren, reported what he had seen, and the two men scrambled together up to the summit of the hill.

The moment was made for heroism, but Warren himself was an unlikely hero. He was certainly brave enough, having proven himself a sturdy West Pointer, graduating second in his class, who had seen service in the regular army in a campaign against hostile Sioux in 1855 and as commander of the 5th New York Volunteer Infantry (Duryee's Zouaves) at Big Bethel and Gaines's Mill, where he was wounded. Mostly he was known, however, as a skillful cartographer and a capable engineer. Yet something about Warren rubbed people—particularly his superiors—the wrong way. Years spent in the army conducting topographical surveys in the West gave him an independent streak that made him sound overly opinionated and occasionally insubordinate. Fastidious and pedantic, he liked to question orders or use his discretion to change them as he saw fit.

Nor did he look the part of a hero. Short and willowy, he appeared to be no more substantial in body than a young boy, or as some remarked, a young woman; his uniforms tended to hang off him as if they were several sizes too big. An artillery officer described him as "dark complexioned, with black eyes, and long, straight black hair; he has a little of the look of an Indian," a reference to Warren's high cheekbones, prominent forehead, and narrow eyes.[13] In the high command, his fellow officers respected his ability as an engineer, but disliked his arrogance and insolence. Warren's temper was legendary, and when his anger boiled over he sputtered out profanities that, said one colleague, "made my hair stand on end."[14]

But Warren was a true believer, which worked a great deal in his favor. His patriotic ardor was pure and undiluted. He had faith in the cause of the Union, and believed with a certainty that God would ultimately grant success to the North. He also saw slavery as a sin that had necessitated the great cleansing by blood; the war, he asserted, would wash away the sins of a guilty nation. A week before Gettysburg, he had written to his wife: "God smites a nation for the sins of its rulers. We suffer now for the sin of slavery and we must suffer still till favor, ambition[,] avarice and

Brigadier General Gouverneur K. Warren, Army of the Potomac

envy[,] hatred and malice shall all disappear under God's chastening influence[,] and patriotism and purity alone survive."[15]

On the rocky western face of Little Round Top, Warren learned that no Federal troops occupied the hill, other than a handful of signalmen with their semaphore flags, a crew that had assumed Lieutenant Jerome's vacated station on the summit. "I saw," wrote Warren years later, "that this was the key of the whole position and that our troops in the woods in front of it could not see the ground in front of them, so that the enemy would come upon them before they would be aware of it."[16] The signalmen must have told him that they had seen the enemy massing on Warfield Ridge. Evidently the Confederates they and Roebling had seen so plainly from the hilltop were no longer visible, and Warren wanted to know for sure what the enemy was up to.

As Warren claimed years later, in an account that seems too fantastic and dramatic to be believed, he quickly sent a runner to instruct an artillery captain—presumably Captain James E. Smith, commander of the 4th New York Battery's four guns positioned at the top of Devil's Den, or possibly whoever Smith had left in charge of his two guns located near the southeastern edge of the den, in the low valley later called the Valley of Death—to throw a shell in the direction of Warfield Ridge. Warren watched "as the shot went whistling through the air" and when the sound reached Hood's Confederates it "caused every one to look in the direction of it." That motion, said Warren, "revealed to me the glistening of gun barrels and bayonets of the enemy's line of battle already formed and far outflanking the position of any of our troops."[17] Realizing that the path between Warfield Ridge and Little Round Top itself lay undefended by Federal troops, Warren scribbled a hastily written note to Meade and asked that a division, at the very least, be sent to the defense of Little Round Top. He also sped a message to Sickles requesting troops from the Third Corps.

As Warren assessed the circumstances and sent his dire pleas for help, Smith and his four guns at Devil's Den continued to hammer the enemy with uninterrupted artillery fire. The bombardment was not all one-sided, however. "The accuracy of the enemy's aim was astonishing," Smith admitted, commenting on the skill of the Confederate gunners. But his men were holding their own. "Every shot told," he said, "[and] the pieces were discharged as rapidly as they could be with regard to effectiveness, while the conduct of the men was superb."[18]

Warren, still standing on the rocks of Little Round Top, feared for the vulnerability of the army's left flank and the opportunity that existed for the enemy to sweep unimpeded up the slopes of the hill and roll up the Federal flank along the length of Cemetery Ridge. Warren implored the signalmen to keep their flags waving. That, at the very least, might make the enemy think that the hill was occupied by Union troops. Everything, though, seemed to be hanging by a thread. And time, a soldier's worst enemy, was about to work against the Army of the Potomac.

WHILE LAW GOT HIS TROOPS READY to launch the assault from Warfield Ridge, Longstreet rode up through the lingering clouds of artillery smoke and found Hood on the crest of the ridge, overlooking the Bushman

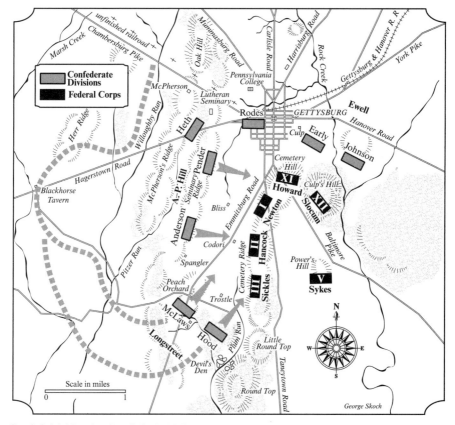

Lee's initial battle plan, July 2, 1863

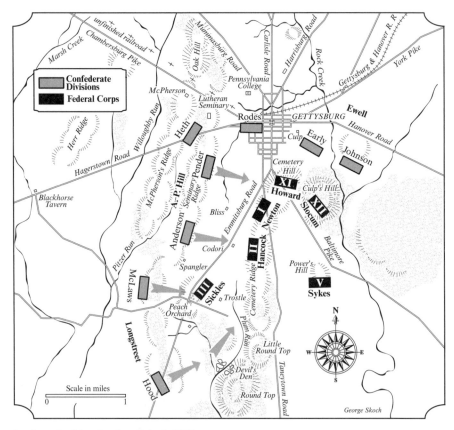

Lee's revised battle plan, July 2, 1863

and Slyder farms below. Despite his failure to get Longstreet to approve his tactical suggestion of swinging around to the rear of the Union left, Hood repeated his protests in person to Longstreet and asked the general to reconsider his request. Longstreet was stern in his reply: "We must obey the orders of General Lee." With this, Longstreet rode back toward McLaws's position. Captain Barziza of the 4th Texas noticed him sitting his horse "like an iron man with his spyglass to his eye, coolly watching the effect of our [artillery] shots. Limbs of trees fell and crashed around him, yet he sat as unmoved as a statue."[19]

Meanwhile, Hood rode to a favorite place in the lines, near his beloved Texans of his old brigade. Before giving the order to advance, he made a brief speech to the men. No one remembered exactly what he said; of those who recorded his words, each seemed to hear something different. According to one Texan, an officer in the 1st Texas, Hood exclaimed: "Forward, my Texans, and win this battle or die in the effort!" Another Texan thought Hood said: "Fix bayonets, my brave Texans; forward and take those heights!" John West believed Hood shouted, "Forward—steady—forward." Whatever the precise words he spoke, his message had been plain. "The ball," said one Texan succinctly, "had opened."[20]

Toward the Confederate far right, where the 15th Alabama waited tensely near the edge of some woods on the high crest of the ridge for Hood's orders to be passed down the line, Colonel William Oates found himself preoccupied with two matters that the high command cared nothing about. Greatly concerned for the welfare of his men, particularly the overwhelming thirst that the Alabamians were suffering after their long marches under a merciless sun, Oates sent off a detachment of twenty-two men, two from each company in the regiment, carrying canteens with the order to find water and return to their places in the line. The detachment had not yet returned, and Oates began to get nervous about their absence, given the fact that the order to advance could be given at any moment.

And then there was his brother. Oates saw that John looked even worse than he had earlier in the day, and it seemed evident that the marching and countermarching had nearly done his brother in. Oates ordered John to the rear on sick call, but the pallid lieutenant refused to obey. "Brother," he said, "I will not do it. If I were to remain here [i.e., out of the battle] people would say that I did it through cowardice; no, sir, I am an officer and will never disgrace the uniform I wear; I shall go through, unless I am killed, which I think is quite likely."[21] Knowing better, William Oates nevertheless relented and let his brother stay in the ranks. He would regret his decision for the rest of his life.

The attack was about to begin. Captain Thomas J. Goree, a Texan on Longstreet's staff, rode down the length of Hood's line, pointing to Little Round Top and exhorting the men to take it. "We will do it," the Texans replied. The Texans and Alabamians shed their personal belongings—knapsacks, blanket rolls, and haversacks—and moved forward at the quick step, with officers dashing along its front, urging the men onward, shouting to the men to guide center and dress their ranks. "The men sprang forward as if at a game of ball," observed William Ward of the 4th Alabama, but most of the troops—while energetic and aroused by the cry of battle—felt that gnawing emptiness in their stomachs that comes with knowing that the gods of war now held each man's fate in their hands.[22]

Among the Alabamians, Colonel Oates led his regiment down the slope of the ridge, but with great misgivings. Not only was his brother unfit for combat, but the water detail had not yet returned when the order to advance was given. "It would have been infinitely better to have waited five minutes for those twenty-two men and the canteens of water," Oates wrote after the war, "but generals never ask a colonel if his regiment is ready to move." Lieutenant Oates kept up with his company as best he could. The 15th Alabama rushed forward through an open field for a distance of three or four hundred yards and then, as Colonel Oates recalled, "down a gentle slope for quarter of a mile" and into the Plum Run valley below.[23]

The rough terrain, made up of swales and ditches, threw the attack into confusion, and the Confederates scrambled to maintain their lines as they hurriedly took down fence sections or stumbled over rock outcroppings in their front. As the Alabamians ran down the ridge, they picked up speed, and soon Law's brigade separated from General Robertson's Texas brigade, and while the Texans broke into a double-quick to keep up with their comrades to the right, Robertson thought that Law had prematurely ordered a charge "a full mile from the enemy's line of battle."[24] Meanwhile, the Texans encountered the buildings of the Bushman farm in their path, and their lines divided to allow them to pass around the structures. As a result, the gap between the Texans and the Alabamians widened. The disorder in the lines was only the beginning of a greater chaos to follow.

For major ellis spear of the 20th Maine, details (what he occasionally referred to as "surly facts") were something important, something to pay attention to. History, in his estimation, was filled with such details, small matters that might seem trivial and inconsequential on the surface, but that otherwise might speak volumes about people and events in the past. "The preservation of these details," he wrote after the war, "is of great importance, not only for the special interest which attaches to them, but because they illustrate the larger actions and will be of value to future generations, as showing the very body and features of the time." In this sense, Spear thought it was "interesting, and not unprofitable, to know that the Father of his Country in some wrathful mood swore roundly; or that the Philosopher of the Revolution, in his younger days, trudged the streets of Philadelphia with a loaf of bread under each arm; or, when older, was very gay and festive in the gay and festive capital of France."[25]

It was of no small importance, or coincidence, that Spear spoke of Washington and Franklin with admiration, even as he acknowledged that little churlish facts about these historical figures made them seem more human. Flawed or not, these men who had founded the nation were, in Spear's estimation, true heroes. Every Fourth of July, said Spear, the Old Revolutionaries marked the occasion by celebrating the Declaration of Independence and by remembering the "seven long years of bitter wasting war, of poverty, want, hardship, danger, anxiety, of hatred to a foreign foe, waging war on our own soil, and with the rejoicing was the feeling of sweet triumph over the enemy; and many now living can remember when the name of British was odious in this country." The war being waged by the North against the South called for the same sense of commitment, the same duty to one's country and to the values of the American Revolution, although the struggle was aimed not at driving away a foreign enemy but at bringing "rebellious citizens" back into the fold, "to put down faction and restore harmony."[26]

Spear was not an abolitionist, nor did he actively espouse the antislavery cause prior to the outbreak of the war. The time he spent in Maryland and Virginia, before the Gettysburg campaign, gave him an opportunity to see the strange fruits of slavery in the South and to come into contact with slaves who had taken advantage of the war and expressed an eagerness to "go North." He felt a great sympathy for their plight. But he also suffered from the racial prejudices that afflicted most white men of his time, including the proclivity to see African Americans in stereotypical terms that were none too favorable. From time to time, for instance, Spear referred to the tendency of blacks to move with animation or show "their spacious grins."[27]

But there was more humanitarianism in Spear than met the eye. Not only did he wish for the Union to subdue the "misguided" citizens of the South and "compel them to obey the laws," he also hoped that the war would achieve "the extinction of an obsolete, unprofitable and hateful system of slave labor." In waging this conflict, he said, the North did not simply fight for itself or for the cause of Union. "We did not contend only for ourselves," he wrote more than twenty years after Appomattox, "but for humanity. Not less in the cause of humanity was the destruction of slavery. In that respect also we builded better than we knew when we resolved to uphold our government."[28]

These were the great and compelling ideas that had brought acting Major Ellis Spear to Gettysburg, where he now lounged listlessly in an open field near the Baltimore Pike with his comrades of the 20th Maine. Still feeling weak from fever and diarrhea, Spear welcomed the chance to rest, if only because it kept him from the discomfort of sitting a horse. He took off the belt that held his holstered revolver and placed it across his horse's saddle. Suddenly, like a thunderclap out of the blue, the pounding of artillery broke the afternoon silence, and the men of the 20th Maine were no longer drowsy. The rumble of the guns came from the direction of Sickles's Third Corps, which now became engaged in a fierce artillery duel with Longstreet's batteries.

To what Chamberlain called "the awakening bugle," the entire Fifth Corps, responding to orders issued by Meade himself, quickly got into formation and moved from the Baltimore Pike, with Vincent's Third Brigade in the lead, traveling at the double-quick along farm roads and across farm fields, through "thorn-hedges, stone-fences, [and] miry swamps," toward the southwest. "The rebel shells came over among us thick and fast," reported Corporal William T. Livermore of Company B, "but on we marched at a step between quick and doublequick until some fell exhausted."[29]

The 20th Maine, along with Vincent's brigade, soon found itself at the edge of a wheatfield (what would later be known as *the* Wheatfield) to the east and beyond sight of the Emmitsburg Road. There Vincent's Third Brigade paused to receive its next orders. Not far away Union forces were already battling desperately for a pile of huge boulders called Devil's Den, and Chamberlain, Spear, and the men of the 20th Maine waited to be ordered into battle line. "The sound of the battle in front," Spear remembered, "[was] developing more and more and sharper and clearer."[30]

In their imposing farmhouse on the Taneytown Road, Jacob Weikert and his family heard the noise of battle increase in the distance and began worrying about their safety. When the battle had broken out to the northwest of the Weikert farm on the morning of July 1, the family members hoped that their farm, nestled in the protective shadow of the Round Tops, would be spared the ravages of war. Residing in the house was Jacob, sixty-six years old, his wife, Sarah, sixty-one, and at least two children, Rebecca, nineteen, and David, fourteen. One of the Weikerts' married daughters, Henrietta Shriver, had brought her two children from Gettysburg to the farm during the afternoon of July 1, after the first day's battle had heated up to a rolling boil. Accompanying Mrs. Shriver was her neighbor, Matilda (Tillie) Pierce, a fifteen-year-old girl who lived on Baltimore Street with her parents and attended the Young Ladies Seminary in town. By the time Tillie arrived at the Weikerts', the farm—including the house, a carriage house, and a huge bank barn—had been turned into a field hospital.

Tillie watched as a steady stream of Union soldiers flowed in front of the house toward the reverberations of battle. Suddenly a caisson exploded in a flash of light and with great noise directly in front of the farmhouse, and Tillie stood shaking in fear as she witnessed an artillery teamster being thrown high into the air and landing in a wheatfield nearby. A group of soldiers rushed to the wounded man and carried him into the house. As he passed by, Tillie saw that his eyes had been blown out "and his whole person seem[ed] to be one black mass." The first words she heard him utter were: "Oh dear! I forgot to read my Bible to-day! What will my poor wife and children say?"[31]

Soon she was fetching water from the Weikert well and standing by the roadside to offer drinks to the endless procession of soldiers. "Before night," Tillie recalled, "the barn was filled with the shattered and dying heroes of this [first] day's struggle." She and Becky Weikert went to the

Tillie Pierce

barn to see what was happening. "Nothing before in my experience had ever paralleled the sight we then and there beheld," she wrote. "There was groaning and crying, the struggling and dying, crowded side by side, while attendants sought to aid and relieve them as best they could."[32] Tillie and Becky retreated from the barn in tears.

But the next day Tillie, composed once more, assumed her post fetching water for the passing soldiers. Standing at the garden fence, she gave a mounted officer some water in a tin cup, only to be told later that the officer was General Meade. The men gave him three cheers. Meade bowed gallantly to young Tillie, saluted the soldiers, and then rode rapidly away.

By THE TIME LONGSTREET'S ARTILLERY opened its prodigious cannonade against the Union left, Lee had returned to Seminary Ridge and taken up his former position near the Seminary itself, where he sat on a tree stump and waited for the day's battle to unfold. Almost as soon as the guns began their tremendous clamor to the south, Ewell's batteries, by a prearranged signal, opened up in a great new crash along the Union right that shook the summer air and threw shot and shell screaming over Cemetery Hill and Culp's Hill. Occasionally, reported Colonel Fremantle, Lee squinted through his field glasses. But the gentle rolling country around Gettysburg was shrouded in a thick haze of powder smoke, and for a time daylight grew dim and gray as the July afternoon seemed to change abruptly to a muted dusk.

During the afternoon, while the smell of powder and death fell heavily over the countryside, Major General J. E. B. Stuart arrived in Gettysburg and reported to Lee. Stuart's cavalry had been out of touch with the Army of Northern Virginia since June 25, when he had taken his cavalry on a wild and mostly unsuccessful expedition behind Union lines. In the course of Stuart's adventures, he had aroused Northern public anxieties about marauding rebels and had captured 125 Federal wagons, but he had gained no tactical advantage for the Army of Northern Virginia. When Stuart reached Seminary Ridge that afternoon, having ridden ahead of his troopers, Lee greeted him coolly and without enthusiasm. "Well, General Stuart," said Lee in what has become the traditional account of the meeting, "you are here at last."[33] The meeting was so brief that Fremantle failed to notice it at all.

As the battle grew hotter, Lee maintained his poise and his aloofness. The agitation he had displayed earlier that morning was gone now. On the stump, as he listened to the slow irregular pulsations of battle in the distance, he appeared alert, but resigned. He had blind faith in his army. As he was fond of saying, and believing, "All this will come right in the end."[34]

5

A Wild Rush

I N THIS SUMMER OF 1863, a summer of wilting heat and crucial battles, it seemed like the war would never end. It had been going on
for twenty-seven months—twenty-seven dreadfully long months of
death and destruction and desolation, and the men who were fighting it
had learned very little in all that time, except that war was cruel and shattered men's lives. Generals still ordered massed infantry charges across
broken terrain and against high ground held by the entrenched or fortified enemy. The long ranges of artillery and rifled muskets meant that
the attackers could be very nearly decimated before they even reached
the enemy's works. Technological improvements in weapons thus had far
surpassed tactics, making this Civil War a modern war, and a particularly
bloody and deadly one at that.

But there was more to it than the futility of frontal assaults and the relative accuracy of revolving minié balls that could crush limbs and end
lives in an instant. Soldiers of both North and South failed to take into account that the landscape over which they fought often determined the
outcome of battles and prevented the armies from winning decisive victories over their enemies. Generally speaking, Civil War battles were fought
in confined spaces, in close quarters, with woods and hills and swales and
streams making tight spaces even tighter. There was little room to maneuver, and close-order infantry tactics, based on the military principle of
concentration, would mean that casualties would assuredly be high in the
battles between Union and Confederate armies, but this lack of maneu-
verability also often meant that the death blow, the final decisive check-
mate, could not be delivered—by *either* of the armies in contention.

And the terrain wore men out, long before they got into effective rifle range with the enemy. When Hood's division launched its assault, the visible enemy, at that moment, lay approximately one thousand yards away (Smith's Federal guns atop Devil's Den) or, in the case of Little Round Top, where there was no visible enemy but which would soon be quickly manned by Union defenders, almost fifteen hundred yards away. The farm fences, stone walls, stream beds, woods, brambles, rock out-croppings, orchards, farm buildings, and other natural and man-made features of the landscape served to break up brigade battle lines, regimental formations, and company cohesion.

In fact, Hood's battle lines began to disintegrate almost as soon as his men took their first steps off Warfield Ridge after hearing the command to advance. General Law sent five companies of skirmishers from the 47th and 48th Alabama ahead of the battle line. Part of their job was to tear down fences and clear the way for their comrades behind them. Yet the advance of the skirmishers seems not to have been well coordinated, and they passed around the base of Big Round Top to the east, thus

The view from the crest of Little Round Top, looking north

removing themselves entirely from the battle. The 47th Alabama advanced in its main line down the slope of the ridge, but soon broke into the double-quick well ahead of any order to do so. Soon the regiment led the line by a "distance of fifty to a hundred yards," bragged Colonel James W. Jackson, the 47th's commander.[1] The 4th Alabama also broke into a trot, encouraged not only by the acceleration of the 47th on its right but also by several officers who urged their men forward.

Over the broken terrain, the Alabama brigade stumbled, confronted fences still in place, scaled stone walls, and lost its footing while trying to negotiate crop rows in planted fields and avoid boulders and small groves of trees that dotted the landscape. As the 47th Alabama pulled ahead of the other Alabama regiments, the Texas regiments to the left moved out with determination but confronted many of the same obstacles that were tripping up the Alabamians.

Robertson's orders had been to keep his Texas brigade "well closed" on his right to Law's left. As the Alabamians lurched ahead, outpacing the Texans, Robertson discovered, much to his surprise, that his own brigade could not possibly maintain his left on the Emmitsburg Road, as he had been instructed to do, while also keeping his right connected to the Alabamians. The roadway veered off at an angle that prevented him from staying on its course; moreover, Law's brigade kept pulling off to the right, when it should have been aligning on its left. As a result, Robertson "abandoned the pike" out of necessity and attempted to close on Law's brigade.[2]

Like a wave being divided on shore by a breakwater, Robertson's left regiments—the 1st Texas and the 3rd Arkansas—lost their connection with the right regiments, the 4th and 5th Texas; the first two regiments headed toward Houck's Ridge and Devil's Den, while the latter two regiments closed on Law's brigade and made way for the Slyder farm and, beyond the farmyard, the small gap that lay between the boulders of Devil's Den and the low ridge that formed the northwestern base of Big Round Top. Robertson ordered his brigade forward at the double-quick, trying desperately to keep up with Law's rapid advance, but his force was being hit heavily by skirmish and artillery fire that tore his ranks apart. There was nothing for Robertson to do but to lead his right two regiments in a charge against "the line of the enemy" on Houck's Ridge and Smith's Federal artillery at Devil's Den.[3]

Meanwhile, Union troops from the 2nd U.S. Sharpshooters, posted behind fences in the Slyder farmyard, stone walls, and other cover near the base of Big Round Top, and in the woods on Houck's Ridge, opened fire on the approaching Confederates with a menacing and deadly accuracy. The Plum Run valley became a hornet's nest with bullets whining and buzzing all around the advancing butternut lines. With the Confederates in the open, they also became fair targets of Smith's battery on Devil's Den. Thick smoke rolled "in billows" over the battlefield as Smith and his gunners took advantage of the silence of the Confederate artillery, which had been forced to cease fire while the infantry troops moved forward.[4]

John West, in the 4th Texas, recalled charging ahead across the valley toward Plum Run, "yelling and whooping." But the lines, he said, became "broken and confused." Captain Barziza of the 4th Texas described how the regiment advanced "in a wild, frantic and desperate run, yelling, screaming and shouting; over ditches, up and down hill, bursting through garden fences and shrubbery, occasionally dodging the head as a bullet whistled by the ear . . . On we go with the same speed, jumping over and plunging through creeks, pulling through mud, struggling through underbrush, still keeping up the loud, irregular and terrible Confederate yell. Shells and grape shot, canister and minié balls, came hurtling through our ranks, bursting, screaming, whistling—still that same wild, reckless, unhesitating rush towards the [enemy]."[5]

The fire from the Federal sharpshooters and cannon had become so hot that the Texans and Alabamians could not bear to stay exposed to the enemy's decimating spray of lead and iron. One shell, reported a veteran of the Texas brigade, killed and wounded fifteen men in the 4th Texas. Lines became a jumble and ranks split apart. Eventually, as Sergeant Valerius C. Giles of Company B, 4th Texas, explained, the regiments "lapped over each other," and the advancing lines became hopelessly tangled.[6]

After reaching a stone wall that divided the Bushman property from the Slyder farm, the 47th Alabama was so exhausted and disorganized that it suddenly halted its advance, and the men fell out to rest. Colonel Jackson, mustering all of his own strength, which was waning quickly, let his men catch their breath, ordered them over the stone fence, but could not keep up with them. He collapsed, found his way to the rear, and left the regiment to the command of Lieutenant Colonel Michael J. Bulger. Captain Leigh R.Terrell of Law's staff rode up to Bulger and informed him that he was to "take charge of the Redgment and conduct it in the fight."[7]

While his division spread across the Plum Run valley, the men staggering and reeling from the slaughter caused by Federal guns and sharpshooters, Hood remained near an orchard in the vicinity of the Bushman farmhouse to watch the battle's progress. No doubt he saw his attack beginning to fall apart under the enemy's merciless fire and from the effects of broken terrain. If he was about to set matters right, he never got the chance. Over his head, about twenty or thirty feet above him, a shell exploded with violent force, and shrapnel cut deeply into his left arm. He nearly fell out of his saddle, but he "was caught and eased down by his aides who instantly had dismounted," recalled Lieutenant Colonel Phillip A. Work, commander of the 1st Texas. Hood was taken to the rear on a litter, and his absence from the field meant that his division would lack a commander for some time, because Law, to whom the division command would fall, could not be immediately located. General Hood remembered experiencing "deep distress of mind and heart at the thought of the inevitable fate of my brave fellow-soldiers."[8] He lost the use of his left arm for the rest of his life.

LUCKILY, Warren had sent his messengers from the summit of Little Round Top to hustle reinforcements to the hilltop. While wave after wave of Confederates charged through the Plum Run valley, Warren could hear the awful clamor of battle rising to a higher pitch, could hear the shouts of the soldiers in faded butternut as they grew closer, and could see great and ragged clouds of smoke billowing up in the summer sky. But little else was plainly visible. Standing atop a flat rock on the summit of Little Round Top, eyes fixed to his field glasses, despite the veil of dense battle smoke, he spent several nervous minutes wondering if his urgent appeals for help would be answered or ignored.

One of Warren's aides, Lieutenant Ranald S. Mackenzie, galloped to General Sickles to request that troops be sent to Little Round Top in all haste. Sickles refused to give up any of his men to reinforce the flank, asserting, as Mackenzie later reported, "that his whole command was necessary to defend his front, or words to that effect."[9] Warren's other messenger, Lieutenant Chauncey B. Reese, got a better response to the call for help. Reese made straight for General Meade, who by this time had returned to his headquarters on the Taneytown Road, and handed him Warren's request in writing for a whole division to be rushed to the hill. Meade immediately instructed General Sykes, whose Fifth Corps was already on its way toward the Union left, to provide reinforcements for Warren and to hold a defensive line along Cemetery Ridge that would terminate on Little Round Top.

Alfred Waud's drawing of
Warren on Little Round Top

The Round Tops: Little Round Top is on the left, Big Round Top on the right.

Frustrated by Sickles's refusal to help, Lieutenant Mackenzie sped off to find troops that would be willing to provide the needed assistance. In the already mounting chaos of battle that swept across the wide plateau that stretched from the Wheatfield to the Peach Orchard, Mackenzie came upon General Sykes as the Fifth Corps commander was seeking out Major General David B. Birney, leading the First Division of the Third Corps, to suggest that Birney's troops close up to the left and connect themselves to the Fifth Corps divisions now moving up. After listening to Mackenzie communicate Warren's desperate call for help, Sykes agreed without hesitation to send one of the brigades in Brigadier General James Barnes's First Division of the Fifth Corps. Satisfied at last that reinforcements would be rapidly dispatched, Mackenzie returned to Little Round Top to report the news to Warren. Without delay, and without informing headquarters of his battlefield decision, General Sykes sent a captain from his staff to locate Barnes and order him to march one of his three brigades to the summit of Little Round Top. At last Warren's plea would be answered.

Mackenzie's report must have been reassuring to Warren, but the engineer could not yet assume that all would be well. No Union troops could be seen hurrying to the hill. The promise of help would only be worth something so long as the Federal reinforcements reached the summit before the Confederates did. Before him, as if depicted in a panorama painted on a broad canvas, Warren witnessed through shifting pockets of gray-and-white smoke the unfolding second day's battle in all its glory and horror. As the Confederates made steady gains across the landscape below him, Warren's anxiety deepened. What would happen if help did not arrive in time?

ALL THROUGH THE SULTRY AFTERNOON, as the day grew hotter and the prospects of battle began to simmer like a pot of water ready to boil, the skirmish line of the 2nd U.S. Sharpshooters regiment prowled through the woods and fields along the western base of Big Round Top searching for the enemy. Major Homer R. Stoughton, in command of the regiment, had been ordered to take his men to the far left of Brigadier General J. H. Hobart Ward's Second Brigade of the First Division, in Sickles's Third Corps. Stoughton placed his troops in skirmish line formation just beyond Plum Run. Company F, which was made up of New Hampshire men, was posted among the Slyder farm buildings and along a stone wall that ran from the tiny stone house to the formidable wooden barn. Company B, with Michigan men in its ranks, was placed farther south near the edge of Bushman's Woods. Companies E and H, containing men from Vermont, took cover behind a stone wall and rail fence along the Slyder lane that led westward and eventually connected with the Emmitsburg Road. Stoughton then sent scouts forward to determine what the Confederates were up to.

The sharpshooters enjoyed a shining reputation as an elite unit in the Army of the Potomac. Under the overall command of Colonel Hiram Berdan, the 1st and 2nd U.S. Sharpshooters were comprised of soldiers from various states who had passed a rigorous test of marksmanship—placing ten consecutive shots within a ten-inch circle at two hundred yards. Dressed in distinctive green frock coats, trousers, and forage caps, the sharpshooters stood out from their blue-coated comrades in the army. Berdan armed his men with Sharps .52 caliber breechloading rifles equipped with special sights and double-set target triggers. These rifles enabled the sharpshooters to fire and load at a rate three times faster than infantry riflemen armed with muzzle-loaders.

Leaving his skirmishers in the vicinity of the Slyder farm, Stoughton rode forward about half a mile in front of his lines to see if the enemy could be found. The discovery came almost instantaneously. Having spotted Hood's division forming along the crest of Warfield Ridge, Stoughton came galloping back to his lines. At the Slyder farm, the New Hampshire boys in Company F held firm behind their stone wall and watched for signs of the approaching enemy. "We did not have to wait long," remembered Sergeant Wyman S. White of Company F. Advancing without pause toward them, emerging from the battle smoke like gray ghosts, came "a solid mass of rebels" that "spilled over a ridge" and extended well beyond the view of the sharpshooters to their right.[10]

The oncoming enemy lines were impressive and unnerving. "They came yelling and firing and struggling over fences and through the timber," wrote White in his diary. The Confederates, dressed in their butternut uniforms, "had the appearance of a plowed field being closed in mass formation until they got within good fighting distance to our line, when they broke into line of battle formation three lines deep." Bullets came whacking in, hitting the stone wall and forcing the sharpshooters to keep their heads down. When the Confederates came in close enough, the sharpshooters laid down a murderous fire that mangled Hood's lines and held back, at least for a while, the crashing assault waves. "We took the matter very coolly," boasted Sergeant White, "[and] many a brave Southron threw up his arms and fell."[11]

The sharpshooters' skirmish line, however, could not withstand the Confederates' brisk return fire or the surging butternut tide. "We were obliged to fall back or be either killed or taken prisoner," wrote White.[12] When the enemy reached a distance of about one hundred yards from the sharpshooters, Stoughton ordered a retreat, and the green-clad companies fell back in detached groups, keeping up their fire as they withdrew. Companies E and H—Stoughton's right wing—retired toward Devil's Den, while companies F and B—the left wing—found shelter behind a stone wall and boulders at the base of Big Round Top, with Plum Run now positioned between them and the approaching enemy. Here the sharpshooters waited, letting their breechloaders cool down, while the Confederate lines marched beyond the cover of the Slyder farmyard, now wreathed in smoke, and moved steadily closer to the stream bed and the shaded slopes of Big Round Top.

Closer to the emmitsburg road, across the crop fields of the Bushman and Rose farms, the 1st Texas and 3rd Arkansas regiments pushed relentlessly forward and lost sight completely of Robertson's other two regiments, the 4th and 5th Texas, which had closed on Law's brigade in the advance down into the Plum Run valley. The Confederate attack had become dangerously fragmented, but the left wing of Robertson's brigade could only move forward against the Federal battery that continued to belch canister and solid shot into the ranks of the 1st Texas and the 3rd Arkansas. Soon the gap in Robertson's brigade became too wide to fill, and the terrain—broken ground of swales, stone walls, fences, woods, rock outcroppings—forced the two wings to march in completely different directions toward entirely separate targets.

Federal skirmishers from the 2nd U.S. Sharpshooters greeted Robertson's left wing with a bristling rifle fire that slowed the Confederates' pace from a double-quick to a hesitating walk. Desperately the 1st Texas on the right and the 3rd Arkansas on the left advanced toward a skirt of timber. The 3rd Arkansas halted and opened fire on the sharpshooters, dispersing the Federals and clearing the way for Robertson's men to reach the protection of the woods. But the artillery blasts from Devil's Den and scattered musket fire continued to maul the Confederate lines. A soldier in the 3rd Arkansas recalled how the man next to him fell from a bullet in the head: "I caught him as he fell against me, and lead him down, dead. As I straightened up to move on, that same familiar 'spat' which always means something, sounded near, and looking around, I saw Bose Perry double over and catch on his gun. He did not fall, however, but came on, dragging his wounded leg, and firing as he advanced."[13]

With the Confederate assault unraveling minute by minute, General Law realized that his own Alabama brigade had diverged too far to the right, so he decided to close the gap by taking the two regiments on the extreme left of the Alabama brigade, the 44th and 48th Alabama, marching them behind the advancing lines of the 15th, 47th, and 4th Alabama, and the 4th and 5th Texas, and swinging them into position to bridge the space between the left of the 4th Texas and the right of the 1st Texas. Such a complicated maneuver was not easily accomplished under fire, and William Oates, leading his men of the 15th Alabama through the planted fields of the Slyder farm, looked to his right to discover—much to his surprise—that the 44th and 48th Alabama were no longer there.

Almost at once, General Law galloped up to Oates, reined in his horse, and told the colonel that his regiment now constituted the extreme right of the Confederate line. As Oates remembered the conversation with his superior, Law "directed me to hug to the foot of Round Top on its west side & pass up the valley between the two mountains until I found the federal or Union left & to turn it if possible to do all the damage I could." Law also let Oates know that Lieutenant Colonel Michael Bulger, now in command of the 47th Alabama, advancing to the 15th's left, had been instructed to close up with the 15th, and, "if separated from the left of the brigade" to act under Oates's overall command.[14]

As the 44th and 48th Alabama got into position to the left of the 4th Texas and made themselves ready to assault the Union defenses at Devil's Den, Hood's battle line was thus mostly restored and the severe gap that had opened up among his brigades was finally closed. Disaster had been averted by the quick action of General Law, but the movement of his two right regiments put Oates and the 15th Alabama in a perilous situation. Having been previously pressed to the left by the 44th and 48th Alabama, the removal of those two regiments from his right allowed Oates's own right wing to swing forward, creating a "converging" line; Oates set his sights on getting his regiment between Devil's Den and the base of Big Round Top, as Law had ordered him to do, but this meant his regiment must now advance by purposefully closing on its left. In doing so, this put the 15th Alabama, and the 47th Alabama to its immediate left, on a course headed nearly due north, with the western face of Big Round Top to the Alabamians' immediate right.

Meanwhile, confusion among the Confederates had not entirely been eradicated. On Warfield Ridge, General Henry Benning obeyed the orders he had received from Hood to follow Law's brigade into battle by maintaining a distance of four hundred yards between the Alabamians and his Georgians. When his men stepped off the ridge, a line of Confederates were ahead of him, about four hundred yards away as prescribed. He followed that line, halting twice to sustain the required interval between his men and Law's advancing brigade. Within a short time, Benning could see that the Confederates in his front were in trouble, and he ordered his brigade forward in an assault, but it was only afterwards that he learned he had inadvertently followed Robertson's left wing—the 1st Texas and the 3rd Arkansas—into battle, rather than Law's Alabama brigade, which had been shrouded from his view by dense trees and thick battle smoke. Benning saw Robertson directly ahead of his lines, but he could not see the enemy at all.

Tige Anderson, watching Benning's brigade cascade down the slopes of Warfield Ridge, commanded his men to do the same and, after receiving a request for support from General Robertson, succeeded in coming to the aid of the 1st Texas and the 3rd Arkansas. Union batteries in the Peach Orchard, however, cut through the Georgians with devastating effect and caught them in an enfilade fire that toppled Anderson's lines nearly from end to end. Making perfect targets with their left unprotected, Anderson's men wondered where McLaws's division was and why it had failed to appear on the battlefield. Coming up on the far left of the 3rd Arkansas, the Georgians passed through a wheatfield and into some woods and became immediately engaged with Union troops from Brigadier General J. H. Hobart Ward's brigade in the Third Corps.

From the top of Devil's Den, Captain Smith's Federal battery kept up its unremitting fire. When the enemy emerged from the woods in line of battle, about three hundred yards from Smith's left flank, his cannoneers opened with canister, but with little effect. The rocks surrounding Devil's Den offered excellent cover to the Confederates and gave protection to their own sharpshooters who picked off Union gunners. "We used canister without sponging," explained Smith years later, and rammed the charges as rapidly as possible, but the enemy kept coming. Realizing that he faced a choice between saving his guns or delaying the enemy, he decided to "consume the time it [would] take to remove the guns in fighting them," hoping to hold back the Confederates for precious minutes that ultimately would seem like hours.[15] Looking to protect his vulnerable left, he had asked for the 4th Maine, under the command of Colonel Elijah Walker, to be posted on his flank and to his rear. In response to Smith's request, General Ward ordered the 4th Maine into the valley separating Devil's Den and Little Round Top, over the very strong objections of Colonel Walker.

In short order, the 44th and 48th Alabama regiments moved up on Smith's left, his weakest point. After being pulled from the Alabama brigade's right, the two regiments had moved east of the Slyder farm buildings and advanced into the woods. Colonel William F. Perry, in command of the 44th, was determined to obey Law's orders and silence the enemy battery that had caused so much damage to the Confederates' lines. Reaching the edge of the woods, Perry instructed his regiment to wheel "so as to face to the north," and the Alabamians moved directly forward to the sound of Smith's guns.[16] But a stone wall, defended bravely by remnants of the 2nd U.S. Sharpshooters and skirmishers of the 4th Maine, proved to be a formidable obstacle, so Perry wheeled his regiment again, this time to the left, and extended his line to the base of Big Round Top.

But, given the rough terrain marked by plentiful boulders, the banks of Plum Run, and dense woods, the 44th and 48th Alabama could not maintain a contiguous line, and the two regiments broke into two wings, right and left. Perry led his 44th through the boulders and woods toward Smith's blazing battery, but he could not hold his entire regiment together, and it, too, divided into two wings. The left companies of the 44th advanced toward Smith's guns, while the right companies, linking once more with the 48th Alabama, marched toward the position defended by the 4th Maine, at the edge of the gorge between Devil's Den and Big Round Top, what would later become known as the "Slaughter Pen."

Enemy fire, brisk and deadly, caused Perry and his 44th Alabama to seek shelter behind the trees and rocks. The Alabamians, however, returned the Federal fire with gusto. All the while, Smith's guns—the four Parrotts on the crest of Devil's Den and the other two Parrotts near Plum Run—continued to roar in earnest and throw case shot into the Confederate ranks. Musket fire from the 4th Maine kept the Alabamians mostly pinned down. "Our principal loss was in this place," reported the adjutant of the 4th Maine, "the men expending on an average 25 rounds."[17]

For the next twenty minutes, the exchange of fire between the 44th Alabama and the 4th Maine filled the valley with quick spurts of flame that cut through the blue fog of powder smoke.

CONFUSION REIGNED SUPREME for Private John West and the 4th Texas as they forded the Plum Run and reached the foot of Big Round Top. Every man was exhausted. Having moved through the broken ground of the Plum Run valley and into the brambles and tangled woods that lay between Devil's Den and Big Round Top, the Texans had passed east of the small cluster of Slyder farm buildings and had surged into the woods while still under a ruthless enemy fire. To the right, the 5th Texas advanced with the 4th, both regiments trying to maintain some semblance of order by moving forward together, their right closed tightly on the left of Law's brigade.

In the mad dash across the Plum Run valley, the Texas regiments had lost contact with the brigade's two left regiments, and their own lines had crumbled under the insane fury of the enemy's artillery and sharpshooter unremitting fire. "Our men [were] tumbling out of ranks at every step," recalled J. Mark Smither of the 5th Texas, "knocked over by the Enemy's sharpshooters who lined the side of the mountain." Now, as they entered the shelter of the woods, the trees and boulders broke their lines apart even more; no one could tell for sure where the Texas lines ended and the Alabama lines began. "We were," declared Val Giles of the 4th Texas, "a badly mixed crowd."[18]

At some point after crossing the Slyder lane, the Texans kept moving toward the foot of Big Round Top, veering to the right to maintain the link with Law's brigade, while the 44th and 48th Alabama rolled behind them to the left. From a stone wall at the base of the hill, the 2nd U.S. Sharpshooters hit the Texans with a steady rifle fire that revealed how little the woods would protect them from the enemy's persistent peppering. But the 4th and 5th Texas, despite the chaos in their lines, moved directly toward the sharpshooters behind the stone wall, and their relentless advance convinced the Federals that there would be no stopping these Confederates this day. As the sharpshooters withdrew, and the Texans clambered over the stone wall, Private West watched as Lieutenant Joseph Smith of his company wet a handkerchief in Plum Run and tied it around his head to keep cool. Within a split second, Lieutenant Smith fell dead from a minié ball. "He was killed in twenty feet of me," West wrote home, "just after we crossed the branch—shot through the head, the bullet passing through the folds of his handkerchief on both sides."[19]

To the right of the Texans, the Federal sharpshooters at the base of Big Round Top were still waiting to menace the approaching lines of Law's Alabama brigade. With the 44th and 48th Alabama regiments now removed from the right flank, the 15th Alabama occupied the far right of Law's line. Oates, who had been squeezed to the right, was forced to advance his regiment almost due north, which put the Federal sharpshooters, shrouded under the shade of the green wooded slopes of Big Round Top, directly on his right flank. Suddenly the sharpshooters opened with a smashing volley. Undaunted, Oates and the 15th Alabama continued marching toward the small gorge between Devil's Den and Big Round Top. The sharpshooters delivered another volley into the flank of the Alabamians. This fire brought down several men, including the regiment's lieutenant colonel, Isaac Feagin, who fell with a shattered knee. Realizing he could not ignore this threat any longer, Oates deployed his right company to threaten the sharpshooters and drive them from their position behind the stone fence. Given the fact, however, that the sharpshooters were not exactly parallel with his battle line and had delivered both a frontal and right oblique fire against the Alabamians, Oates decided further to change direction to the right, and on his order "the seven companies of the Forty-seventh swung around with the Fifteenth and kept in line with it."[20]

The men of companies B and F, 2nd U.S. Sharpshooters, must have been surprised when nearly two regiments of Alabamians broke off from their advancing brigade lines and stood nearly face-to-face with them. Oates led his companies directly up the western face of Big Round Top, but the Federal sharpshooters tried their best to hold back the Confederate tide. Sergeant White described how the sharpshooters blocked the advance by taking advantage of the cover of boulders and trees: "An occasional lull in the fire would be followed by a terrific volley and the bullets would snap on the rocks and spat on the trees and glance off with a peculiar screech."[21] The uphill advance of the Alabamians dislodged the sharpshooters, but the Federals gave up ground grudgingly. Oates noted how the retreating sharpshooters "kept up a lively fire on my advancing line, which returned it but without much effectiveness"— or so he thought. White, who was on the receiving end of the Alabamians' fire, believed that "our loss was considerable" as the sharpshooters fell back.[22]

Oates and his troops—including Billy Jordan and his comrades in the 15th's Company B—scrambled up the steep hillside, "catching to the bushes and crawling over the immense boulders." For men who had already marched twenty-five miles that day, the climb up Big Round Top was a terrible ordeal. "Rocks and crags," wrote Oates, covered the hillside "thicker than grave stones in a city cemetery." The Federals moved back up the hillside, but, as Sergeant White observed, the sharpshooters retired "no faster than we were obliged to." In pursuit, Alabamians dropped from fatigue, thirst, hunger, and the human inability simply to take one step farther. "The ascent was so steep and rugged," wrote a soldier in the 47th Alabama, "that in many places the men could only advance one abreast, and then were to be lifted by their companions from one acclivity to another."[23] The battle lines of both the 15th and the 47th fell into complete disarray, yet the Alabamians continued to scale the hill, inch by inch, foot by foot.

Halfway up the hill, the Federal sharpshooters suddenly dispersed, vanishing "as though commanded by a magician." The sharpshooters, said Sergeant White, had held out long enough and had begun to think that they were "fighting the whole rebel army unsupported."[24] White and Company F retreated around the hillside toward Little Round Top; Company B, comprised of Michigan men, withdrew around the southern slope of Big Round Top. Oates, ignoring Law's orders, pushed his men to the hill's summit. At the top, Oates allowed his men to rest after their hard climb, knowing they were too exhausted "to make a good fight." Then dreams of glory took hold of him. On this high hill, he believed he could win the battle for the Army of Northern Virginia. "Within half an hour," he thought, "I could convert it into a Gibraltar that I could hold against ten times the number of men that I had."[25]

The arrival of Law's adjutant, Captain Terrell, who had managed to ride his horse up to the summit, shook Oates out of his pipe dream. Annoyed and bewildered, Terrell wanted to know what Oates was doing on this hill and why he had halted. Oates explained that his men needed rest, but he also argued the case for keeping his regiment on the hilltop. After listening patiently to Oates's proposal, Terrell informed him that Law—who was now in command of the division—had ordered the 15th Alabama "to press on, turn the Union left, and capture Little Round Top, if possible, and to lose no time."[26] With that, the adjutant spurred his horse and rode down the hill.

So Oates reluctantly obeyed his orders and led his men down the northern face of Big Round Top, skirting around a huge precipice near the summit, and finding the descent as difficult as the ascent had been. Down went the Alabamians, with faint clankings and low moans, their lines fractured by the trees and the rocks, down into the dark uncertainty of the wooded saddle between the Round Tops, down toward the only numbing reality that soldiers ever know—blood and the specter of death.

6

UP COMES VINCENT

THE BOOMING OF THE GUNS sounded distant, like the repeated slamming of an unlatched cellar door in a strong wind. When word reached the 140th New York that the Fifth Corps had been ordered to the front as reinforcements for Sickles's Third Corps, it was evident that a battle was in the making. Lieutenant Porter Farley shook off his weariness and knew that there would be no more songs sung that afternoon. Weed's brigade, aroused from its rest near Rock Creek, behind Power's Hill, formed quickly into columns and marched over fields and farm lanes in a determined lunge to connect with the Taneytown Road and find an expeditious route to Sickles's battlefield.

When the Second Division, commanded by Brigadier General Romeyn Ayres, stepped off, it was led by the First and Second Brigades, comprised entirely of U.S. Regular regiments. Behind the Regulars came Weed's Third Brigade, although the precise line of march of its regiments is uncertain. Probably O'Rorke's 140th New York, with O'Rorke at its head riding his little brown horse, and Farley cantering beside him as the dutiful adjutant, led the other three regiments of the brigade: the 146th New York, the 91st Pennsylvania, and the 155th Pennsylvania.[1] Leaving the brigade under the temporary command of O'Rorke and guided by his staff officer, Captain Azor S. Marvin Jr., Weed rode ahead of his brigade to find Sickles and determine his precise orders, while the Third Brigade moved quickly down the Taneytown Road toward the south.

Cutting across farm fields and shuffling due south from Power's Hill, Weed's brigade moved in a parallel line to Cemetery Ridge, out of sight to its right, until it came upon a farm lane that took it to the Wheatfield Road, which intersected with the Taneytown Road to the northeast of

Little Round Top. As it hurried west along the rough farm lane toward the Taneytown Road, the brigade marched by a field hospital, with its distinctive red flag waving overhead, where Third Corps' surgeons stood, hands in pockets, waiting for their patients to arrive. The scene for Weed's soldiers was ominous. "Attendants and stewards, holding suspicious-looking parcels and instruments, looked very sober as they moved silently about," recalled the historian of the 146th New York.[2] A battery came rumbling down the narrow lane, its horses galloping at breakneck speed, and the brigade split itself in two, like the Red Sea opening on Moses' command, to let the bounding guns go through.

Lieutenant Farley thought it odd that the rising noise of artillery fire could be plainly heard, although "it still had a distant sound" to it, while the sound of musketry could barely be heard at all. "It must have been owing to the intervening hill [i.e., Little Round Top] or the direction of the wind, or both causes combined," mused Farley many years later. But as the 140th New York crossed the Taneytown Road and followed the Wheatfield Road that ran along the northern base of Little Round Top, Farley at once detected minié balls whistling over the hill "through the high air above us." Very soon, he knew, the 140th would confront the "full fury" of the battle as it "burst upon us."[3]

Across the sun-warmed boulders of Devil's Den and in the dull green patches of woods around it, death—immortality striking sharp and early, as Emily Dickinson would have phrased it—had found a rugged place to dwell. For the dead soldiers who lay upon the bleak ledges and beneath the silent trees, solitary dark figures in the sunlight and the shadows, there would be no tomorrow. But death had not yet mustered all of its recruits. The fight for Devil's Den was about to reach a murderous crescendo.

On the northern shoulder of Houck's Ridge, above the plateau where Smith's Parrotts continued to spew fire and lead, Ward's brigade fought to hold back the 3rd Arkansas and the 1st Texas in a clamorous fight that lasted more than an hour. In the woods belonging to John Rose, a prosperous farmer, the 3rd Arkansas became entangled in a contest with the 86th New York, which successfully drew the Arkansas regiment away from the goal of taking and silencing Smith's battery. That left the work of storming the Federal guns to the 1st Texas, which forged ahead through the dense thickets and the dim woods, repeatedly trying to dislodge the

Union lines holding Houck's Ridge. Every time that General Robertson, accompanying his right wing, thought that his men had broken through the enemy line, "another fresh [line] would present itself, the enemy reinforcing his lines in our front from his reserves at the base of the mountain [i.e., Devil's Den] to our right and front, and from his lines to our left."[4] Actually Ward's brigade—made up of the 4th Maine, most of which was covering Smith's left, 99th Pennsylvania, 124th New York, and 86th New York—confronted the Confederates without immediate additional reinforcements, except for some beneficial fire delivered against Robertson's left flank by the 17th Maine of Colonel Philippe Regis Denis de Kerenden de Trobriand's brigade near the Peach Orchard. Much later in the fight, as the Federal lines began to disintegrate, de Trobriand sent in the 40th New York (the "Mozart Regiment") and Brigadier General Andrew A. Humphreys spared the 6th New Jersey from his Third Corps division to stave off a renewed and reinforced Confederate assault.

"The carnage," as one soldier in the 1st Texas admitted, "was frightful." In about twenty minutes, the 20th Indiana lost more than half its strength. Among the Confederates, Colonel Van Manning of the 3rd Arkansas went down with a head wound. A private in the 1st Texas recalled how "the blood and brains" of the man beside him were suddenly "scattered over my face and hat." The acting major of the 1st Texas, Captain J. R. Woodward, fell with a wound "while gallantly discharging his duty." Casualties in the Union ranks multiplied with the passing of every minute. In the 99th Pennsylvania, almost 40 percent of the regiment fell in the struggle for Houck's Ridge. At the end of the slaughter, the highest ranking man in Company G of the 124th New York was a corporal. Captain Smith described the contest as "hard, persistent, determined fighting."[5]

Whether Houck's Ridge and Devil's Den would remain in Federal hands came down to the courage of the 124th New York (the "Orange Blossoms"), which was not lacking. As the 1st Texas surged to within one hundred yards of the 124th, Colonel A. Van Horne Ellis ordered his men to fix bayonets. At Chancellorsville, where the regiment had lost nearly 40 percent of its effective strength, Colonel Ellis had urged his men: "Let the little girls of old Orange [County] hear a good report of this day's work." Now the New Yorkers were faced with another day's hard work. When the Confederates came to within fifty yards of Smith's guns, the New Yorkers rose up in an instant and let loose with a "crash of riflery" that thinned the ranks of the Texans and drove them back. Recovering from the musket blast, the Texans reformed and advanced again, but they gained ground slowly, step by step, and no longer was the Rebel Yell heard echoing up the slopes of the ridge or across the bloody earth contained in a triangular field to the east of the ridge and Devil's Den. There was "no time," said one Texan with a dry wit, "for shining shoes."[6]

In the center of this maelstrom, Ellis decided it was time for his regiment to charge. He called up for the officers' horses, and he and the regiment's major, James Cromwell, got in their saddles. "The men must see us to-day," said Ellis. Shortly, Ellis nodded his command, Cromwell waved his sword, and the 124th New York lurched forward at the double-quick, bayonets glistening before them as they rushed down the rocky western slope of Houck's Ridge and into the triangular field. Later, those who survived the charge remembered it for its great ferocity: "Roaring cannon, crashing rifles, bursting shells, hissing bullets, cheers, shouts, shrieks, and groans were the notes of the song of death which greeted the grim reaper, as with mighty sweeps he leveled down the richest field of grain ever garnered on this continent."[7] The Texans fell back approximately two hundred yards, shocked and thrown off-balance by the force of the attack. Cromwell shouted out a victorious whoop, but his exuberance was premature. As the Texans reformed along a rail fence and the battle smoke began to drift away, the stout men of the 124th New York looked in dismay as a second line of Confederates moved up, ready to assist the Texans in another assault.

This second line was Benning's Georgia brigade, which had belatedly advanced across the meadows of the Bushman and Slyder farms, and now at last was about to perform its duty as support troops. It poured "a terrible fire" into the Union lines that, to one officer in the 124th, "seemed in an instant to bring down a quarter of our numbers." Major Cromwell, defiant and undaunted, continued to wave his sword above his head, but a bullet soon found him and he toppled from his saddle. Ellis saw Cromwell fall. "My God! men!," he screamed. "Your major's down; save him! Save him!"[8] His men held their ground. In moments, Ellis was consumed by the dingy gray smoke that hugged the field. When he emerged again from the clouds, like a warrior god descending to earth from the heavens, a bullet hit him in the forehead and he fell dead among his men, his horse galloping off into the ranks of the attacking Confederates. Recovering the bodies of Cromwell and Ellis, the 124th retired to its original line and waited for the next assault.

The intense pressure on Smith's battery and the Union defenders of Houck's Ridge was increased by the steady advance of Perry's 44th Alabama in its fight with the 4th Maine on Smith's left. Perry's slugging match with the Maine regiment got some assistance from Sheffield's 48th Alabama, which deployed in open ground to Perry's right. When the 48th Alabama opened fire it was only some twenty paces away from the enemy. To protect his flank, Colonel Walker of the 4th Maine refused his line and a protracted fight lasting almost half an hour ensued in the area later called the "Slaughter Pen." The Confederates, particularly the 48th Alabama, sent "a biting musketry fire" into the 4th Maine, which "suffered [a] large loss."[9] All at once, Perry ordered the 44th Alabama forward and the Confederates swept over boulders and poured into the lines of the 4th Maine. Perry's men, working around to the left, raced for Smith's guns, three of which still remained on the level ground above Devil's Den.

Smith's position was now untenable. As the first wave of soldiers from the 44th Alabama flowed through the crevices between boulders and wrestled with the Union gun crew on the ridge, Smith appealed to the 124th to lend a hand: "For God's sake, men, don't let them take my guns away from me!"[10] But the 124th could spare no help, for it was hotly engaged again trying to hold back the Georgians and Texans in their front, and eventually the 124th withdrew with most of its ranks practically decimated. In the heat of the fighting being waged by the 4th Maine, below the rocks of Devil's Den, Colonel Walker, realizing that Smith was still up on the ridge, withdrew from his position below and, in an audacious move, charged his men straight up the slope to assist the wavering Federal lines on Houck's Ridge. With this, Smith decided he could hold out no longer, and rather than trying to remove his three remaining guns, he ordered his men to retreat and take their firing implements with them. Smith's Parrotts were now fair game.

Every man—Union and Confederate—tried to do his duty that day, and every survivor thought he understood perfectly how the battle had been fought, but the swirl of combat and the terror of close contact with the enemy caused a carousel of chaos and bewilderment that clouded men's minds and jumbled their memories; almost every Confederate regiment in the vicinity of Devil's Den that afternoon, for instance, took credit for capturing Smith's guns. More than likely, it was the 1st Texas that actually seized Smith's three Parrotts after successfully advancing with the Alabamians and Georgians and driving off the remaining Federal infantry on the southern lip of Houck's Ridge.

As the men of Perry's 44th Alabama swarmed across the plateau where Smith's guns stood silent, they captured some forty Federals found behind boulders and between the rocks. But the Alabamians were under fire from Union artillery—Smith's two remaining guns on a hillock behind Houck's Ridge and possibly Hazlett's guns, which by this time had reached the summit of Little Round Top—and, just as Perry escaped a serious wound from an exploding shell, it appeared as if the 4th Maine was forming for a counterattack. In the nick of time, Benning's Georgians swept forward, and the battle raged anew between Yankees and Rebels, with neither side being able to claim true victory or admit sorry defeat. The 17th and 20th Georgia regiments moved past the 44th Alabama, which was nearly fought out by this time, and on the right the 2nd Georgia sprang forward to engage the wilting Federals. The 124th New York, broken and limping, was struck by the 15th Georgia and the 1st Texas. "The whole line was alive with burning powder," remarked an officer in the 4th Maine.[11] The Maine boys put up a stiff resistance. Colonel Walker suffered a wound in the foot, and his men held on only by the skin of their teeth. Walker later observed with pride that two shell pieces and thirty-two bullets had lacerated the 4th's colors and a shell fragment had broken the colors' staff.

Despite the onslaught of the Georgians, the 6th New Jersey rushed into the fray, spraying bullets into the 44th and 48th Alabama in the gorge between Devil's Den and Big Round Top and into the Georgia regiments on Benning's right. Smith's two Parrotts, belching canister, also did considerable damage, and Smith himself said he saw a Confederate battle flag drop "three different times from the effect of our canister." General Benning complained that the "shells of the enemy . . . were incessantly bursting along the summit of the peak [Houck's Ridge], and every head that showed itself was the target of a Minié ball."[12] As the 6th New Jersey moved up, trying to link with Ward's defensive line, the 4th Maine withdrew out of necessity—the Confederate advance was too strong for it to withstand.

Behind the 6th New Jersey came the 40th New York, which charged ahead through Smith's caissons and limbers toward Devil's Den and the approaching Georgians and the 48th Alabama. Although the Confederates fell back to Devil's Den and the protection of the woods along the base of Big Round Top, the 40th New York was not able to gain a new lodgement on Houck's Ridge or retake the rocks of the Den. Eventually the 40th fell back, concerned that its flank might be turned. The retreat of the New Yorkers was supported by the 6th New Jersey. Eventually the Federals found shelter in Rose's Woods, but the Confederates succeeded in pushing the Union line back to the Wheatfield. One Texas veteran declared without hesitation that the fight for Devil's Den had been "one of the wildest, fiercest struggles of the war."[13]

Captain Smith took his remaining section of two guns to the Wheatfield, placing them near Captain George B. Winslow's Battery D, 1st New York Light Artillery. From there, Smith led his caissons and limbers, loaded with his wounded, back to the Union rear along the Baltimore Pike. He had done what he could to hold back the Confederate attack, and his efforts, while unsuccessful in the end and disheartening because of the loss of his three guns, ensured that the troops of Hood's division who captured Devil's Den and Houck's Ridge would be too spent, too battle sore and weary, to help their comrades in the unfolding assault on Little Round Top.

WHILE THE 20TH MAINE and the rest of Colonel Strong Vincent's Third Brigade waited near the edge of the Wheatfield for orders, Major Ellis Spear, still feeling ill and fatigued, watched with concern as stragglers and wounded men moved methodically toward the army's rear. Ahead, through a screen of trees, the blunt sounds of what Spear could only assume was "a severe struggle"—the fight for Devil's Den—could be distinctly heard.[14] The men grew restless as the intensity of the battle noise increased. The waiting dragged on for what seemed like an eternity.

At the head of the brigade was Colonel Vincent. His brigade led the three brigades of Barnes's division that day, with the 44th New York assuming the lead position in the order of march.[15] Young and handsome, Vincent was a Pennsylvanian, born in Waterford and educated in Erie. For a time, he worked in his father's iron foundry in Erie, earning a physical strength that suited his given name. He studied for two years at Trinity College in Hartford, Connecticut, and then transferred to Harvard College, from which he was graduated in 1859. He was not, however, a brilliant student. He also earned admonishments on his record for missing chapel and smoking in Harvard Yard.

Vincent was of medium height, and Private Oliver W. Norton of the 83rd Pennsylvania, who served as Vincent's brigade bugler and flag bearer at Gettysburg, thought he was "a gentleman by nature."[16] With a strong voice and a quick mind, he commanded attention. After receiving his degree, he passed the bar and began to practice law in Erie. In April

1861, he married Elizabeth H. Carter, a tall, dark-eyed schoolmistress whom he had met while a student in Hartford. The wedding took place in Jersey City, New Jersey, just a few days after Vincent had enlisted as a private in a three-month regiment, the Wayne Guards. After the Guards disbanded, Vincent returned to Erie and helped to raise the 83rd Pennsylvania regiment, receiving a commission as its lieutenant colonel.

He later rose to the 83rd's command and the rank of colonel after the death of the regiment's senior officer at Gaines's Mill. Only twenty-seven years old in July 1863, he had assumed brigade command on May 18, when Colonel T. B. W. Stockton had resigned. Although inexperienced at brigade command, Vincent was admired by the men of the 83rd Pennsylvania and respected as both a tough disciplinarian and a hard fighter.

Of the Confederates, Vincent wrote home in spring 1863 to his wife, Lizzie: "We must fight them more vindictively, or we shall be foiled at every step. We must desolate the country as we pass through it, and not leave the trace of a doubtful friend or foe behind us; make them believe that we are in earnest, terribly in earnest." But this battle at Gettysburg

Colonel Strong Vincent, Army of the Potomac

worried him like no other battle had before, and Oliver Norton sensed that Vincent may have had a premonition of his own demise. While the brigade passed through Hanover on July 1, with the drummers beating a marching rhythm and the flags rippling in the breeze, Vincent bared his head and turned to his adjutant general, saying: "What death more glorious can any man desire than to die on the soil of old Pennsylvania fighting for that flag?"[17]

As Vincent sat his horse waiting for orders near the Wheatfield, with the crash of battle rising higher and higher in the distance, he spied a courier headed toward the brigade, spurred his horse, and rode out to meet him. "Captain, what are your orders?" asked Vincent of the courier. The captain replied, "Where is General Barnes?" Annoyed, Vincent reiterated: "What are your orders? Give me your orders." The courier finally answered, "General Sykes told me to direct General Barnes to send one of his brigades to occupy that hill yonder," and the captain pointed to Little Round Top. Vincent knew that Barnes was absent from the division at that moment, so he decided to act on his own. "I will take the responsibility for taking my brigade there," declared Vincent, and he immediately rode down the length of his column, found and informed Colonel James C. Rice, commanding the 44th New York, "to bring the brigade to the hill as rapidly as possible," and then turned his horse about and galloped off toward Little Round Top, Norton accompanying him with the brigade headquarters flag.[18]

In the oppressive heat of that late afternoon, Vincent and Norton rode to the foot of Little Round Top's northwest slope, but discovered that ascending the hill from that direction would be impossible. They returned to the Wheatfield Road, raced along the northern base of the hill, and must have missed by minutes the arrival of Colonel O'Rorke and Weed's brigade column led by the 140th New York. Vincent turned his horse into the woods, reached the southern base of the hill, and found the spur of land, "partly covered by scattered boulders and smaller rocks," that would later bear his name.[19] Using this spur as his access point, he rode up a ridge through woods and emerged at the hill's summit, where a narrow platform of earth overlooked the slopes of Little Round Top's western face, which was littered with immense boulders and rock outcroppings.

Toward the southern edge of the summit, Vincent halted and looked around while Norton scrambled to catch up with his superior. Norton reined up behind Vincent, holding the flag. Out of nowhere, shells exploded to the right and left of Vincent and Norton, and the colonel remarked calmly to his aide, "They are firing at the flag, go behind the rocks with it."[20] Norton quickly did as he was told. Vincent joined him behind the cover, dismounted his horse, and went forward into the rocks to determine how he would place his brigade. The brigade commander's sword was still strapped to his saddle.

The brigade, now in motion toward Little Round Top, followed a route similar to the one taken by Vincent and Norton, marching along a farm lane, skirting the northern base of the hill, and cutting across its eastern face and up the wooded slopes. Many years later, Ellis Spear remembered Little Round Top and its rocky crest as having the appearance of "a long barn roof." It was separated, he said, "from the higher hill of Great Round Top by a level space, a sort of broad gap all covered with half grown oaks."[21]

As Vincent's column hurried up the hillside, shells burst above the brigade's regiments, including the 20th Maine, and Colonel Chamberlain feared the day could become a hard one for his mother if any of the shells exploded too close to him and his two brothers. He sent his brother Thomas back to the rear to keep the stragglers moving, and he told his brother John to begin setting up a hospital aid station for the wounded behind the battle lines. The shells continued to explode in the trees, showering branches down onto the men and wounding many of them. In the 16th Michigan, a shell took off the head of Adjutant Rufus W. Jacklin's horse, and the animal fell midgallop, "a mass of quivering flesh." But the soldiers also took a beating as the enemy shells continued to rake the treetops. "Many of our men," recalled Private Elisha Coan of the 20th Maine Regiment's color guard, "were killed or wounded by the falling limbs." A private in the 44th New York said glibly, "Say, if I ever get out of this, I shall resign."[22]

Moving up an old logging trail at the double-quick, Vincent's brigade—led by the 44th New York, followed by the 83rd Pennsylvania, 20th Maine, and 16th Michigan—streamed forward in column of fours.[23] Tensions ran high. The chaplain of he 20th Maine, Luther French, witnessed the beheading of Jacklin's horse and ran to Captain Atherton W. Clark, commanding the 20th's Company E, babbling about what he had seen. Clark interrupted French abruptly and shouted: "For Christ sake Chaplain, if you have any business attend to it." As the brigade near the crest, the troops recognized that they were about to hold a commanding position on high ground. A soldier in the 44th New York perceived that a defensive line on Little Round Top would give the Union forces a decided advantage. "I think we have got them shure this time," he wrote to his sister. Each man had been issued sixty rounds of ammunition. The "ball," wrote Ziba Graham of the 16th Michigan, was about to open.[24]

On the summit, Vincent—holding a riding crop given to him by his wife—greeted Colonel Rice, who had ridden on ahead of the brigade. Rice, who was called "Old Crazy" by his men, tended to get overly excited during combat and make mistakes.[25] Like Vincent, he was a practicing attorney when the war broke out. A graduate of Yale, Rice was a volunteer soldier who, despite his excitability, showed courage and resoluteness under fire. Vincent relied on him to help deploy the brigade across the hillside. Making a quick assessment of the ground, Vincent decided to position his regiments in an arc that would begin on the southern slope of the hill and stretch around to the rocky western face.

The brigade probably halted, extending for a quarter of a mile or so from the head of the column to the rear, to wait for Vincent's orders. Vincent walked the ground with his regimental commanders and showed them where their men would form in line of battle. At first he directed the 16th Michigan, under the command of Colonel Norval E. Welch, to hold the ground at the extreme left of the brigade, down along the spur between Little Round Top and Big Round Top. Next in line came the 20th Maine, with the 83rd Pennsylvania to its right, and the 44th New York on the extreme right of the brigade line. But as the 16th Michigan took up its position, Vincent changed his mind and shifted the regiment to the extreme right, beside the 44th New York, where the 16th would occupy a pile of boulders and outcroppings along the western face of the hill.

After the war, the tale was told that Vincent changed his mind and moved the 16th Michigan from a position on the left that separated the 83rd Pennsylvania from the 44th New York to the far right in order to fulfill a request made by Colonel Rice. According to some veterans, Colonel Rice asked Vincent to move the 16th Michigan and place the 83rd Pennsylvania and the 44th New York—the so called "Butterfield Twins"— next to each other in the battle line, for the two regiments had "always fought side by side in every battle, and I wish that they may do the same today." Vincent supposedly replied: "All right, let the Sixteenth pass you."[26]

But it is unlikely that Rice ever made such a request. In the first place, the two regiments were never known in the brigade as the "Butterfield Twins," a reference to the time when the Third Brigade was under the leadership of Brigadier General Daniel Butterfield. In the second place, the two regiments never fought side by side until the afternoon of July 2. In the third place, the 83rd and the 44th were already side by side. Moving the 16th Michigan from its position did not alter the deployment of the 83rd and the 44th. The tale implied that Vincent had initially placed the 16th Michigan between the so-called Butterfield Twins. But that simply was not so. The story of the "Butterfield Twins" was pure mythology. Vincent did, however, shift the 16th Michigan from the extreme left to the extreme right of the brigade. His tactical reasons for doing so are not known or knowable.[27] The change put the 20th Maine, in Private Coan's words, "on the left of the brigade and the extreme left of the army."[28] Vincent's redeployment of the 16th Michigan kept the 83rd Pennsylvania and the 44th New York as the two center regiments in the brigade battle line.

Colonel Rice described the brigade line as "nearly that of a quarter circle" with the right "thrown forward somewhat to the front of the ledge of rocks," making the right "more exposed than the other parts of the line." "Each rock," wrote a historian of the 83rd Pennsylvania, "was a fortress, behind which the soldier[s] instantly took shelter." As the lines were formed, one private felt the thrill of fighting for once on home ground, which sparked lofty thoughts of heroism and personal sacrifice: "We are fighting on our own native soil, and as for me, I will never [leave] this position alive while there is an enemy in front."[29]

Vincent personally supervised the placement of his regiments. To Colonel Chamberlain, he said: "I place you here! This is the left of the Union line. You understand. You are to hold this ground at all costs." Chamberlain replied that he understood, but he would soon learn that he had little idea what holding the left flank of the Army of the Potomac "at all costs" actually meant. To bring his men into position, Chamberlain bellowed: "On the right by file into line." It took a while for the regiment to perform this formation, which was more suited for the parade ground than a hillside battlefield. The 20th Maine, said Private Coan, "was formed in an open level space comparatively free from rocks and bushes but in our front was a slight descent fringed by ledges of rock, and our side of the hill was covered with boulders."[30] Because the regiment lacked field officers, Chamberlain assigned Captain Atherton Clark of Company E to command the right wing, and acting Major Ellis Spear the left.

With his brigade now on line, Vincent directed his regimental commanders to send out skirmishers. Colonel Welch of the 16th Michigan sent out two companies, Brady's Sharpshooters and Company A, a deployment that was made before the 16th Michigan was rapidly shifted from the left of the brigade line to the right. In the 44th New York, Captain Lucius S. Larrabee took his Company B forward and deployed his men into a skirmish line. Larrabee functioned under a dark cloud this day. Earlier, he had told two other officers of the regiment that "since the last battle I have known that I would be killed the next time I was under fire." So strong was this premonition that he left his valuables with the regiment's quartermaster. As he moved forward with his company, a comrade called out wishing him luck. "Good bye, Billy," replied Larrabee, "I shall never see you again." Under the command of Captain David P. Jones, Company A of the 83rd Pennsylvania went forward as skirmishers. Chamberlain ordered Captain Walter G. Morrill to lead Company B forward as skirmishers into the trees below the regiment's line; the intention was for Morrill's company to link up with the skirmishers of the 16th Michigan. Morrill thought he had been told to cover the regiment's front and left flank, so he moved to the left, disappearing into the woods, but his effort "to connect on the right with the 16th Michigan" failed.[31]

The men of Vincent's brigade tried to settle down, waiting nervously for the enemy to appear. Chamberlain released the pioneers, provost guard, cooks, and walking sick for combat duty. On the 20th's left, Spear worked to straighten the line as he watched the trees anxiously for moving forms. For some strange reason, Chamberlain, while "observing and meditating as to the impending and the possible," left his regiment, which might have come under fire at any moment, to visit Colonel Rice and the 44th New York toward the front of the hill. The two men, incredibly, walked to the right of Rice's regiment, where they could gain a clear view of the Plum Run valley below. From this vantage point, Chamberlain and Rice could see the enemy overrunning Devil's Den, which Chamberlain later described as "a smoking crater." Below them, the Confederates were "pressing past the base of the Round Tops," and it looked like every enemy line "was rolling toward us in tumultuous waves."[32] The two colonels looked at one another, said nothing, and silently returned to their places in their respective lines. Those enemy waves were about to come crashing with a roar onto the rocks of Little Round Top.

* * *

IN THE MASSIVE, EIGHT-ROOM STONE HOUSE of Jacob Weikert on the Taneytown Road, all was turmoil and upheaval. Tillie Pierce watched that afternoon in awe as column after column of blue-clad soldiers marched past the house toward Gettysburg. In an open field just to the east of the farmstead, the army parked its artillery and ammunition trains. She observed soldiers stacking oblong wooden boxes, which looked "ominous and dismal," along the roadside.[33]

During the afternoon, several officers asked to go up to the roof of the house to observe the battlefield, and Tillie obliged by leading them up through a trapdoor and onto the roof, where they "looked through their field-glasses at the grand panorama spread out below." The officers even let Tillie look through their glasses. What she saw, she said, "was wonderful and sublime." The landscape for miles around "seemed to be filled with troops; artillery moving here and there as fast as they could go; long lines of infantry forming into position; officers on horseback galloping hither and thither!" It was, she wrote more than twenty-five years later, "a grand and awful spectacle."[34]

With the passing hours, the gruesome reality of battle drew nearer to the house. Heavy cannonading could be heard in the distance, but the threatening sounds soon became amplified and eventually thundered "so terrible and severe that it was with great difficulty we could hear ourselves speak." Tillie and the Weikerts were "terror-stricken," and some soldiers suggested that they evacuate the house and find shelter at another farmhouse nearby. They abandoned the house so quickly that Mrs. Weikert forgot to remove a loaf of bread baking in the kitchen oven. As they fled down the road, a rude soldier told Tillie that Gettysburg was on fire "and all the people in it." She broke down in tears, but was comforted by other, more compassionate soldiers who assured her that the armies always allowed "helpless and innocent citizens to get out of a place, and never to destroy them."[35] They felt sure her parents and sister were still safe in the town.

Before the civilians arrived at their refuge, Mrs. Weikert sent old Jacob back to the farm to collect some personal treasure she had forgotten. In the meantime, Tillie and the Weikert women were told they could not stay where they had been sent. So they returned to the Weikert farm, coming upon Jacob as he trundled down the road carrying a brand-new quilted petticoat—Mrs. Weikert's prize possession. Panting, they entered the farmhouse, none the better for their "wild goose chase," as Tillie called it.[36]

While they had been out of the house, Dr. Clinton Wagner, chief surgeon of the Second Division, Fifth Corps, began setting up a field hospital in the house and around the farmyard, augmenting and expanding the aid station that had been established there the day before. He was assisted by Dr. John Shaw Billings, the famous army surgeon and statistician who later planned Johns Hopkins Hospital. Billings recalled that when he got to the Weikert house, "I found it unoccupied and bearing evident traces of the hasty desertion of its inmates. A good fire was blowing in the kitchen stove, a large quantity of dough was mixed up, [and] the bake-pans were greased."[37] He immediately put his attendants to work baking bread and heating water. Tillie was pleased to find upon the family's return to the house that Billings's men had actually removed the loaf left baking in the oven before the bread had turned to cinders.

But the Weikerts could not have been pleased by what they found after having been gone from their house for only a short time. According to Dr. Cyrus Bacon, the medical staff "had ransacked the house and secured operating tables, cloths for dressing, etc." Rifling through the clothes cupboards upstairs, the men brought down a variety of items to be used by the surgeons, including "a neatly worked lady's chemise." When Rebecca Weikert saw that her chemise was being used as a placemat for surgical instruments, she demanded it back, but Bacon refused to give it up unless she could find something to replace it with. After a few minutes, Rebecca returned with another article of clothing, and the chemise was returned to her.[38]

By this time, though, old Jacob Weikert had had enough. Disturbed that his well might be emptied by thirsty soldiers, insistent doctors, needy wounded, and the overly generous women in his company, he removed the crank handle from the well's bucket winch and carried it with him as he, his family, and Tillie Pierce took cover in the house's dark and musty cellar. They did not feel safe. "The very earth beneath our feet trembled," wrote Tillie.[39] Crouched in the damp cellar, Tillie and her Weikert companions trembled as well.

Outside it seemed like the world was coming to an end. Indeed, the ensuing fight for Little Round Top was about to resemble—as one soldier phrased it so graphically—"the warring of Milton's fiends in Pandemonium."[40]

7

THROUGH THE VALLEY OF DEATH

F OR CIVIL WAR SOLDIERS, there were two kinds of death: *ordinary death* (that disturbing but commonplace and natural occurrence, in which relatives and friends were taken from the land of the living) and *war death* (that sudden and unpredictable force that violently struck down soldiers by the random thousands in camp or in combat).[1] Ordinary death came to the elderly, the ill, the victims of accidents and other mishaps, and a sad percentage of children, including newborns, infants, and toddlers; war death indiscriminately took young men in their prime without warning, without mercy, without apparent divine purpose, and always with a grim brutality. All that war death seemed to accomplish was to end the lives of men well before their time and to spread misery and suffering across the land—loss and sorrow brought about in the name of a cause, noble or ignoble, it didn't seem to matter much in the end.

Private John West and his comrades of the 4th Texas, ever since stepping off Warfield Ridge, had repeatedly come upon war death and all its terror as they moved across the broken terrain of the Plum Run valley and into the small gorge of dark shadows and muffled noises that divided Devil's Den from the lower shoulder of Big Round Top. Now, as the Texans and Alabamians continued to advance and the fighting showed no signs of abating, they were about to confront war death to a much greater degree than they had experienced it before, and watch it consume lives with such an unrestrained intensity that they would never be able to forget this baleful afternoon for the rest of their days. Some of these men, though, had little time left to live, so their memories of the horror that they and their comrades were about to encounter would soon be totally and eternally obliterated. There would be no ordinary deaths in Gettysburg this day.

The afternoon still held the heat, like a tin roof, although it was nearing six o'clock, and the shadows had begun to lengthen over the battlefield. A professor in town had recorded the temperature at 82 degrees Fahrenheit four hours earlier, but in the direct sunlight it was probably 10 or 15 degrees hotter than that, even at this hour—which the advancing Confederates of Law's Alabama brigade and Robertson's Texas brigade might have confirmed had they been given the chance, but they were too busy trying to pick their way around boulders as big as ambulance wagons and bounding across the meandering Plum Run as they passed through the gorge at the foot of Big Round Top. "It was extremely hot," said West, stating what was obvious to all.[2]

This much could be said: despite the unbearable heat, the Texans had successfully driven away the remnant Federal sharpshooters who had taken cover behind a stone wall and who now had scattered when the Confederate lines drew close and threatened to overwhelm the marksmen. But the Texans still faced some stiff fire directed against their front and left flank. The 4th and 5th Texas regiments pushed on, trying to maintain order in the lines, but the rocky ground broke their lines apart as effectively as enemy canister might have done. Any attempt "to preserve anything like line of battle," declared a soldier in the 5th Texas, "[was] impossible." Some of the Texans, giving up their lines entirely, took cover behind the huge boulders, where, remembered one soldier in John West's regiment, "a person could shield himself from the minnie balls."[3] These solitary soldiers began operating as snipers, picking off Federals on Houck's Ridge and Little Round Top.

Through the timber and thick overgrowth that covered the low shoulder of Big Round Top, the 4th Texas on the left and the 5th Texas on the right drove through the woods, storming a rail fence that the Texans believed was protecting an enemy force, only to find the fence undefended when they reached it. To the right of the 5th Texas, the 4th Alabama stuck like glue, having become separated from the 47th and 15th Alabama when Oates decided to pursue the scattering enemy sharpshooters up the slopes of Big Round Top. In the 4th Alabama, men dropped from wounds, fatigue, and the paralyzing heat. Some men simply fell behind, never to be seen again. Fording Plum Run, Sergeant William Ward took notice of a private, Billy Marshall, who stooped at the stream, "supporting himself on his left hand, without kneeling, holding his musket in his right, and drank as an animal might have done." That was the last that Ward ever saw of Marshall. "His body was never found," reported Ward, "and no one has ever heard of Billy Marshall since that day."[4]

Together the Texans and Alabamians swept across the heavily wooded shoulder, shaded by the trees that gave them some blessed relief from the scorching sun as they tumbled forward through the dreary forest of second-growth timber and fallen deadwood. Ward recalled how the dead trees "formed a natural abatis, through which passage was difficult"— especially since the men had been ordered to advance at the quickstep (the Texans were hurrying at the double-quick), which proved impossible to achieve. The boulders offered even greater obstacles. The rocks created "a natural breastwork," as Ward described it, and "over and through this the line had to mount."[5] Men scaling boulders using hands and knees could not possibly retain their places in line, and the pretense of an orderly advance shattered yet again as broken terrain and natural barriers threw the advancing regiments into complete disarray.

To their left and rear, the struggle for Devil's Den reached its height as the wild crash of battle reverberated through the woods, ricocheting

Little Round Top, as seen from Houck's Ridge

off the rocky landscape. Despite the shade from the trees, the men still felt trapped in a furnace. The sun slanted in through the branches and leaves with enough intensity to make the woods as hot as the open spaces. Sweating and fatigued, yearning for water, most of the Confederates were dehydrated and panting; to some it seemed like they might never slake their thirst or catch their breath. Ahead of them, out beyond the somber shadows and the unnatural heat of the dappled woods, awaited more fighting, more blood, more death.

When they finally passed out of the woods and emerged once more into the bright unmerciful sunlight, they saw before them a majestic and intimidating sight. Rising up from the floor of a level valley was the massive western face of Little Round Top. Across its cleared slopes gigantic boulders were strewn from the bottom to the top of the hillside, as if some ancient god had sown the hill with rocks instead of seeds. More ominously, the Texans and Alabamians could plainly see their foes positioned behind ledges and brush and wedged into the crevasses formed by rocks and trees. Most of the Confederates regarded the hill "a high mountain," as Private West called it in his letters home.[6] Although the crest of Little Round Top stood only 170 feet above the floor of the Plum Run valley below it, the hill itself rose steeply halfway up its slopes, leaving behind a more gradual ridgeline that ran nearly from the banks of the stream in the valley to a cluster of boulders and rock outcroppings along a vertical ledge about twenty-five yards below the frowning crest.

Ahead of the broken but relentless Confederate lines fled the Federal sharpshooters, the remnants of Company F, 2nd U.S. Sharpshooters, who were yielding the ground slowly and reluctantly. Some of the sharpshooters, the most stubborn among them, turned coolly around as they retreated, firing a shot or two into the butternut regiments and then turning their backs on the enemy and calmly walking away. The sharpshooters, showing an utter lack of concern for the enemy practically crawling up their backs, sauntered into the wooded saddle between Little Round Top and Big Round Top and entered the lines of the 83rd Pennsylvania, whose left companies dipped down close to the shaded floor of the valley.

Without benefit of skirmish lines, Hood's Texans moved inexorably forward, but a new line of Federal skirmishers suddenly appeared ahead of them, having just received their orders from Colonel Vincent to push forward beyond the brigade's battle line. These skirmishers from the 44th New York and the 83rd Pennsylvania (and possibly the 16th Michigan) offered the advancing Confederates "a sharp contest," in the words of Major John P. Bane of the 4th Texas.[7] About two hundred yards ahead of Vincent's battle line, the blue-coated skirmishers resisted the surging gray clumps of Confederates with rippling volley fire that momentarily halted the Texans in their tracks.[8]

Doleful Captain Larrabee, commanding Company B of the 44th New York, led his men forward in the line of skirmishers, despite his overwhelming sense of doom and his certainty that he would not survive this battle. Conquering his premonition of death for the moment, he did his duty and commanded his men down into the little valley that lay between the Round Tops. Ahead the New Yorkers spotted the jumbled ranks of Hood's Texans, and they let loose a volley that caught the enemy by surprise and threw the Confederates into confusion. Quickly, however, the Texans regained their composure and answered the Federal fire with a shattering volley of their own. Larrabee, who saw that he could not advance any farther, decided to withdraw his men just at the moment when the enemy volley struck his line. He was shot through the body and instantly killed, the first officer of the 44th New York to die in combat. His poignant prediction to this friends—"I shall never see you again"— had come true.[9]

Unable to resist the steady enemy riptide that now crashed upon them, the Union skirmish line immediately broke apart. Unintentionally colliding into the skirmishers' rear, the Confederates took a number of prisoners before the Federals could figure out just what was going on. In haste, the remaining skirmishers fled back up to the protection of the brigade stretched out among the ledges and rocks along the uneven slope of the hill. Quickly the Texans and Alabamians, who had advanced in columns of fours, reformed in a battle line as best they could, with the 4th Texas on the left, the 5th Texas in the center, and the 4th Alabama on the right.

With little delay, the Confederates followed the retreating enemy skirmishers across the open ground between the wooded shoulder of Big Round Top and the rising ridges of Little Round Top, staying as close to the heels of the fleeing Federals as they could. In this advance, Colonel John C. G. Key and Lieutenant Colonel B. F. Carter of the 4th Texas fell with severe wounds, leaving Major Bane in command. With grim purpose, Private John West bounded forward across the Valley of Death and soon discovered, with the rest of his comrades, that the large boulders at the base of Little Round Top made it impossible to maintain the battle lines that just minutes before had been so painstakingly adjusted. The huge rocks formed defiles, which, as Lieutenant Colonel King Bryan of the 5th Texas pointed out, "not more than 3 or 4 men could pass abreast, thus breaking up our alignment and rendering its reformation impossible."[10]

It was rough going—so rough, in fact, that the Texans found it difficult to fire up into the enemy ranks as they stumbled around the boulders and loose rocks at the base of Little Round Top. The Federal line exploded in a blaze of musket fire that killed and wounded numerous Confederates. William Fletcher of the 5th Texas saw the colors fall five times. When the colors went down for the last time a piece of the flagstaff struck him in the face and fell between his feet, causing him to lose his balance. Angrily, he gave the stick "a kick and said a curse word, and passed on." The climb up the hillside, wrote Colonel R. M. Powell of the 5th Texas, "was so difficult as to forbid the use of arms." Private J. Mark Smither of the 5th thought the rocks were a formidable barrier. "We could hardly have gone over them," he later wrote his mother, "if there had been no Yankees there."[11]

Over on the left with the 4th Texas, John West saw the mass of rocks littering the western slope of Little Round Top and concluded that "a mountain goat would have revelled" in the site of such rugged terrain. He quickly learned that scaling these rocks might have been possible for a man without the accouterments of a soldier; as it was, West had discarded his blanket and personal belongings—everything except his musket and cartridge box—but he still could not make much headway up the slope, especially with the heavy enemy fire pouring down on him and his comrades. Amid the smoke and noise of battle, he perversely remembered an alliteration learned in childhood: "Round the rude rock the ragged rascal ran." But few of the Texas rascals were successfully running around any rocks that terrible afternoon. One of West's fellow Texans complained that the boulders, in fact, were "as large as a meeting house."[12]

The din of battle grew so loud that few men could hear the orders being shouted by the officers along the ascending lines. Major Jefferson C. Rogers did, however, hear Colonel Powell of the 5th Texas call out: "Swing up the left, Major Rogers." Rogers yelled back: "I'll do it, Colonel, by jingo"—and just then the racket of battle ceased completely so that "by jingo" could be heard by every Confederate on the rocky slopes, which, in turn, produced a hearty round of laughter among the Texans. But most spoken words were drowned out by the deafening sounds of battle. "Private soldiers," said Val Giles of the 4th Texas, "gave commands as loud as the officers. Nobody paid any attention to either." The ground, reported

Captain Barziza, was now "strewn with the dead and dying—the warm blood yet pouring from them."[13]

In the 5th Texas, the men were pulling each other up and over the rocks. A private in that regiment, Rufus K. Felder, dodged bullets and believed that Lee must have been mad to order this assault. "He came very near loosing his whole army by it," said Felder to his mother in a letter written only a few days after Gettysburg. Private Smither had similar thoughts, although he blamed "Bullhead Longstreet" for the reckless attack on such a strong position. West had to agree that this attack seemed like pure folly, but he put the case more positively. "General Lee," he wrote home after the battle, "never would have attacked the enemy in their position on the mountain side except for the splendid condition of his army, and his confidence in its ability to accomplish anything he chose to attempt."[14]

ACROSS THE SOUTHWESTERN HILLSIDE of Little Round Top, the Texans took cover behind the boulders and opened up with an intense musket fire that stung the Federals above them. The men in John West's regiment found the enemy fire so withering that they could not move forward without exposing themselves to what Val Giles remembered as a deadly "rain of Minié balls that were poured down on us." To the right, in the 5th Texas, Private Smither noticed his regiment's commander, Colonel Powell, urging his men forward by "waving his sword and cheering."[15] At Powell's side, a lieutenant was hit and stumbled, but the colonel caught him and helped him to the ground. As he stood up, Powell was struck in the left side, the bullet passing out of his back. Smither caught him and managed to get the colonel to cover behind a boulder.

Watching his men get as close to the enemy as twenty-five yards, Lieutenant Colonel Bryan of the 5th Texas decided that the regiment could go no farther without reinforcements, and he went looking for Colonel Powell to get the commander's next orders. He moved toward the center of the Confederate assault line, passing "many officers and men who had fallen, having discharged their whole duty like true soldiers," when he finally discovered Powell, who lay wounded on the ground.[16] As Bryan approached the regiment's commander, he was struck in the arm; but he did ascertain that Powell was still alive, even though it appeared that the colonel's wound was mortal. Bryan could not staunch the flow of blood from his own wound, so he left the field and turned command over to Major Rogers.

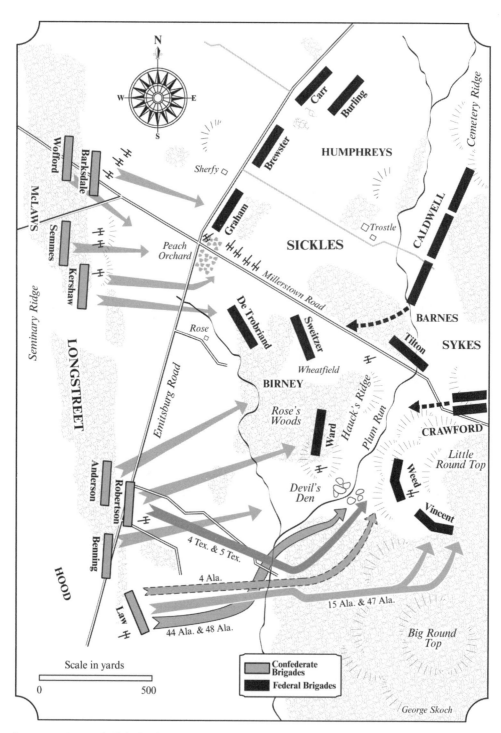

Longstreet's assault, July 2, 1863

Rogers assessed the situation and assumed a place behind the regiment's color guard, telling his men to aim carefully. The enemy was close enough, in William Fletcher's opinion, to shoot the Texans in the top of the head without much difficulty. Enveloped in smoke and noise, Rogers suddenly realized that the 4th Texas to his left had fallen back and the 4th Alabama to his right had failed to emerge from the woods, leaving the 5th Texas alone on the steep slopes of the hill. At once the major ordered a withdrawal "to an open space about 50 yards in rear." When the Texans reached shelter, Major Rogers learned that nearly two-thirds of the men in the 5th Texas had been killed or wounded. After the war, Captain Barziza lamented poetically about the frightful number of Texas casualties and "the death dew upon the brow of the dying soldier." At the time, however, his thoughts were more focused, more practical, less romantic. In his diary, he recorded simply and matter-of-factly: "Charged the enemy posted in strong position behind rocks upon the top of a hill. We fought them about an hour."[17]

Rogers saw, before pulling his men back, that the 4th Alabama was not to his immediate right as he had expected it to be, because the Alabamians had become pinned down in the woods and among the boulders near the saddle of land that connected the two Round Tops. The enemy volleys from below the crest of Little Round Top had caught them in an enfilade fire that stopped the Alabamians cold and forced them to take cover behind trees and boulders. Sergeant William Ward was among "a long line of us" who fell from one of these deadly volleys, and almost immediately he felt "a sharp, electric pain in the lower part of the body" as he sank to the ground. His only thoughts were: "This is the last of earth." He blacked out, but soon regained consciousness and heard the continuing "clash of musketry at close range."[18] Ward discovered that he could no longer use his legs, so he dragged himself behind a large boulder, four or five feet high. One of Ward's messmates, Sergeant John Mosely, joined him behind the rock, but Ward admonished him to move forward with the rest of the regiment. Mosely did, inching ahead with the stalled advance of the 4th Alabama, and met his death some fifty yards shy of the Federal line.

Lieutenant Colonel Lawrence H. Scruggs, commander of the 4th Alabama, had dropped from exhaustion soon after crossing the Plum Run valley and moving into the gorge beyond the Slyder farmhouse, so command of the regiment devolved upon Major Thomas Coleman. The major retracted his lines and established a rallying point among the rocks where Sergeant Ward had taken cover. "Halt here, boys, and let us make a stand at this place," Ward heard an officer call out.[19]

It is not entirely evident how the next assault by the Texans and Alabamians came about. The wounded Colonel Powell was not present among the reforming lines of his regiment, but he believed that the second attack happened spontaneously in response to someone in the ranks saying that the Texans should charge them again. Acknowledging that he had received orders to advance again, Major Rogers, in command of the 5th Texas, did not reveal who had given those orders or how they had been delivered to him. However it happened, the Texans and Alabamians shouldered their way around the boulders and between the trees at the foot of Little Round Top and placed themselves under the flaming muskets of the enemy.

By this time, artillery had arrived to buttress the Union defense of Little Round Top, and the booming guns shook the air and spewed clouds of smoke into the Valley of Death. Although the muzzles of the Federal cannon could not be lowered sufficiently to spray ordnance directly into the advancing lines of the Alabamians and the Texans (the Union gunners aimed their fire instead toward Devil's Den and Houck's Ridge), the presence of the guns on Little Round Top helped to discourage the Confederates in their uphill onslaught. Getting up the hill was difficult enough; but even if they should succeed, the Confederates knew now that they would face musket fire *and* cannon fire before they could reach the top of the hill.

What could possibly have motivated these seasoned soldiers to give this hill another try? Orders, of course, were orders, and to disobey them could mean shame, punishment, or, at the very least, the flat of an officer's sword on one's backside. But more than orders moved these men. A stalwart belief in their cause—the hope and promise of Southern nationhood, the desire to defend their homeland, and even the anticipation of a nascent slaveholding republic built on the foundation of white supremacy—did spur them along, supplying them with the ideology and the ideals they needed to face the enemy's guns and wage the risk of giving up their lives for a dream. But beliefs and ideas and dreams do not often go buzzing through men's minds as they move into combat. They are the high thoughts that come after a battle, when one can bathe in the glory of one's own miraculous survival. Mental pictures of hearth and home, family, wives, and children could work to deter men about to go under fire, but they could also encourage them forward by giving soldiers the determination to win one more battle, and with every victory came the realization that a rail ticket home might be closer at hand. For the Texans and the Alabamians who came out of their cover and groped up the hillside for a second assault on the Union lines, most of their thoughts must have focused on raw survival, the immediate task before them, the strength and accuracy of the enemy fire, and, for the pious at heart, the inscrutable will of God.

Those who obeyed the order to advance were among the most reliable of their regiments—the best soldiers who rarely shied away from a fight or fell to the rear in battle. Because of this, they were also the ones most likely to fall from wounds, for it was the bravest and the best who were killed and maimed; but when they fell, the somewhat less courageous suddenly found themselves in the front ranks, and they would be the next to fall. In a battle such as this one, where the odds were stacked so neatly in favor of the defenders and so pitifully against the attackers, it was a certainty that the most lionhearted in the grey regiments would soon be counted among the casualties; given the steady sheet of bullets coming from above, however, it would be a miracle if anyone trying to climb those slopes came out of this maelstrom alive.

In the heat of battle, Civil War soldiers experienced an incredible self-centeredness that comes with the likelihood of meeting one's end. Sometimes the frenzy of battle produced a mesmerizing state of mind, a rage and audaciousness, in which the soldier lost himself and became detached from any sensibility of danger. Under those circumstances, an individual soldier might become caught up in the violence to the extent that he conceived of himself as a solitary agent of destruction, what Confederate cavalryman Thomas Rosser called "fury's mad delirium."[20] Not every soldier forgot himself in combat or became a killing machine, but many Civil War soldiers confessed a peculiar exhilaration that sometimes came in battle and motivated them to advance into the dire straits of fire and blood that any man in his right mind would otherwise want to avoid at all costs.

Unit cohesion might motivate some of these soldiers to move forward in battle, for fear that their comrades might brand them cowards if they did not, and some consolation might thus have been achieved in the strength of numbers, which enabled individual soldiers to feel less isolated. But ultimately these Texans and Alabamians, like all other Civil War soldiers (and perhaps all soldiers since the dawn of time), acted as their own solitary entities with most of their inner focus targeted on the ways in which they might avoid the enemy's fire, elude the mayhem, and survive the whole horrible ordeal. The Confederate soldier, wrote Carlton McCarthy, who later in the war served with the Richmond Howitzers in the Army of Northern Virginia, "fought for a principle," but he also admitted that the typical Southern warrior "was an individual who could not become the indefinite portion of a mass, but fought for himself, on his own account."[21]

So in the middle of combat, with bullets flying, men screaming, and chaos descending over the entire scene, covering the landscape in willowy shrouds of black and crimson, most soldiers could think—if they thought any coherent thoughts at all—only of the two fundamental fears that all warriors must confront sooner or later: the fear that death may come to you at any moment, and the fear that you may be the one who causes the death of another living person, no matter how much you claim to detest that individual as your sworn enemy. War is hell not because it brings sorrow and hardship to those who wage it. War is hell because it turns human beings—ordinary men with otherwise ordinary powers—into angels of death.

Hell now stood only yards away for the Texans and Alabamians. For this second assault, the Texans, who ended up back at the foot of the hill picking their way around the boulders—knew how to use the huge rocks to their advantage, hiding until they were ready to shoot at the blue targets above them. The problem was that the rocks prevented the attack from gaining any real momentum, and groups of Confederates, or sometimes just single soldiers, inched their way between the massive boulders and tried to get a foothold on the slope that would let them, at the right moment, lunge at the Federal defenders with some power behind the thrust. Unfortunately, the enemy succeeded in keeping the Texans at a good distance and forced the butternut lines, such as they were, to remain in clumps or to take solitary cover behind the rocks, which now were heavily pocked with small indentures and white creases where numerous minié balls had ricocheted off into oblivion.

The second assault, in fact, was so disorganized that there was little or no coordination between the two Texas regiments and no real communication with the 4th Alabama. Some of the Texas soldiers didn't even realize that a second attack was under way; others found themselves behind the same rocks they had used for cover in the first assault, and, after the war, the separate advances up the slopes of Little Round Top blurred in their memories into a single charge. A few Texans from Company K of

The Confederate attack on Little Round Top

the 5th Texas had not earlier withdrawn from the hillside, waiting anxiously for the rest of their regiment to return after reforming; these three officers and eight men stood their ground on the slopes, suffering terrible casualties as the bullets whizzed around them. They were joined by men who had been separated from their own companies and regiments, and one soldier from the 5th Texas recalled that the minié balls flew in such quantity that it seemed like "a man could hold out a hat and catch it full."[22]

To the far right of the Texans, the 4th Alabama again hit the southern slopes of the hill and tried to gain ground, but volley fire, rippling from one end of the enemy lines to the other, kept them back and forced them to take cover in the vicinity of the boulder behind which William Ward had earlier found refuge. Captain William Robbins tried to hold the 4th's right flank steady as his company advanced, took a fearful mauling, and fell back to find cover. Adjacent Robert T. Coles described the battlefield as "inaccessible to man."[23] Confusion reigned everywhere. The men were exhausted. Casualties mounted. Every man, if he had not realized it already, began to see that they simply could not carry the heights in front of them.

Among the Texans, things were no better. All order and discipline had vanished in the thick battle smoke that hugged the ground. "Every fellow," wrote Val Giles, "was his own general." To make matters worse, Confederate artillery was firing into the ranks of the 4th Texas. "Their shells were bursting behind us, in the treetops, over our heads, and all around us," remembered Giles with some bitterness. The gunners, he said, had cut their fuses too short. Nothing, said Giles, "demoralizes troops quicker than to be fired into by their friends." In the 5th Texas, William Fletcher advanced "without a murmur" with his comrades, "knowing what was ahead of us if we went far," and soon enough they reached "the danger point," where they received a hammer blow from the enemy muskets above them. "The men," wrote Fletcher, "about faced near as if ordered and marched back." Desperately the regiment's officers tried to halt the retreat, but their orders were unheeded. Near Fletcher, a lieutenant squealed from the pain of having had his big toe shot off. "He made more racket than I ever heard from one wounded man," noted Fletcher uncharitably.[24]

Major Rogers was trying to hold this second assault of the 5th Texas together, even as his men began to leak toward the rear. He later praised the regiment, writing that "the coolness and determination of the men and officers were equal to the occasion."[25] But he could not ignore the fact that the soldiers under his command, no matter how brave and resolute, knew that they faced an impregnable enemy position. His immediate circumstances, however, had less to do with the courage and fortitude of his troops than with the fact that once again, to his right and left, the 5th Texas had been left on the slopes without any support. Thinking he was about to be flanked, Rogers ordered his men to retire, although the spontaneous retreat described by Fletcher probably compelled Rogers's action as much as any real threat from the Federals, who remained solidly behind the cover of the rock ledges below the crest. The 5th Texas withdrew because the men had decided they could not face the whistling bullets and the unremitting fury that lay before them.

So the Texans, with depleted numbers and battered bodies, limped back again to the skirt of woods along the shoulder of Big Round Top, where they hoped to rearrange their lines yet one more time while gaining some respite from the firestorm that encircled the summit of Little Round Top. These regiments of Hood's division—which formed the only brigade of Texans in Lee's army, a proud brigade that Hood himself had previously commanded in battle—enjoyed a brilliant combat reputation as Lee's shock troops, but today it was the Texans who received the shock and who, no matter how hard they tried, could not successfully drive the enemy from the field as they had done so many glorious times in the past. Nevertheless, these Texans, as John West so keenly observed from the moment he had joined their ranks, were a hearty bunch with rowdy dispositions—and stubborn beyond all reason. They would give it another try.

No one was particularly happy about having to go up that hill again. Off to the far right, beyond the woods where the 4th Alabama had taken cover, the noise of battle thundered and swelled—an indication that the 15th Alabama and the 47th Alabama, after a prolonged absence, had joined the fight for the hill along its southern slopes. In the waning light, as twilight dimmed the world around them and mercifully sent the blazing sun to its rest behind South Mountain, the men of Law's and Robertson's brigades braced themselves for yet one more attack.

Attempts to reform the lines within the protection of the woods proved futile; no order existed among companies, let alone regiments. Behind the Texans and Alabamians, Confederate forces successfully overran Houck's Ridge and forced the Federals to abandon their defense of the Valley of Death, where the water that trickled through Plum Run now ran pink in the fading dusk. Joined by the 48th Alabama to their left, the 4th and 5th Texas veered more purposefully to the left as they advanced up the hill and looked to outflank the Federal defenders who held the extreme right of the Union line. This put the Texans even more out of touch with the 4th Alabama, but the added weight of the 48th Alabama might just make the difference in this third assault.

While the Texans moved forward, leaning into the enemy fire as one might lean into a hard rain, a courier from General Law appeared out of nowhere and found Major Rogers. The aide saluted Rogers and said: "General Law presents his compliments, and says hold this place at all hazards." In reply, a perturbed Rogers screamed: "Compliments, hell! Who wants any compliments in such a damned place as this! Go back and ask General Law if he expects me to hold the world in check with the Fifth Texas Regiment!" The men pushed on, with frightful results. The dead and wounded covered the hillside. Captain Barziza described the mindset of the determined Texans: "Cold, heat, rain, fatigue and danger are alike disregarded, and even God himself is, for the time, forgotten."[26] Suddenly Barziza went down with a severe wound as the Texans came to within twenty-five yards of the enemy lines.

In the 5th Texas, the color guard had already been obliterated, so Sergeant W. S. Evans of Company F took the regiment's flag and rallied the men forward, up a rough defile toward the exposed right flank of the enemy. Amazingly, with superphysical fortitude, the Texans scrambled up through the rocks, getting closer and closer to the Union lines. How close they came to penetrating the enemy's defenses is clouded by the fog of war. Some Texan accounts indicate that they were held in check about twenty-five yards below the Federals' flashing muskets; other descriptions of the battle suggest that some Texans got to within ten or twenty paces of the enemy. What is certain that the last great lunge of the two Texas regiments, supported by the 48th Alabama, very nearly crumpled the right flank of the Union lines on Little Round Top.

By some miracle, it looked like the Texans would accomplish the impossible. Above them, the men of the 4th and 5th Texas could see the Federal lines waver and splinter. They continued toward the top, men falling in agony with every step. No one fired; they saved their shots for the struggle that would take place on the crest above them. An iron will carried them forward. It appeared through the fluttering veils of smoke as if the enemy forces holding the extreme right flank were now falling back, breaking apart. The Texans kept on climbing. And in the thin and sullen light of twilight, as these men from the Lone Star State pushed themselves beyond all human endurance, victory seemed amazingly, wondrously, within their grasp.

8

Shouting the Battle Cry

O N THE BARREN SUMMIT of Little Round Top, field glasses in hand, Gouverneur K. Warren waited nervously for Union troops to arrive and defend the hill. But at that very moment, when Warren's anxiety was at its height, Vincent's brigade was actually taking position on the hilltop, only a few hundred yards from where Warren stood. How this could have happened, how Warren could have failed to know that approximately thirteen hundred men—boisterous, clanking, grunting men who took no particular care to get into position quietly or invisibly—were deploying across the upper reaches of the southern and southwestern face of the hill, remains one of Gettysburg's most perplexing mysteries.

After the war, Warren insisted that he did "not see Vincent's brigade come up," although later that afternoon he did learn that the brigade had moved up the hill "behind me through the woods and taking their post to the left (their proper place) I did not see them."[1] No one has ever explained how he could have avoided seeing or hearing Vincent's men. He was too good an officer—and too capable at engineering, topography, and reconnaissance—to have missed them. But miss them he did.

Perhaps he had become distracted. He reported that he stood on a rock watching the enemy movements below and as he did so the minié balls had begun "to fly around us."[2] Toward his rear, he saw a battery struggling to move its guns up to the summit; elated by this sight, Warren propelled himself down the eastern slope of the hill to give whatever assistance he could to the intrepid gunners. It was Lieutenant Charles E. Hazlett's Battery D, 5th U.S. Artillery, and Warren—whose head was spinning by this point and who later could not quite reconstruct events in the

131

sequence that they had unfolded—took hold of one of the guns and labored with the gun crew to get the piece over the rocks and up the steep and wooded hillside. As Warren and the artillerymen fought the natural obstacles of trees and ledges and boulders, Vincent's men, below the hill's summit, fired their first volleys as the enemy came into view. Whatever his lapses, Warren proved his mettle this day.

So, too, did Colonel Strong Vincent, who looked to his men as they settled into position across the rocky crest of Little Round Top. He was made of stern stuff. In his heart, a flaming spirit seemed to burn; he possessed a pent-up energy and verve that made him appear to be everywhere at once. Admired and respected by his men, he was not always an object of their deep affection. Oliver Norton, his bugler, at first sized him up as "a dude and an upstart." Later, Norton's opinion of the young officer mellowed, and he soon came to believe that "no officer in the army was more thoughtful and considerate of the comfort and health of his men."[3]

The men, in fact, were inspired by Vincent's patriotism. On Washington's birthday, 1862, Vincent read George Washington's farewell address to his troops, which could not have been easily endured by the 83rd Pennsylvania, for the address was lengthy, and it must have taken

Lieutenant Charles E. Hazlett, Battery D,
5th Regiment, U.S. Light Artillery

Vincent quite a while to read the entire speech aloud; nor could it be said that Washington's farewell was particularly relevant to the times. But in Washington's heartfelt words, in the first president's sincere articulation of the principles of duty, self-sacrifice, and love of country, Vincent himself must have found some profound meaning—enough for him to feel called upon to share Washington's retirement message with his men and to hope that they, too, might gain a greater sense from it of the high stakes for which the Civil War was being fought.

No sooner had Vincent's regiments formed into line than the Confederates succeeded in pushing back the Federal skirmish lines and advancing through wisps of smoke and fading streaks of sunlight toward Little Round Top, hitting the Union lines with a great shock of gunfire. Vincent's men could see the enemy lines, what looked like three columns swinging out into battle formation, advancing toward them. They could also hear the Rebel Yell, that blood-curdling, shiver-provoking howl that seemed to be a cross between a fox yelp and the cry of the banshee. A soldier in the 83rd Pennsylvania thought that the yell sounded "as if all pandemonium had broken loose and joined in the chorus of one grand, universal war whoop."[4]

"If we had been five minutes later," wrote Private Charles Salter of the 16th Michigan, "the enemy would have gained the ridge we were on, and turned our left flank, and it would have been very hard to drive them from it." The Confederate assault struck in the center of Vincent's line, solidly in the front of the 44th New York and the 83rd Pennsylvania. For about a half hour, the fight became an exchange of long, crashing volleys in the deadly twilight. Almost at once, the hillside was covered in a thick, blinding smoke, and the men on each side strained to see their targets; often they gave up and fired aimlessly into the clouds, hoping by chance to hit a foe. Sergeant Charles Sprague of the 44th New York remembered that at first he could see the enemy "zig-zag among the trees down the hill." Instantly his regiment opened fire without orders. Of the Confederates, Sprague said that "I never saw them again distinctly," and the musket smoke obscured every man's vision. "Once in a while," he remarked, "they would get very close and a red star of flame would jump right out of the smoke at every discharge."[5] Those were the times when men would be hit and fall to the ground.

Norton the bugler stayed as close to Vincent's side as he dared, observing, as he followed his commander, that the Confederates were "held in check by our fire, but they continued to swarm along the slopes of the hill," edging slowly toward the north. When the smoke cleared sufficiently to see the enemy, the New Yorkers and Pennsylvanians fixed their sights and fired away. "The first thing I saw of them," remembered one New York soldier, "three men came out in sight and I took aim at the center one and he threw up his arms and went down, but as others were firing at the same time I do not know who hit him."[6] The Federal thanked the heavens for the rocks on the hillside—rocks that hid the wily Confederates but also provided life-saving cover for Vincent's men.

Vincent jumped atop a rock behind the 83rd Pennsylvania to survey his line and assess the force of the attack upon it. He didn't like what he saw. Although the Confederates seemed to stall about forty or fifty yards beneath the Union defenses, the enemy revealed a firm determination to make its way up the hill, no matter what the obstacles proved to be. Shaken by the enemy's resoluteness, Vincent called for his adjutant, Lieutenant John Clark. "Go," he told Clark, "and tell General Barnes to send me reinforcements at once; the enemy are coming against us with an overwhelming force."[7] He also sent runners to find additional ammunition. From his perch, Vincent could see most of his line, except for the right flank of the 16th Michigan, which was hidden by the bulge of the hillside.

Over there, the Michigan troops experienced a somewhat lighter push by the Confederates, but the fighting was still intense and deadly. The men were firing their muskets so rapidly that they were fouling. "I used one gun as long as I could," remembered W. W. Colestock, "and then picked up a dead comrade's and used it the rest of the day." A private in the 83rd Pennsylvania proudly noted that the enemy had been "handsomely met by our boys." Vincent's men were holding up their own, pounding the Confederates mercilessly, letting nothing go to chance, save the luckless fate of those who fell dead and wounded. The blue battle line, recounted Captain Amos M. Judson, laid down "a sheet of smoke and flame."[8] The Federals, with their faces blackened from the biting of cartridges and wearing smudges like those found on chimney-sweeps, stood firmly, shoulder to shoulder, with a grim and murderous intent.

Finally the Confederates withdrew, limping back down the slopes and into the relative invisibility of the smoke-filled valley below. Captain Judson marveled at how the enemy had at last reeled and staggered, falling back "in confusion." Fearful as that assault had been, ruminated Philander Platt of the 83rd Pennsylvania, he "felt not the least dismayed, or disturbed about being driven out of our position, as it appeared that every man in the brigade was imbued with the same spirit."[9] Others continued to be watchful and nervous, wondering if the Confederates would attack again and when the assault might occur.

There was only a short lull between the enemy advances. Many of the soldiers on both sides later blended the assaults together in their minds and in their memories, a testament to the fact that the attacks came close upon the heels of one another and that there was hardly any time for the Federals to catch their breath, regain their composure, tend to their wounded, and adjust their lines. The fight for Little Round Top, in the hazy light of memory, seemed more like one continuous volcanic eruption, one seamless episode in bloodletting, one black and endless nightmare. No one could see all of it; no one could understand much of it. But what was at stake formed clearly in the minds of the Union defenders across the hillside. As Captain Judson later described it: "It was a death grapple in which assailant and assailed seemed resolved to win or fall in the struggle. The enemy had everything to gain if they carried the position; everything to lose if they failed."[10]

Vincent's men also had everything to lose if they failed to hold back the Confederate tide. While they possessed a commanding position on high ground, there was nothing written in the heavens that said they would be the victors this day, nothing that preordained a Union victory and a Confederate defeat. What made these men of Vincent's Third Brigade, these ordinary farmers and physicians, merchants and attorneys, from such disparate states as Pennsylvania, Maine, New York, and Michigan, brace themselves for another attack and find the courage to retain their lines, keep their wits about them, and grit their teeth for another assault? Put another way: why did these men put themselves in jeopardy, offer up their very lives, for this insignificant hill that rose like a rocky blister in the placid farm country of central Pennsylvania? If their lines gave way, as General Warren, Colonel Vincent, and Captain Judson had perceived, it might certainly lead to the terrible defeat not only of their brigade and their regiments, but of the entire Army of the Potomac—or so they believed, and not without justification. But the army was used to mistakes, used to failure, used to defeat. It had been pummeled by Lee's Army of Northern Virginia in one contest after another; one more defeat seemed, in the reckoning of things, hardly to matter.

And yet it did matter. It mattered very much to these men in blue and to their own sense of what was right and what was wrong. It mattered in their hearts, where the flames of patriotism burned as brightly for many of them as the fire that had inspired Strong Vincent to read Washington's words to his men on a cold February day that, in the heat of this July afternoon, seemed to belong to a previous millennium, when the war was still new and the earth had not yet swallowed up so many young men. What now held these men on this hillside, in no small part, still had everything to do with George Washington, love of country, and the very idea of the Union itself. Inside them burned a fiery commitment to a cause, a loyalty to their nation, and a devotion to an ideology that, as Lincoln put it so well, sought to prove "that popular government is not an absurdity."[11] The compelling force of ideology, the lure of ideas as opposed to emotions, moved these men to stand on these slopes and fight side by side, offering their lives not so much to their country as to the ideas that defined the essence of their country—ideas that still sound like melodious and glorious trumpets in full splendor and that stir the American soul down to its deepest recesses: liberty, democracy, freedom, and equality.[12]

Unionist ideology was not necessarily any more compelling than the Confederate ideology that had motivated Hood's division to risk death on the slopes of Little Round Top. And yet Northern ideology, which had to a great extent wrapped itself around the political ideals of the Republican party, did appear to be more dynamic, more uplifting, more energizing, perhaps because it encompassed the high virtues of free labor, free soil, and free men. After Gettysburg, James Rice, who commanded the 44th New York as a colonel, believed that the battle had "resolved the greatest political problem of this age and of all ages to come—a problem no less than whether the United States should be all free or all slave—whether the flag of oppression should flaunt in every breeze, or the banner of freedom, in the name of Christ, be set up forever throughout the land."[13] Like many other Northerners, Rice likened the Union cause to a crusade fought not only for the sake of freedom, but also for godly values and Christian morality.

Such inspiring beliefs were not held by officers alone. A corporal in the 83rd Pennsylvania, Henry Lytle, wrote home just before Gettysburg to encourage his brother not to lose faith in the Union cause: "Do not be caried away by fear or excitement but let that dormant spirit be fired to deeds of valor, and let the invaders learn by experience that there is yet a sound core in the despised mudsills of the northern states. Hoist up the old flag, send up a petition to the ruler of all for strength, and then let the defiant spirit of the old northlanders come forth."[14] With sentiments like these to bolster them, Union soldiers found that ideas and beliefs could actually propel them into combat and sustain them, giving them the strength and the purpose to face the next test, fight the next battle, and strive for victory.

But, like their enemy, Union soldiers did not rush to the charge or huddle together on the defensive, as they were doing this day on the slopes of Little Round Top, thinking foremost of the noble virtues of the republic, the joys of liberty, or the moral superiority of their cause. By the summer of 1863, the Federals had seen so many pointless deaths, so many failed campaigns, so many useless assaults that they had begun to harden themselves to the deaths that came in such abundance with every battle and to abandon most of their lofty notions of war's romance and glory. After Fredericksburg, a Pennsylvania chaplain in the Fifth Corps wrote: "The phrensy of soldiers rushing during an engagement to glory or death has, as our boys amusingly affirm, *been played out*. Our battle-worn veterans go into danger, when ordered, remain as a stern duty so long as directed, and leave as soon as honor and duty allow."[15]

Civil War soldiers on both sides had to balance the demands of duty, the commitment to ideology, and the desire for self-preservation. Through-out the surviving passages of Ellis Spear's Civil War diaries (the diaries for 1861 and 1862 have been lost), he never once makes any mention of the Union cause, the ideas or values for which he as an individual was fighting, the controversy over emancipation, or even Abraham Lincoln, apart from recording the fact of the president's assassination. Instead, Spear's diaries, like so many other diaries written by enlisted men and of-ficers on both sides, resemble a farmer's journal, noting information of a practical nature, a record of when crops are planted and harvested; in Spear's case, he noted the army's movements, the weather, his maladies and those of his troops, and other quotidian details of soldier life. It is al-most impossible to know what Spear was thinking in combat, for he left no specifically introspective memoirs of his Civil War experiences; the memoirs he did write after the war never provide a picture of how he felt or what he thought during the height of battle.

Other soldiers writing after the war publicly suppressed—or tried to—whatever trauma they had experienced on the battlefield, and they managed, at the same time, to transform their memories of combat into recollections of honor and glory. Colonel Joshua Chamberlain was some-one who could always make war sound grand, bloodless, and incredibly romantic. Chamberlain claimed that he never felt fear in battle. Soldiers, and particularly officers, he said, have other things to think about during combat. "The instinct to seek safety," he wrote, "is overcome by the instinct of honor." War, in his estimation, was mostly chivalry and honor. As a result, he thought that the effects of war upon an individual were beneficial, not deleterious: "In the privations and sufferings endured as well as in the strenuous action of battle, some of the highest qualities of manhood are called forth,—courage, self-command, sacrifice of self for the sake of something held higher,—wherein we take it chivalry finds its value."[16]

Of course, a good number of Union soldiers did write more revealing and realistic accounts of the war and the parts they played in it, but the point is that for most soldiers, North and South, combat was such a great ordeal, an intensive physical and emotional experience that resembled nothing else in their lives, that every soldier had to develop for himself the personal and individual means by which he survived his encounters with unbridled violence, rivers of blood, and the countless deaths of comrades on the battlefield. All soldiers may have wanted to be heroes, but the reality of battle meant that fear would have to be confronted time after time (no matter what Colonel Chamberlain seemed to think), and no one—even the bravest of men—could necessarily predict how he might deal with an all-consuming timidity that could conceivably descend upon him without warning.

To fight battle after battle, a soldier's fear had to be conquered, or at least managed, to a degree that would enable these huge armies to assemble themselves and march headlong into the muzzles of cannon yet one more time. But, tellingly, some soldiers who stood as the epitome of courage in one battle—as Strong Vincent was doing atop his rock on the slopes of Little Round Top—might run in fear from the battlefield in the next, and the steadiness and endurance of each individual soldier seemed to depend on intangibles and unknowable forces that existed deep in his heart and mind. Ideology might have helped to motivate the Union soldiers on Little Round Top to fight this battle in the name of a good cause. But ideology did not necessarily keep them in their places, behind their shelters of rocks and trees, firing their muskets until the barrels became so fouled that they could no longer ram a cartridge down to the breach.

One Union soldier perceptively—and no doubt pretty accurately—estimated that the percentage of heroes and cowards in the army could be broken down to a mixture of soldiers who were brave, timid shirkers, and something in between. He believed that about 10 percent of the

Northern army were "arrant cowards" who had to be forced into combat, another 10 percent were notably courageous, and that about 80 percent could be counted somewhere in between the extremes of bravery and cowardice.[17] Most Civil War soldiers accepted the fact that someone could be brave one minute and a coward the next, for combat was an ever-changing set of circumstances that kept men constantly off balance and unable to know the outcome of the struggle at hand. The variables of combat meant that anyone could run in battle, even the most stalwart and dependable of soldiers.

More than anything, group cohesion helped soldiers to stay on the firing line, to remain firmly within that large percentile of soldiers who were neither overtly brave nor exceptionally pusillanimous. What helped to provide enormous cohesion in Civil War companies, the basic fighting unit of every regiment, was the fact that soldiers were usually recruited from the same community and knew one another as friends, neighbors, and fellow parishioners before the war began. Cohesion was further solidified by the social integration that occurred within companies; sometimes relatives belonged to the same company and regiment, and often men who had known one another before the war formed themselves into messes and other smaller groups, including prayer associations and social clubs, within a company. Homogeneity in companies and regiments in turn buttressed loyalty to the Union cause by reinforcing ideology as a group dynamic and by cementing bonds between soldiers that helped them stand the devastation and horror of combat; in the group, in the strength that came from everyone sharing in the same experience, individual soldiers often found the necessary courage to get them through the terrible ordeal of battle.

In some instances, the pressure brought by peers in one's company or regiment might provide the motivation for an individual soldier to march into the hell of combat, if only to avoid condemnation by his comrades after the battle or for fear that his cowardly acts might be reported to friends and loved ones back home. That same group dynamic, however, could occasionally prove the undoing of a unit as a whole, compelling entire companies and regiments to retreat or to crumble apart in the middle of a fight because if everyone withdrew at once, no single individual could be criticized for cowardice. Nevertheless, the cohesion of companies and regiments led most usually to a reinforcement of bravery on the battlefield and provided a primary motivation for soldiers risking their lives—beside their neighbors—in combat as they fought to uphold their ideological beliefs, to survive the terrors of battle, and to protect their friends and messmates from harm.

The will to fight, and the courage required to do so, came from a matrix of motivational factors—ideology, group cohesion, and survival instincts—that worked together to keep soldiers on the battlefield, even after combat had depleted their ranks and removed the messmates to whom they, as individual soldiers, wanted to prove themselves. All in all, however, it was the socioeconomic and demographic characteristics of the company, particularly in Union armies, rather than ideological commitment and morale, that help to explain why soldiers fought and why, if they were fortunate enough to survive, they were willing to fight again and again. Group cohesion, more than any other factor, allowed Civil War soldiers to face the malignant and distorted landscape of death that came with every battle.[18]

Another important factor also helped the Union soldiers along Vincent's brigade line to face the enemy with added resolve and fiery willpower. These men, especially the soldiers in the 83rd Pennsylvania, were fighting on their native soil, Northern territory. In every other battle fought by the Army of the Potomac, the fighting had taken place south of the Mason-Dixon line, in Virginia or Maryland, in places considered to be enemy soil or "Southern" lands. At Gettysburg, the entire army now had the opportunity to defend its homeland, to do battle in a Northern state, on fields and hills belonging to Union citizens, to protect Northern families and friends from the barbarian invaders. When the men of the 83rd Pennsylvania marched north in the days before the battle and approached the border of the Keystone State, they realized, as Captain Judson explained, "that they were about to enter the threshold of their native State and fight upon her soil" and "their enthusiasm knew no bounds." Private William Brown of the 44th New York declared that the Confederates "have made a mistake in invading old Pennsylvania."[19]

Along the irregular ledges of Little Round Top, the men of Vincent's brigade also enjoyed another advantage that allowed them to fight the enemy with a cohesion and unity that otherwise might not have been possible had the battle taken place in an open field or across a broad meadow. The terrain of the hill worked to keep the Union troops in position as they defended the slopes; not only did the scattered boulders and jumbled rocks provide cover for all of Vincent's regiments, the landscape made it possible for them to hold together, to maintain the semblance of battle-line formation, to effect a shoulder-to-shoulder defense in the face of the enemy's more diffused and fragmented assaults. Captain Judson pointed out that Little Round Top "was most admirably adapted for a defensive position." After the battle, another Union soldier admitted that the relatively small losses in his regiment were "owing to our being protected by high rocks."[20]

As the men along Vincent's line waited for the next Confederate assault, boulders and trees actually seemed of little comfort. Battle smoke weaved its way between the rocks and over the ledges, clutching the earth like a low fog on a summer's morning. If the enemy continued to drive as doggedly up the slopes as it had before, rocks and ideology and honor and group cohesion might make very little difference. If this hill were lost, no one could be quite certain what would happen next. But Vincent's men were determined, as was Vincent himself, to stop the enemy before it could reach the crest. This war had now come down to an enormous slugging match between two powerful armies about to become legends on the gloomy slopes of an insignificant hill in the farm country of central Pennsylvania.

EVEN THOUGH THE CONFEDERATES had withdrawn after their first assault to regroup in the woods below Little Round Top, small knots and clusters of the enemy remained behind some of the boulders on the hillside, enough of them, in fact, to create a steady musket fire and some serious cause for concern among Vincent's men. One soldier in the 83rd Pennsylvania pointed out that the lulls in the fighting weren't noticeable; the battle, he said, pretty much went on "without intermission." But the Confederates had been held back, and Private Brown of the 44th New York contentedly affirmed that "the men stood as firm as the granite boulders" that protected them.[21]

The situation was changing rapidly. While the Confederates gathered for a second attack, Lieutenant Charles Hazlett's battery arrived at the northern foot of Little Round Top, and men began straining their backs in the herculean task of getting the six ten-pound Parrotts up the slopes to the open face of the crest. Captain Augustus P. Martin, the Fifth Corps Artillery Brigade commander, was responsible for sending Hazlett's battery to the hill. Together the two officers had conducted a reconnaissance near the Wheatfield, looking for good ground on which to place their guns. While sizing up the field, Hazlett said to Martin: "I have just received bad news from home and I would rather someone else lead off today." What the bad news was, he didn't say. Then he made an even more startling statement. "I have a premonition," he said, "that this will be my last battle." Somewhat taken aback by Hazlett's remark, Martin tried to reassure him by explaining that he had great confidence in the young lieutenant and that he preferred "to have him go on the field with me." Later Martin remembered that Hazlett often said that "if he should fall in battle he hoped it would not be in a skirmish or small engagement, but in a big battle."[22]

Martin then noticed Little Round Top, and he suggested that Hazlett try to get his battery up to the summit, although he was unsure if guns could be moved up the "rough and rocky" slopes. The two men galloped to the northern side of the hill, rode with some difficulty up through the rocks and trees, and reached the crest. Once there, the two artillerists did not see General Warren, but they agreed that the hill was of extreme importance to the Union army. It was, wrote Martin long after the war, "one of the most formidable and important artillery positions on the entire field of battle."[23] Meanwhile, the battery followed the two men up the hill, although the crews and drivers experienced one difficulty after another in dragging the Parrotts up such steep slopes.

As the battery approached the foot of the hill, the caissons were halted and parked off to the left, where it was hoped they would be safe. The limbers pulling the guns went up the hill through the woods on the east side, wheels spinning, "at a trot, with spurs and whips vigorously ap-

Hazlett's battery on Little Round Top

plied," remembered Lieutenant Benjamin F. Rittenhouse, the battery's second in command. By this time, the Confederates' second assault had begun in earnest, so "everything was red hot," with "each man and horse trying to pull the whole battery by himself." As the hill became steeper, the horses gave out, and the guns had to be wheeled by hand up to the crest. One artillerist thought that the sappers had "cut a road . . . through the woods for us," but he must have assumed that an old logging road that ran up the hillside had been especially blazed for Hazlett's battery. In any event, the road proved to be inadequate, and the hill was "very steep and too dangerous for horses on top."[24] Some of the guns tipped over, but the men righted them again, grabbed hold of rim and spokes and trail, and pushed and pulled with all their might.

Near the top, Hazlett's men were joined by General Warren, who put his back into the work, and a dozen or so stragglers from Vincent's brigade were found, according to Captain Martin, "loitering behind the boulders," and were pressed into service. Together the artillerists and infantrymen lifted the Parrotts over the rocks and onto the ledges of the crest. Although Warren had learned of the battery's arrival and had helped to lift the guns over the large boulders that divided the open space on the crest from the wooded portion of the hill, he could not fathom how the artillery had so miraculously appeared on Little Round Top. "Martin," he asked, "how the h——l did you get those guns up here?"[25]

Hazlett, still on horseback, supervised the placement and sighting of the guns. Four of the Parrotts had reached the top of the hill; the two remaining guns in the battery would arrive in a short while, but the restrictions of space on the crest—limited to a narrow shelf of rock, where Hazlett's cannon were placed in two sections of two guns each—meant that the remaining section would never be deployed on the summit.[26] Three cannoneers were shot while getting the guns into position. There was not a great deal of room on the summit to place the guns without fear that on recoil, they might topple back down the hill. But Hazlett chose his placements carefully and with an eye toward shelling enemy targets across the Valley of Death in Devil's Den and on Houck's Ridge. Warren was impressed with Hazlett and his coolness under fire: "There he sat on his horse on the summit of the hill, with whole-souled animation encouraging our men, and point with his sword toward the enemy amidst a storm of bullets—a figure of intense admiration to me, even in that desperate scene . . . There stood the impersonation of valor and heroic bravery."[27] With haste, the crews began loading their weapons and readying them for action.

By now the second Confederate assault had reached once more to within fifty yards of Vincent's line, and bullets came flying over the hill like an endless swarm of bees. If Warren had not been aware of Vincent's brigade before, he certainly must have taken notice now. The enemy "poured in a deadly fire upon our troops," reported Captain Judson of the 83rd Pennsylvania. Vincent saw one of his men skulking behind some rocks and used his riding crop "freely over his shoulders as he drove him back into the ranks." One soldier in the 44th New York had a bullet pass through his haversack as he wondered what motivated the Confederates to come "rite up upon us." Later, from some Texan prisoners he learned that "they thought we was greene malittia and by rushing rite up we would run." But, he said gleefully, "they was sadly disappointed in this." Private Salter of the 16th Michigan thought it was "the most desperate fighting I ever saw."[28]

On the crest, Warren discussed with Hazlett about how the Parrotts could be used effectively on this high ground. "It was no place for efficient artillery fire," wrote Warren after the war, for the muzzles could not be sufficiently depressed to rake the Confederate infantry moving up the hillside, and he told Hazlett that as the battle raged below them. "Never mind that," replied Hazlett. "The sound of my guns will be encouraging to our troops and disheartening to the others, and my battery's no use if this hill is lost."[29] While the two officers talked, a musket ball struck Warren in the neck. Although the wound bled profusely, it was not serious, and Warren simply pressed his handkerchief to the gash to stop the bleeding.

With Hazlett's guns in place, Warren decided to get more infantry reinforcements for Little Round Top, so he left the crest and rode down the northeastern slope toward the road at the foot of the hill. Behind him, Hazlett's guns opened fire and the entire hill erupted into a blazing inferno. When Hazlett's first Parrott let loose its fire and smoke and screaming iron, the gunner had pulled the lanyard with the words, "Take that, damn you!"[30]

9

DOWN THIS WAY, BOYS

THE SUNLIGHT WAS WANING as the fight for Little Round Top heated up. The soldiers who fought to possess the hill found no respite from their work as the light dimmed and shadows disappeared. The Southerners—clambering uphill in their second assault—came on like a juggernaut. But Vincent's men held firm, letting the boulders and the slanting ledges give them shelter while they hammered down a concentrated fire that, as Oliver Norton reported, "laid the rebels in heaps" on the hillside. Norton had left Vincent's side, found a discarded musket, and joined in the fight on the right with the 44th New York. "The old Third Brigade," he wrote home with pride after the battle, "fought like demons."[1]

Hazlett's battery was in full swing now, pounding the Confederates across the valley with shot and shell without pause and making a terrible racket that shook Little Round Top with what seemed like the sounds of the earth's creation. As the guns went into action, infantrymen in Vincent's brigade took time to cheer Hazlett and his artillerists. "No military music," wrote Eugene Nash of the 44th New York, "ever sounded sweeter [than the roar of Hazlett's guns] and no aid was ever better appreciated." "There was one Continual roar of artillery and musquetry all along the whole lines," wrote an infantryman in the 83rd Pennsylvania, and the Confederates wavered under the weight of so much lead and iron.[2]

Among the men of the 44th New York, William Brown kept up his musket fire against the enemy, repeatedly loading and firing as if he were going through the manual of arms. When the men discovered that they were using up all the rounds in their cartridge pouches, they obtained more from their dead and wounded comrades around them. Sergeant

Sprague recalled with vividness how he felt as the Confederates advanced: "I don't think any one was afraid, now, or cared for anything but getting rid of his cartridges. We were not good marksmen; I suppose if we had been we should have been deliberate and made less smoke and done more execution. Target practice had been very little attended to."[3]

In the 16th Michigan, one soldier lamented that "in the short space of 5 minutes [we] lost a great number of men and officers." But it was not simply the casualty rate that made this combat distinctive from other struggles the men had made in earlier battles and on other battlefields. This fight seemed to be bringing out the worst in men on both sides. As the Union soldiers observed with admiration the determination of the Confederates as they worked their way once more up the steep slopes of Little Round Top, the bluecoats nevertheless displayed their own brand of fierce obstinacy. Out of the inner core of these soldiers came forth a destructiveness, a passion for virulence, that ended up surprising themselves. Charles Salter of the 16th Michigan could not fathom the outpouring of pure venom and brutality that he saw all around him—a bloodlust that made him wonder about his own humanity. "It seemed," he wrote in a letter after the battle, "as if every man, on both sides, was actuated by the intensest hate, and determined to kill as many of the enemy as possible, and exerted up to an enthusiasm for exceeding that on any field before that we have been engaged in."[4]

As hard as they tried, the Confederates could not break through the Union defenses and they retreated once more, carefully backstepping down the slope, receding purposefully like a broken wave of brown and gray to the protection of the thick woods along the shoulder of Big Round Top. Colonel Rice of the 44th New York remembered that the Confederates retreated "and stretched themselves behind the rocks, panting for breath."[5] But musket fire continued to be exchanged between the two sides, even as the Confederates rested and reformed. The Federals had a slight advantage in this sporadic exchange of musket fire, for in firing from above, they tended more times to hit their targets than their enemies who often aimed high and sent their bullets buzzing over the heads of Vincent's men.

The continuous fire from both sides meant that the wounded remained where they had fallen on the hillside and behind the ledges. Their cries and moans could be distinctly heard along Vincent's brigade front. But even among Vincent's regiments, the wounded could not be removed to the rear. "So fierce was our own fight," explained Ziba Graham of the 16th Michigan, "that we could spare no men to take off the field our own wounded."[6]

When the third Confederate assault smashed against the Union defenses, it did not seem as if this attack was any different from the enemy's two previous attempts to take the hill. The steady progress of the Confederates up the slopes was met, as it had been met so readily in the other two assaults, with crippling volleys of musket fire from the Federals behind the ledges. Enemy dead and wounded fell in tangled heaps that writhed and heaved in agony. But slowly it must have become apparent to the Federals in Vincent's brigade that this latest assault had shifted the enemy's emphasis from the center of the Union defense—the ledges defended by the 83rd Pennsylvania and the 44th New York—to Vincent's vulnerable right and left flanks.

Having gained added weight to their attacking force with the addition of the 48th Alabama, the 4th and 5th Texas swerved to the far right of the Federal line and, with their combined strength, scrambled over the rocks and through the low bushes and collided with the exposed flank of the 16th Michigan, where that regiment's commander, Colonel Norval Welch, had attempted to harden his defenses by refusing his right companies into a salient. At the same time, the 4th Alabama veered toward Vincent's left, through the low saddle that divided the two Round Tops, when it was joined fortuitously by the 47th Alabama, which had finally made its way over the lower slopes of Big Round Top while accompanying Oates's 15th Alabama in its fruitless pursuit of elusive Federal sharpshooters. Together the 4th Alabama and the 47th Alabama struck the unanchored left flank of the 83rd Pennsylvania and the hovering right wing of Vincent's rear guard, the 20th Maine.

The Confederates hit the 16th Michigan, Vincent's right flank, with about the same impact as a locomotive crashing full speed into a stone wall. How these nearly spent Texans and Alabamians could have mustered the energy necessary to deliver such a stunning blow is beyond comprehension. In the ranks of the 44th New York, the men perceived that the enemy had found a new route up the slopes, following a small ravine to the right of the New Yorkers, and the regiment, as Lieutenant Colonel Freeman Connor explained, "turned our fire upon those who had advanced in the hollow to our right." Another soldier in the 44th New York later glumly recorded in his diary that "the carnage was dreadfull." But it was not enough to halt the Confederates. Dumbfounded by such utter courage, the men of Vincent's brigade marveled at the enemy's direct attack upon the 16th Michigan's flank and the guns of Hazlett's battery. These Confederates, said William Brown, were coming on again "with more fury" than they had displayed before, if that were possible. Never before had he experienced such a "dreadful hail of Bullets all around me."[7]

But the 16th Michigan was getting the worst of it. While cheering on his men and waving a sword above him, Lieutenant Wallace Jewett of Company K went down from a ball that penetrated just over his right eye and traveled clean through his head. The Confederates swarmed through what one Michigan officer called "those wild looking rocks and trees," and the regiment's lines began to waver as the enemy, despite Welch's defensive salient, overlapped the Federal flank. Frantically Ziba Graham collected whatever ammunition he could find among the wounded; meanwhile, some of the wounded took up the task of loading rifles for the men who could still fire. Graham said he would never forget "the bravery, heroism and the fearful grandeur of it all." In the murderous storm of lead, the 16th Michigan's colors went down, "enveloping the fallen," as one soldier described the scene, "with their silken folds like a funeral pall." All of the regiment's color guard, save one member, fell dead. When a wounded brave sergeant lifted the colors, he cried out that he was content to die under the flag's "silvery stars."[8] And so he did.

Every man has his breaking point, and so does every regiment, no matter how brave, no matter how tested, no matter how proud. There was only so much these Michigan men could stand. As the Confederates crammed their way through the boulders and reached the 16th Michigan's battle line, it seems likely that a hand-to-hand struggle ensued, although only the Federal records mention such close combat; the Texans and Alabamians apparently did not recall getting into the Union lines and wrestling at close quarters with their foes. In any event, Charles Salter asserted that the encounter between the Michigan soldiers and their enemies at this crucial moment on Little Round Top involved a "close hand to hand fight" that left the regiment with numerous casualties and drained of its strength. Another Michigan veteran recalled that "the hand-to-hand struggle" became a desperate one using "the most modern weapons of destructive warfare"—that is, "sabres clashed, bayonets crossed, guns clubbed, stones hurled with barbaric strength, death welcomed in a teeth-a-set and hand-to-throat embrace."[9]

The Michigan boys tried to hold their position, steeling themselves against the strength of the Confederate attack, leaning into the fight as one might do in shouldering a door closed against a strong wind. But the enemy streamed through the short brush and around the smaller boulders on the 16th Michigan's flank, taking advantage of terrain that was less rough and a slope that was less steep where it met the shelf of ledge defended by the Federals. The Confederates pushed forward, wrote Oliver Norton years later, with "courage" and "overwhelming numbers." Among the Michigan ranks, one soldier watched in horror as his comrades "fell thick and fast" around him.[10]

Death was all around. For those soldiers who miraculously missed being hit by enemy bullets, they saw their comrades go down along the rocky ledges, entangled with dead and wounded Confederates. In Charles Salter's place in the line, men fell one after the other. Salter was hit in the cheek by a piece of rock that knocked him down and made him bleed profusely. His comrades assumed he was a dead man, and some of them even reported Salter among the regiment's fatalities, but Salter survived and later wrote gleefully that "they did not get rid of me quite so easily as that after all."[11] Of the 263 men of the 16th Michigan engaged in the fight that day, 23 died, 34 were wounded, and 3 went missing.

Some of the ferocity of Civil War combat came from the fear of dying; one fought harder, more brutally, and with more determination, hoping that the production of enough enemy dead would persuade his foes to retreat to safety. But, in the protocol of warfare, retreat was a sign of cowardice, so individual soldiers became killing machines to prove their courage and confront the reality of death with a savagery that, in the end, only escalated the violence rather than diminished it. As quickly as they could, men loaded their muskets, fired, and loaded once more. Death, or more precisely, the fear of death, led soldiers to embrace brutal responses on the battlefield and gave soldiers something to contemplate beyond their own private fear that this might be their last battle. In that sense, Civil War soldiers fought more vigorously against death, and the indiscriminate manner in which death would call its victims at random, than they did against their human enemies. Death was the real foe on Little Round Top, as it was on every other battlefield of this cruel war.

In this harvest of death along the hillside, something suddenly went terribly wrong in the Michigan line. Without warning, the regiment's colors, which had fallen to the ground several times with the near demise of the entire color guard, pulled back to the rear, perhaps because of the pressure being applied by the enemy or perhaps because of someone's foolish order. Colonel Welch, commanding the regiment, later implied that Major General Sykes or Brigadier General Weed called for the Michigan line to "fall back nearer the top" of the hill, which was unlikely. Welch later maintained that a lieutenant, upon an "entirely unwarrantable assumption of authority," gave the order for the colors to fall back, and when he did, the regiment was thrown into confusion and withdrew from its position along the ledge, giving ground to the steady hammering of the enemy.[12] The faltering of the 16th Michigan immediately created a crisis on Vincent's right, for it appeared that his entire flank was about to cave in.

Vincent saw the trouble, jumped from his high perch on a rock behind the 83rd Pennsylvania, and ran to do whatever he could to buttress his right. Using the riding crop his wife had given him as a whip, Vincent tried to drive the men from the 16th Michigan's right wing back into line, but as he did so he was struck by a minié ball, which had passed through his left groin and lodged in his left thigh. He fell to the ground, still conscious. "This is the fourth or fifth time they have shot at me," he said to the men who had gathered around him and were hustling to carry him toward the rear, "and they have hit me at last."[13]

Now the crisis on Little Round Top had become even more pronounced, even more desperate, for not only had the right flank of Vincent's line fallen apart, leaving a wide gap where the right wing of the 16th Michigan had once stood, but Vincent himself was down, badly wounded, perhaps mortally so. The Confederates, weary and growing weaker with every step, groped their way over the rocks. Apparently nothing could be done to plug their breakthrough or halt their relentless advance.

WITH LIEUTENANT ROEBLING at his side, General Warren, his neck stinging from the bullet wound he had received only moments before, rode his gray horse down the northeastern side of Little Round Top toward a dirt road that ran along the base of the hill. He was looking for reinforcements to send up to the hilltop, but he had no idea what he would find or which units might be available to provide assistance. Behind him the tumult of battle rose higher and higher over the crest of Little Round Top.

At the foot of the hill, Warren could see a column of soldiers marching along the rough road toward the Peach Orchard, and even from a distance he recognized that this was General Weed's brigade, the same brigade Warren had commanded before becoming chief engineer of the army. Almost immediately he saw Colonel O'Rorke riding at the head of the 140th New York, and while he was still some distance away, perhaps fifty yards, Warren called out that the Confederates were coming over the hill and he needed a regiment to meet them. O'Rorke explained that "General Weed is ahead and expects me to follow him." "Never mind that," said Warren impatiently, "bring your regiment up here and I will take the responsibility."[14] Satisfied that he had found the reinforcements necessary to blunt the Confederate attack, Warren rode off to locate more troops and direct them toward the hill.

At the base of Little Round Top, Colonel O'Rorke without hesitation turned his regiment up the hill and followed Lieutenant Roebling, whom Warren had instructed to guide the 140th New York up to the summit. The New Yorkers moved at the double-quick in column of fours. "We went flying up the hillside," remembered Sergeant Henry Cribben, "as fast as its rocky face would permit." As they drove up the slope, the column's formation was broken when two of Hazlett's Parrotts, the last section to be moved up the hill, rolled through O'Rorke's regiment, sending infantrymen bounding off to the left and right. One soldier remembered that "we . . . had to do some lively dodging to keep from being run over."[15] When the cannon had passed, the New Yorkers realigned themselves and continued their sprint up the hill. Farley rode beside O'Rorke, their horses struggling to negotiate the slope, and the young lieutenant suddenly realized that the regiment had not been ordered to load its muskets before racing up the hillside. The 140th New York, therefore, was going into battle with their rifles empty.

When the regiment reached the top, the men were out of breath and before them they could see, as Farley later described the scene, "war's wild panorama spread before us." The air, he said, "was saturated with the sulphurous fumes of battle and was ringing with the shouts and groans of the combatants." As soon as the lead companies of the 140th reached the crest, "bullets came flying in among us." The regiment was moving to the right in front, and Farley worried once more about those empty muskets. Directly ahead of them, the New Yorkers saw that the enemy was outflanking Vincent's line just to their left, and the Confederates were not stopping on the ledge below the summit, but were quickly coming up a ravine toward the crest and Hazlett's guns. "Bloody work was ready for us at our very feet," thought Farley.[16]

When O'Rorke and Farley arrived just above the struggling entanglement of Vincent's men and the advancing Confederates, the colonel saw that the ground was too rough for horses. "Dismount Farley," shouted O'Rorke and threw his reins to the regiment's sergeant major nearby. As soon as O'Rorke was off his horse, he drew his sword and yelled, "Down this way, boys."[17] Farley obeyed O'Rorke's order, but by the time he had dismounted the lead companies of the regiment were already running over the crest and down the slope toward the enemy, and Farley was quickly separated from O'Rorke by this mass of men. After Farley successfully handed his horse over to someone, he found himself surrounded by the second company in the regiment's column, so he took charge of directing the men to the fight below. He also became aware that the whole regiment could not possibly flow down the hillside in a charge without becoming a huge mob, and he began forming other companies into a defensive line along the shelf on the summit.

O'Rorke took a few minutes to get his regiment in shape before plunging it into battle, probably by having his men perform a tricky maneuver—made all the trickier if done on a battlefield rather than a parade ground—to "front" into battle line and then about-face in order to confront the enemy. Captain Joseph Leeper remembered O'Rorke shouting out: "Face to the rear; forward, follow me." Yet even with these hasty efforts and these fancy maneuvers, the regiment was not aligned perfectly or into as solid a battle line as was the norm in most Civil War units preparing to go into battle. "It was not known by the officers or men of the left wing that the right wing had been deployed, so thick were the rocks on the hill," remembered one soldier from Company K.[18]

Even if O'Rorke managed to get his regiment to "front" as he wanted it to, it is doubtful that all the companies executed the maneuver with equal skill or completeness. No matter how skillfully this may have been done, the terrain would soon throw the advance of the 140th New York—one of the largest regiments in the Army of the Potomac—into shambles. Some of the companies did, however, take advantage of this delay in their movement to load their weapons. But probably most of the soldiers in the lead companies, A and G, went into the fight with unloaded muskets.[19]

With practically no order at all in the line, and the advance looking more like a busy crowd forging ahead along a city sidewalk, the lead companies streamed blindly after O'Rorke, who led them down the western face of the hill toward the enemy. Like an avalanche, the New Yorkers hit the Confederates with a force that was totally unexpected and overwhelming. Just as the Texans and Alabamians thought victory was in their grasp, Paddy O'Rorke and the 140th New York slammed into them "with all the same moral effect upon the rebels," wrote Farley after the war, ". . . as if our bayonets had been fixed and we ready to charge upon them." Sergeant Cribben recalled that the Confederates, when they were struck without warning by the New Yorkers, had reached the upper ledges of the hillside to within thirty feet of the summit. "You had ought to have seen our boys fight after that," wrote one soldier to his father. "Nothing could exceed their bravery."[20]

Meanwhile, the rest of the regiment's companies, coming abreast of Vincent's line and finding their own place among the boulders, loaded their muskets and directed a murderous fire down into the splintering Confederate ranks. Even though the enemy had been stunned by the impact of the 140th New York's charge down the hillside, the Texans and Alabamians returned fire with a deadly effectiveness. Casualties among the New Yorkers were high—a consequence, Farley believed, of going into combat without loaded weapons and as a disorganized crowd of men rather than in fully and properly formed battle lines. Among the enlisted men, twenty-six were killed and eighty-nine were wounded. Numerous officers fell dead on the slope; several others were severely wounded. The greatest losses were in Company A, the lead company that followed O'Rorke directly into the maelstrom.

At once the Confederate assault began to dissolve. The left wing of the 140th New York pursued the retreating enemy down the hill. The regiment, according to one infantryman, "lost men very fast." Samuel Hazen was struck in the neck by a minié ball, which made a gash that bled and burned. "It was the closest shave I ever had," wrote Hazen several decades later, "and the man who fired it was not over 50 feet distant, although I expect he belonged in Alabama."[21] Within the space of only a minutes, the 140th New York took up an impressive defensive position along the upper ledges of the western face of Little Round Top, forming a V-shaped line that faced to the west and to the south.

Struck by the massive blow of the 140th's assault, some of the Texans and Alabamians quickly threw up their hands in surrender; others rushed into the Federal lines, almost as forcefully as if they were taking up the assault again, to offer themselves up as prisoners. Captain Joseph Leeper believed that about two hundred prisoners fell into the hands of the regiment. In the wild fighting, the men in butternut who did not give up scrambled down the hillside and retreated in disorder to the protection of the wooded shoulder between Big Round Top and Devil's Den. "The Rebs," wrote Captain Milo Starks of Company A with pride, "were never so neatly defeated before."[22]

As Paddy O'Rorke valiantly led his men into battle, surging down the hill toward the shelf of rock so recently vacated by the right wing of the 16th Michigan, he paused for a moment to cheer his men on and wave them forward. When he did, he was struck in the neck by an enemy bullet, which probably pierced the spine at the base of the brain. O'Rorke, killed instantly, slumped to the ground. Samuel Hazen of Company G claimed that the Confederate who had hit O'Rorke was immediately singled out and brought down in a rain of minié balls fired from companies A and G; the dead Confederate, said Hazen, was later found with seventeen bullet wounds. How this could have been known in the chaos that prevailed on the hillside is not made clear, but such stories must have given some comfort to the survivors of the 140th New York, who had lost their beloved and brave commander in the flash of a moment. When Lieutenant Farley learned of O'Rorke's death, he could hardly keep himself from falling apart. "Up to that time in my life," he recalled, "I had never felt a grief so sharply, nor realized the significance of death so well."[23]

Passing its fallen colonel, who lay sprawled across the rocks, Company A ran down into the thick of the fight, and Captain Starks, who would receive four wounds that day, placed his men into line by company to fill the gap left by the Michigan boys. Company G filed to the left of Company A and closed on the right flank of the 16th Michigan. Then the remaining companies descended the slope and extended the 140th New York's defensive line to the right and back up the slope toward Hazlett's guns. The threat on Vincent's right was now over. But to the left of the Third Brigade, up along the wooded slopes where the 20th Maine was already engaging a determined enemy, another crisis was reaching a blazing crescendo, for the ultimate fate of Little Round Top, as yet, had not been decided.

A FEW HOURS EARLIER that afternoon, Ewell's bombardment of the Union right began precisely on schedule, at about four o'clock, when the sound of Alexander's guns near the Peach Orchard reverberated northward and informed the commander of the Second Corps that Longstreet's assault against the Federal left was about to step off. If Ewell had unwisely exercised his discretion the evening before by failing to attack Cemetery Hill and Culp's Hill, he responded to Lee's orders on the afternoon of July 2 with no lapse in timing or judgment. According to Lee's orders, Ewell was to "make a diversion" in favor of Longstreet's First Corps as soon as he heard those guns open; he was also to convert the diversion "into a real attack if an opportunity offered."[24] On Benner's Hill, located east of Cemetery Hill and northeast of Culp's Hill, Major Joseph W. Latimer's artillery battalion, which he commanded because of the absence of the wounded Lieutenant Colonel R. Snowden Andrews, let loose and opened the barrage on the Union defenses. The Federal batteries answered almost immediately, and Benner's Hill became what one Confederate artillerist called "a hell infernal."[25]

A newspaper reporter described the scene in the Evergreen Cemetery: "There came a storm of shot and shell; marble slabs were broken, iron fences shattered, horses disemboweled. The air was filled with wild, hideous noises, the low buzz of round shot, the whizzing of elongated balls and the stunning explosion of shells overhead and all around. In three minutes the earth shook with the tremendous concussion of two hundred pieces of artillery." Colonel Charles S. Wainwright, artillery chief of the First Corps, watched as enemy artillery shells "ploughed up two or three yards of men, killing and wounding a dozen or more." Yet he also admitted, while narrowly escaping harm himself, that he seemed to feel indifferent to the danger around him during the barrage, but afterward he realized that it was neither bravery on his part nor true indifference that led to his response; rather, he said, his lack of concern about his own safety stemmed from "an unconsciousness" of the real danger that existed all around him.[26]

For all the noise and smoke, and for all the serious damage and casualties inflicted by the Southern shells that rained down in the vicinity of the cemetery, the Confederate bombardment never severely threatened the Union position on Cemetery Hill and Culp's Hill (only thirty-eight of Ewell's eighty guns went into action), and at no time did Meade feel anxious enough to draw troops away from his imperiled left in order to defend his right. The artillery duel lasted some ninety minutes before Latimer was forced to abandon his exposed position on Benner's Hill. All that it seemed to accomplish was to strike down young Latimer, "the boy Major," with a mortal wound after most of his battalion had pulled out. As a diversion, Ewell's cannonade failed; what's more, Ewell delayed sending in his infantry until well after Longstreet's assault had reached its zenith to the south. So, no matter how well timed Ewell's guns had been in opening the demonstration on the Union right, his later actions meant that Lee's hope for coordinated infantry attacks against the Army of the Potomac would be dashed.

Yet, at the same time that the bombardment of the Union right made the ground tremble on Cemetery Hill, and the fight along the Union left for Little Round Top filled the air with flame and smoke, Longstreet's forces were also making progress along the Emmitsburg Road, where McLaws's division attempted with considerable success to shatter Sickles's salient at the Peach Orchard. But the Confederate initiative along the Emmitsburg Road, like so many of the Southern efforts that day, was hampered by confusion and misunderstandings. McLaws believed that Longstreet wanted him to delay his advance until Hood's division had captured Devil's Den. Before going down with a serious wound, Hood sent McLaws an appeal for assistance, and the dogged resistance of the Federals changed circumstances to such a degree that the original battle plan no longer could be put into effect.

General Longstreet, impatient with the slow unfolding of events, took matters in his own hands, improvising the battle plan on the spot, and personally ordered Brigadier General Joseph B. Kershaw's South Carolina brigade of McLaws's division to advance. Yet much of the delay in sending McLaws's division forward rested on Longstreet's own shoulders. Longstreet's intention was for Kershaw's right wing to go to the aid of Hood's troops who were trying to drive the Union defenders from the Wheatfield, and for his left wing to advance, as planned, toward the Peach Orchard in an effort to roll up the defensive line of Sickles's Third Corps. McLaws, however, believed that Longstreet had ordered his brigades to "incline to the left" before the division reached the battlefield and without informing him that such an order had been given.[27]

At about five o'clock, when a prearranged artillery signal was sounded, Kershaw's men jumped a stone wall in their front and moved forward "with great steadiness and precision," followed in good order by Brigadier General Paul J. Semmes's brigade.[28] On foot, Longstreet accompanied Kershaw's brigade to the Emmitsburg Road and watched the charge begin; he then returned to his horse, mounted, and rode farther to the left, where Brigadier General William Barksdale's Mississippians were waiting to go in. Frustrated by Lee's insistence on this flank attack, and annoyed by the fact that the Federals were not where they were supposed to have been, Longstreet seems to have translated his feelings into action, first by becoming sullen and testy, next by stepping on McLaws's toes, and then by allowing himself to get closer and closer to the actual fighting. In all, he had the energy of a caged tiger wanting to escape the confines of its cell.

Meanwhile, Barksdale had been pleading with McLaws to let him charge. Now, to Longstreet, the Mississippian continued his entreaties, fairly "chafing" to get his men into action. "I wish you would let me go in, General," said Barksdale. "I would take that battery in five minutes." Longstreet, now with less impatience than he had demonstrated earlier to both Hood and McLaws, replied: "Wait a little, we are all going in presently."[29] But the delay in sending in Barksdale's brigade proved deadly, for the South Carolinians had by now advanced far enough to have their left flank unprotected, enabling the Federal artillery in the Peach Orchard to pour a devastating enfilade fire into Kershaw's lines. Finally McLaws sent orders for Barksdale's Mississippians to advance, and Longstreet released the brigade—although the sequence of these orders could very well have been reversed, for no precise or reliable account exists of how McLaws and Longstreet were handling the command of McLaws's brigades after Kershaw went in. Taking up a position in front of his brigade, Barksdale led his men forward toward the Peach Orchard.

While Kershaw's right wing—assisted by Anderson's Georgians and reinforced by Semmes's Georgia brigade—slugged it out with Federal forces at a small stony hill on the west side of the Wheatfield, a struggle that lasted for an hour and that swayed back and forth across the Wheatfield as the two sides alternately gained the upper hand on this small patch of ground, Barksdale's Mississippians crashed through the Union infantry lines west of the Emmitsburg Road and streamed relentlessly across the road to the north of the Peach Orchard. Sickles's salient at the orchard had been shattered, and the Mississippians, urged on by the pugnacious Barksdale (who would later fall mortally wounded in the charge), rushed toward a gap in the Union line on Cemetery Ridge.

Longstreet sent the brigade of Brigadier General William T. Wofford in next. These Georgians passed through a Confederate battery to begin their advance and received hearty cheers from the cannoneers as they marched forward. Having held himself in check for most of the afternoon, Longstreet now rode to the front of Wofford's brigade to lead it personally into battle. The Georgians shouted out a cheer for Longstreet. Somewhat discourteously he replied, "Cheer less, men, and fight more." Wofford's brigade veered slightly to the right and followed Semmes's men toward the hotly contested Wheatfield.[30]

From his vantage point near the Trostle Farm, Union General Sickles could see with dismay that Longstreet's divisions were breaking through the fragile Union defenses from the Emmitsburg Road to the Wheatfield. Confederate batteries concentrated their fire around the Trostle house, where Sickles and his staff tried to avoid the heavy downpour of shells. While he worked feverishly to patch up his disintegrating lines, he was sitting his horse near the Trostle barn when a round ball struck him in the right knee with such apparent gentleness that the impact did not frighten his mount. But Sickles's leg had been badly mangled by the ball. Either he fell off his horse or his men helped him to the ground, where a tourniquet was quickly applied to stop the bleeding. Pale and in shock, Sickles was placed on a stretcher, and he worried that he might be hit again by enemy shells or even captured. When Major General David Birney rode up, Sickles called out to him: "General Birney, you will take command, sir."[31]

A sip of brandy from a flask he took from his pocket and some drags on a cigar seem to have strengthened him somewhat and eased the shock he was suffering. While he waited for an ambulance to arrive, he propped

Brigadier General Stephen H. Weed, Army of the Potomac

himself up on the stretcher to show everyone that he was still alive. After the ambulance pulled up, he was carried to it while puffing away on his cigar. Finally he was taken to the rear, where the leg was amputated above the knee in a Union field hospital later that day.[32] Sickles was out of the battle, and, for that matter, out of the war.

Along the length of the Union line, from the Trostle farm to the Wheatfield, from the Peach Orchard to Devil's Den, the Confederate assault gained ground, not exactly as Lee had planned it or even as Longstreet had revised or improvised it, but the results seemed in the end to be the same: a successful rolling up of the Federal left that would, with just a bit more effort, eventually lead to a destruction of the Army of the Potomac in detail. But even as the Confederates swept inexorably toward triumph, Longstreet's attack began to lose momentum and became unglued. At the very moment Longstreet's men imagined winning the laurels of victory, General Meade was calling up troops from Hancock's Second Corps to reconstitute the Union left and replace the shattered Third Corps—reinforcements that ultimately would break the Confederate advance, throw it back on its heels, and deprive the enemy of any decisive outcome that day.

While the daylight slowly melted into twilight, the fight for Little Round Top had not as yet been finally settled. Reinforced by the 140th New York and the rest of Weed's brigade, Vincent's men—minus Vincent himself—continued to spar with the persistent Texans and Alabamians who had been repelled from the hill three times that afternoon. Hazlett's guns kept up their steady booming, Union soldiers held their ground behind formidable boulders directly beneath the crest of the hill, and the struggle for Little Round Top began to shift from the open western face to the wooded, but steep, slopes toward the southeast, where a wooded saddle lay between the two Round Tops. Although the Confederates assumed that victory would soon be theirs, the day—and the fight for Little Round Top—was not yet over.

10

A Sorry Place

ON THE REVERSE SLOPE OF Little Round Top, acting Major Ellis Spear and his comrades in the 20th Maine waited expectantly for their turn to go into action. To their right, beyond what they could see of the 83rd Pennsylvania, with its lines drooping down into the shallow dark valley that divided Big Round Top from Little Round Top, the staccato sounds of musket fire could be heard along with the human screams and metallic clangs of battle. The regiment had gotten into battle line only a short time before Spear began to hear Hazlett's battery pounding on the other side of the hill. "We had then," he wrote long after the battle, "no knowledge of how the battle was going, except that we seemed to be holding up our own."[1]

Unlike the other regiments in Vincent's brigade, the 20th Maine had no vantage point from which to watch the unfolding struggles for Devil's Den, the Wheatfield, and the Peach Orchard. From where he stood, Spear could see through the trees to the "steep and thickly wooded side of Big Round Top, two or three hundred yards distant." The 20th's line, he said, was formed on the higher part of the southern slope of Little Round Top, "partly amongst the boulders, and with boulders and trees on the sloping front, faced squarely to the left." A regimental historian later wrote with approval that "our men appeared to be as cool and deliberate in their movements as if they had been forming a line upon the parade ground in camp."[2]

Company B of the regiment (consisting of sixty-five men from Piscataquis County in Maine), which Colonel Chamberlain had sent out beyond his lines to protect the 20th Maine from flank attack, went through the woods toward the left. They were looking to connect with

160

the skirmishers of the 16th Michigan, whom they could not find, and did not have a chance to deploy before, according to one Maine veteran, "a large force of the enemy was soon seen marching rapidly to the left through the ravine in our front." The approach of the Confederates happened so quickly and took Company B so completely by surprise that the skirmishers were forced to find cover and "secrete themselves behind a stone wall." Captain Walter Morrill ordered his men, who had started up the rear slopes of Big Round Top, "to march by the left flank so as to uncover the enemy, and at the same time to guard against flank movements on the left."[3]

As Company B worked its way in short order through the thin woods, it came upon a dozen or more men from the 2nd U.S. Sharpshooters, dressed in their green uniforms, part of the contingent that had confronted Oates's 15th Alabama down near the base of Big Round Top and had skirted around the big hill to escape the clutches of the hill-climbing Alabamians. The sharpshooters asked permission to stay with Morrill, and he readily granted it. Together Morrill's Company B and the sharpshooters settled down behind the stone wall and waited for the enemy to make its appearance.

From Spear's position on the left of the regiment, he listened as musket fire off to the right rippled down the line of the 83rd Pennsylvania. Corporal William T. Livermore "heard terrible musketry on our right which rolled along, coming nearer and nearer." Even from where Spear stood, he could see the legs of enemy soldiers moving through the bushes down the steep slope of Big Round Top. Spear wondered what might have happened to the regiment's skirmishers, because they had not fallen back with the onslaught of the enemy. The Confederates—who had thrown out no skirmishers of their own—approached with no awareness that the Federal defensive line extended above them beyond the left of the 83rd Pennsylvania, and the 20th Maine completely surprised them, opening on them with a devastating volley. "Hesitatingly," one veteran later wrote, "they replied, and finally came to within twelve yards of us, and then the bloody struggle ensued." At first only the right companies of the 20th Maine were engaged, but as more of the enemy force emerged from the woods, the firing along the Federal line drifted toward the left. "The action," wrote Colonel Chamberlain more than twenty years after the battle, "was quite sharp and at close quarters."[4]

Emerging out of the woods and striking the 20th Maine's right wing was the 47th Alabama, under the direct command of Lieutenant Colonel

Michael Bulger but under the overall command of Colonel William Oates of the 15th Alabama. The 47th had not scaled the high summit of Big Round Top, as Oates's 15th had done. Instead, they had skirted across the western slopes of the big hill and had come over a ridge that compelled the regiment to approach Little Round Top through the wooded saddle almost precisely from the south and at the point where the 83rd Pennsylvania's left flank failed to link up with the 20th Maine's right. Bulger's Alabamians, like most of Law's Confederates that day, found the terrain broken and rough, so that they could not maintain formation as they drove toward the Federal defenses on the ledges above them. One veteran of the 20th Maine described the attack of the 47th Alabama as striking Chamberlain's line "squarely in front" while opening "a murdering fire on our unprotected line."[5]

From the start of its engagement with the bluecoats on Little Round Top, the 47th Alabama found itself caught between an effective enfilade fire from the Pennsylvanians on their left and the Mainers on their right. With only seven companies involved in the advance (three companies had been sent forward as skirmishers, before the advance of Law's brigade began on Warfield Ridge, only to be captured by the enemy), the 47th lacked the necessary manpower to plunge out of the woods and drive a wedge between the two Union regiments that sent fire and lead down on their heads. As it laid down its heavy fire, the left wing of the 83rd Pennsylvania pulled back some distance up the hill—a maneuver made possible by Chamberlain's having already refused his line. "We retreated with a backward step obliquely to the left so as to close up the gap left in the right of the 20th Me.," remembered one veteran of the 83rd Pennsylvania.[6] With the gap closed, the Confederates approached to within twenty feet of the 83rd Pennsylvania's left wing, but their charge crested when the Pennsylvanians opened with a devastating enfilade fire.

For Chamberlain and his men of the 20th Maine, the first exchange of shots with the enemy "did not seem . . . *very* severe." The fire was certainly "hot," but Chamberlain said that they "gave them as good as they sent, and the Rebels did not so much attempt at that period of the fight to force our line."[7] In fact, the Maine boys successfully kept the Alabamians at a distance, forcing Bulger's men to take cover behind the ubiquitous boulders and trees near the base of the hill and along the edges of the saddle. Chamberlain later thought that he had been hit by two full brigades of Hood's division. But, at the most, the seven companies of the 47th Alabama may have been assisted by the right companies of the 4th Alabama, which meant that the force of the Alabamians' assault equaled the strength of a typical Confederate regiment, not a brigade.

While the musket fire raged along the front of the 20th Maine, Chamberlain's attention was diverted, first in one direction, then in another. Nervous officers came running up with reports of happenings both real and imagined. But the men stood firm, displaying good discipline and solid courage under fire. "Scattering bullets came singing through the trees," wrote Livermore in his diary. Then he caught sight of a Confederate and fired at him. At the same instant, "a sheet of fire and smoke belched forth from our line." Livermore heard Chamberlain yell out from behind him, "Boys, hold this hill!" The enemy came up to within twenty-five yards of the 20th Maine's line, some of the Alabamians taking cover behind boulders and trees, just as their butternut comrades had done in the fight along Vincent's right. As the engagement spread, said Livermore, the Rebels "kept up a murderous fire, which was returned by us." When the Alabamians realized they had collided with a Federal regiment, they let rip with the Rebel Yell all along their front. "We braced for the shock," remembered Elisha Coan of the regiment's color guard. Bullets clipped the twigs and leaves in the trees above the 20th Maine, and as the enemy got closer, the bullets flew lower and lower. The first casualties among the Maine men began to fall. Then "our line burst into flames," said Coan, "and the crash of musketry became constant."[8]

Colonel Oates's attention was also diverted as he and his men of the 15th Alabama descended the precipitous northern face of Big Round Top and heard the noise of battle growing louder below them. In plain view through the trees, Oates could see, some two hundred yards away, a Federal wagon train parked behind the Round Tops and close to the Taneytown Road. Tempted by what he thought would be an easy prize, Oates foolishly reduced the size of his force again (having lost his canteen detail earlier that afternoon) and ordered Captain Francis K. Shaaff to take Company A and "surround and capture the ordnance wagons"; then Shaaff and his men were to drive the wagons into the Confederate lines.[9] It was a risky plan. More to the point, Oates's lust for the Federal wagons made little sense under the circumstances. He and his regiment were about to engage with the enemy. And he would need every man jack of them.

Chamberlain and Oates both shared an additional distraction as their respective regiments began to confront one another. Each had to worry about the welfare of his younger brother in the battle line. Chamberlain had sent his brother John, a noncombatant visiting the regiment, to help set up an aid station in the rear, but Thomas, his brother who served as a lieutenant and the acting adjutant of the 20th Maine, remained at the front. Oates somehow had managed to get his brother, also named John, up and over Big Round Top—no mean feat given John's debilitating rheumatism. While he worried about John's welfare, Colonel Oates had larger concerns—the advance of his own regiment and the seven companies of the 47th Alabama that Law had placed under his overall command.

Coming through the saddle and out of the dense woods that covered the verdant slopes of Big Round Top, Oates and the 15th Alabama suddenly found themselves the unexpected targets of a scorching ripple of musket fire coming from the right wing of the 20th Maine along a rocky ledge above them, only some sixty paces away. "I did not see a single man of the Maine regiment," wrote Oates long after the battle, "until we received their fire." He reported that his line halted, but did not break. But, Oates said, the Federals laid down "the most destructive fire I ever saw."[10] Among the 15th Alabama's left companies, Billy Jordan and his comrades in Company B took some of the heaviest fire from both the 20th Maine's right wing and enfilade fire from the 83rd Pennsylvania's left wing. As the Alabamians were cut down, men clumped together to fill the place of the fallen.

Jordan expected to be shot at any moment. So far, he had not fired his musket once in the Confederate advance. On the hillside above him, he "saw the enemy plainly" and very deliberately stepped behind a small tree for cover. Jordan fired his musket, taking careful aim toward the enemy lines, but he never revealed if he thought his shot had hit anything or anyone. That was the only time during the afternoon that Jordan pulled the trigger; for the rest of the battle, he devoted himself to staying alive. Across the narrow saddle between the two Round Tops, he could see that some of his friends had take refuge behind some large boulders, just beneath the flaming rifles of the 20th Maine. The saddle, he said, "had no undergrowth, had a few trees dotted about, [and] no rocks for protection." Jordan decided to join his comrades behind their formidable shelter. "I was in a very exposed position at that time," he wrote; he did not hesitate, however, and he ran across the little valley "as speedily as possible."[11] He got across to the boulder without being wounded and took his place next to seven fellow Alabamians.

From above, the Federal fire rose to a fearful intensity. Jordan and his friends could do nothing but remain huddled behind their rock. No opportunity presented itself for returning the enemy's fire. It took all their

The attack of the 15th Alabama on the 20th Maine, Little Round Top

endurance, all their courage, to keep their heads down, hear the startling volleys as they erupted overhead, and listen to the bullets as they went singing through the air over their heads or struck the boulder with loud smacks and pings. With Company B, Oates's other left companies became pinned down after emerging through the thick woods, and the musket fire from the right wing of the 20th Maine was so sweeping, so potentially murderous in its relentless hammering, that the battle line of the 15th Alabama quickly dissolved and devolved into small clusters of men who, almost instinctively, crammed themselves together to gain the feeling of protection that comes from being in a group. Behind his boulder, Jordan still felt uneasy and unsafe. The enemy, he wrote, "could see every movement we made, [and] they would shoot down" every time Jordan or one of his friends made any move in an attempt to gain more protection from the rock.[12]

Yet the assault of the 15th Alabama hit Chamberlain and his men hard, perhaps even harder than Oates realized. Chamberlain thought he had his hands full just dealing with the 47th Alabama and its unwitting advance into the gap between the 20th Maine and the 83rd Pennsylvania.

He also believed that some portion of the Texas regiments had swung around to the south of Little Round Top and joined the assault against the 20th Maine. When Oates and his regiment flowed out of the woods and across the saddle, Chamberlain decided that yet another "new line" of enemy soldiers, as he later referred to Oates's force, were reinforcing the other Confederates in the assault upon his solitary regiment. The advance of the 15th Alabama, Chamberlain told Oates years later, struck the 20th Maine as a "really heavy blow" that made his regiment "reel" from the shock.[13] To get a better look, Chamberlain mounted a large boulder near the colors, which gave him "a full view of the enemy," and from this vantage point he "perceived a heavy force in rear of their principal line, moving rapidly but stealthily toward our left." He realized he had only a moment to act. "If a strong force should gain our rear," he mused in a magazine article published in 1913, "our brigade would be caught as by a mighty shears-blade, and be cut and crushed."[14]

Major Ellis Spear saw this danger, too, and he rushed to inform Chamberlain of the Confederates' apparent swing beyond the 20th Maine's left and toward its rear. He suggested to the colonel that "it seemed best to bend back two [left] companies to meet the threat upon that flank."[15] Chamberlain agreed and decided to "refuse" his line, that is, to extend his battle line to the left and swing it back to form a salient on the hillside.

To do so, he called his company commanders together and told them the plan: "to keep the front fire [on the right wing] at the hottest, without special regard to its need or immediate effect, and at the same time, as they found opportunity, to take side steps to the left, coming gradually into one rank, file-closers and all." He ordered "the right wing to move by the left flank, taking intervals of a pace or two, according to the shelter afforded by rocks and trees, extending so as to cover the whole front then engaged." At the same time, he and Spear "moved the left wing to the left and rear, making a large angle at the color[s]," which were placed at the point "where our left had first rested."[16] Some of his companies, especially on the right wing, "were brought into [a] single rank when the nature of the ground gave sufficient strength or shelter." As a result, his defensive line resembled more "a horse shoe" than a right angle, given the uneven terrain.[17] It was Chamberlain's intention to have his right wing hold off the 47th Alabama and the left companies of Oates's 15th Alabama, while his left wing blocked any attempt by Oates to outflank the 20th Maine.

Although the maneuver was risky, especially in the face of an assaulting enemy, the men of the 20th Maine—well drilled and diligently trained—"admirably executed" the movement, so effectively, said Chamberlain, "that our fire was not materially slackened in front, and the enemy gained no advantage there, while the left wing in the mean time had formed a solid and steady line in a direction to meet the expected assault."[18] With sincere admiration, he wrote in 1913: "Of rare quality were my officers and men." Taking the colors in hand, he moved them to mark the new center of the regiment. He was sorry, however, to place the color guard out of necessity in an exposed position "on the smooth and open slope." It was upon this salient that "a most deadly fire" fell during the fighting that ensued. Wrote Elisha Coan of the regiment's color guard with intended irony: "The calm of the early afternoon had been succeeded by a cyclone."[19]

The line of the 20th Maine was refused just in time. Almost at the very instant that the Maine soldiers assumed their new positions, Oates's Alabamians appeared before them and opened fire with a thunderous musket volley. Spear recalled the "uproar of musketry, the cloud and smell of battle smoke" as a "tense excitement" ran through the ranks. But the men, he said, were extremely well poised despite the mayhem that surrounded them. There was no shouting; instead, the men of the 20th Maine were quietly "loading and firing as fast as possible." Chamberlain watched from his rock as the Confederates, "having gained their desired point of attack[,] came to a front, and rushed forward with an impetuosity which showed their sanguine expectations." When the Alabamians encountered the 20th Maine's new defensive line, Chamberlain said, their astonishment was evident. Instead of meeting "an unsuspecting flank," they came upon "a firm and steady front."[20]

Captain Samuel Keene, commanding Company F, was worried that the Confederates were getting "pretty near," and he thought "we were getting into a sorry place." But he proudly described how "our boys stood their ground, however exposed to [the] terrible fire of musketry."[21] In Company H, Corporal Nathan S. Clark recalled how "a dreadfull roar" swept over the hillside as the Confederates "came round on our left." But the 20th Maine was not the only Federal regiment in trouble. One Maine soldier remembered how his Company C, on the left wing, "was swung back so we could see down the line for some distance in rear of [the] Brigade[,] by which I could [also] see several [men] falling." Obviously, wrote this private, the regiments of the Vincent Brigade "were getting Roughly handled."[22]

After receiving the Federals' smashing volley, Oates saw that his best opportunity was to move as much of his regiment as he could to the right and try to overlap and outflank the 20th Maine's left. He directed his men in column through the lower wooded slope of the hill, but he could not maneuver his men fast enough. Along the ledge above him, Oates could see the bluecoats shifting their position in response to his flanking movement. So when the 15th Alabama broke out of column and formed into battle lines, Oates quickly ordered it to assault the Federal line and drive it from the ledge, hoping at the same time to pour an enfilade fire down the enemy line that would help to relieve his own three companies pinned down among the boulders to his left and the seven companies of the 47th Alabama that were caught in a crossfire. The 15th Alabama, said Oates, "executed a full half wheel & gained the rockey higher ground first occupied by the Maine men." But his men could not hold the position, for the enemy fire "was so destructive that my line wavered like a man trying to walk against a strong wind," and, as a result, his troops slowly retired from this advanced position.[23]

Just at the time that Oates led his seven companies at the center and on the right of his line into this first attack on the 20th Maine, the 47th Alabama began to fall apart, riddled by the overwhelming Federal firepower from behind the rocks above. While the smoke prevented him from seeing off to his far left, Oates nevertheless realized with dismay that "the left of the Forty-seventh Alabama was disconnected—I know not how far—from the right of the Fourth Alabama, and consequently the Forty-seventh was outflanked on its left, and its men were being mowed down like grain before the scythe."[24]

Oates was under the impression that the 47th Alabama had been placed under his command, but Lieutenant Colonel Michael Bulger of the 47th assumed full responsibility for leading his own regiment into battle (and did not bother to coordinate his efforts with Oates). As he urged his men forward, Bulger was amazed to see a staff officer ride through the churning storm of battle and inform him that General Law wanted Bulger to "charge the enemy." Bulger, somewhat nonplussed by the aide's timing, answered: "Tell General Law that I am charging to the best of my ability."[25]

With this, Bulger and his men resumed their advance. The regiment successfully broke through the rocks at the base of Little Round Top, and Bulger ordered his troops to charge the enemy "with a yell, which was obeyed with a will." According to Bulger, his men almost reached the top of the hill and engaged in hand-to-hand fighting with the Federals. It is unlikely that either of these things actually took place, for the 47th Alabama was halted in its charge by a wall of musket fire that could not be penetrated. At the height of the attack, while waving his sword and cheering his boys onward, Bulger was hit by a bullet to the chest. To keep from falling, he backed into a tree and lowered himself to a sitting position on the ground. For a few minutes, there was a lull in the shooting and, Bulger remembered, "silence prevailed for a while."[26] Then his regiment surged forward again, a desperate fight erupted across the hillside, and the Federals once more succeeded in driving the Alabamians back. In fact, the 47th retreated in haste, routed by the enemy, and abandoned the wounded Bulger on the battlefield. Major James Campbell, who assumed command of the regiment, attempted to rally the men and prevent the rout, but the steady stream of men toward the rear proved to be unstoppable.

Rushing to his left, fully aware that a crisis had developed there, Oates also tried to hold the 47th Alabama in its place. He wanted to reform the regiment and send it forward to strike the Federal line again, but nothing could block the retreating men who headed with speedy determination up the slopes of Big Round Top and toward the safety of the Confederate rear. Seeing that there was nothing more he could do, but fretful that his own left flank was now entirely exposed, Oates returned to the center of his line, where his brother John stood shoulder-to-shoulder with the men of Company G, the old "Henry Pioneers," the same company Oates had raised in Abbeville, Alabama, and had mustered into service during the summer of 1861. With his three left companies—including Billy Jordan's Company B—held in check by "a most galling fire" from the enemy, Oates decided to order another charge by his center and right companies against the 20th Maine's left wing. Said Oates many years after the battle: "With no one upon the left or right of me, my regiment exposed, while the enemy was still under cover, to stand there and die was sheer folly; either to retreat or advance became a necessity."[27]

Over on the Federal left, where the men formed a defensive line along a high ledge behind sparse second-growth trees and fewer boulders than could be found along the regiment's right, Spear tried to hold his men together, although many of them had gravitated into small clusters behind whatever trees and rocks afforded them shelter. His line was not so much a continuous string of men, standing side by side, as it was a series of clumps of men, huddled here and there, along a fairly long front that was barely straight. Worse, when the enemy had pushed the 20th Maine back from its original position, it forced the Federals to leave many of their fallen dead and wounded in a no-man's land between the contending lines. Private Coan, standing with the colors at the center of the regiment, lamented over the fact that the maimed "were before our eyes[,] writhing in the agonies of their terrible wounds." During the very brief lull between enemy attacks, the soldiers of the 20th gathered loose rocks and tree branches and constructed a low breastwork for shelter. "This helped us but little," remembered Chamberlain, "[for] it served chiefly to mark the line we were bound to maintain."[28]

When the next Confederate attack came, Spear and his men were ready. "The grey line surged up the hill enveloped with battle smoke," Spear wrote afterward. The roar of the muskets "drowned out all words of command, and you could only see the line thinning as men fell." Spear

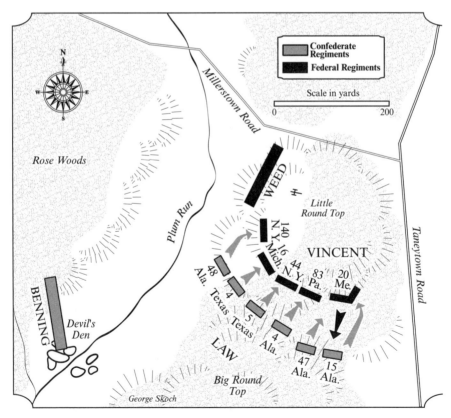

Law's attack against the Union left, late afternoon, July 2, 1863

watched as men tossed their cartridges on the ground "that they might be more readily snatched, evidently intending to stay as long as there was any left, and they did not return their ramrods but stuck them in the earth, after loading."[29] Coming up the steep slope, he saw the Confederates creeping forward and taking shelter behind boulders, but he thought that the enemy was generally overshooting their targets.

Oates could not know that his men were overshooting. It was enough to get them organized and galvanized to move forward toward the enemy's steady sheet of flame blazing down from above them. He gave the command to charge, but the noise of battle was so great that his men could not hear him. Near him, Captain James Henry Ellison of Company C, wearing a new jacket turned with gold lace that Oates had given him before the Gettysburg campaign, put his hand to ear and asked Oates to repeat his order. Colonel Oates did so, and Ellison called out, "Forward, my men, forward!" They were his last words. A ball passed through his head, killing him instantly. Oates, who regarded the officer as "one of the finest specimens of young manhood I ever beheld," watched as Ellison fell on his back, "gave one quiver[,] and was dead." The men of Company C gathered around their dead officer, despite the fact that they were exposed, as Oates put it, "to the most destructive fire at the time."[30] Oates told a lieutenant to get the men in line and order them forward.

Passing through the line, Oates waved his sword and shouted as loudly as he could: "Forward, men, to the ledge!" Although he claimed that his troops "promptly followed" him "in splendid style," at least one veteran described how Oates mounted a rock and discharged all six cartridges of his revolver "in the face of the enemy," but none of the men would advance with Oates in the charge, except one, a private named William R. Holloway.[31] The private got up on the rock with Oates and remarked, "Colonel, I can't see them." Oates directed Holloway to look under the smoke. Doing so, Holloway at last saw the enemy, kneeled down, took deliberate aim with his musket, and fired. As he took his gun down from his shoulder, a bullet smashed into his temple and through his head. Oates caught him in his arms, laid him down on the ground, and took up Holloway's musket, firing "a few rounds myself."[32] Then Oates went to another part of the line.

Despite the reluctance of the Alabamians, they finally followed Oates up toward the ledge held by the Federals. In this second assault, the 15th Alabama lost many of its best men; the regiment's casualties were becoming frightful. But over among the three left companies, where Billy Jordan of Company B remained safely behind the cover of a boulder and the Henry Pioneers (Company G) faced the solid center of Chamberlain's salient, the 15th Alabama suffered some of its worst casualties. It was at this place, between the angle in his own line and the gap that existed between the 15th Alabama and the 4th Alabama, some two hundred yards away to the west, that Oates said he "lost the greatest number of my men."[33] During one of the regiment's surges forward, Captain Henry C. Brainard of Company G attempted to lead his men up a ledge of rock when he was hit by enemy fire. He fell exclaiming: "O God, that I could see my mother!" Then he died.[34]

The ill Lieutenant John Oates, who had traveled so far this day and had somehow found the wherewithal and the courage to carry on despite his maladies, assumed command of the company and urged the men forward. Within five minutes of Brainard's death, however, Lieutenant John Oates fell in a downpour of bullets; he had been struck seven times in the legs and, ironically enough, in the hips, where his rheumatism had grown so painful. Lieutenant Isaac H. Parks of Company I, who had been John's schoolmate, ran to him and dragged him to cover behind a boulder, probably somewhere in the vicinity of the rocks just below the center of the 20th Maine's line. As Parks pulled John to shelter, an eighth bullet carried away one of the wounded lieutenant's little fingers. Lieutenant Oates was mortally wounded. At about the same time, Lieutenant Barnett H. Cody of Company G, one of the Oates brothers' boyhood friends, also went down with a fatal wound. At the time, Colonel William Oates did not know that his brother and so many of his friends had fallen in such rapid succession. He would soon learn that for all his efforts to keep his younger brother safe, for all his pleadings earlier that afternoon for John to stay out of the battle, his brother now lay behind a boulder bleeding with multiple wounds, clinging to life.[35]

The 15th Alabama struck Chamberlain's center with all the force of a sledgehammer, and the enemy came to within ten paces of his line, "where," said Chamberlain, "our steady and telling volleys brought them to a stand." Meanwhile, under trees that were becoming defoliated and barked by minié balls, Spear tried to hold the left wing steady against the formidable pressure applied by the Confederates. At one point, Spear's wing swayed backward a few steps, as the enemy surged forward, but the Maine men quickly regained their composure and resumed their line. The enemy, said Spear, "crept forward & took shelter behind boulders, and fired on us from some partial covering." He thought the Confederates got closer to his line than they otherwise might have because the boulders "afforded them some shelter." But his men "readjusted themselves among the rocks" and held firmly while "firing rapidly."[36]

He worried, though, that the force of the Alabamians' attack and their persistent movement around the 20th's left would result in the entire regiment being outflanked, so he went to the center, where Chamberlain was, and asked for two companies to reinforce his wing. Chamberlain agreed to transfer Companies E and I to the left. On hearing the order, the two companies fell back from the right wing in confusion, almost causing a collapse of the 20th's right flank. Quickly Chamberlain countermanded his own order, later explaining that he feared the transfer of the two companies "was likely to be misconstrued into a retreat." The left wing, he said, would have to hold on as best it could.[37]

The movement was indeed misconstrued, at least by Oates. When Oates saw the confusion on the enemy right, he concluded—falsely, as it turned out—that his left companies had succeeded in pushing the 20th Maine's right wing back off the rock ledge and had possibly accomplished a breakthrough. In later years, Oates adamantly affirmed that he had driven back both Chamberlain's left and right. To William Robbins, a former major of the 4th Alabama and a member of the War Department's commission that administered the Gettysburg National Military Park, Oates wrote in 1904: "Just as sure as your name is Robbins and mine Oates my regiment not only overlapped his [Chamberlain's] left flank but drove the 20th Maine from that position back to where I showed you[,] and his right as well as his left was forced back but not so far."[38]

While Spear was at the center of the 20th's line, requesting the additional two companies from Chamberlain that ultimately were never sent, he noticed that "most of the color guard were knocked out." Private James A. Knight of Company G was on the ground; Spear knelt down and asked him where he was hit. "Right through me," he answered feebly. Spear admiringly observed as Color Sergeant Andrew J. Tozier picked up a musket, while keeping the colors upright and tucked into his left arm, and stood loading and firing at the enemy. In Tozier's mouth was a piece of cartridge paper that he chewed like a cud. Chamberlain sent his brother Tom to find men who could rally around Tozier and support his heroic stand.[39]

Seeing the colors so courageously snapping through the battle smoke and so nobly defended by the valiant Tozier, Chamberlain later thought that the entire episode was "a stirring picture," something out of the romantic days of knights and the "songs of chivalry."[40] But the reality of the Confederate advance was about to come crashing down on his regiment. Worried that the enemy might succeed in turning his left, Colonel Chamberlain sent word to Captain Orpheus S. Woodward, commander of the 83rd Pennsylvania, for reinforcements to plug up the gap between the two regiments. Woodward, however, had enough going on along his own front, and he replied that he could not provide any help to the 20th Maine.

Out to the very far left and rear, hidden behind their stone wall and the tumbling clouds of musket smoke that swelled through the woods, Captain Morrill, his men of Company B, and the dozen or more green-coated snipers from the 2nd U.S. Sharpshooters, remained quietly in their hiding place and out of touch with the regiment. As yet, even with the attempts so far by the Confederates to move around the main body of the 20th Maine's left flank, Morrill—who had armed himself for combat with a musket, which was unusual for an officer—apparently could not see the enemy clearly or closely enough to bushwhack the Confederates from behind. He sent out flankers to protect his small force from surprise attack, but for the moment he and his men waited for the enemy to get in closer and become easier targets.

On the left wing, where the Confederates had obviously decided to target their greatest effort by attempting to outflank or break through the 20th Maine's line, Spear looked to his men and accepted the fact that he would be receiving no reinforcements. He must do with what he had. The musket fire, he noted, "was hot and men were falling." As his men were wounded, they dropped out of the ranks, some heading for the rear, some too disabled to move from where they had fallen, but the left wing's defensive line remained solid and strong. The regiment, he later wrote in his journal, was behaving "nobly."[41] The men of the 20th Maine would have to keep up their noble behavior, and their deadly musket fire, if they expected to survive what was about to take place in the gathering twilight along the bloody and darkening slopes of Little Round Top.

11

Everywhere Men Torn and Broken

To the men who fought there, the struggle for Little Round Top felt like it would never end. Seconds seemed like minutes; minutes crawled like hours. Even the victories—large and small, military and personal—that happened on the hillside that afternoon were only partial and not entirely decisive. With the arrival of the 140th New York at a crucial moment, the center and right regiments of Vincent's brigade turned back the battering assaults of the Texas and Alabama regiments who attempted to take the hill from the west and the southwest. However, the fighting along these slopes did not cease with the retirement of the Confederate forces back into the protection of the woods and boulders along the shoulder of Big Round Top. Even as Colonel James C. Rice of the 44th New York assumed command of the Third Brigade, after learning that Vincent had fallen, the Texans and Alabamians from the rocks and trees below were continuing an effective long-range fire of musketry against the Union defenders. In the exchange of rifle fire that replaced the massed assaults of the enemy up the ragged slopes of the hill, the battle seemed far from over or decided.

The sharpshooting was annoying—and deadly. Porter Farley said that everyone defending the hill felt the stinging effects of the Confederate sharpshooters, but Hazlett's cannoneers suffered the most, for they were more exposed to this continuous fire than the infantrymen who remained planted behind boulders, trees, and hastily constructed stone walls. The Confederate shooters, he wrote, "seemed swarming in the tree-tops and behind the rocks over in the direction of the peach orchard." The losses were heavy. "Man after man," Farley recalled, "fell under this murderous sharpshooting." A soldier in Farley's regiment later

175

explained to his loved ones back home that his "life and health" had been preserved, but the 140th New York's position on the hillside was "so open to sharpshooters that our loss was very severe."[1]

"Crazy" Rice behaved in a conspicuously sane fashion that afternoon. Hoping to avoid panic among his troops, he passed along the line and notified the brigade officers that Vincent had fallen and that he had assumed command. He spoke to every regimental commander—except, perhaps, Chamberlain, whose regiment was by this time heavily engaged—and assured them, as he wrote in his official report, "of my determination to hold the line to the last." He received word from each regiment, including the 20th Maine, that ammunition was running low. Having no aides or staff officers to assist him, he pressed into service several officers and men behind the firing line "and made them pledge their honor that they would deliver in person every order that I should send by them." He then sent four runners with orders to procure ammunition for the brigade. The ammunition, he said, "came promptly, was distributed at once, and the fight went on."[2]

Below the smoldering crest of the hill, along its craggy western face, the rest of Weed's brigade came up to join the 140th New York and extend the Federal defensive line across the ledges to the north. After General Warren had commandeered O'Rorke's 140th New York and removed it from the brigade column by sending it up to the summit of Little Round Top, the remainder of Weed's brigade—comprised of the 146th New York, the 91st Pennsylvania, and the 155th Pennsylvania—had continued its march to reinforce Sickles at the Peach Orchard. On the way, Weed halted his regiments and ordered the men to load their muskets. One soldier in the 91st Pennsylvania assumed that the brigade was "heading right for where the strife was most terrific."[3] When the brigade arrived to the east of the Peach Orchard, the battle smoke was so thick that General Weed rode ahead to find out from Sickles precisely where he should deploy his regiments, and he ordered his staff to bring the column along at a slow pace. Suddenly the brigade came under enemy fire, and Weed's men suffered their first casualties of the day.

Knowing that O'Rorke and his men were speeding to the hill's rescue, Warren spurred his horse toward the head of Weed's moving column; finding it, he halted the brigade and ordered it to await further instructions. Sending word for Weed to return to his brigade, Warren then rode forward, found General Sykes, the commander of the Fifth Corps, and told him about the desperate crisis on Little Round Top. Perturbed that

The western face of Little Round Top

Weed's brigade was not already on the hill, Sykes immediately sent word for Weed to get his men to the hilltop as quickly as possible. Warren's job was done. Believing that he had sent all the necessary reinforcements he could find to hold Little Round Top, he galloped to the north to look for Meade and give a report of his various activities.

Shortly Weed returned to his column, riding in the company of Lieutenant Edgar Warren, the general's brother, who served as Weed's aide. Weed seems to have already received Sykes's order by this time. With haste, he turned his brigade around and by a countermarch led it back to Little Round Top at the double-quick. Now the brigade was under heavy enemy fire, and the wounded fell out of the column as it hurried along. The regiments began to fall apart even before they reached the hill, for the rapid movement was making it difficult to keep the column together and hold the men in proper formation. As the brigade moved uphill, maintaining the double-quick as best it could, it encountered Hazlett's men as they manhandled their battery's last gun over the rocks; some of Weed's men fell out to help lift the Parrott into place, and, as a result, caused even more disorder in the brigade's column.

Surviving accounts attest to the confusion: various survivors gave bewildering and contradictory testimony about the marching order of the brigade, with some asserting that the 146th New York led the way up the hill, and others insisting that the 155th Pennsylvania occupied the head of the column. A private in the 146th New York recalled that the scene along the slopes as Weed's brigade scrambled and panted up to the top "was one of wildest confusion." The forced march up the northern side of the hill, he said, "was hard on our men, with a hot July sun beating down upon them." Weed's troops were out of breath when they reached the brow of the hill, yet they were still determined "to 'do or die.'" One veteran of the 155th Pennsylvania, however, reported that the confusion continued to reign after the brigade had reached the summit. "All semblance of order was soon lost," he wrote, "[with] each man taking care of himself as best he could."[4]

The fog of war, which had already enshrouded so many of the events that took place on Little Round Top this day, now tightly enwrapped itself around Weed's brigade. Amid all the other points of confusion, there are also conflicting statements as to what happened when the brigade finally did gain the crest. Some soldiers described in dramatic terms how the brigade arrived in the nick of time to avert the turning of the 140th New York's right flank by a swarm of Confederates who held fast to the ledges below the brow of the hill. Several veterans of the 146th New York claimed that their regiment rather than the 140th New York pushed the Confederates off the western slopes of Little Round Top. One New Yorker from the 146th contended that his regiment had engaged in bloody hand-to-hand combat with the Confederates. "The bitter conflict," he wrote, "was carried on tenaciously, with butts of guns, bayonets, and even stones with which the ground was plentifully supplied, being used as weapons."[5]

Some of Weed's men told of a lull in the battle that lasted thirty minutes or more; others believed that the Confederates launched yet another assault after the brigade had been deployed on the hillside. Veterans of the 155th Pennsylvania claimed that the enemy attacked them and got close enough, within thirty feet or so, to enable the regiment to use its outmoded smoothbore muskets that fired buck-and-ball shot. "The whole regiment fired a volley into them," declared one Pennsylvanian, "and they soon turned their backs."[6] But a man in the 91st Pennsylvania recounted the same enemy attack and said that Hazlett's cannon drove the Confederates back to the woods from which they had come.

Almost as soon as the brigade reached the hill's crest in a jumble of regiments and companies, Weed personally looked to straightening out his lines and putting his men into better order. He deployed the 91st Pennsylvania on the left so it connected with the right of the 140th New York, put the 146th New York next in line beside the 91st Pennsylvania, and placed the 155th Pennsylvania on the far right flank. While Weed was making sure his regiments had regained order and his lines were secure, General Sykes arrived on the hilltop to see for himself how the defensive efforts there were faring. Called "Tardy George" in the old army, Sykes on the afternoon of July 2 was punctual and conscientious enough to get his troops where they were most needed.

Meanwhile, more Federal reinforcements moved up to occupy the ground to Weed's right, off beyond the 155th Pennsylvania. They were Brigadier General Samuel W. Crawford's division of Pennsylvania Reserves, which took up a strong position on the northwestern slope of Little Round Top. Watching the arrival of Crawford's division with Weed was Captain Augustus Martin, commander of the Fifth Corps' artillery brigade, who had remained on the hill after Hazlett's guns had gone into action. The two officers were good friends, and they viewed the grand panorama of battle as it spread across the fields and woods and swales below them. "Martin," said Weed, "I would rather die on this spot than see those rascals gain one inch of ground."[7] Martin didn't like what he had just heard. Soldiers get nervous when their comrades talk about death and dying, and already Martin had heard Hazlett describe his own premonition of doom. Now Weed seemed to be tempting fate with his ill-chosen words. No doubt feeling uncomfortable, Martin left Weed and walked over to where Sykes and a group of officers were watching the battle with keen interest.

Death hovered like a dark cloud over Little Round Top as the afternoon light faded into grayness. When Captain Martin happened to turn around, he saw that Weed was reeling and falling to the ground. He had been struck by a sharpshooter's bullet, and he lay on the rocks, paralyzed from the shoulders down. He fell near Hazlett's guns, and Lieutenant Rittenhouse rushed to the general's side. "I am cut in two," said Weed. Then, weakening, he murmured: "I want to see Hazlett." Rittenhouse sent word to Hazlett who rode quickly to where Weed lay, dismounted, and knelt beside the general. Weed gave Hazlett, a close friend from the days when the general served in the artillery, instructions about the payment of some debts he owed to his fellow officers, pulled him closer to say something more, when Hazlett was suddenly hit in the back of the head by a minié ball and slumped over the general, dead. Horrorstruck, Weed exclaimed, "Poor Hazlett! He has gone before me!"[8]

More men now gathered around the two fallen officers, who were carried behind some rocks while everyone waited for the stretcher-bearers to arrive. Weed maintained consciousness throughout this ordeal, and he anxiously tried to express his last wishes to the men huddled around him. He asked the quartermaster of the 140th New York to give the ring on his finger and his pocketbook of letters to his fiancée, the daughter of Simon Cameron, the famous Pennsylvania Republican. Knowing that his end was near, he told his subordinates he wanted Colonel Kenner Garrard of the 146th New York to assume command of the brigade. His adjutant general tried to comfort Weed. "You will be all right soon, general," he said. But Weed demurred. "By sundown," he asserted, "I will be as dead as Julius Caesar."[9] In a short while, Weed became delirious, and he was carried to the rear.

Colonel Garrard took over the brigade, as Weed had requested, and reported to Sykes, who still stood on the crest watching the battle roll across the far hills and fields. What the two men said to each other was not recorded, but the two of them stood bravely on the boulders "as cool," wrote one officer, "as if witnessing a review." Others noticed Garrard's composure and found it reassuring. In battle, said another officer admiringly, Garrard was "as cool as when in camp."[10] Garrard took up Weed's work of deploying the brigade, restoring order to the ranks, and strengthening the lines. Meanwhile, the desultory crackling of muskets and the thundering of Hazlett's guns, now under the command of Lieutenant Rittenhouse, continued on the summit of Little Round Top, while the light grew pale and the flashes of fire began to look like strokes of heat lightning in the summer sky.

THE OFFICERS of the Fifth Corps, alive and slain, had done what they could to keep Little Round Top from falling into the hands of the Confederates, and heroism—or blind courage—was not in short supply among their numbers. In the end, though, victory would depend as it always must in every war, in every battle, on the stamina, the bravery, and the ability of the enlisted men, the ordinary soldiers, the rank and file, many of them by now hardened veterans, who had marched through dust and rain to reach this hill and sacrifice their lives if they had to for their cause. The rest of what happened on Little Round Top, as the dull orange sun descended behind the azure horizon of South Mountain, would be up to them and how well they could steel themselves against the relentless Confederate attacks and sniper fire. For those soldiers with less combat experience, such as the relatively untested men of the 20th Maine, this fight would prove their fortitude and show the rest of the corps and the army as a whole what they could do and what they could stand.

Along the base of the smoking southern slopes of the hill, Colonel William Oates was discovering that these Maine boys could stand quite a lot. His repeated attacks against the 20th Maine sputtered out one after the other and forced his men to disperse into groups and clumps as they sought cover behind trees and boulders. Over on the 15th's left, Billy Jordan and his comrades remained behind their boulder and did not dare try to peek over it to see what was going on. Jordan and the men with him were, for all purposes, out of the fight, for they could not hear the commands of their company officers—never mind the orders issued by Oates himself—and they could not retreat from their stronghold, either.

In all, the Confederates attacked the Maine regiment five times. None of the surviving accounts, including the ones written by Oates and Chamberlain, describes precisely the surging fight for this portion of Little Round Top; nor do they delineate with any degree of accuracy the events that happened in each of the separate charges. Instead, the various recollections of the fight are confused and written without a clear awareness of chronology or timing. Everything, in other words, seemed to be happening at once, and the muddleheadedness found in participants' accounts reflects the chaos that prevailed along the southern and eastern slopes of the hill.

Chamberlain tried to sum up what had happened: "The two lines met, and broke and mingled in the shock. At times I saw around me more of the enemy than of my own men. The edge of conflict swayed to and fro—now one and now the other party holding the contested ground. Three times our line was forced back, but only to rally and repulse the enemy. As often as the enemy's line was broken and routed, a new line was unmasked, which advanced with fresh vigor."[11] Oates did not receive any reinforcements, as Chamberlain had assumed, but it seemed to the men of the 20th Maine that these Confederates could not possibly be the same soldiers who attacked them again and again. Surely no human could have such determination, such physical strength. But the attacks kept coming. According to Oates, the two contending forces surged back and forth several times, more than the three occasions that Chamberlain remembered: "We drove the Federals from their strong defensive position; five times they rallied and charged us—twice coming so near that some of my men had to use the bayonet—but in vain was their effort."[12]

The separate thrusts made by the 15th Alabama, and the resurging responses by the 20th Maine, occurred without the luxury of breathing spells between the actions or any convenient lulls or lapses. As a result, the survivors came to remember the contest as pure bedlam, and the separate attacks became blended together in their minds—the mesmerizing experience of combat, the whirl of events, everything rapidly moving, the world all out of focus beyond one's immediate reach, the endless ragged popping of rifles, the constant screams and shouts, the moans of men in anguish, blue smoke thick and choking, lips and throat as dry as paper, lungs gasping for air, hands trembling uncontrollably, heart pounding, chest heaving.

All of these things, and more, happened at once. The bullets kept flying, buzzing, whistling until they hit a tree, a stone, or a man. Everything moved at incomprehensible speed, while at the same time every human motion appeared to take place in slow gesticulation, like dancers pirouetting in a ghoulish ballet or people in a horrible nightmare running endlessly for safety and never attaining their destination. Blood flew in every direction; no one on that hillside could escape the splattering of blood and flesh and the shattering of bone and teeth. Every man's cheeks were covered with the greasy grime of black powder and the dark gray soot of war. Among the dead and wounded, the faces bore ghastly expressions of shock, surprise, dread, and fear. The wounded called for water or for their mothers. The dead stared with agate eyes toward the sky.

During one of the 15th Alabama's lunges forward, Oates bolted toward a large boulder "about forty steps up the slope" with his men following right behind him. They crashed into the 20th Maine's left wing, the Maine men fell back a few steps and then regained their equilibrium and counterattacked almost immediately. Hand-to-hand fighting broke out all along the intertwined lines. About ten feet from the huge boulder, Oates stopped and watched as a Maine soldier tried to yank the 15th Alabama's colors out of the hands of the color-bearer. As the color-bearer stepped back, resisting the grasp of the Federal soldier, Sergeant Pat O'Connor, a fiery Irishman, rammed his bayonet through the head of the Maine infantryman, who fell dead. Oates wrote later with understatement that the incident "impressed me beyond the point of being forgotten."[13]

As the fighting intensified on the 20th Maine's left, Spear kept his men together and fighting. Sometimes it was necessary to hold them in place by grasping his sword with both hands, one near the tip and one near the hilt, and pressing it against the backs of the men. He had taken his sword from its scabbard, but, before dismounting his horse, which had been taken to the rear, he had forgotten to retrieve his belt with its holstered revolver. With no firearm, he did battle against the enemy as best he could. "I smelt the hot smoke," he remembered later in life, "[and] the faces of the men were set." Already he was proud of them and the courage they were showing. "How they worked," he said.[14] Some of the men were firing so rapidly that their muskets clogged.

Colonel Chamberlain recalled that during one of the enemy surges, the Confederates reached to within ten yards of his lines. Between the contending sides lay the dying and the dead. Chamberlain sent messengers to the rear with "reports of my condition, that my ammunition was exhausted, and that I could hold the position but a few minutes longer."[15] Along Spear's wing, his ammunition was not depleted, but his men were nearly spent with fatigue and his casualties were mounting. When the Confederates fell back, Chamberlain took the opportunity to have his men collect cartridges from the dead and wounded, friend and foe. Panicking officers came dashing up shouting that the regiment would soon be annihilated, and some of the men, fearing the worst, began facing to the rear.

The fighting continued with no halt; in fact, the combat grew more and more bloody. "The edge of the fight rolled backward and forward like a wave," wrote Chamberlain. "Squads of the enemy," he said, "broke through our line in several places, and the fight was literally hand to hand." The sounds were strange and frightening. There arose, he said, a "strange, mingled roar—shouts of defiance, rally, and desperation; and underneath, murmured entreaty and stifled moans, gasping prayers, snatches of Sabbath song, whispers of beloved names; everywhere men torn and broken, staggering, creeping, quivering on the earth." In a moment of crisis, he ordered his brother, Lieutenant Thomas Chamberlain, to plug up a gap in the line. "The fire down there at this moment," said Colonel Chamberlain, "was so hot that I thought it impossible for him to get out alive." So he sent Sergeant Reuel Thomas, the regiment's special orderly, after Thomas, and the two men eventually returned "with personal proofs of the perilous undertaking."[16]

The men continued to fetch cartridges from the fallen, and some even took advantage of the shifting tide to get better Springfield muskets from the Confederates to replace their own Enfields. Somewhat glee-fully, Chamberlain noted that "the rebels were then met with their own bullets." Other men found time to build up rude shelters out of loose rocks and tree limbs, anything that could serve as even a low breastwork. The struggle, said Chamberlain solemnly, "became desperate and bloody in the highest degree." Even as the men fought bitterly to stand their ground, trying with all their might to kill their foes, small acts of kindness were performed to aid the wounded, give a comrade the last sip of water from a canteen, or send a smile of encouragement to a pal in the ranks. At one point in the melee, Chamberlain saw a Confederate officer go down with a wound; eventually the lines shifted so that the officer lay behind the 20th Maine line. Chamberlain later told how he assisted the wounded man by sending him "to the rear and out of danger."[17]

After the war, Chamberlain admitted that he expected never to leave the hill alive. He was hit twice. The first wound occurred when a bullet hit a rock below the arch of his right foot that tore open his boot and cut his instep. Another minié ball struck his sword scabbard, bending the steel sheath and bruising his left thigh. He would learn after the war that at least two Confederates got him in their sights and tried to kill him, but one hit instead a soldier who walked in front of Chamberlain at the cru-cial moment, and the second found that as a result of a "queer notion" he could not pull the trigger, even though he had a clear shot. All around him, the Maine soldiers were falling. He was proud of his men. They fought, he said, "with a desperation never excelled on the field of battle."[18]

Trying to care for his men in any way he could, he found Private George Washington Buck wounded with a great hole in his breast, lying on the ground and looking skyward. Buck had been demoted unjustly, losing his sergeant's stripes, by a bullying quartermaster who punished him for refusing to perform a menial personal service. Now Buck was mortally wounded, the blood flowing out of him, and Chamberlain bent over him to say a few words. The colonel spoke first: "My dear boy, it has gone hard with you. You shall be cared for!" Buck whispered, "Tell my mother I did not die a coward." Chamberlain told him: "You die a ser-geant. I promote you for faithful service and noble courage on the field of Gettysburg!"[19] Then Buck died.

The carnage on the hillside continued, most of it unconnected to the romance that Chamberlain always managed to see on a battlefield. At the center of the 20th Maine's salient, the colors remained stationary, as though fixed in stone; Tozier and the two remaining members of the color guard—for one of the guard was dead and the other wounded—budged not an inch despite the howling storm of musket fire all around them. In Company C, Private John O'Connell slipped into deep despair. "It was only a question of time," he wrote, "when every man must fall before the superior fire of our Enemy so greatly outnumbering us." On the left, Spear became increasingly concerned about how long his men could hold on. Half of his wing had fallen, and the line was full of gaps. "If it continued long," he said, "our men would all be down, or their ammunition exhausted."[20]

Less than twenty-five yards away, Colonel Oates knew as well that his men could only take so much. Captain De Bernie Waddell, the regiment's adjutant, asked Oates for permission to take forty or fifty men from the right wing and advance to some rocks, where they could then pour an enfilade fire down on the 20th Maine's left flank. Knowing this might be the only way successfully to turn the enemy's left, Oates approved the plan. Waddell led his detail far around the right and took cover behind a ledge of rocks, although the flank fire seemed not to deter the enemy or force its withdrawal. At this moment, in what must be regarded as perfect timing, Company B of the 20th Maine and the small contingent of sharpshooters behind their stone wall finally decided to join in the fight, and they laid down what Oates called "a withering and deadly fire" in the rear of his line. "While one man was shot in the face," wrote Oates, "his right-hand or left-hand comrade was shot in the side or the back." Some men, he said, "were struck simultaneously with two or three balls from different directions."[21]

Oates realized that his position was becoming rapidly untenable. He sent the regiment's sergeant-major to the left with a request that Colonel Bowles of the 4th Alabama shift his men to the right and come to the aid of the 15th Alabama. The sergeant-major returned shortly and reported that he could not find the 4th Alabama or any other Confederate troops to the left. Oates now knew that he could expect no help. The 15th Alabama had no reserves; Company A, sent out to capture the Federal wagons parked behind the Round Tops, had vanished, and the regiment's casualties were heavy and growing. Two of Oates's captains, Frank Park and Blant A. Hill, informed him that Federal troops were closing on the 15th Alabama's rear. Oates ordered Park to find out the size of the enemy force. When he returned, he had only bad news. Two regiments carrying two battle flags, reported Park, were coming up behind the Alabamians, and Oates himself thought at that moment he could see the enemy lines halting behind a fence about two hundred yards away. What he saw, of course, and what Park had mistakenly counted as two regiments, were the blue-coated men of the 20th Maine's Company B and the green-coated marksmen of the 2nd U.S. Sharpshooters behind their stone wall, although it is possible that he had caught a glimpse of Colonel Joseph W. Fisher's brigade of Pennsylvania Reserves, detached from Brigadier General Samuel Crawford's Third Division of the Fifth Corps, as it moved across the Weikert farm on its way to assist in the defense of Big Round Top. Oates also came to believe that dismounted Union vedettes had also arrived in his rear. He began to feel like the famous Captain Nolan of the Light Brigade at Balaklava.

"It seemed," recalled Oates in his later years, "that the regiment was doomed to destruction." Captains Hill and Park recommended that Oates order a retreat. All around the dead and wounded lay strewn across the ground. The regiment's casualties, said Oates, "were then nearly as great in number as those still on duty." The battlefield was a sickening sight: "The blood stood in puddles in some places on the rocks; the ground was soaked with the blood of as brave men as ever fell on the red field of battle." Not wanting to face the reality of his situation, however, Oates still hoped for reinforcements. He told his captains: "Return to your companies; we will sell out as dearly as possible." Hill said nothing. Park smiled, gave a crisp salute, and said: "All right, sir."[22]

One reason that kept Oates from withdrawing his regiment was personal: he knew his brother was probably bleeding to death, nestled between boulders on the hillside, and he did not want to leave him to die in the hands of the enemy. But he finally saw that he had no choice. He decided to order a retreat, but he knew that it would be impossible for the 15th Alabama to retire in order. He sent Sergeant-Major Norris on another mission, this time to inform all the small islands of men along the line that the signal would be soon given to retreat and that "every one should run in the direction from whence we came, and halt on the top of the Big Round Top Mountain." Norris went down the line, but failed to inform Waddell and the detail on the far right that the withdrawal was about to take place, perhaps because the sergeant-major was not told the detail was there. Oates then waited for the latest surge of the 20th Maine to happen, for the enemy to regain its previous position along the ledges, and for the firing to die down. So doing, he hoped to "give my men a better chance to get out unhurt."[23] Then he ordered the retreat.

At the same instant, the 20th Maine had also reached a moment of truth. Chamberlain believed his ammunition was running out, and despite Rice's claim that he saw to the replenishment of ammunition among all the regiments in the brigade, the 20th Maine seems to have been forgotten. Sending out runners to get more cartridges, Chamberlain was disappointed when they returned empty-handed. It was then, he said, that "our ammunition *utterly failed*." Every available man was called up to the firing line, including walking wounded, drummers, and other noncombatants in the regiment. "For God's sake hold that front," commanded Chamberlain, whose nerves were now frayed and whose options were becoming quickly narrowed. Chamberlain thought he heard a commotion over on the right, but the Alabamians burst forth up the slope and attacked his left one last time. This time the enemy did not rush up and throw itself into the Maine line. Instead, the Confederates stood back and fired from a distance, preferring not to engage in a hand-to-hand conflict. When the enemy was within fifty feet of the 20th Maine, the Federal fire slackened to practically nothing. "Every round," said Chamberlain, "was gone."[24] Yet the men from Maine held their ground and repulsed this latest Confederate attack.

After the war, Chamberlain estimated that at least fifty thousand bullets had been exchanged between the two sides in this fight, and while his estimate may be fantastically high, given the fact that each man in the 20th Maine had been issued only sixty rounds, he may be excused the exaggeration, for the musket fire was, by any measure, intense and fairly continuous. Nevertheless, the entire supply of ammunition for the regiment had not been exhausted, as Chamberlain apparently supposed. Spear would later report that the left wing had not expended all its cartridges, and along his line his men kept up a steady fire against the Confederates. But the crisis was real enough. A third of the regiment had fallen. So many of his men were dead and wounded that Chamberlain worried that the regiment might not be able to mount an effective defensive. Worse still, Chamberlain could hear to the rear "a great roar of musketry," and he feared that the brigade line and Hazlett's battery behind him were caving in.[25]

Knowing that the enemy would soon try another assault, Chamberlain observed his men turning their muskets upside down and grasping them by the barrels in anticipation of using them as clubs against the Confederates. Through the rolling smoke, he could see that the center of his salient, where the colors still could be seen, "was nearly shot away." He could also see below him the enemy forming in the low shrubbery and rocks for what he believed was another assault. "It was manifest," he explained after the war, "that we could not stand before the wave that was ready to roll upon us." Even the men in the ranks realized that time was running out. "Our line," said Private Coan in the color guard, "was melting away like ice before the sun."[26]

In desperation, Chamberlain decided to order a bayonet charge. He tried to warn the companies on the left of what he was about to do, but Spear never received any word from Chamberlain. Then Lieutenant Holman S. Melcher of Company F interrupted the colonel with a request to move his men forward to rescue some wounded men who were caught between the contending battle lines and who were calling out for help. Chamberlain told the young lieutenant to take his place with his company; he was about to order an advance of the entire regiment. Melcher fled to rejoin his company. Chamberlain shouted out: "Bayonet!" and the word rippled down the line, to the right and to the left. "The click of the steel," noted Chamberlain, "seemed to give new zeal to all." But he never got the opportunity to give the order to advance; if he had, he later said, no one would have heard it anyway. The 20th Maine moved forward without orders and began running down the hill. "With fixed bayonets and a yell," remembered Corporal Livermore, "we rushed on them, which so frightened them, that not another shot was fired on us." It was, recalled Private Coan, "a wild mad charge."[27]

Chamberlain had assumed a position near the colors, and as the regiment advanced, he moved forward with the color guard, or what little remained of it. It was his impression, as he later reported to his superiors, that "the two wings [of the regiment] came into one line again, and extending to the left, and at the same time wheeling to the right, the whole Regiment described nearly a half circle, the left passing over the space of half a mile, while the right kept within the support of the 83rd Penna." The charge, he said proudly, "was like a cyclone."[28] Chamberlain, who sprang down the hill with the apex of his regiment, suddenly came upon a Confederate officer who, in one hand, held his sword in a gesture of surrender, and in the other hand, held a Colt revolver aimed at the colonel's face. The Confederate pulled the trigger, the pistol clicked on an empty chamber, and Chamberlain put his own saber tip to his foe's throat. The enemy officer quickly surrendered.

On the left, Spear experienced the charge—or remembered it, at any rate—in a much different manner than did Chamberlain. He had received no orders about a general advance, no matter what Chamberlain himself asserted in the years after the war, and stood amazed as he heard a shout of "forward" coming from the center and saw the lines of his comrades advancing down the hill to his right. "The left took up the shout and moved forward," Spear wrote, "and [with] every man eager not to be left behind, the whole line flung itself down the slope through the fire and smoke and upon the enemy."[29]

Without warning, the 20th Maine came barreling down the bloody hillside just at the very moment that Oates gave his order for the 15th Alabama to retreat. The clamor of the charging Federals, the cries of the wounded, and the continuing racket of musket fire from both sides meant that hardly any of the Alabamians heard Oates shout out the order to withdraw. Waddell and his men off to the right certainly did not know what was going on. And Billy Jordan, crouched behind his boulder, only became aware that the 15th Alabama was falling back when he saw men racing toward the rear. "When the signal was given," Oates admitted, "we ran like a herd of wild cattle."[30]

Some of the men headed toward Big Round Top, as Oates had directed, but others took off in whatever direction seemed to make sense. Waddell and his detail off on the right saw the rest of the regiment go and they followed as quickly as they could, suffering some casualties as they ran for the rear. A good number of the Confederates, particularly those who ran east toward the Weikert farm, where Tillie Pierce and the Weikert family were waiting out the battle, ended up falling into the hands of Spear's pursuing companies and Merrill's Company B boys. The mayhem was such, however, that Confederates also managed to pick up a few prisoners. Oates insisted that during the retreat his own men captured three dismounted Union cavalrymen.[31]

As Oates raced up the steep wooded slopes of Big Round Top, his mind in turmoil as he tried to cope with the fact that he had left his wounded brother behind on the field of battle, one of his infantrymen ran beside him, his throat spattering blood from a wound made by a bullet. His windpipe was entirely severed, said Oates, but the man made it up the mountain, only to die in a field hospital that night or the next morning. When Waddell reached the foot of Big Round Top, he met Captain Shaaff and Company A, which now emerged from the woods and their unsuccessful detour to capture the Federal supply wagons. Where Shaaff and his men had been all this time was never properly explained. Waddell took charge of things and ordered Company A to take a stand on the slopes of Big Round Top, checking the Federal pursuit up the hillside.

Below the summit of Big Round Top, Oates, who by this time was physically drained and emotionally distraught, attempted to reform his regiment but discovered that was not possible because the men had scattered during the withdrawal and many of them were busy helping wounded and disabled comrades. Overcome "by heat and exertion," he fainted and fell. He would have been captured, he later recounted, but two of his men carried him up to the summit, where the regimental assistant surgeon revived him. Oates temporarily turned command over to Captain Hill, telling his subordinate to lead the regiment down to the base of the hill in the vicinity of the Slyder farm, where the companies could reform and assume a defensive position. It was just about "deep dusk" when the 15th Alabama went down the western slope of Big Round Top and bivouacked in an open field just beyond Plum Run.[32]

When the retreat began, Billy Jordan was faced with a dilemma. He could try to run with the other Alabamians but risk getting shot by the Federals as he did so, or he could stay where he was and let himself get captured. Six of the eight men who had hidden behind Jordan's boulder ultimately surrendered. But Jordan at least wanted to make an attempt to escape. "I determined never to be a prisoner, as I preferred death," he wrote. So he took off running from his boulder, leaning over slightly (by which he hoped to make himself a smaller target), and headed in a left oblique direction. Above him, the Union troops fired a volley, which miraculously missed him. "There was not a thread cut on me that I ever knew of," he said, "but [I] expected to be riddled with bullets."[33] He went about a hundred yards and heard a man calling hello. It was Elisha Lane, a young soldier from Jordan's own company, who had been shot through his thigh while trying to escape. Lane threw his arm around Jordan's neck, and at that moment John Hughes, who had found shelter with Jordan behind the big rock, came up, and the two of them managed to get the wounded man over Big Round Top to the bivouac near the Slyder farm. There the litter bearers carried Lane away to a hospital. Jordan later remarked that the men who stopped to surrender saved the others who made it up Big Round Top, for the Federals took such a delight in their prisoners that they became distracted from the pursuit.

But acting Major Spear seemed less than distracted as he and his men flew down the hillside and pursued the fleeing Confederates. Following the lead of the companies to his right that had bounded down the hillside, Spear scaled a boulder and found two Confederates on the other side, both of whom stood up suddenly, holding empty muskets. Having only his sword in hand, he worried for a moment that these two enemy soldiers might contest his capture of them, but they ended up offering no resistance and compliantly headed to the rear. Spear and his men chased the retreating Alabamians into a farm lane and caught up with them at a worm fence that stopped them dead in their tracks. Some of the Confederates were shot down as they tried to climb the fence, but most of the enemy silently and sullenly surrendered. It was then that Spear realized that Morrill's Company B had been "firing into the rear of the enemy during the fight and more effectively as the enemy fell back in confusion before our charge."[34]

The charge, said Spear, "was easier to start than to stop." The men had run down the hill with "more vigor than order." The enemy was simply swept away by the 20th Maine's charge. Decades later, the historian of the regiment described how the men of the 20th pursued the Confederates "like avenging demons." Spear was particularly proud of the accomplishment of his regiment. "It was an extraordinary act, to charge as we did leaving our place in the line of battle without orders from the brigade commander or some higher officer," boasted Spear. Telling the story of the charge to a child forty-seven years later, Spear said that the Confederates "all seemed to remember something they had left at home, and they ran like mad intending to go in the direction of home and their mothers." One soldier wrote in his diary that the Confederates "had but little time to choose between surrender and cold steel, so the most of their front line dropped their rifles and steped to our rear for safety." Corporal Livermore marveled at how the Maine men took prisoners "by scores." For those too far away to be captured, he said flatly, the Federals gave them "deadly shots in the back."[35]

Chamberlain, understandably, was exuberant about his regiment's victory on Little Round Top. Two years after the battle, he told a newspaper correspondent: "If our whole brigade could have joined in the charge, I doubt not Hood's whole brigade would have fallen. Our men were exultant. They were on the road to Richmond, and could not be stopped." The men finally did stop, of course, before reaching Richmond, but not before they had swept the little valley between the two Round Tops clean of any remaining Confederates, including some stragglers and lost souls from the 4th and 5th Texas. The enthusiastic infantrymen of the 20th Maine ended the pursuit of the enemy when they had reached the front of the 44th New York. But there the chase was taken up by the 83rd Pennsylvania and the 44th New York, who cleared the broken terrain in their front of any remaining Confederates. The enemy, as Colonel Rice later wrote, "was repulsed with terrible slaughter."[36]

"It was a bad smash-up," Chamberlain confessed several decades later, referring to the clash between the 20th Maine and the 15th Alabama, "but we won the day."[37] Indeed, the day was almost over. By the time Chamberlain had stopped his men in their wild pursuit, the amber glow of twilight, gentle and dim and full of gloom, had already descended like a veil over Little Round Top.

12

TWILIGHT

UNDER THE PALL of twilight, the outcome on Little Round Top was still in doubt. Sporadic firing continued as the light waned and darkness crept through the sky. The acrid smell of battle smoke still lingered in the air, thick enough in some places to choke a man if he breathed too deeply, and the aroma of death, sickeningly sweet and foul, was wending its way across the broken battlefield. Death took the leading role in the drama this day; the battle had become a veritable theater of death. And it was not over.

The Confederates still had more work to do. Although Longstreet's forces had successfully taken Devil's Den and the ridges and woods around it, the Peach Orchard, and a long section of the Emmitsburg Road, and while their attack had slowed and lost most of its punch in the raw twilight, they still threatened to overrun the remaining Union defenses near the Wheatfield, along the center of Cemetery Ridge, and onto the northern ridges of Little Round Top. The tattered but determined remnants of Kershaw's, Semmes's, and Wofford's brigades from McLaws's division, and some Georgians from Tige Anderson's brigade of Hood's division—the crack Southern troops who had so effectively demolished Sickles's salient and driven their far more numerous foes back in retreat—were now moving steadily in the direction of Little Round Top.

To meet this threat, the Union commanders had set up some formidable obstacles. More guns had been moved up to defend Little Round Top, namely Captain Frank C. Gibbs's Battery L, 1st Ohio Light Artillery, which placed one section to the right of Hazlett's battery and south of the Wheatfield Road on the north slope of Little Round Top, and the other two sections north of the road, overlooking the broad expanse of the Valley of Death. The ground, broken and rocky, was not suited for the placement of artillery. Gibbs and his men had to get the Little Round Top section into place by hand, although their efforts required less herculean labor than Hazlett's gun crews had earlier performed.

General Sykes also ordered his Third Division, consisting of two infantry brigades of Pennsylvania Reserves under Crawford's command, to assist Vincent's and Weed's Fifth Corps brigades on Little Round Top. These Pennsylvania Reserves, who were itching to get into the fight to defend their home state, had been detached on June 25 from duty manning the defenses of Washington, D.C. Crawford's division, which had proven itself on many battlefields and had taken exceptionally high casualties at Fredericksburg the previous December, had been marching since the early morning of July 1 with only a few hours' rest.

Crawford, a native of Pennsylvania, had only been in command of the reserves since May. He was rather an odd duck. A graduate of the University of Pennsylvania medical school, Crawford had served in the old army as an assistant surgeon. He was stationed at Fort Sumter in Charleston harbor in April 1861, when the fortress was besieged by Confederate forces, so he witnessed the outbreak of the war and later decided to join in the fight as an infantry commander. After Sumter, Crawford first received a commission as major of the 13th U.S. Regiment, and then, in the spring of 1862, promotion to brigadier general. After recuperating from a wound he received at Antietam, he was given command of the Pennsylvania Reserves in Washington. Ambitious and petulant, he yearned for recognition and advancement.

Given his burning desire for the main chance, Crawford was not about to waste an opportunity like the one being offered him at Gettysburg. When Meade ordered Sykes to bring his Fifth Corps to Sickles's assistance, Crawford trailed behind Barnes's First Division and Brigadier General Romeyn Ayres's Second Division of Regulars. Almost getting lost on the way to the battlefield, the two brigades of the Pennsylvania Reserves finally reached the northern slopes of Little Round Top, where Crawford received an order to send one of his brigades as reinforcements for Vincent and Weed. He dispatched the brigade under Colonel Joseph W. Fisher to aid Vincent, while he retained one of Fisher's regiments, the 11th Pennsylvania Reserves, to remain with Colonel William McCandless's brigade along the northern end of the hill.

Brigadier General Samuel W. Crawford, Army of the Potomac, leads his Pennsylvania Reserves in an attack across the Valley of Death.

Crawford deployed his regiments in two lines with the 1st Pennsylvania Reserves in the first line on the far left, just below and to the right of Gibbs's artillery section, the 11th Pennsylvania Reserves in the center, and the 6th Pennsylvania Reserves on the right. In the second line, the 13th Pennsylvania Reserves was positioned on the left, and the 2nd Pennsylvania Reserves on the right. Although Colonel McCandless was technically in command of the First Brigade, Crawford later said that the colonel "was not to be found . . . until all was over," so the general assumed direct command of the regiments.[1] Somehow the 98th Pennsylvania, which belonged to the Third Brigade and to Major General John Sedgwick's Sixth Corps, became confused in its approach to the battlefield and found itself detached from its brigade and standing to the left rear of the 11th Pennsylvania Reserves.

No sooner had Crawford gotten his lines in order and told his men to lie down on the ground than the Confederate skirmishers came into sight, followed by thick columns, although the mass of enemy troops looked to be in considerable disarray. Between Crawford and the oncoming enemy, however, were retreating regulars from Ayres's divisions, who had been earlier placed in position for a brief time on the northern slopes of Little Round Top and then sent forward into the fight for the Wheatfield. Driven back by the Confederates, the regulars—who had lost 50 percent of their men—now came streaming toward the safety of the rear, if the rear could only be found. Coming off the field, they passed through Crawford's newly formed lines. The regulars, wrote an officer in the 13th Pennsylvania Reserves (also known as the "Bucktails"), "came back stumbling over us as we lay hugging the ground closely to avoid the shower of bullets." Crawford reported that "the plain to my front was covered with fugitives from all divisions, who rushed through my lines and along the road to the rear."[2]

Waiting for the moment when the field of fire would be clear—minutes that seemed interminable to Crawford and his men—the reservists watched as the enemy advanced farther toward the Federal battle lines, with the enemy skirmishers almost reaching the base of the hill. It is quite possible—given the shambles in which the Confederates and the retreating regulars found themselves, and the great difficulty that existed for anyone who tried to identify friend from foe in the deepening twilight—that the Confederates actually swept up a short distance on the hillside. Major Henry D. McDaniel of the 11th Georgia, one of Tige Anderson's regiments, reported that his men "vigorously pressed" the retreating Union regulars "to the very foot of the mountain, up the sides of which the enemy had fled in the greatest confusion."[3]

Colonel Samuel Jackson of the 11th Pennsylvania Reserves remarked that it seemed as if nothing could stop the Confederates; in fact, they looked to him like an "irresistible mass of living gray." The Pennsylvanians, however, held their places and did not flinch, despite the enemy onslaught. Through the valley echoed the Rebel Yell as the enemy advanced, already triumphant and expecting complete victory. E. M. Woodward of the 2nd Reserves described the scene: "Our battery to the right belched forth its sheets of flame and smoke, hurling its missiles of death over the heads of the flying mass into the enemy. Immovable and firm stood the Reserves, resting on their arms."[4]

But the Confederate attack was losing steam, although it did not appear that way to the waiting Pennsylvanians. In nearly total disarray, exhausted and with little order to their ranks, the butternut waves lapped forward with fierce determination, but with little power behind their thrust. Still, their rifle fire was deadly and their threat potent. In Crawford's lines, men were wounded from the enemy bullets that sprayed the front ranks of the reservists. Even while Crawford held back his musket fire, Gibbs's battery opened with canister that cut through the advancing Rebels like a scythe. Captain George Hillyer of the 9th Georgia could not keep his men going forever: "Our little band, now thinned and exhausted by three and a half hours' constant fighting, made a gallant attempt to storm the batteries, but the enemy being again heavily re-enforced, we were met by a storm of shot and shell, against which, in our worn-out condition, we could not advance."[5]

Finally the battered U.S. regulars finished limping through Crawford's line and the front was cleared for action. Crawford, filled with energy and longing to get into the fight, ordered his regiments to open fire up and down the line. From the ranks of the Pennsylvania Reserves exploded two tremendous volleys that tore into the approaching Confederates. It was, by itself, wrote one Confederate, "a fatal blow." The musket fire forced the Confederates to "halt and hesitate."[6] Smoke filled the valley, and the Confederates became screened by the battle fog.

Riding a "spirited" blood bay horse, Crawford found himself next to the color guard of the 1st Reserves. He leaned over and seized hold of the flagstaff, but the color bearer, Corporal Swope, refused to let the general have the flag. "I can't give you my colors," Swope said. Crawford, with some annoyance, replied: "Don't you know me, I am your General? Give me your colors."[7] The corporal gave up the colors, but he insisted on grabbing the general's pant leg and holding on, hoping, one supposes, that by so doing he could stay near his cherished flag and protect it from any harm.

The general, firmly gripping the colors and holding them high, rode a short distance to the front of the reserve brigade. Crawford ordered an immediate advance, crying out: "Forward Reserves." With a "simultaneous shriek from every throat, that sounded as if coming from a thousand demons, who had burst their lungs in uttering it," boasted one veteran, "on swept the Reserves." The brigade "advanced in gallant style," wrote Colonel McCandless, who seems to have been with his regiments after all, and soon "charged at a full run down the hillside and across the plain, driving the advancing masses of the enemy back."[8] The enemy was wiped from the hillside and pushed relentlessly across the level ground and a marshy field. Beyond the marsh and creek, a high grassy hill rose up before the charging Pennsylvanians, but they scaled it with relative ease and continued pushing the enemy back through a belt of woods and toward the open space of the Wheatfield.

When the order to charge was given, the Bucktails (13th Pennsylvania Reserves) were still in the process of forming their lines. Seeing the regiments on their right preparing for an advance, the Bucktails moved forward "in a somewhat broken line," as one Pennsylvanian remembered, "but when they received the order to charge every one of those veteran soldiers quickly found his place, and as if by magic they presented a solid and unbroken line to the enemy." According to this soldier, the enemy advanced so far up the slopes of Little Round Top before the Pennsylvania Reserves began their counterattack that the Bucktails had to grapple, hand-to-hand, with the Confederates as the brigade moved forward. The struggle, however, "lasted but a short time," and the Rebels retired quickly from the hillside in confusion.[9] The Bucktails followed on the heels of the retreating enemy and took many prisoners as the regiment swept across the shallow valley to a stone wall on the edge of the Wheatfield.

At that stone wall, the Confederates attempted a last-ditch stand. But the momentum of the Pennsylvania Reserves was too much to halt. With little effort, the Pennsylvanians rushed the stone wall and drove the enemy from its shelter. Some of Crawford's men ran far beyond the wall, chasing the Confederates into the Wheatfield itself, but the general called them back, not wanting to overextend himself or push his luck. Arriving at the stone wall on his bay mount, Crawford discovered that Corporal Swope—from the color guard, the man who had grabbed hold of his pant leg—was still beside him clutching his trousers. The Pennsylvanians realized their success and let loose with "one loud shout of victory [that] ran through the valley, and over the hills."[10]

In the attack, the second line of the Reserves, consisting of the 13th Reserves and the 2nd Reserves, had been led to the left, while the front line attacked nearly straight ahead across the valley. The Bucktails advanced far beyond the point reached by Crawford's first line; ahead of the other regiments, the Bucktails received a galling enemy volley into the regiment's right-center. In the middle of this chaos, Colonel Charles Frederick Taylor, much admired among the Bucktails, discovered a small contingent of Confederates, some two hundred or three hundred men, firing from a stand of timber nearby. A Federal officer demanded their surrender and most of the Southerners threw down their muskets. But one Confederate, toward the rear of the ranks, shouted: "I'll never surrender to a corporal's guard."[11] With that oath, his comrades picked up their muskets and opened fire. A bullet struck Colonel Taylor in the

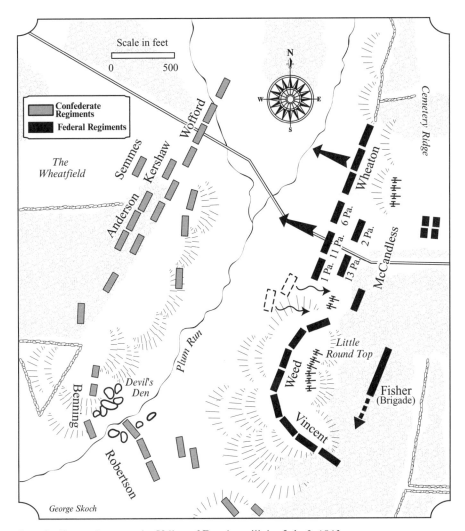

Crawford's attack across the Valley of Death, twilight, July 2, 1863

heart. The Bucktails replied by pouring several volleys into the Confederates. About fifty enemy soldiers threw down their weapons, and the remaining Confederates quickly bounded to safety within their own lines.

While the Bucktails moved to the left during the assault, so too did the Sixth Corps' 98th Pennsylvania, which joined Crawford's Pennsylvania Reserves in the counterattack. As the reserves stepped off to their right, the men of the 98th Pennsylvania sent up "a ringing cheer" and "swept down the face of the hill, meeting the rebels as they came pushing forward." Company K of the 1st Pennsylvania Reserves was composed of recruits from Adams County—local boys who, according to one veteran, "chased many a rabbit all over these hills, and gathered berries in these valleys, [and] played 'hide and seek' among these rocks and boulders" and now fought with vigor to defend their homes and hearths.[12] They swept the retiring Confederates from their front with admirable courage and determination. Eventually the regiment reached the stone wall, where Crawford had halted the advance, and the work of the 98th Pennsylvania was over.

Scattered musket fire continued to crackle in the timber near the Wheatfield, along the crest of Houck's Ridge, among the rocks of Devil's Den, in the tangled woods on the northern shoulder of Big Round Top, across the wide expanse of valley through which Plum Run flowed, and up and down the rocky and wooded slopes of Little Round Top. Even darkness didn't bring an end to the sporadic fire. But as the black night took Little Round Top into its grip, the fighting for the day had ended, and finally, as darkness consumed the battlefield, it could be said at last that the hill had been saved for the Union. But the cost could not be immediately reckoned. Only in the daylight would the full death toll be known. One thing was certain. The angel of death had done fearsome work at Little Round Top that day.

NIGHT CAME GENTLY, soft as sable, in stark contrast to the fiery day. The black night provided protection, finally, from the sure eyes and accurate aim of the Confederate sharpshooters who still occupied the rocks of Devil's Den and the woods near the base of Big Round Top. All across Little Round Top, the Union soldiers had their hands full preparing breastworks, caring for the wounded, and burying the dead. There were bodies everywhere.

Behind the lines there was constant movement, an unceasing flow of couriers, walking wounded, stretcher bearers, ambulance attendants, and stragglers who, like men in a daze, wandered through the night toward some uncertain destination. On Little Round Top, the Union forces there had to do something about the numerous prisoners they had taken throughout the afternoon and into the evening. Colonel Rice reported that his entire brigade captured "over 500 prisoners, including 2 colonels and 15 commissioned officers, together with over 1,000 stand of arms belonging to the enemy."[13] The enemy prisoners had to be escorted to the rear and placed in the hands of the provost marshal.

The two Confederate colonels mentioned by Rice were Colonel Powell of the 5th Texas and Lieutenant Colonel Bulger of the 47th Alabama. Both men had been wounded and were found by the Federals on the battlefield. After the fighting had ended, Bulger was approached by a Federal enlisted soldier who demanded his surrender. Bulger answered crisply: "My good fellow, is it possible that you are a federal soldier, and in the army of the United States, and yet you do not know that a private is not authorized to disarm an officer he captures?" When the soldier admitted that he did not know the protocol, Bulger sent him off to find an officer of the nearest rank to lieutenant colonel. Colonel Rice returned and said apologetically, "Colonel, my duty requires me to ask for your arms." Bulger gladly handed over his pistol and sword, remarking: "That's a very fine sword. I have had it on a short time. It was captured a short time ago from the lieutenant colonel of the Twenty-second Maine, and presented to me day before yesterday."[14] Incredibly, Bulger recovered from his wound, served time in a prisoner-of-war camp on Johnson's Island, and was exchanged in the spring of 1864.

The surviving men in the 5th Texas also assumed that their colonel had died where they had left him. But Powell was stronger than they had assumed, stronger than he had even realized. When Union soliders found him, he was lying conscious on the western slope of the hill, surrounded by other wounded Confederates. He was carried from the rocks where he had fallen and placed near a badly wounded Union officer who had steadfastly refused to give up his colors during the battle. Later the wounded prisoners were moved to an open field and spread out on the ground. "There we lay," wrote Powell, "forlorn, wretched, ragged and battered."[15] In the night, it began to rain. Powell and his fellow prisoners shivered without blankets, most of them probably suffering from shock. Eventually Powell received treatment for his wounds from Federal doctors who told him he would soon die. Like Bulger, however, he eventually recovered. He also was shipped as a prisoner of war to Johnson's Island, where he remained until January 1865, when he was transferred to Fortress Monroe in Virginia. He was paroled a month later.

The Federal victory on Little Round Top did not necessarily ensure that the left flank of the Army of the Potomac was no longer vulnerable. Just before night fell, Colonel Rice ordered the 20th Maine to move to the summit of Big Round Top in an effort to anchor the Union left flank. Out of the approximately five hundred men that Colonel Chamberlain had led into the fight, only 198 could be counted after the charge. Six captains had commanded the 20th Maine's ten companies; now there were three. All of the officers in Company C had been wounded. When Rice asked Chamberlain to take the remainder of his regiment up to the top of the big hill—after having heard Colonel Joseph Fisher, who led the other brigade of Crawford's Pennsylvania Reserves, turn him down—the Maine colonel knew his men were tired and nearly spent. But he also knew that the flank must be protected, and he approached his exhausted men by saying, "Boys, I am asked if I can carry that hill in front," half expecting that the men would refuse to follow him. According to Corporal Coan, every man "sprang to his feet as one man," and Chamberlain threw out a skirmish line and led his men up the steep, wooded slopes of Big Round Top.[16]

Spear remarked that the order to ascend Big Round Top left the regiment "no time in which to bury our own dead, and we were compelled to leave them in other hands."[17] Once he reached the top of the hill, he sought out a tree where he could sit with his back to it and get some rest. He was weak from the exertion of combat, his malarial flare-up, diarrhea, and lack of food. Almost as soon as he sat down, Spear fell instantaneously asleep. He had no blanket, so when he awoke halfway through the night, he was shivering and his teeth were chattering. One of his men shared a blanket with him for the rest of the night; the blanket and the other man's body heat took away his chills.

In the terrifying night, when the slightest sound could set a man's heart racing and make his mouth go instantly dry, the 15th Alabama reassembled itself in a cleared field down the western slope of Big Round Top near the Slyder farmstead—not all that far away from the lines of the 20th Maine. Oates had regained his strength and taken command of the regiment again, but his heart was heavy. Somewhere in the dark, his brother remained where he had fallen, suffering from his wounds. But beyond the personal concern that fretted Oates, he also took notice of his weary men and the shattered state of his regiment. He ordered the roll called and discovered, much to his horror, that of the more than four hundred men he had led into battle that day (which did not include the detached water detail and Company A), only 223 were present for duty. More than half of the regiment's officers had been left on the battlefield; only nineteen answered the roll. Even though more men drifted in after the roll was taken, Oates's regiment nevertheless suffered close to 35 percent casualties in the fight for Little Round Top. In the 47th Alabama, losses were considerably less. Of the 347 men who went into the fight, the 47th lost 44 men killed, wounded, and missing.

The night was filled with the moans of the wounded, the startling sounds of sudden movement in the woods and over the rocks, and the bedeviling uncertainty that breeds understandable fear in soldiers who must remain on a battlefield in the darkness. Despite the bright moon above, the trees of the Round Tops blotted out the moonglow and kept the hills immersed in pitch blackness. "It was a solemn and lonely night," remembered Billy Jordan, who had found his way back to the 15th Alabama's bivouac after delivering his wounded comrade to the field hospital in the Confederate rear. Of the forty-two men in his company who had gone into the attack on Little Round Top, only eight survived unharmed. During the night, Oates ordered Company B, or what little remained of it, out on picket duty. Luckily, Jordan said with unintentional irony, "there was no disturbance or interruption by the enemy, everything being as quiet as a graveyard."[18]

But the men of Oates's regiment caused their own disturbance. Some of them, concerned about the large number of wounded left behind including Lieutenant John Oates, volunteered to go out into the dark without orders, back to the scene of the fighting on Little Round Top, and try to retrieve as many of their fellow Alabamians as they could find wounded on the ground. They reached the hill without being detected, managed to collect a few wounded officers (not young Oates, however), and suddenly ran into a Federal picket line. The Union troops opened fire. The rescue party had to abandon their wounded comrades and run to the safety of the Confederate lines. Colonel Oates later said: "I am sorry that I do not remember the names of those brave men who voluntarily went within the enemy's lines to relieve and save from capture [our] wounded comrades."[19] Out beneath the rocks of Little Round Top, where puddles of blood remained as ghastly evidence of the combat that had raged there, John Oates spent an unimaginable night alone with his pain and fear. For him, there was no certain knowledge that he would ever see the sun again.

BEFORE THE SUN HAD FULLY SET, Confederate efforts elsewhere on the battlefield brought the fighting for the day to a close. Along the low elevation of Cemetery Ridge, Barksdale's assault finally collided with a

formidable Union defensive line and sputtered out, while a Union counterattack, effectively undertaken with terrifyingly high casualties by the
1st Minnesota, turned back an attack launched near the Union center by
a brigade of Alabamians, from Hill's Third Corps, led by Brigadier General Cadmus Wilcox. Other troops from Hancock's Second Corps also
successfully stopped a heroic charge by Brigadier General Ambrose R.
Wright's Georgia brigade, also of General Hill's Third Corps, that streamed
across the Emmitsburg Road and into the open farm fields not far from a
distinctive copse of trees in the center of the ridge. But when Wright's
men reached the crest of Cemetery Ridge, Hancock threw in reinforcements from his own corps and from the First Corps—some of them urged
on by General Meade himself, waving his hat over his head and calling
out, "Come on, gentlemen"—and halted the Confederate attack as darkness spread over the bloodied fields. Meade was elated by the outcome.
When the shooting had stopped along the ridge, someone pointed out
that the day had been a pretty close call. "Yes," said Meade, "but it is all
right now, it is all right now."[20]

Everything, however, was not all right. A battle for Cemetery Hill and
Culp's Hill had begun with a Confederate artillery barrage that broke
the silence along the Union right flank at around the same time that
Longstreet had launched his attack to the south. Now, in the growing
darkness, it had become an infantry struggle for possession of the two hills
that formed the barb in the Union army's fishhook line. Ewell, in ordering
his infantry forward, had gotten a late start, perhaps in accordance with his
orders, but much later than Lee had expected, and much of the fighting
did not take place on the northern hills until dusk had fallen, Longstreet's
assault down along the Emmitsburg Road had run its course, and night
had begun to draw its heavy curtains. Coincidentally, the attack on Culp's
Hill, which was intended to initiate an *en echelon* assault first by Major
General Edward ("Allegheny") Johnson's division (Stonewall Jackson's
old division) against Culp's Hill and then by Major General Jubal Early's
division against Cemetery Hill, took place when Meade had made the
hills more vulnerable by pulling some of Major General Henry W.
Slocum's Twelfth Corps troops to the southern portion of the battlefield in
anticipation of their use as reinforcements in the Union defensive positions behind Sickles's shattered lines. Left to defend Culp's Hill was a
lone brigade commanded by Brigadier General George Greene, a descen-
dant of General Nathanael Greene, George Washington's capable second-
in-command during the Revolutionary War.

When Johnson's Confederates struck Culp's Hill at about 7:00 P.M., Greene had extended his lines and put his troops behind strong entrenchments and breastworks. Red flashes from the muskets streaked through the darkness, and the fight became heated and intense. In the dark and the smoke, men could barely see their comrades beside them; the enemy was practically invisible. Just in time, though, Federal reinforcements from the Eleventh Corps and from the Second Corps arrived to shore up Greene's lines, and while the Confederates were successful in occupying some of the Federal works along the lower slopes of the hill, Greene's men held their ground and prevented Johnson's forces from capturing the hill. Later the absent brigade of the Twelfth Corps returned to man the lines. More confused fighting broke out in the black night when the Federals discovered that their entrenchments had been captured by Confederates. Finally both sides decided to disengage and wait for the morning and daylight.

At roughly the same time that Johnson ordered his division to storm Culp's Hill, Jubal Early sent two brigades of his division forward against East Cemetery Hill and the formidable Union defenses that slanted across the hill's eastern brow and crest. Early's brigades struck the base of the hill and fierce fighting broke out along the Federal lines, which in this sector were defended by troops from the luckless Eleventh Corps. The Confederates drove through the gathering darkness with remarkable determination, breaking the defenses and making some of the Eleventh Corps troops flee in retreat yet one more time; many of the Eleventh Corps men did, however, bravely stand their ground. As a result, the Louisianians and North Carolinians moved steadily up the slopes and reached two Union batteries installed behind lunettes cut into the hillside. There, in the moonglow, cannoneers wrestled with Confederate infantrymen in a bloody hand-to-hand struggle. Some of the artillerymen drew their revolvers and fired into the faces of their foes. The fight for the hill was excruciatingly brutal and deadly. One of Early's brigadiers, Colonel Isaac Avery, fell with a mortal wound. Before he died, and while the battle still swirled around him, he scribbled on a scrap of paper addressed to his friend, Major Samuel Tate: "Major: Tell my father I died with my face to the enemy."[21] In the end, Federal reinforcements from the Eleventh and Second Corps flowed into the fight and repulsed Early's forces by running them off the slopes.

By midnight, the fighting at Gettysburg had died down. Under the phosphorus moon and the twinkling stars, the night carried the sounds of wounded men all along the scrambled lines of both armies as they cried out for water, for help, for God's mercy. From Culp's Hill to Big Round Top, the situation was the same: the armies had fought with all their might, giving up thousands of lives, and gaining little for their mortal efforts. At the end of the day, the Army of the Potomac remained in its strong defensive position, its flanks now strengthened and fortified, and the final outcome at Gettysburg had been all but sealed. Lee would have to work one of his miracles to crush the Union army in whatever fight was left to come. His greatest challenge was the same one he had faced and not fully met on July 2: to get his now depleted army and his various lieutenants to coordinate their efforts and correct their fumbling ways in whatever course they might follow when daylight returned to the scarred and desolate battlefield, bringing with it the certainty of more fighting and the surety of more death.

BEHIND THE ROUND TOPS, along the Taneytown Road, the field hospitals churned with activity as the surgeons and their assistants tried to deal with the overwhelming number of wounded men that kept arriving for treatment. In the Weikert house, Drs. Wagner and Billings did what they could for the Fifth Corps wounded who filled the house and every available space in the barn and outbuildings and the nearby orchard. Under the bright moonlight, the straight rows of maimed men, laid out in the adjacent fields with no protection from the night air, looked like a strange, silvery crop of human forms. Near the farmhouse, piles of severed limbs began to grow into formidable mounds, creating a hideous spectacle: a miniature mountain range of discarded arms, legs, hands, and feet. Billings said he performed a huge number of operations; he couldn't remember how many exactly. But he felt certain that he had "received and fed 750 wounded," and he worked through the night without pause.[22] A yellow flag had been placed outside the house to mark it as a hospital site.

The price paid by the Army of the Potomac for defending Little Round Top was very high. Five Union heroes of the hill were brought to the Weikert farm. The bodies of Lieutenant Charles Hazlett and Colonel Paddy O'Rorke were laid in the yard.[23] Lieutenant Porter Farley, who accompanied the party that carried O'Rorke to the Weikert yard, could not deal with the reality of his commander's death. He admitted years later: "I choked with grief as I stood beside the lifeless form. I had known and loved him well, and in these last few weeks better than ever, my position as his adjutant naturally leading to intercourse of the most familiar kind, as day by day we ate our soldier's fare together and often at night slept with the same blanket covering us."[24]

The dying Colonel Strong Vincent had been carried to the house and laid in a bed after having being struck down on Little Round Top. His bugler, Oliver Norton, went to visit him during the night. When Norton arrived at his side, the colonel looked "very pale," and he was unable to speak. With his eyes, Vincent seemed to want to know the outcome of the battle. "The boys," said Norton, "are still there, Colonel."[25] Vincent's eyes lighted up and he smiled.

Vincent lingered on for several days. Generals Sykes and Barnes came to visit him. He asked for his wife to be sent word of his condition with a request for her to come to Gettysburg. A message was sent, but it did not reach Vincent's wife in time. He suffered severe pain, but he tried not to show it. "I presume," said Vincent, "that I have done my last fighting."[26] He grew so weak that he could no longer speak. On July 7, a telegram from President Lincoln, commissioning Vincent a brigadier general, was read to him, but he could not acknowledge whether he understood that the president had promoted him for bravery in the line of duty. Vincent died later that day. His body was transported to Erie for burial.

Tillie Pierce's head was swimming with all the excitement and horror she witnessed inside the house and outside in the farm yard. Through the dreary night, she was appalled at the number of wounded who were brought to the farmyard. "The scene," she wrote, "had become terrible beyond description." She volunteered, nevertheless, to assist the doctors and nurses. One soldier, who sat on the floor of the house as he cared for a wounded man beside him, beckoned her and asked for a slice of bread. After bringing him a piece, Tillie sat down and asked the wounded man if he was hurt badly and if he suffered much. The soldier answered yes to both questions, and added that he hoped in the morning he would be better. Tenderly, Tillie offered to do anything she could for him. "Will you promise me to come back in the morning to see me?" he asked. She said she would, and the man smiled.

When she returned the next day, the sun was already high in the sky. She hurried down to the room where she had left her wounded friend. An attendant was by his side. But Tillie immediately saw that the wounded man had died during the night. "Do you know who this is?" asked the attendant. "No sir," Tillie replied. "This," said the attendant, "is the body of General Weed." She would "never forget that name," wrote Tillie many years later.[27] Weed's prediction had come true. He was as dead as Julius Caesar. His body was taken out in the yard and placed next to Hazlett's and O'Rorke's. Vincent's body would later fill the row. Little Round Top had been very expensive indeed.

13

Night of the Dead

Three was nothing but the night, an interminable night of sadness and sighs. In the darkness (an utter blackness unknown to people living in the age of electricity), the shadow of death passed invisibly over the battlefield, claiming more victims, casting itself over the weak forms of the pitiful wounded who lacked the will or the strength to crawl away from death's immutable shroud. Heaviness could be found in the hearts of all men on the battlefield that dreadful night, a heaviness like the one described by the Psalmist, but without the promise of uplifting joy in the morning. In so many respects, it seemed like the world's last night.

Among the Texans, worn out and reduced in number by the cost of battle, John West spent an uncomfortable night without a blanket, pondering the great "slaughter of our men." He had asked his friends to safeguard his Bible and "the little tin cup, which baby gave me" in case he should fall in battle. He retrieved those items now. Looking around for a discarded blanket, he was lucky to find one and settle down for the night. "I started from Texas to find a fight," he wrote later to his wife, "and I have made a success of it." Then he begged his wife to kiss the children for him. In a different letter, he confessed to his brother: "Suffice it to say that I have endured more than I believed myself capable of."[1] But he was heartsick; he missed his wife, his children, home, and Texas. And he had no idea if he would ever see them again.

After dark, Lieutenant Colonel Phillip Work, commander of the 1st Texas, sent to the rear three Parrott guns his regiment had captured from Smith's 4th New York battery on Houck's Ridge, near Devil's Den. He was unable, however, to remove the three other guns that had fallen into the Texans' hands. Work took comfort in the fact that while he couldn't move the pieces, neither could the enemy get them back, for they were well protected by a potential musket fire that kept the Federals "in check."[2]

The men of the 4th and 5th Texas rested on their arms that night. For some of the soldiers, the dreary darkness was hellish. Val Giles of the 4th Texas wrote: "Alexander Dumas says the devil gets in a man seven times a day, and if the average is not over seven times, he is almost a saint. At Gettysburg that night, it was about seven devils to each man." Officers and men could be heard cursing and arguing, the wounded wailed in pain, and sporadic musket fire broke the occasional silence. Giles supposed that not a single man on the battlefield "cared a snap for the golden rule, or . . . could have remembered one line of the Lord's Prayer."[3]

Most of the Texans who had fallen in the attack on Little Round Top were out of reach, so their comrades were forced to listen to their groans and calls for help through the hideous night. Many years later one man in the 4th Texas lamented: "It has been forty years now, and I don't remember the names of my own company that were lost."[4] He wanted to remember, but he could not. Perhaps it was just as well. The casualties in Hood's division were enormous. In Robertson's brigade, the Texans suffered mightily. Of the 479 effectives who went into the fight with the 3rd Arkansas, 182 were killed, wounded, or missing. The 1st Texas had a fighting strength of 426 men before the battle; at Gettysburg, the regiment lost 97 men. Casualty rates were even higher in Private West's 4th Texas. Of the 415 men that accompanied West into combat, 112 were killed, wounded, or missing. But the 5th Texas suffered the worst casualties in the entire brigade. That regiment marched 409 men into battle; it lost 211 during the fighting, or nearly 52 percent of its effective strength.

Law's brigade, which took up a position along the base of Big Round Top to the right of the Texans, fared no better. Oates was depressed by the 34 percent of his men he had lost on Little Round Top. Other regiments in the brigade lost fewer men, but the casualty figures were still appalling. The 4th Alabama went in with 346 men and lost 87; the 44th Alabama had 363 effectives going into combat and suffered 94 casualties; the 47th Alabama lost 44 casualties out of a battle strength of 347; and the 48th Alabama, with 374 effectives, came out of the fight with 102 dead, wounded, and missing. Things were worse in Tige Anderson's brigade. His Georgians had been slaughtered. The 8th and 9th Georgia regiments each lost more than 50 percent of their men. The 11th Georgia, which went into the battle with 310 men, came out of it with only 109, suffering a casualty rate of almost 65 percent.

Confederate dead in the Slaughter Pen

Entangled in the statistics were the human stories of suffering, pain, and hardship. Captain Barziza of Company C, 4th Texas, mused about the cost of the assault on Little Round Top: "The price of liberty is not only 'eternal vigilance,' but oceans of red blood. To die a freeman, or to live a slave, is often the bitter alternative, and infamous is he who hesitates in the choice. The reward is greater than the sacrifice; and upon the dreadful ruin which war inaugurates and leaves behind, the Temple of Liberty is reared, fair, firm, proud, blood-cemented, and baptized in fire."[5] Those were high-flying words, the kind of words behind which Civil War soldiers hid their true feelings, their deepest emotions.

But not all Confederates could take such a philosophical and bloodless view of their situation. Private William Fletcher of the 5th Texas, for example, found himself struggling with profound discouragement as the night wore on. He reflected on the day's events. In his estimation, "it looked as though our officers were blind." How could anyone have ordered such a senseless attack against such a strong position? Why hadn't they tried to swing around the Federal flank? Through the dead hours of the night, Fletcher felt safe enough behind his pile of stones, provided

A dead Confederate soldier in the Slaughter Pen

he didn't move or raise his head. It was not a heartening place to be, especially after such a dreadful and bloody day. "I was at the time," Fletcher confessed, "on the dark side of life's thoughts." Another Texan expressed his feelings straightforwardly: "At Gettysburg we suffered defeat, bloody, terrible and disastrous defeat."[6]

Across the Valley of Death, where Plum Run now flowed pink in the bright moonlight, the Federals occupying Little Round Top spent an equally miserable and weary night, although the realization of their victory did help to boost their spirits, if only temporarily. The 44th New York, wrote one of its officers, had "fought one of its hardest battles and gained its greatest victory." The struggle for Little Round Top, he said, "was the greatest fight I have ever been in." An enlisted man in the regiment told his cousin, "This is the hardest summer's work I ever did in my life and probably harder than we will have to do again."[7]

The Federal casualties seemed to defy comprehension. Among the highest were those of the 20th Maine: 125 out of 386 men who participated in the fight, a casualty rate of slightly more than 32 percent. In the other regiments of Vincent's brigade, the losses were less severe, but dra-

Dead Confederate soldiers in woods near the Slaughter Pen

matic nonetheless. The 16th Michigan lost 60 men out of 263; the 83rd Pennsylvania, 55 out of 295; and the 44th New York, 111 out of 391. Battery D, 5th U.S. Artillery, suffered 13 casualties out of the 68 men who manned the guns. Weed's brigade was also hit hard. The 140th New York, which arrived at a crucial moment on the crest of the hill, was down 133 men out of 449; the 146th New York, 28 out of 456; the 91st Pennsylvania, 19 out of 220; and the 155th Pennsylvania, 19 out of 362. Losses were lighter in McCandless's brigade of the Pennsylvania Reserves, which had been led in its heroic charge by General Crawford. The 1st Pennsylvania Reserves experienced 46 casualties out of 379 in the regiment; the 2nd Pennsylvania Reserves, 37 out of 233; the 6th Pennsylvania Reserves, 24 out of 324; and the 13th Pennsylvania Reserves, 48 out of 298. The 98th Pennsylvania of Wheaton's brigade, Sixth Corps, which assisted the Pennsylvania Reserves in the charge across the Valley of Death, had 11 casualties out of 351 men who went into the battle.

Of these casualties, 181 men lost their lives defending Little Round Top. In the 20th Maine, Captain Samuel Keene of Company F felt the shock of these losses. His company suffered seven killed, twelve wounded,

Union dead on the southern portion of the battlefield

and three missing. His casualties, he said, "were the most severe of any company." Of the dead, he wrote: "Poor fellows, I lost some of my best and bravest men. God help and console the afflicted friends." Private Harlan P. Bailey in Company G wrote home to report that the 20th Maine "is getting very small." After the battle, his company stacked arms with only twelve men present.[8]

But the survivors of the fight for Little Round Top, Union and Confederate, seemed to believe the cost was worth it. "I think with little help now we can brake the Back Bone of this Rebellion," wrote an officer in the 44th New York.[9] Few of the men who lived through the battle thought that their effort was meaningless, that they had fought for nothing, that their efforts on the slopes of Little Round Top lacked significance. On the contrary, the old veterans of both sides recalled the struggle with a certain lust and wrapped their memories in the protective shields of glory, romance, duty, and courage. To the veterans who looked back on the battle, sometimes as many as twenty-five or fifty years after the fact, every man who fought there was a hero.

But that is not the way soldiers described the struggle for Little Round Top immediately after its conclusion. In letters, diaries, and journals, these men wrote very specifically of casualties, of friends who had fallen, of neighbors who had been lost. Consistently, as if working from a primer, they expressed two fundamental reactions to what they had just experienced. The first was a heartfelt gladness, an exhilaration, that by the grace of God they had survived it all, as if some miracle had been performed in their individual favor. The second, and the saddest, was a deep lamentation that by the will of God so many of their comrades had been killed, wounded, or captured. Among those lost, they mentioned those soldiers whom they knew the best, their messmates or the young men they had grown up with back home. In the gloom of the night, their thoughts focused on their own mortality, either by grasping the reality that they personally had escaped death or by comprehending the actuality that some of their comrades had not.

In the 44th New York, Sergeant E. R. Goodrich of Company A went out on picket duty and took stock of what he saw around him. "The ground was literally covered with dead and wounded," he wrote. Many of them were Texans. He spent the night "attending to the [enemy] wounded, giving them water, fixing them in easy positions, cutting off shoes and helping them in every way I could." It was hard labor, emotionally taxing. Some of the men were "crying, some praying, some swearing and all wanting help." The calls of water from the wounded were constant. One soldier in the 44th tried to help a wounded Confederate by giving him a drink of water, but the man died in his arms. He was able to comfort two other wounded Texans, wetting their wounds and covering them with a blanket. The Federal picket line that night was a miserable place to be. "That was the most lonesome picket duty I ever did," admitted the New Yorker.[10]

Many of the Confederate casualties were beyond reach, however, in the no-man's-land between the lines. When the cries of the wounded "became fainter," recalled William Brown, "we knew that their lives were fast passing away."[11] Those closer at hand often received help from the Federal soldiers in the advanced line. In the 83rd Pennsylvania, the men carried in the Confederate wounded on their backs and supported others as they limped along. Down in front of the rocks earlier defended by the 20th Maine, there were approximately fifty enemy dead strewn across the slope, and the wounded—including John Oates—were also plentiful. Confederate prisoners provided the labor to carry the 20th Maine's wounded to the rear. But details from the 20th brought in the Rebel wounded despite the fact that enemy sharpshooters still pelted the area with minié balls.

Along the western face of the hill, Weed's brigade worked diligently to build a breastwork out of stones and to collect their dead and wounded. Nearly all the surviving Federal letters and memoirs speak of building stone walls during the night and strengthening the defenses of Little Round Top in anticipation that the enemy might try again to capture the hill. But it was the cries, the moans, and the whispers of the wounded that the soldiers most remembered, often in such a way that suggested the haunting reality of the night. The wounded would, "in piteous tones . . . call out their name or company and regiment," recalled one soldier in the 91st Pennsylvania. Sleep was nearly impossible, despite the physical and emotional fatigue of the soldiers. "We lay on our guns," remembered an artillerist in Hazlett's battery, "but could not sleep." The cries of the wounded were deafening. "Some were praying," wrote the cannoneer, "some were swearing, and one was preaching and exhorting the men to forgive their enemies." It took nearly two hours for the wounded of Weed's brigade to be brought in by details from the different regiments and by ambulance crews. For Lieutenant Benjamin Rittenhouse, who had assumed command of Hazlett's battery, it seemed as if "there were spirits flitting from Little Round Top to Devil's Den and back, all night."[12]

In the hospitals, the Union and Confederate wounded suffered just as much, if not more, than they had on the slopes of Little Round Top. Sergeant Charles Sprague of the 44th New York, wounded in the fighting, spent a night of terror in a stone house, probably the Weikert house, behind Little Round Top. It was one of the longest nights of his life. "I heard every tick and every stroke of the old clock as I lay in the old parents' bedroom," he wrote. Around him "rows of men of all ranks and of both armies covered the floors, each one seeming to have his own peculiar groan or cry." Shouts of "mother" and "water" seemed to be syncopated with the ticking of the clock. Beside him, a wounded man snored through the night muttering "pop" and "mom" in his sleep. So far no one had bothered to look at Sprague's wounds, and he did not receive any medical attention until the following day when the chaplain of the 83rd Pennsylvania "saved my life" by giving him "a tumbler of whisky."[13]

A soldier in the 140th New York found chaos as well as human suffering in the hospitals. The wounded were "in a horrible condition." No one had given them any treatment, their wounds had received no dressings, and they lay out in the open with no shelter. The injured soldiers waited and waited, but still no doctors came. "Some one must be to blame for this," asserted the New Yorker with indignation. The fault, he thought, could be attributed to the division's chief surgeon, whom he called the "chief butcher." All the other surgeons, the "young butchers," were under his charge. But the doctors, always in short supply, were working as hard as they could. Cyrus Bacon, a surgeon in the 16th Michigan, simply noted in his journal: "Operations, amputations, etc."[14] Exhausted and overwhelmed by the endless rows of patients, Bacon did not get any rest until nearly midnight, when he fell asleep under an apple tree.

Under the protection of night's black mantle, Federal burial parties from different regiments were sent out to find their dead on the hill and bury them. Soldiers considered burial details the worst kind of duty, for they inevitably brought on depression and a demoralization among the men forced to transport the dead, dig their graves, and cover them over with dirt. James Woodworth in the 44th New York helped bury his dead captain. Four men from another company in the 44th carried four of their dead comrades from the field and buried them. "It was hard, I tell you," wrote one of the soldiers in the burial party. "They had stood right up beside us in the ranks all through everything until now."[15]

A burial party from the 140th New York, which included John Huntington, dug graves on the slopes of Little Round Top for the six dead in its company. Describing this task to a friend at home, Huntington remarked: "I will say that we have done well to live through so much hardship." On the eastern hillside, Porter Farley witnessed the burial of twenty-six of his comrades from the 140th in "a row of inanimate forms lay[ing] side by side beneath the trees." There was, he said, no funeral ceremony, and only the shallowest of graves could be dug. "In the darkness of the night," he wrote, "silently and with bitter dejection, each company buried its dead."[16] The burials went on through the night. The Confederate dead were left where they lay. The night was warm, and occasionally the snipers on both sides fired into the dark, never really knowing if their bullets would hit anything at all. Overhead, the moonlight flickered through the dark trees, and it cast an eerie light down on the gray rocks of Little Round Top.

An unfinished Confederate grave

All through the dark hours, the soldiers on both sides confronted the fruits of war, the wounded and the dead scattered across the rough landscape—a purgatory of boulders, loose rocks, and tangled undergrowth. The dead beckoned their living comrades. Hidden in the dark, they waited to be discovered—soldiers who had sacrificed themselves in the summer sunlight and who lay now in the shimmering moonlight, dark corpses in silent, eternal repose—men who would never see another sunrise, boys who would never see their mothers again. To their surviving comrades, the loss of their friends, their messmates, brought on a deep and harrowing sadness. "The exultation of victory," said Farley, "was soon chilled by the dejection which oppressed us as we counted and realized the cost of all that had been won."[17]

Rarely did the men who survived a fight feel elation for very long; rarely did they possess the energy to celebrate their victory. Mostly there was sadness and a feeling of profound emptiness: sadness at the sight of death and destruction that covers the battlefield; sadness at the loss of one's friends, comrades, brothers-in-arms; emptiness from realizing the high price of war, the toll in human lives that have been spent so that you may stand, still breathing, still blinking, still thinking, while so many others lay lifeless before you. The survivors of the battle would experience a heartsickness that came from knowing that the place of a comrade, a friend, was, as Captain Barziza of the 4th Texas wrote, "forever vacated, his battles fought, his marches ended, his future fate mysterious, unknown, and . . . dreadful."[18]

But the survivors must carry on. "Stern duty," said Barziza, "bids the survivor to forget," although forgetting everything or one's closest friends was impossible.[19] When friends were lost in war, in fact, they never seemed quite gone. They were always there, marching by one's side, or perhaps they were off with another unit on detachment, or had simply fallen behind and would catch up at nightfall. The battlefield dead remained as something more than specters in the lives of the war's survivors, even long after the war was over. They came to the living in dreams, they appeared vividly in remembrances, and they endured for as long as the survivor—the friend, the messmate—lived his natural life. In the memories of their friends, the dead were not the ghosts of the past or the hauntings of a nightmare. They were always with the veterans, tenting on the old camp ground. "The *past* and the *future* meet in the memory of the dead," wrote George B. Taylor, a Virginian, in 1863. "The sweetest and brightest link in the chain that stretches back over the past, binds us to the dead; and that chain stretches forward to eternity and attaches itself to the throne of the living God." In this way, said Taylor, "death joins on to life; and all that is sacred in memory connects itself with all."[20]

The struggle for Little Round Top, like each of the escalating battles of the Civil War, battles that kept getting bloodier and more costly one after the other, forced Northerners and Southerners alike to deal with death in ways that had not existed before, to confront the horrible realities of so many young men dying away from their loved ones, in the throes of agony, and beyond the consolation of family or friends. In the nineteenth century, the people living in the North and the South were accustomed to death and the rituals of death in ways that modern Americans are not. Death played an important role in antebellum life, defining the boundaries of the life cycle, the manifestation of religious beliefs, and the very meaning of life itself. Unexpected death was ubiquitous, taking infants and mothers especially. Christian devotion, however, promised rewards after death, the reward of eternal life, so Americans thought often of death and wrote about its frequency, of its being a natural path toward salvation.

Americans in the Civil War era also regarded death, including burial customs, within the context of a romanticized and sentimentalized culture. The expectation was that death would occur at home, in a family setting, with loved ones at the beside at the hour of passing. Family and friends would comfort the dying, reassuring them that all would be well after their death, that they would be remembered, and that life would go on for the living. In this way, loved ones affirmed the reality of death, faced its consequences directly, and informed the dying of an unlikely recovery, thus preparing themselves as well as the dying for the imminent actuality of the end of life. In reply, the dying person would offer comfort and express his or her willingness to enter the gates of heaven and enjoy a new unity, and a more intense spiritual relationship, with the Lord.

The Civil War helped to transform the American way of death, which had largely been a personal and private drama, into a ceremonial and public ritual. Death visited nearly every American household during the war, touching nearly every community, every family, every individual. In time, the losses became unbearably plentiful, and as the war ground on, mashing lives like a great killing machine, it seemed as if the deaths would never stop. These fatalities forever changed the nation and the people who survived the war. No one could calculate what the loss of this life might mean to their loved ones, community, state, and nation. No one could ever really know what these dead men might otherwise have contributed to their world; no one could know the descendants they never procreated—perhaps brilliant scientists, great statesmen, natural teachers, humble workers—who might have changed the world for the better. No one could really comprehend the loss that mankind experienced with the deaths of these soldiers, Northerners and Southerners. The loss, in fact, was immeasurable.[21]

Nothing could prepare Americans for the magnitude of death and destruction that the Civil War produced from 1861 to 1865. Battlefield and field hospital deaths violated all of the American assumptions, cultural expectations, and norms about death. Soldiers could not die "ordinary" deaths, nor could they participate in the comforting dialogue between the dying and assembled loved ones. War deaths occurred away from family and friends, in isolated and unknown places like Gettysburg and Sharpsburg and Manassas. At the time of death, the battle might be in its full fury, so that there could be no one to console the dying or help him cross over into paradise. The dead on the battlefield might become unrecognizable, thus losing their identity completely in the moment of death.

At home, loved ones would feel shock when they received news of a death in the family or among friends; they, too, could not participate in the dialogue of comfort between the dying and those who kept the death watch at bedside. They often could not know where their lost soldier had been buried, or even whether his grave was identified. Some households, of course, never received word that their soldiers had died; they reached that conclusion only after failing to receive word or waiting endlessly for him to come home. Worse, there was no way of telling whether their soldiers had passed peacefully, with full acceptance of God's will, into the hereafter, and many loved ones at home were left with unsettling suspicions that their soldiers had died violent deaths and had suffered great pain, heartache, and loneliness before the end finally came. The thought that soldiers died anonymous deaths brought great torment to families and friends at home. It was none too pleasant a thought for the soldiers themselves, who feared dying alone and being thrown into a mass, unmarked grave.

Sentimentalizing death allowed Americans to deal with its reality by domesticating it, reducing its horror, and covering it with a layer of romance. The picture of heaven created during the war years stressed the domestic bliss of the afterlife and promised that life, although in a dramatically different form, would continue after death. The end of life thus was a process, a transforming means by which the individual reached spiritual fulfillment and contentment. Sentimentalism also enabled Americans to deal with the disturbing anonymity of soldiers who died on battlefields far removed from the home front and in places most people had never heard of before. The sentiment that sprang out of the Civil War tended to idealize war death and reduce the trauma of anonymous death for the comrades and loved ones who still walked among the living.

The hope was for a "good death" (sometimes referred to as an "honorable death"), whether on the battlefield or not. A good death taught a positive lesson about life, revealed the piety of the dying individual, consoled the loved ones in their loss, and generally reaffirmed the truth of Christ's resurrection and the promise of life after death for all those who truly believed.[22] But a good death, or an ordinary death, was not possible on the battlefield or in the field hospital, at least not according to the accepted cultural mores that called for a dialogue between the dying and his loved ones at the death bed and that stressed the importance of funeral rites, a church burial, and mourning rituals. Yet the war brought about changes in these mores to the extent that soldiers died "good deaths" after all, or so it seemed, and the proof of that was often shared by comrades who wrote letters of condolence to fallen soldiers' families or, in some cases, close friends. Unattended deaths and the upheaval they might cause in the minds and hearts of those Americans who remained on the homefront were overcome in many instances by letters of condolence that confirmed how well the soldier had died and how much, despite the altered circumstances of the battlefield and hospital, his death could be viewed as a good death.

Letters of condolence typically contained accounts of the last moments of the deceased that deliberately disclosed how the soldiers had died a good death, that is, a death with specific purpose, a death that at once revealed the religious faith, the innate goodness, the inspiring last words, and the brimming patriotism of the fallen. A soldier struck down in battle, no matter how much of a reprobate he might actually be, could not die a bad death. "I couldn't imagine," wrote one soldier in the 8th Illinois, "the soul of a soldier who had died in the defense of his country being consigned to an orthodox hell, whatever his opinion might be of the plan of salvation."[23] Through letters of condolence, the relatives and friends of dead soldiers became linked with the deceased and the places where they had ended their lives; despite the often great distances between battlefield and home front, these letters closed the gap and gave the bereaved a sense of closeness that partially mitigated their absence from the sides of those whom they had lost. These letters often became the only proof, the only manifestation, that the dead on America's battlefields had not died for nothing.

An officer in the 44th New York, Orsell C. Brown, found it his "painful duty" to send news to a father of his son's death on Little Round Top. Brown's letter followed the pattern of almost every other letter of condolence written during the Civil War, for it contained stock ingredients, almost as if the writer were following a recipe, that included the writer's regrets ("painful duty"), a description of how the son had died in battle, references to premonitions of death by the deceased, reassurance that the dead soldier had performed his military service nobly and gallantly, evidence of the dead man's virtues and sterling character, information about the burial, and spiritual consolation that the dead son was now residing in heaven.

Brown said that the lieutenant's death had caused a "deep gloom and [a] sadness" that hung over the regiment. Lieutenant Dunham, "a noble man" in whom Brown had taken a personal interest and whom he called his "best friend," had died bravely, struck by a minié ball under the right eye, "while nobly and gallantly urging his men to duty." Brown assured the father that his son had died instantly and did not suffer. All of young Dunham's personal effects were in Brown's hands, and he promised to send them home to the father at the first opportunity. Before he died, Lieutenant Dunham had given his father's address to Brown, informing his fellow officer that "I might have to tell you of his death—and dear sir, so it has proved." The company buried the lieutenant under a peach tree "in his blanket and poncho, and his burial place [was] plainly marked."

After the burial, said Brown, he passed the lieutenant's grave and he halted a few minutes to remember his friend. "Freely did the tears course down my cheeks," he wrote, "to think that poor Dunham was never more to be with us; that his well loved form was made to lie low by the hand of some cursed traitor." Brown made sure he set down accurate directions to the grave site, so that it could be found at a later time. He wanted Dunham's father to know that his son "was highly appreciated by his company and all officers, particularly the Colonel." "Be assured," Brown said, "that Lieut. Dunham fell in a noble cause, and God has called him home." And then, Brown added a touching note of heartfelt emotion, departing from the usual contents of such letters of condolence. "Sad and lonely without our friends," he wrote solemnly, "I cannot but weep with you."[24]

All soldier deaths, then, were good deaths in the sense that soldiers died for the cause, Union or Confederate, and patriotism and loyalty to one's country were seen as things worth dying for—noble ideals that often came to be regarded as sacred in their own right. In fact, the prevailing sentimentalism of the age often united patriotism and Christianity into a single entity. Walt Whitman, writing of a dead soldier in a poem entitled "A Sight in Camp in the Day-Break Grey and Dim," believed that the young man looked familiar: "I think this face of yours is the face of Christ himself."[25] In this sense, an honorable death could also be a courageous death, what Oliver Wendell Holmes Jr. called a "soldier's death."[26] Many years after the battle, a veteran of the 155th Pennsylvania and the fight on Little Round Top declared: "We know that every deed of peerless valor, every act of patriotic devotion, every example of exalted self-sacrifice, even unto death and martyrdom, offered in the Nation's defense is lifted above all vulgar destiny and will live as long as the Republic honors her heroes."[27] The stigma of dishonor and cowardice was sometimes regarded by soldiers as a worse fate than death itself. Godliness was a source of courage, so a pious soldier would be much more likely to display courage on the battlefield than not.

Soldiers became resigned to the fact that God would either protect them or single them out for sacrifice. With their lives resting so firmly in God's hands, soldiers realized that there was little they could do to change their fates. It would do well, of course, to find cover in the midst of a hail of bullets; but it was also true that divine will determined whether one was hit, whether one would die. Soldiers found comfort in maintaining their antebellum ideas of death and their faith in a Christian god. To do otherwise meant confronting the realities of death that they saw around them. It was easier to harden themselves against death or to understand it in spiritual terms. Either way, it was better not to think about it at all. Many soldiers came to see death without emotion, regarding it as commonplace, refusing to dwell on death itself in their letters or conversations, forcing themselves to become indifferent to the death that so often surrounded them. The vast harvest of death produced by the Civil War required soldiers to develop a stoicism and a fatalism by which they hoped to protect themselves from the harsh reality of death and a sense of their own fragile mortality.

Yet many of the deaths they encountered on the battlefield could not be dismissed or ignored; worse, they had a personal impact on the soldiers who survived. Describing the battle to his father, Charles Brandegee of Weed's brigade informed his parent that the fight had resulted in "a great loss of both officers and men." Never before had he "such an opportunity of seeing the glory, i.e., the horrors of war." In front of his position on Little Round Top, he counted "30 dead rebels." Another soldier, this one from the 44th New York, agreed. "Great is the slaughter," he wrote his sister. "Oh, it is awful." Not only Federals saw the battle as bloody and murderous. Rufus Felder, a Texan, put the matter very plainly to his mother: "The slaughter on both sides was terrible."[28]

The soldiers dealt not only with the massive and overwhelming carnage they had helped to create on Little Round Top. By necessity, they confronted as well deep personal grief, personal losses. Among the dead were messmates, acquaintances, admired officers; in some cases, the dead were friends they had known since boyhood. Private Mark Smither of the 5th Texas informed his mother simply, but not without feeling, that his friend, James A. McDade, had been killed on Little Round Top. "He was a noble boy," said Smither. An infantryman from Rochester in the 44th New York wrote home to inform his father that "John Evans, son of Evan Evans, who lived across the Square," was killed. Erastus Harris of the same regiment let a mother know that her son, Chester Smith, had died in battle and was buried in one of two trenches on the reverse slope of Little Round Top. Hoping to offer consolation in his letter, and provide some greater meaning to her son's otherwise senseless death, Harris wrote: "He fell defending the cause of freedom and he sleeps on a soil unpoluted by the footsteps of a slave."[29]

Losing friends made war just as hellish and depleting as having to face an enemy volley. After the contest for Little Round Top, Captain Frank Park of the 15th Alabama performed his "painful duty" of telling Benjamin Gardner that his son, Samuel, had fallen at Gettysburg. "During the struggle," Park explained, "your brave boy received a minnie ball in the head, which killed him instantly." Unfortunately, said Park, the body was left on the field after the Alabamians retreated, and that fact had made Park grow sad and melancholy. "In the death of your son," he wrote, "I have lost a pleasant associate and friend, the service of a faithful, vigilant and brave soldier, and you a noble boy." Having affection for someone made death all the more difficult. "I am afraid I thought too much of Sam," Park confessed.[30]

Colonel William Oates assumed the agonizing responsibility of writing a letter of condolence informing the father of Lieutenant Barnett C. Cody, one of Oates's childhood friends, of his son's death from wounds received during the fight for Little Round Top. Understandably, Oates found it difficult to separate his friendship and his duty as a commanding officer, so his letter blended elements of his dual relationship with the deceased. Bud Cody died in a Union hospital on July 23, 1863, hanging on to his life by a thread for nearly three weeks after the battle was over. Cody's death—and the death of Oates's brother John, who died in the same hospital two days after Cody died—nearly unhinged the colonel; the grief was too much for him to bear. "I feel discomfited and exceed[ing]ly gloomy—even reckless and miserable," Oates told the Reverend Edmund Cody, Bud's father.

Little Round Top, for Colonel Oates, was a personal catastrophe, not only because of his failure to lead his regiment to victory there, but more because of the price he and his men had had to pay in their bloody assault. "I have not only lost my dearest relative on earth," said Oates, "but two of my dearest friends." Young Cody was "my dear Boy friend." Oates acknowledged that he loved him with the same tender feelings he had felt toward his own brother. The loss was unbearable, for Bud Cody had been a rare man of great merit and virtue: "Noble and manly in bearing, brave, honest, reliable and true[,] he challenged the admiration of all who knew him. Strict in discipline, accurate in drill and obedient and respectful to superiors[,] he was unsurpassed as an officer by any in the Confederate army of his age." Not a religious man himself, Oates offered some thoughts he knew the Reverend Cody would be thinking: "Poor Boy[,] he has gone to a better world." Then Oates wrote something startling: "Your loss is truly great—but not so great as mine." He admitted that the Reverend Cody had lost his son, but "I have lost my dearest relative and two of my best friends and sadly do I feel my own bereavement."[31]

Obviously, such letters of condolence served a double purpose—to inform families at home that their fathers, husbands, sons, and brothers had died on the battlefield, and to allow the writers to express their own feelings about that loss, often in very personal, very private ways. Some soldiers might have been able to harden themselves to the reality of death that became so much a part of their lives, so much a part of being in the army, so much a part of serving in this cruel war; but, clearly, oth-

"An Incident of Gettysburg—The Last Thought of a Dying Father"

ers could not. Orsell Brown and William Oates felt what so many of their fellow soldiers experienced after the fight for Little Round Top: a sad, lonely emptiness that death had laid upon them and that they could not easily shake off.

Something unusual was happening. Just at the moment when this war was becoming more brutal, more costly in human lives than anyone ever could have imagined, the old hardened attitude of the soldiers toward death was breaking apart, cracked by the sheer multitude of deaths and the desperate style of fighting that would now dominate the battlefields. Soldiers were finding, although they may have been as unaware of it as Brown and Oates, that the old defenses against sadness and heartache would not work anymore, would not enable them to wall off their emotions, maintain their stoicism, and act as if the deaths that occurred all around them could be ignored. The hard war that now had emerged in 1863, and that would grow even harder in the coming months, shattered their dispassionate armor against feeling emotional pain and a deep sense of loss. The war and all its inhumanity had laid those emotions bare, and Brown and Oates could not help slipping out of the accepted conventions, the old devices that had protected them from sorrow and grief. Brown and Oates, and so many of their comrades, had come to experience the very real pain of war—a pain that could not be avoided, that had to be felt, and that would grow worse as the war continued to cut its swath through America. For at the bottom of the feelings that Brown and Oates expressed with such heartfelt sincerity in their letters of condolence to the fathers of their lost comrades was a very real fear of their own demise, the very real possibility that a minié ball could strike them down without warning and add their own names to the casualty lists on as bleak a night of the dead as they had endured at Gettysburg.

A titanic engagement between two mighty armies for a relatively insignificant hilltop towering above the lush farm fields of Pennsylvania, the struggle for Little Round Top was one of the great and legendary encounters between the Blue and the Gray in this nation's worst cataclysm, the Civil War. But it was, in the end, something more than that, something greater than the battle itself and larger than the story of who saved the day and who lost it, who fought here or there and who didn't. It was, and still is, the heart-wrenching story of how ordinary men—thousands of men like Brown and Oates—lost their best friends to war and came face-to-face with their own mortality.

14

WAITING FOR TOMORROW

SOMETIME AROUND NINE O'CLOCK, when the warm and almost suffocating night had attained a silver glow under a glaring moon and
the winking stars, General Meade called for his officers to meet at
the Leister house to determine the shape of the army in the aftermath of
this hard-fought battle and to decide what its next step should be. An
hour earlier, he had telegraphed General Halleck in the War Department: "The enemy attacked me about 4 P.M. this day, and, after one of
the severest contests of the war, was repulsed at all points." As for the
morrow, Meade was vague. "I shall remain in my present position to-morrow," he said, "but am not prepared to say, until better advised of the condition of the army, whether my operations will be of an offensive or
defensive character."[1]

His weary generals filed into the tiny house, gathering in one of its
two cramped rooms. A single candle on a table lit the meeting. Twelve
generals attended the gathering: Winfield Hancock, commander of the
left wing; Henry Slocum, who normally commanded the Twelfth Corps,
but who now claimed titular command of the right wing; John Newton,
who took John Reynolds's place as commander of the First Corps;
John Gibbon, assigned to command the Second Corps in Winfield Scott
Hancock's absence; David Birney, who assumed command of the Third
Corps after Sickles was wounded; George Sykes, commander of the Fifth
Corps; John Sedgwick, in command of the Sixth Corps; Oliver O. Howard,
commander of the Eleventh Corps (who arrived late); Alpheus Williams,
who was in temporary command of the Twelfth Corps (who wished to be
dismissed because Slocum was present, but Meade asked him to stay);
Daniel Butterfield, Meade's chief of staff; Gouverneur Warren, chief

engineer; and Meade. If Henry Hunt, chief of artillery, and Alfred Pleasonton, cavalry commander, had been invited, they did not attend, perhaps because duties required them elsewhere. Warren, totally exhausted from his heroic activities, slept through the entire meeting.

The meeting began informally, "in the shape of conversation," wrote Gibbon, with the generals reporting on the events that had occurred to their troops during the battle that day. Their reports included an estimate of their effective troop strength, which added up to approximately fifty-eight thousand men. In the course of the discussion, almost all of the generals thought it would be best for the army to remain where it was and face whatever Lee was going to throw at it tomorrow. Only General Newton expressed some reservations that "this was no place to fight a battle in," but Gibbon dismissed his objections as relating to "minor details of the line." Despite Newton's opinion, said Gibbon, "it soon became evident that everybody was in favor of remaining where we were and giving battle there."[2]

As the meeting progressed, Butterfield suggested making the proceedings more formal and create a record of the discussion, thus turning the gathering into a council of war, and Meade agreed. Butterfield posed three questions to the assembled generals: "1. Under existing circumstances, is it advisable for this army to remain in its present position, or retire to another nearer its base of supplies? 2. It being determined to remain in the present position, shall the army attack or wait the attack of the enemy? 3. If we wait attack, how long?"[3]

The generals did not hold back in responding to the questions. In answer to the first question, Gibbon said carefully: "Remain here, and make such correction in our position as may be deemed necessary, but take no step that looks like retreat."[4] Newton, who had earlier articulated some reservations, now answered essentially as did Gibbon, and the two men now sparred playfully as to whether Gibbon was agreeing with Newton or vice versa. All the other generals agreed to stay and fight. Hancock couldn't see how the army could retire at all, even if it wanted to get closer to its supply base.

To the second question, Gibbon wanted to refrain from attacking the enemy, preferring to let the Confederates initiate an assault against the Union lines. Howard said to wait for an attack until 4:00 P.M., implying that if the enemy did not attack by then, perhaps the Army of the Potomac should consider striking the Confederates. Hancock didn't want to attack "unless our communications are cut." Sedgwick thought the army should wait for an attack "at least one day," but even if the Confederates did not attack the Army of the Potomac, he was unsure if the Federal army should assault the enemy at all.[5]

The third question produced greater differences among the respondents. Gibbon said the Union army should wait until Lee made a move. One day was the time Williams, Birney, and Sykes voted to wait. Sedgwick thought they should wait at least a day, but Hancock answered that they couldn't wait long. The army, he said, "can't be idle." Newton was worried that if the army waited too long for the Confederates to act, the enemy might find an opportunity "to cut our [supply] line." Howard clarified his earlier answer to the second question by saying: "If [they] don't attack, attack them."[6]

To all the questions, Birney had to answer that he just didn't know what to say. The Third Corps, he explained, was all "used up, and not in good condition to fight." Gibbon agreed with Birney's assessment, afterwards confirming the fact that "the Third Corps had been badly defeated, and rendered for the time comparatively useless."[7] Slocum, on the other hand, was assertive in his answer to all three questions: "Stay and fight it out."[8]

As these interrogatories were posed and the answers given, Meade remained mostly silent, except to make a brief comment here and there; otherwise he listened intently to the opinions of his generals. Several times he was interrupted by couriers delivering messages, and the generals could hear artillery firing coming from the direction of Cemetery Hill, where the Confederate attack on that position was being repulsed in the darkness. When all the responses had been given to the three questions, Meade said, "in a decided manner": "Such, then, is the decision."[9]

Meade meant, of course, that the army would stay and fight on the defensive. With that pronouncement, the meeting ended, and the generals left the little house and went back to their commands. As the room emptied, Meade stopped Gibbon for a moment. "If Lee attacks to-morrow," he said, "it will be in your front." Gibbon's "front" was the center of the Union line along Cemetery Ridge. He asked Meade why he thought so. "Because," Meade said quietly, "he has made attacks on both our flanks and failed, and if he concludes to try it again it will be on our center." In reply, Gibbon said he hoped Meade was right, telling the commanding general with confidence that if Lee hit the Second Corps on July 3, "we would defeat him."[10]

*   *   *

LEE HELD NO COUNCIL OF WAR THAT NIGHT. At 7:00 P.M., he had received a report from Longstreet that announced: "We are doing well."[11] The report must have arrived at the very hour that Longstreet's assault was actually becoming unstitched. Lee seems not to have been in the best of moods that night. Someone who saw him at the army's headquarters regarded him as "not in good humor over the miscarriage of his plans and his orders" by both Longstreet and Ewell.[12] Lee saw the day as accomplishing only "partial successes." Major Walter Taylor, an officer on Lee's staff, expressed the view of headquarters about the day's events, and in so doing probably captured the source of Lee's frustration that night: "The whole affair was disjointed. There was an utter absence of accord in the movements of the several commands, and no decisive result attended the operations of the second day."[13]

More than that could have been said. While morale among the men remained high, an air of failure and uncertainty hung over Lee's army that night. Longstreet did not visit Lee's headquarters that evening, although that was his custom after a fight. Lee had as yet received no reports of losses during the day, so any plan he devised for Friday, July 3, would have to be done without such basic information. A. P. Hill reported to Lee in person during the night of July 2, the one corps commander whom Lee probably needed to see the least. Longstreet and Ewell both sent summaries of the day's actions and its results.

But Lee's mood shifted from disgruntlement to optimism before the night was over. Sometime after 10:00 P.M., another visitor to headquarters believed "the commanding general looked well." He further described Lee as being "all himself, and never appeared to better advantage." When he heard that Hill had arrived at headquarters, Lee greeted him by shaking his hand and saying: "It is all well, General. Everything is well."[14]

Of what had been achieved that day and what tomorrow might hold, Lee later wrote: "The result of this day's operations induced the belief that, with proper concert of action, and with the increased support that the positions gained on the right would enable the artillery to render the assaulting columns, we should ultimately succeed, and it was accordingly determined to continue the attack." His idea for July 3 was to resume the fighting begun the day before. "The general plan," he said, "was unchanged." According to this plan, "Longstreet, re-enforced by Pickett's three brigades, which arrived near the battle-field during the afternoon of the 2d, was ordered to attack the next morning, and General Ewell was directed to assail the enemy's right at the same time."[15] Lee sent his orders to Longstreet and Ewell that night.

Longstreet, always genuinely proud of his First Corps, praised the men in his two divisions for all they had accomplished that day. It was, he said, "the best three hours' fighting ever done by my troops on any battle-field." To Fitzgerald Ross, an Austrian officer traveling with the Army of Northern Virginia, Longstreet said that evening: "We have not been so successful as we wished," and attributed the shortcomings of the day to Hood's wound and to Barksdale's death.[16]

But there was folly in how Lee and Longstreet spent that night. Lee made his decisions in the dark, literally and figuratively. Longstreet failed to speak to his chief that night and clarify what was expected of him on the morrow, later pretending never to have received orders from the commanding general at all. But Porter Alexander, the First Corps' key artillery officer, described riding to Longstreet's bivouac that night and learning that "we would renew the attack early in the morning."[17] Both Lee and Longstreet badly neglected their duty as Thursday melted into Friday. Lee went to sleep around midnight. Longstreet, if he got any sleep at all, slept at his headquarters in a field west of the Emmitsburg Road. The moon, a great white ball in the sky, rose and fell with the passing hours. Neither Lee nor Longstreet, working at cross purposes as so many of the Confederate leaders did at Gettysburg and presuming things that generals should never presume, bothered to let Pickett know that his division would be needed at dawn. In the morning, at daybreak, it would be too late to correct their many errors.

THE NEW DAY ARRIVED with an awful portent: the sound of musket and artillery fire breaking the morning silence and the still air with crackling and thundering intensity. The battle noise arose around Culp's Hill and signified the determination of the Union army to take back the trenches it had lost to the enemy the night before. At about the same time, cannon fire erupted as Confederate batteries opened near the Peach Orchard, but the artillery demonstration ended long before the more ominous battle sounds around Culp's Hill faded out. On Little Round Top, every soldier who awoke to the rumblings of gunfire in the distance had to wonder if the battle would flare up again around him on this hill—the place that yesterday had been a whirlpool of bitter, deadly combat.

Daylight came on July 3 without the blowing of heavenly trumpets, which must have been something of a disappointment for the survivors on both sides of the struggle for Little Round Top. It meant that today would be like all other days, and it might even mean that another battle would have to be fought, just as it had been yesterday, and just as it might be tomorrow, and the next day, and the day after that. The war was going on. And so, too, would all the destruction, sorrow, and death. To these soldiers, Union and Confederate, these battlewise, seasoned soldiers who awoke on the third of July and felt the stifling heat on their faces even before the sun could rise very high in the sky, the day of jubilee was beginning to seem like a wistful mirage on the horizon, a hazy dream that resided a very long way down the road.

Through an early morning mist, Lee rode to the right of his line, probably assuming as he cantered along that the guns he heard coming from the direction of Culp's Hill were the first heralds of Early's attack on Culp's Hill. But when he joined Longstreet, he could see for himself that Pickett was not up yet. Fearing that Lee might still be "in his disposition to attack," Longstreet tried to anticipate him by saying, "General, I have had my scouts out all night, and I find that you still have an excellent opportunity to move around to the right of Meade's army, and maneuver him into attacking us." He was just putting his own plan into motion when Lee had arrived. Lee must have been furious, but he simply said, pointing his fist in the direction of Cemetery Ridge, "The enemy is there, and I am going to strike him." Longstreet did not believe another attack attempting to roll up the Federal line from its left flank would work any better on this day than it had the day before. He claimed years later to have said to Lee: "General, I have been a soldier all my life. I have been with soldiers engaged in fights by couples, by squads, companies, regiments, divisions, and armies, and should know, as well as any one, what soldiers can do. It is my opinion that no fifteen thousand men [the nominal size of the First Corps] ever arrayed for battle can take that position."[18]

Lee's anger could only have gotten worse, although his style was not to display his emotions to anyone. His intention was to have Longstreet's three divisions—Hood's, McLaws's, and Pickett's—drive up the Emmitsburg Road from the Peach Orchard. Longstreet protested, pointing out that if Hood and McLaws moved up in that direction, their flanks and rear would be dangerously exposed to the enemy. Lee agreed and decided to keep Hood and McLaws where they were, while adding to the attack column by taking troops from Hill's corps. The entire assault, however, would remain under Longstreet's overall command. But the goal of the actual attack was changed, too. Instead of renewing yesterday's fighting, now the object of the attack was to hit the Federal center on Cemetery Ridge. To do otherwise would mean having to move too many troops around the battlefield to get them into proper position. A charge on the Union center would mean that Pickett's division would occupy the right wing and Hill's divisions the left wing of the attack.

As an improvised battle plan, made necessary because of so many variable factors (and, one might add, so many mistakes in judgment), the assault on the enemy center left much to be desired. Porter Alexander later wrote: "I think that all military engineers, who will study that field, will agree that the point selected for Pickett's attack was very badly chosen—almost as badly chosen as it was possible to be." Longstreet was morose. "Never was I so depressed as on that day," he said. "I felt my men were to be sacrificed, and that I should have to order them to make a helpless charge."[19] Lee was hopeful of success or else he would not have ordered the charge in the first place.

Below Little Round Top, where the Texas brigade had held its position through the night following its repulse the day before, Private John West, hidden behind some rocks, spent the morning and the early afternoon dodging enemy minié balls. "Every now and then," he remembered, "Yankee bullets would come pretty thick amongst us." One bullet, he said, "went through my beard and struck a rock half an inch from my head, and a piece of the bullet hit me on the lip and brought the blood."[20] Having gotten his Bible back from friends who had kept it in case he fell in battle, he now read passages to himself, including one Psalm that he did not identify. He was still hungry, but other companies in the 4th Texas received rations in the morning. He would not eat again, beyond finding a little bread for himself, until July 6.

On the lower western slopes of Big Round Top, Billy Jordan was startled that afternoon when a tremendous cannonade erupted to the north, "the heaviest artillery firing that I ever heard."[21] Lee had ordered a massive bombardment of the Union center to clear the way for Longstreet's infantry assault. At about the same time that the guns shook the earth to the north, Union cavalry arrived in the vicinity of Big Round Top and deployed south of the hill, throwing out skirmishers to determine the strength of Confederate defenses there. Later that afternoon, while Pickett's charge surged and waned, a brisk fight between the Federal cavalry and Texas and Alabama regiments in Hood's division—now under the command of General Law—broke out in earnest, with Law successfully warding off the attack on the Confederates' far right flank.

The 15th Alabama became engaged with the enemy cavalry, inflicting some heavy casualties on the troopers. As Jordan put it, "several saddles of the enemy had been emptied."[22] A skirmish line from the regiment killed the Union cavalry commander, Brigadier General Elon J. Farnsworth, although Colonel Oates believed for the rest of his life that Farnsworth committed suicide when faced with the prospect of being captured by the Alabamians. Closer to Devil's Den, West and his fellow Texans "heard terrible musketry on our left" when the contest between the Federal cavalry and Law's division flared up. They could not see through the woods, but they supposed for a time that the Confederate flank had given way. The Texans were moved to an open field to prevent their own line from being flanked and threw up breastworks in anticipation of an enemy attack, but no Union forces ever appeared in their front. Finally darkness ended the fighting along the Confederate left.

On the summit of Little Round Top, where the boulders and formidable stone walls constructed during the night protected them, the Federal troops watched in awe as the stupendous spectacle of the artillery duel swept across the landscape between Seminary and Cemetery Ridges below them and to the north. Porter Farley and the rest of the 140th New York had been on alert since dawn, waiting for a possible Confederate attack, but no assault came and the slopes of Little Round Top remained peaceful, except for the occasional sniper fire on both sides that disturbed the morning. Off in the distance, they could hear the fight for Culp's Hill being waged. Soon the entire battlefield fell quiet, which brought on, in Farley's words, "hour after hour of tedious suspense." From the hilltop, the New Yorkers could see Confederate troops massing along Seminary Ridge and artillery being placed in position. Suddenly the enemy guns opened fire with "a terrific cannonading." After a while, the Union artillery replied. Farley described the explosive scene: "No language can exaggerate the mighty storm of shot and smoke and sound which for nearly two hours filled the air." But the enemy fire was directed at Cemetery Ridge and not at Little Round Top. "We suffered nothing from it," said Farley.[23]

For Ellis Spear and his comrades in the 20th Maine, there was little to see, although the gigantic crash of the cannonade could be plainly heard by everyone in Gettysburg that day. Spear remembered that the noise sounded like the Confederates had put into action "every battery they had." Earlier that morning, the regiment had been relieved and moved from the crest of Big Round Top to the left center of the Union line. There the 20th Maine enjoyed a place of relative safety. "Not much of the shelling reached us," wrote Spear, "but the air in front of us was full of bursting shells, and the uproar was immense."[24] At one point, Spear saw General Meade riding by.

As the climax of the Gettysburg battle was unfolding, Lieutenant Ziba Graham of the 16th Michigan received permission to get a troublesome tooth extracted in the rear of the army. What distressed him more than the extraction, which proved to be painful, was the endless wounded, mired in misery and crowding every hospital. "I saw the boys who were wounded from the fight of the day before," he said. "Poor fellows, without a murmur they were patiently waiting their turn for examination, whilst their precious life's blood was slowly ebbing away." Out of this experience came a simple lesson: "No soldier but of iron nerves should ever leave the front to see the sufferers."[25]

On his way back to join his regiment, Lieutenant Graham went seeking a drink of water and wandered into the farmyard of the Weikert house on the Taneytown Road. The surgeons had moved their hospital to another location, farther back from the front, but had left some fifty wounded and thirsty Confederate soldiers at the farm. Graham found the well but saw immediately that the crank had been removed. Asking a Confederate captain about the missing well crank, the lieutenant learned that the owner of the farm had removed it so that his well would not be pumped dry by soldiers—particularly Rebel soldiers. Graham stormed into the house and located old man Weikert—whom he described as "a mean Dutchman"—"buried in the bosom of his family, and his family buried in the bowels of the cellar." He ordered Weikert to give up the crank. Weikert refused. But just as he did, a shell struck the house's chimney, and the noise frightened the old man. Graham threatened to shoot him if he did not hand over the crank. Weikert, anxious and unsure of what this young lieutenant might actually do, finally went behind the stairway, retrieved the hidden crank, and gave it to Graham. "I went out," said Graham, quite pleased with himself, "watered the boys, put two of the least wounded in charge of it and then left, receiving the thanks of all."[26]

While the cannoneers on Little Round Top worked their guns during the great artillery duel that served as an overture to Pickett's Charge,

Confederate sharpshooters took potshots at the Union gunners from below. "We could not defend ourselves against them," explained one artillerist in Hazlett's battery, "because the guns of the battery could not be depressed to bring them in range." During the first part of the cannonade, said Lieutenant Rittenhouse, "we hugged mother earth."[27] Near Hazlett's guns, General Warren stood, scanning the horizon with his field glasses and assessing the movements of the enemy on the left and front. At about 2:30 P.M., Captain Augustus Martin, commanding the Fifth Corps artillery, received orders from General Hunt to slacken his fire. All along the line, from Cemetery Hill to Little Round Top, the Federal guns ceased fire; almost as if in response, the Confederate guns did, too.

Within a short time, the Union gunners from their perch on Little Round Top saw an unforgettable sight far below them. The artillery smoke had been whisked away by a stiff but light breeze, and when the last clouds had rolled off, long lines of Confederate infantry could be seen emerging from the woods along Seminary Ridge and forming into battle line across a long front. E. M. Hays, a cannoneer in Hazlett's battery, had his breath taken away by the sight of the long enemy lines making their way toward Cemetery Ridge. "Words are too poor," he wrote, "to express the feelings that possessed my soul as I watched that magnificent line of gray as it swept down and up the slopes." Hays had never seen anything like it: "How my heart leaped and fluttered and my blood rushed and boiled as I gazed in awe upon the steady advance, the grand courage and fortitude of those heroes as they marched into the very jaws of death."[28]

But success would not march with the Confederates that afternoon. As soon as the long, swaying lines of butternut and gray came into range, the guns of Little Round Top opened with a fury and sent shell and solid shot raining down on the enemy. When the lines grew closer, the gunners switched to case shot. Lieutenant Rittenhouse, the battery's second in command, had a perfect angle and range for enfilade fire, which he poured into the Confederate lines and watched as his shells tore through the enemy troops. "It was a grand but awful sight," remembered Thomas Scott of Hazlett's battery. With the almost endless firing of the guns, Little Round Top trembled, acting "as though it had the shakes." The shells hit the Confederates solidly on the right flank. "Many times," recalled Rittenhouse, "a single percussion shell would cut out several files and then explode in their ranks, several times almost a company would disappear, as a shell would rip from the right to the left among them."[29]

The Union cannoneers blasted away until the Confederate infantry was entirely out of range. Then they trained their guns on two enemy batteries that had been run up to the Emmitsburg Road in the hope of silencing the artillery on Little Round Top. Rittenhouse ordered: "Now, boys, turn your pieces to the front, and blow them out of there." And so they did just that. Off in the hazy distance, the artillerists watched as the Confederate wave struck Cemetery Ridge, cresting in a tremendous upheaval of yelling men, bright streaks of fire, and billowing smoke, and then ultimately breaking on the stone wall that ran in front of a distinctive copse of trees, almost in the middle of the ridge itself. There the Confederate assault lost its strength. In awe Rittenhouse and his men looked on, holding their breath, as the enemy kept moving forward, straining to snap the Union lines, "until the boys in blue, and the boys in gray, were hand to hand in deadly conflict, and the stars and stripes, and the stars and bars, waved together and lap[ped] each other, but our main line stood as solid as a rock, and at last the enemy gave way."[30]

Lieutenant Farley of the 140th New York also saw the charge acted out in the natural amphitheater below him. "We saw it all," he wrote, "up to the point where they came into actual collision with our lines and there the hills and trees hid them from us." Not being able to see everything clearly increased the suspense. "The rattle of musketry so long as we heard it told us that as yet the issue was undecided," Farley wrote. But then the firing slackened, "and we could see disorderly groups of retreating men making their way back across the fields."[31]

Down below, in the Valley of Death, Rittenhouse looked on as a regiment of the Pennsylvania Reserves moved forward in an attack aimed at driving the Confederate sharpshooters out of their lairs along Houck's Ridge, Devil's Den, and the woods bordering on the Wheatfield. With great force, but without experiencing much resistance, the Pennsylvanians succeeded in pushing one regiment of Benning's brigade all the way across the Wheatfield, and that parcel of land, which had exchanged hands so many times the day before, at a cost in blood too high to calculate, now fell back into the hands of the Union army. General Crawford later made the charge of the Reserves sound like an act of pure bravery against desperate odds, and while their final assault was not quite what he made it out to be, it ended the fighting in the vicinity of Little Round Top once and for all. Finally, after so many days of volcanic eruption, the rocks and woods became quiet and calm once more. On Little Round Top, the cannoneers no longer had to worry about Confederate sharpshooters.

Still standing on the hilltop, Captain Amos Judson was glad when the fighting ended that day and the Union troops could celebrate their victory. With the defeat of Pickett's Charge, he knew "that the hosts of freedom were destined to prevail over the dark hosts of slavery and rebellion." With the end of the fighting came a great silence. It was, said Judson, "the silence of the grave."[32]

LATE IN THE MORNING of July 3, after missing breakfast and discovering that General Weed was dead, Tillie Pierce and the Weikerts were told that some carriages had been found to take them to a place of greater safety. Some of the soldiers expected hard fighting in the vicinity of the house. At a farmhouse beyond the Baltimore Pike, Tillie and the Weikerts spent the remainder of the afternoon. Tillie could not know what the fate of her own family in Gettysburg might be.

When the fighting subsided, Tillie and the Weikerts returned to the Weikert farm on Taneytown Road. "As we drove along in the cool of the evening," Tillie wrote, "we noticed that everywhere confusion prevailed." The whole country, she said, "seemed filled with desolation." Finally returning to the farmhouse, they found it filled once more with wounded soldiers. "We hardly knew what to do or where to go," Tillie remarked. Mrs. Weikert collected all the muslin and linen she could find for bandages. Tillie found that she had become "inured to seeing the terrors of battle" and now could watch an amputation without flinching. Inured or not, Tillie said the whole scene "was one of cruel butchery." But she stood it and pitched in to help the doctors as much as she could. "Twilight had now fallen," she wrote. Word had spread that the Union army had won a great victory. But they had done so, Tillie said, "at an awful sacrifice."[33]

The extent of that sacrifice was visible to everyone when daylight arrived on July 4, Independence Day. The historian of the 44th New York tried to cope with what he saw: "A cursory view of the battlefield after the battle bore terrible evidence of the conflict. Dismounted guns, disabled gun-carriages and caissons, dead artillery horses, unsightly, unburied soldiers, solid shots, unexploded [shells] and fragments of shells, musket balls, the ground, the trees and scatter[ed] buildings torn by projectiles, fragments of muskets and accoutrement, made a picture horrible to look upon and impossible to describe." From the 20th Maine bivouac, William Livermore went out to watch a burial party at work. Twenty-eight Union dead lay in a row. "The scene," he said, "is revolting."[34]

Porter Farley confirmed that "the sights . . . were hideous and ghastly beyond all description." Bloated and decomposing bodies were scattered over the hills and fields. "Dead horses," he wrote, "lay by dozens, some torn to pieces by exploding caissons or shells, but most of them killed by bullets, and all of them by this time filled with vermin and poisoning the air with a pestilential odor." From the 44th New York, William Brown wrote home that the battlefield was "a dreadful sight." There were "heaps of dead men" everywhere. He felt that he "was in the very midst of Golgotha itself." On the slopes of Little Round Top, where the 16th Michigan had been engaged, Lieutenant Graham walked among the boulders and counted dead Confederates. "Truly, a valley of death!" declared Graham with accuracy.[35]

Occasional rain showers had begun during the night, but by midday thunderstorms rolled through Gettysburg, bringing torrential downpours and strong winds. Ellis Spear endured the rain until his makeshift bed "became a puddle and we found ourselves in a soak." For the rest of the night, he and Captain Clark sat up, unable to sleep. "Whether the battle was over or not we did not then know," he wrote. Lieutenant William H. Crennel of the 140th New York called it "a very queer 4th of July."[36]

That morning, the 20th Maine, assigned to skirmish duty, advanced and crossed the Emmitsburg Road. It was, said Ellis Spear, hardly a Glorious Fourth. Between the Union lines and the road, he wrote, "the ground was strewn with dead horses & dead men." In one place, he remembered seeing nineteen dead horses huddled together. Horses and men, he said, had become swollen, "and the men were black." A sickening odor pervaded the entire battlefield. When the regiment halted for lunch, Spear ate his meal, but the food was not particularly savory "in that corpse infected air." Near where the regiment had halted was a barn that had been hit repeatedly by artillery shells during the battle. The ground in front of it had been plowed into furrows. Enemy dead "lay thick" all around. During the battle, the barn had caught fire "and burned down to the mass of charred hay, on which were the burned remains of men." Outside the barn, Spear reported with disgust, "were half roasted remains of horses & men."[37] The 20th Maine buried the men.

As the day went on, the rain fell in sheets, saturating the battlefield and all the soldiers on it. The soaking rain, wrote Eugene Nash of the 44th New York, "added discomfort to the sorrow felt and shared by the whole army over our loss[es] in battle." The Union soldiers, who saw little evidence of the Confederates all day, began to suspect that Lee's army had quit the field. A soldier in the 83rd Pennsylvania wrote in his diary: "How earnestly I hope that this is the last of the Rebellion. I wish that on this our nations birthday might be witnessed by the world the overthrow of Rebellion and the defeat of all our foes."[38]

His wish was partially granted. On the evening of July 3, Lee had begun to make his plans for a retreat. A wagon train seventeen miles long carrying the army's wounded began its long journey back toward Virginia late in the afternoon of July 4. That night, Lee issued orders for his army to head to the Potomac; by the following night, no Confederates—except approximately seven thousand additional wounded who could not be taken with the army—remained in Gettysburg. At Williamsport on the Potomac, Lee found the river too swollen to cross. But through the night of July 13 and into the morning darkness of July 14, he managed to get his army over the river and back to the safety of Virginia soil before Meade could deliver any kind of blow that hindered the Confederate retreat. The Gettysburg campaign was over.

In the end, credit for the Union victory on Little Round Top must go, quite obviously, to the troops of the Fifth Corps—namely, the men of the different brigades of the Second and Third Divisions. Holding back the Confederates (and not just *any* Confederates, but Hood's division in Longstreet's corps) in such a decisive fashion, saving Little Round Top for the Army of the Potomac, and defending the hill against every assault the Confederates made against it, shaped and limited Lee's battle plan for the third of July. The Federal success at Little Round Top severely narrowed Lee's alternatives on the following day. In that sense, the victory on the little hill was decisive, although not everyone necessarily realized that at the time. It was the fight for Little Round Top that helped ensure a Union victory at Gettysburg.

The soldiers of the Fifth Corps understood they had accomplished a grand thing. One veteran of the 83rd Pennsylvania asserted proudly: "The battle was fought and won by the superior intelligence of the rank and file of the Army of the Potomac." His sentiments were repeated by countless other soldiers in the rank and file. "The battle of Gettysburg," wrote a soldier in the 44th New York, echoing some of the same words used independently by his comrade in the 83rd Pennsylvania, "belongs to the rank and file of the Army of the Potomac."[39] The great battle, and particularly the fight for Little Round Top, was regarded solidly as a soldiers' fight, where the men on the frontline made all the difference. Such a view did not call into question the widespread acknowledgment—and worshipful veneration—of such officer heroes as General Warren, Colonel Vincent, Colonel Rice, Colonel Chamberlain, Colonel O'Rorke, Lieutenant Hazlett, General Weed, General Crawford, and even General Meade. But the Federal soldiers felt, and rightly so, that they had won the struggle for Little Round Top themselves, with their courage, their warrior skills, with their blood, and with their lives, and they voiced that opinion with great gusto.

Summing up the remarkable feat accomplished by his brigade, his corps, his army at Gettysburg, James Woodworth of the 44th New York wrote to his wife: "Everyone *blows* about this army, if the *Army of the Potomac*, would only do so and so, then every thing would go right, when at the same time there isn't a department in the Service that has done as much hard forced marching, or fought so many or such desperate battles. True, yes too true, we have not been [always] victorious, but the fault is not in the troops, for never have men been known to fight as this army has fought, even when we knew we were out Generaled and defeated. Any man will fight when flushed with former victories, but it's only the *heroes* of *this* shattered army that will face the enemy though defeat be certain."[40] But this time, on the slopes of Little Round Top, the outcome had been different. The fighting men had brought the Army of the Potomac to victory.

Along similar lines, Charles H. Salter of the 16th Michigan saw it this way: "All the papers that I have seen yet seem to lay the blame of our former defeats to our former generals, and give the credit of the victory to General Meade. But our army knows this to be not the true state of affairs[,] for we will fight better in Pennsylvania and Maryland than we will in Virginia, for in the present case we are defending our own soil and in Virginia we felt that we are invading the rebel soil. . . . And I contend that it was the Army of the Potomac that won the battle, and not Gen. Meade, and that we would have done just as well, or better, under McClellan, Hooker, or any other general. We are not fighting for generals, but for our country[,] and I hope that [the] Northern people will give the credit of our fighting to the soldiers."[41]

Epilogue

NATHANIEL HAWTHORNE once wrote that "life is made up of marble and mud."[1] After Little Round Top, the lives of the men who fought there and survived the battle assumed different shapes, new features, new proportions, forming themselves into altered sculptures of marble and mud, but all of them were influenced and, to some degree, distorted by what they had experienced on that hill or on the Gettysburg battlefield.

General Meade, probably one of the most capable field generals in American military history, never won the acclaim he deserved for out-generaling Lee, winning the battle, and helping turn the Union war effort in the Eastern theater into a series of pounding and brilliant victories—later driven by the hard determination of Ulysses S. Grant—that began with the defeat of the Army of Northern Virginia at Gettysburg. Meade himself gave the credit for victory at Gettysburg to the men in the ranks. Soon after the battle, he wrote to his wife: "The men behaved splendidly; I really think they are becoming soldiers. They endured long marches, short rations, and stood one of the most terrific cannonadings I ever witnessed."[2]

Meade's reputation also suffered because Lincoln believed that he had failed miserably by allowing Lee to slip across the Potomac in the days following the battle. On July 14, the president wrote Meade a letter, which he decided not to send, that expressed his great disappointment: "I do not believe you appreciate the magnitude of the misfortune involved in Lee's escape. He was within your easy grasp, and to have closed upon him would, in connection with our other late successes, have ended the war. . . . Your golden opportunity is gone, and I am distressed immeasurably

243

because of it." But Lincoln did not remove Meade as commander of the Army of the Potomac, a post the general retained until Appomattox. In July 1869, Meade returned to Gettysburg to unveil the Soldiers' National Monument, which was erected in the center of the National Cemetery. Once again he praised the soldiers of Gettysburg, "the noble spirits who then fought so well, and now sleep the sleep that knows no waking."[3] He even called for the respectful burial of the Confederate dead at Gettysburg. Meade died in 1872, at the age of fifty-six.

As one might expect, Dan Sickles's reputation gained luster as a consequence of Gettysburg. After recuperating from his amputation, he spent most of his time accusing Meade of mishandling the army at Gettysburg, a charge that resulted in a Congressional investigation and much misery for Meade. Although professional army officers decried his blunder on the battlefield, which almost brought destruction to the Army of the Potomac, Sickles managed so effectively to promote his tactical error as a bold and heroic stroke that he won a Medal of Honor for his role in the battle. He was instrumental in getting the legislation through Congress that created the Gettysburg National Military Park in 1894. When he died in 1914, the *New York Times* declared: "Nobody with warm blood flowing through his veins can read the obituary notices of Gen. Sickles without a certain thrill of admiration."[4] The wording of that sentence left some doubt as to whether the editorial writer meant to praise Sickles or applaud his death.

The high point of Gouverneur Warren's military career came at Gettysburg; the low point occurred at the battle of Five Forks, where Warren held command of the Fifth Corps. At a crucial moment during the battle, Major General Philip H. Sheridan, whose temper was legendary, removed Warren from corps command and ordered him to the rear for mismanaging a pivotal assault. When Warren asked Sheridan to reconsider, Sheridan erupted in anger: "Reconsider, hell! I don't reconsider my decisions. Obey the order!"[5] For the rest of his life, Warren tried to win vindication for himself. A court of inquiry finally exonerated Warren in November 1882, although it held that he had indeed moved too slowly at Five Forks. Warren never heard the verdict. He had died the previous August in Newport, Rhode Island. Reportedly his last words were: "The flag! The flag!" Six years later, the veterans of his old regiment, the 5th New York Zouaves, placed a statue of him on the rocks at Little Round Top in honor of Warren's "gallant services." For decades, Warren was known as "The Savior of Little Round Top," a title that remained in vogue until the rise in popularity of Joshua Lawrence Chamberlain's role in the 1990s.[6]

Ironically, Joshua Chamberlain was one of Warren's most ardent supporters, believing that Sheridan had acted maliciously and without warrant at Five Forks. Like Warren, Chamberlain's star rose at Gettysburg and kept rising even beyond his lifetime. After Gettysburg, he received promotions to the rank of brigadier general, which came in the form of a battlefield promotion issued by Ulysses S. Grant, and of brevet major general. At Appomattox, Chamberlain later claimed that Grant appointed him to receive the formal surrender of the Army of Northern Virginia on April 12, three days after Lee's capitulation to Grant in the parlor of Wilmer McLean's house. But Chamberlain exaggerated his role and the supposed honor, which he implied was singular.[7] After the war, Chamberlain went on the lecture circuit in Maine and New England, relating the dramatic story of his heroism on Little Round Top and his role in accepting the surrender of the Army of Northern Virginia. Telling these tales helped to get him elected governor of Maine for four consecutive one-year terms. For the twelve years following his last term as governor, he served as president of Bowdoin College, his alma mater. In 1893, he received the Medal of Honor for his "distinguished gallantry" on Little Round Top. Known throughout Maine as "The Hero of Little Round Top," he died in 1914.[8]

For many years after the war, Ellis Spear admired Chamberlain as a great hero and a great man. The two former soldiers remained close friends for most of those years, exchanging frequent letters and Christmas cards. After Gettysburg, Spear continued to serve with the 20th Maine, usually commanding the regiment and finally receiving his official promotion to the rank of major, besides receiving the brevet ranks of lieutenant colonel, colonel, and brigadier general. With war's end, he found work with the U.S. Patent Office in Washington, D.C., rising through several positions to become commissioner of patents in 1876. He held that office until November 1878, when he resigned to begin a private practice as a patent attorney. Devoted to his alma mater, Bowdoin College, he served as an overseer for several years. Spear's wife, Susan, whom he married in March 1863, died in 1873. Two years later, he married Sarah Keene, the widow of Spear's close friend, Captain Samuel T. Keene, who had been killed at Petersburg. Spear was active in veteran affairs, particular with his fellow survivors of the 20th Maine, and he helped design the regimental monument erected on Little Round Top in

1888. In his later years, he grew increasingly annoyed by Chamberlain's continuous boasting and, while he maintained his friendship with his former commanding officer, he privately dismissed him as an egotist and prevaricator. Although Spear and Sarah made their home in Washington, they frequently visited his birthplace, the ancestral home at "The Farm" in Warren, Maine. Spear died in 1918 at the age of eighty-four. He is buried in Arlington National Cemetery.

Unlike Spear, Porter Farley did not serve through until the end of the war. After Gettysburg, he did continue as regimental adjutant and later became regimental quartermaster of the 140th New York. In January 1864, he married Mary Caroline Bates, his childhood sweetheart. Later that month he was promoted to the rank of captain and given command of the regiment's Company B. He went on sick leave from the regiment in July 1864 to his home in Rochester, New York, and never recuperated sufficiently to rejoin the 140th. He was discharged from the service in August 1864. In 1872, Farley began writing a history of his regiment, focusing much of his attention on the role the 140th New York played on Little Round Top. He put aside his historical research, however, to study medicine, and he received a medical degree in 1874, graduating at the head of his class from the College of Physicians and Surgeons of Columbia University. In 1876, he returned to Rochester and began his medical practice. Two years were spent abroad studying at universities in Vienna and Heidelberg. After establishing his medical practice in Rochester, he published several articles on the history of the 140th New York in local newspapers. He attended the fiftieth anniversary of Gettysburg in 1913 and wrote about his trip for a Rochester newspaper. Six years later, he died.

Little is known about young Matilda J. "Tillie" Pierce, apart from the account she left of her experiences at the Jacob Weikert house during the battle. She successfully reunited with her family in Gettysburg after the fighting was over. In 1871, she married a graduate of Pennsylvania (Gettysburg) College, Horace P. Alleman of Harrisburg. Horace and Tillie moved to Selinsgrove, Pennsylvania, where he practiced law until his death in 1908. They had three children. In 1889, she wrote and published her firsthand account of her adventures during the great battle in a little book entitled *At Gettysburg, or, What a Girl Saw and Heard of the Battle: A True Narrative*. When she died in 1914, a local newspaper noted the loss of a "truly estimable woman, mother, and authoress."[9] The last line in her small book quoted a passage from the Old Testament (Ezra 8:31):

"The hand of our God was upon us, and He delivered us from the hand of the enemy."

One of those enemies was Private John C. West, a devout Baptist, who probably knew the passage from Ezra by heart. The pious Private West did not remain very long in the 4th Texas after experiencing what he did at Gettysburg. Before he saw another battle, he received an honorable discharge in February 1864, took his trusty Bible in hand, and gratefully made his way back to his wife and family in Waco, Texas. After the war, he entered politics and served as Waco's mayor, a justice of the peace, and a member of the school board. He became a charter member of the local chapter of the United Confederate Veterans. Throughout his life, he maintained his belief in God, his adherence to the Baptist faith, and his diligent reading of the Bible. He lived in the same home from 1859 until he died in 1927 at age ninety-three. Thirty years before his death, in a speech delivered in M'Gregor, Texas, on Decoration Day, 1897, West expressed this earnest hope: "In behalf of peace and [the] happiness of posterity[,] let prejudice cease and reason rule."[10]

Such sentiments were categorically rejected by the 15th Alabama's Billy Jordan, who enthusiastically embraced racial bigotry and made it his special cause for the rest of his life. In the months following Gettysburg, Jordan continued to serve with the 15th Alabama, gaining promotions to the rank of sergeant and the honored place of regimental color bearer. In 1864, he was wounded at Fort Gilmer, but he recovered quickly and returned to service. Colonel Oates praised him as "one of the best soldiers in the regiment," who "was nearly always present in the full performance of his duty." After Appomattox, he returned to Alabama to find his plantation intact but all of his slaves freed, or so they thought. Jordan quickly managed to get his slaves working again in an arrangement that deprived them of any wages. Arrested once for refusing to emancipate his slaves and another time for preventing blacks from voting, Jordan told the Federal authorities that he was "damned if the negroes were free."[11] During Reconstruction, he conducted a singlehanded campaign against Republicans, harassing speakers and breaking up party meetings. In 1884, he was elected to the state legislature, where he conscientiously helped to ensure the perpetuation of white supremacy in his state. He died in 1923.

Colonel William C. Oates, Jordan's regimental commander, also worked to perpetuate white supremacy in Alabama after the war and held fast to the racial presumptions of the times, but his life followed a substantially different path from the one chosen by Billy Jordan. When he received word that his brother John had died in a Union field hospital after Gettysburg, Oates became depressed and lethargic. On various battlefields, he suffered a total of six wounds, the last one resulting in the amputation of his right arm. With the war over, Oates rebuilt his law practice and entered local politics. In 1874, he won election to a seat in Congress, which he retained for seven terms. After retiring from the House, he served one term as governor of Alabama, but he later failed to win his highest political goal, a U.S. Senate seat. When the Spanish-American War broke out in 1898, Oates received a commission as brigadier general in the U.S. Army. For several years after the war, he attempted to raise a monument on Little Round Top in memory of his brother John and the other men in his regiment who had fallen on July 2, 1863. After calling in Joshua Chamberlain as a kind of expert witness, the War Department commissioners of the Gettysburg National Military Park entangled the entire affair in red tape and refused to take action on Oates's proposal. Today there is no monument to the 15th Alabama on Little Round Top.

In 1901, as a delegate to the Alabama Constitutional Convention, Oates argued in favor of giving African American men the right to vote, having come to the realization that the white Democratic party should be courting black votes rather than violating the 15th Amendment. His plea fell on deaf ears. During another debate, he expressed outrage at the racial violence that had arisen across the South, especially the incidents of lynching that had grown into an epidemic of brutality. Even though he later supported the new state constitution, with all its provisions against black suffrage, Oates's political career was over. He died in 1910 at the age of seventy-seven, still mourning the death of his brother John and suffering from all the heartache that Gettysburg had brought into his life.

Heartache also came to James Longstreet as a result of Gettysburg. Despite whatever differences he had with Lee about how the battle should have been fought, the two generals remained on good terms until the end of the war. In May 1863, during the Wilderness Battle, a volley fired by Virginian troops struck Longstreet down with wounds in his neck and shoulder. The following October he returned to duty with the Army of Northern Virginia, and fought out the war until the bitter end at Appomattox. Many of Lee's officers appeared at his headquarters to say good-bye. When Longstreet came to him, Lee embraced him warmly. Turning to Captain Goree, one of Longstreet's aides, Lee said: "Captain,

I am going to put my old War Horse under your charge. I want you to take good care of him."[12]

But the war would not end for Longstreet. He moved his family to New Orleans, where he worked as a partner in a cotton brokerage firm and the president of an insurance company. In an interview with William Swinton, a Northern journalist, Longstreet made public his claim of Lee's promise to fight on the defensive during the Pennsylvania campaign and voiced his own disapproval of Lee's decisions at Gettysburg. After Lee's death in 1870, a number of former Confederates, including Jubal Early, William Pendleton, and Walter Taylor, attacked Longstreet for his criticisms of Lee and blamed the Gettysburg defeat on the First Corps commander. This Lee cult, as it became known, sought to silence any criticism of Lee and elevate him to an untouchable pedestal of fame and glory—an everlastingly noble symbol of the Lost Cause.

Lee's proponents found in Longstreet a convenient scapegoat to explain the defeat at Gettysburg. Longstreet tried to defend himself, without much skill and with little success, but the Lee cult also took him to task for becoming a Republican in the late 1860s and taking a political appointment for a New Orleans post from President Ulysses S. Grant, his old West Point friend. Longstreet also dared to suggest that the South should recognize its own defeat and accept the terms of Reconstruction. "We are a conquered people," he wrote. The North had won the war "fairly and squarely."[13] He also proposed that blacks be given the right to vote. His friends deserted him. In 1889, his wife Louise, the mother of his ten children, died. Eight years later, he married a younger woman, Helen Dortch, who would later take up Longstreet's cause with her able pen. In January 1904, after losing a battle against pneumonia, he died at his daughter's house in Gainesville, Georgia, at the age of eighty-two. His last words were to his wife: "Helen, we shall be happier in this post."[14]

General Robert E. Lee, a man of great complexity and warring emotions, never quite grasped what had gone wrong at Gettysburg. He struggled with the very idea that the Army of Northern Virginia had been defeated. Immediately after the battle, he said to Brigadier General Cadmus Wilcox: "Never mind, General, *all this had been* my *fault*—it is *I* that have lost this fight, and you must help me out of it the best way you can." Later that night, showing the signs of great fatigue, he told Brigadier General John Imboden: "I never saw troops behave more magnificently than Pickett's division of Virginians did today in that grand charge upon the enemy. And if they had been supported as they were to have been—but for some reason not yet fully explained to me were not—we would have held the position and the day would have been ours." He paused for a moment and the exclaimed: "Too bad! Too bad! Oh, too bad!"[15]

These statements expressed well Lee's ambivalence about the battle and his disappointment over its loss. On one hand, he took responsibility for the defeat; on the other, he believed that someone had failed to do his duty or something had not happened as it should have. More than anything, though, he could not see that if troops had not been properly supported, or if actions had not been carefully coordinated, the ultimate responsibility for those failures rested on his shoulders as the commander of the army.

For the rest of his life, Lee believed that he had been ill served at Gettysburg, as indeed he had been, and he spoke about it openly. In 1868, he asserted that he had tried for three days to get such a coordination of action, and he mentioned Ewell, Longstreet, and Hill by name as having failed to "act in concert."[16] Two years later, Lee seemed to think that the failure at Gettysburg resulted in part from the government's refusal to send Beauregard north to reinforce the Army of Northern Virginia. Then he admitted that the defeat in Pennsylvania actually occurred because of "a variety of causes," including Stuart's absence and his own inability to "get a simultaneous attack on the enemy's position." In this interview, Lee remarked tellingly that "that if Jackson had been there he would have succeeded."[17] He never let go of the confidence—indeed, the overconfidence—he had in his men, the fighting soldiers of the Army of Northern Virginia. After the war, his soldiers honored that confidence by overlooking his faults and the errors he committed at Gettysburg and elsewhere. They preferred, in fact, not to acknowledge those errors. His men always liked him best as a statue they could praise and worship.

Lee could not reconcile in his own thinking what had happened at Gettysburg. In his mind, and in his heart, the battle kept raging inside him and he could not reach a firm understanding of what had taken place and what had gone so wrong. Unable to break through his ambivalence, which helped to cloud his thinking and kept him from focusing criticism on himself, he utterly failed to see that he had handled the battle—and, indeed, the whole campaign—badly.

His death in 1870 was mourned by the South. Already he was regarded as a saint, an almost godlike figure who epitomized human perfection and the most noble of all qualities. The nation came to think of Lee not only as a Southern hero, but also as an American hero. Over the years, he became a formidable legend, rivaling in his mythical and heroic bearing King Arthur and the Knights of the Round Table. Like King Arthur, Lee remains distant, indistinct, almost unknowable. In death he is as much an American paradox as he was in life.

A BRIGHT, CLOUDLESS MORNING that smelled of wood smoke and freshly harvested fields welcomed Abraham Lincoln when he awoke in Gettysburg on November 19, 1863. He had come to speak about death. Local officials had asked him to deliver "a few appropriate remarks" at the dedication of the Soldiers' National Cemetery, where the remains of more than thirty-five hundred Union soldiers who died in the battle would be laid to rest.[18] The entire population of Gettysburg at the time was only twenty-four hundred souls, roughly 68 percent of the slain Federal soldiers buried in the National Cemetery. Many of these soldiers had fought and died on Little Round Top. Among them were Private Joseph D. Simpson of Company A, 20th Maine; Private B. E. True of Company B, 83rd Pennsylvania; Private Frederick Feight of Company F, 140th New York; Private James S. Rutter of Company B, 1st Pennsylvania Reserves; Private William N. Norris of Company C, 44th New York; Private L. Griswold of Battery D, 5th U.S. Artillery; Sergeant Henry Raw of Company I, 16th Michigan, and many, many others, some of them unknown.

Lincoln's address was part eulogy, part elegy. Having come to dedicate the cemetery in the name of the American people, the president's mind was very much on the dead who were to be buried in this place. A melancholy man, who fought desperately with an inner private darkness, he had personally come to know death well in the span of his life. As a youth, he had lost his beloved mother, Nancy Hanks, to milk sickness. A brother, Thomas, never survived infancy. Lincoln blamed the death of his sister Sarah on her husband's relatives. Depression overcame him in 1835 when a young woman whom he loved in New Salem, Ann Rutledge, died from "brain fever." He told an acquaintance "that he could not bare the idea of its raining on her Grave."[19] When his father died in 1849, Lincoln did not attend his funeral. His second son, Edward Baker, died of tuberculosis in 1850. In 1862, when the war demanded nearly all of Lincoln's attention, his son Willie took ill, probably with typhoid fever, and died. The president was beside himself with grief. Even after Willie's funeral,

Dedication ceremony, Soldiers' National Cemetery, November 19, 1863

he closed himself off in a room and spent long hours weeping. Now, this November, his youngest son, Tad, was in bed at the White House with an illness he feared might prove fatal. The war had already resulted in more American dead than could be easily counted. And the three days at Gettysburg, "a great battle-field of the war," had produced more dead than any earlier battle. Death was much on Lincoln's mind, and never far removed from his mournful heart.

Lincoln accomplished many things in his address. In 272 words, he defined the meaning of the war by linking it to the treasured principles, first set forth in the Declaration of Independence, of liberty and equality. Purposefully his remarks at Gettysburg were meant to echo the goal of freedom propounded in the Emancipation Proclamation, issued the previous January. By making his address an appeal for the future of the nation, he informed the world of what he thought the Union was fighting for—freedom and the preservation of a government "of the people, by the people, and for the people." Out of the sacrifice this war necessitated, Lincoln saw a new nation rising up out of the old, a renewed dedication to old principles, and the survival of the republic by a commitment to complete "the unfinished work" that the soldiers had carried forward at Gettysburg. He wanted to refashion the United States into a more perfect reflection of the country bequeathed to all later generations by the Founding Fathers. The way to do so, he said, was to embrace the great "proposition that all men are created equal." Equality would be the key to ensuring the continuation of American freedom and its republican government. Lincoln wanted the nation to achieve a fulfillment of its highest ideals and its greatest promise out of the dreadful and mournful destruction of "a great civil war." George William Curtis, the editor of *Harper's Weekly*, declared: "The few words of the President were from the heart to the heart. They cannot be read, even, without kindling emotion."[20]

But the ringing words Lincoln spoke at Gettysburg also helped the nation confront the horror of battle, the terrible price of war, face to face. By 1863, the war had already found its way to the doorsteps of every Northern citizen, every Northern family. Lincoln's address now carried the greatest tragedy of that war, the reality of death, across their thresholds and into their homes. In his remarks, Lincoln did not deny death's sorrowful reality. He dealt with it directly while he stood at this "final resting place." The Union soldiers who had fallen at Gettysburg, he said, had given their lives so that the nation itself might live. What's more, those dead had consecrated the ground more than the living could ever do. Those individuals and families who had experienced losses at Gettysburg were not alone, for his carefully chosen words made plain that those losses belonged not just to the dead soldiers' families or to the states, but to the nation as a whole. His address ensured that the dead at Gettysburg had to be reckoned with, had to be honored for their "last full measure of devotion," and his eloquence made certain that they would not be forgotten. "We here highly resolve," he said, "that these dead shall not have died in vain." He hoped the entire United States would affirm that resolution. If it did, then the nation would experience "a new birth of freedom"; out of the dust and ashes of the dead would come, phoenixlike, a new America.[21]

Lincoln's speech was a national message of comfort and condolence to a country that had been bled almost white, a people who had lost their most precious young men, a society that had suffered hardships and sorrows that seemed to have no end. The Gettysburg Address revealed his own profound understanding of death and of how words can console, how they can help the bereaved adjust to death's grim reality, how the light of meaning can be found in death's blackness, and how birth—even rebirth—can spring forth out of the awful snares of death. Like the letters of condolence written by soldiers to the loved ones of comrades who had fallen on the battlefield, Lincoln's address tried to convince the Northern people that their sons had died for a reason, a very good reason, and that they should find comfort in that fact.

Just as religion worked to console the grief-stricken, so too did Lincoln's speech provide the people of the North with comfort, reassurance, and hope. One Union officer, a veteran of Gettysburg who attended the cemetery dedication, was powerfully and spiritually moved by the president's remarks. As Lincoln spoke, the officer realized that the audience stood "almost immediately over the place where I had lain and seen my comrades torn in fragments by the enemy's cannon-balls—think, then, if you please, how these words fell on my ears." What this officer heard brought him to an epiphany: "If at that moment the Supreme Being had appeared to me with an offer to undo my past life, give back to me a sound body free from the remembrance even of sufferings past and those that must necessarily embitter all the years to come, I should have indignantly spurned the offer, such was the effect upon me of this immortal dedication."[22]

Lincoln, in talking about death, very purposely spoke of rebirth. Out of the multitude of deaths at Gettysburg, including the many that had occurred on Little Round Top, Lincoln hoped that something spiritual and tangible, propitious and meaningful, would emerge—a new birth of freedom and a rededication to the country's most fundamental principles. These deaths would not be in vain. Their purpose was noble, precise, and specific. The war would make America a better nation and would make all Americans a better people. These deaths would bring a rebirth, not unlike the life that comes out of death in the New Testament. All the men who had died for the Union cause on Little Round Top and across the bloody battlefield at Gettysburg had actuated the coming rebirth; the dead would thus be "long remembered" for what they had given, for all they had done.[23]

After Lincoln finished his speech, he sat down and listened as a choir sang a dirge. The benediction was made, an artillery salute was fired, and the ceremony was over. The procession reformed and marched from Cemetery Hill back to the center of town. Lincoln lunched at the house of David Wills, one of two local attorneys who had spearheaded the establishment of the National Cemetery and the man who had invited the president to attend the exercises. At five o'clock, Lincoln attended a patriotic meeting held at the Presbyterian Church, but he left the building before the meeting was concluded in order to catch his train back to Washington.

He was not feeling well. A mild case of varioloid, a form of smallpox, was making him ill. The train left Gettysburg at about 7:00 P.M., as a deep twilight melted into night. South of Gettysburg, the dark hulk of Little Round Top stood as a soft black silhouette outlined against the ebony sky. As night closed in, the hill slowly dissolved from view.

Underneath the canopy of purple stars that blinked overhead, the rocks of Little Round Top remained silent and cold in the darkness. Tomorrow would bring another twilight. But never again would the hillside serve as a bloody field of battle or a host to the angel of death. For American soldiers, North and South, there would be only one twilight at Little Round Top to remember and mourn.

NOTES

Abbreviations Used

ADAH   Alabama Department of Archives and History, Montgomery, Alabama

BC   Bowdoin College, Brunswick, Maine

BP   David L. Ladd and Audrey J. Ladd, eds., *The Bachelder Papers*, 3 vols. (Dayton, Ohio, 1994–1995)

CCW   U.S. Congress, *Report of the Joint Committee on the Conduct of the War at the Second Session, Thirty-Eighth Congress, Army of the Potomac, General Meade* (Washington, D.C., 1865)

CRC   Confederate Research Center, Hill College, Hillsboro, Texas

CSR   Compiled Service Records, RG 109, War Department Collection of Confederate Records; Compiled Service Records, RG94, Records of Adjutant General's Office, both NA

DPL   Burton Historical Collection, Detroit Public Library, Detroit, Michigan

DTMM   *Dedication of the Twentieth Maine Monuments at Gettysburg, Oct. 3, 1889* (Waldoboro, Maine, 1891)

FSNMP   Fredericksburg and Spotsylvania National Military Park, Fredericksburg, Virginia

GASSM   *Grand Army Scout and Soldiers' Mail*

GNMP   Gettysburg National Military Park

LC   Library of Congress, Washington, D.C.

LCN   *Lincoln County* (Maine) *News*

MSA   Maine State Archives, Bangor, Maine

NA   National Archives, Washington, D.C.

NP   Oliver W. Norton Papers, Clarke Historical Library, Central Michigan University, Mount Pleasant, Michigan

NT   *National Tribune*

NYPL   New York Public Library, New York, New York

NYSL   New York State Library, Albany, New York

NYT   *New York Times*
OC   Oates Correspondence, Gettysburg National Military Park, Gettys-
         burg, Pennsylvania
OFP   Oates Family Papers, in the possession of Marion Oates Leiter
         Charles, Washington, D.C. (1995)
O.R.   U.S. War Department, *The War of the Rebellion: A Compilation of the Of-
         ficial Records of the Union and Confederate Armies*, 70 vols. in 128 parts
         (Washington, D.C., 1880–1901). All references are to Series 1, unless
         otherwise noted
PHMC   Pennsylvania Historical and Museum Commission, Harrisburg,
         Pennsylvania
PWT   *Philadelphia Weekly Times*
SCWC   Schoff Civil War Collection, UM
SHC   Southern Historical Collection, University of North Carolina, Chapel
         Hill
SHSP   *Southern Historical Society Papers*
SP   Spear Papers, in the possession of Abbott Spear, Warren, Maine
         (1994)
UM   William L. Clements Library, University of Michigan, Ann Arbor,
         Michigan
UMO   Folger Library, University of Maine, Orono
USAMHI   U.S. Army Military History Institute, Carlisle Barracks, Carlisle,
         Pennsylvania

Works cited by author and short title in these notes will be found fully
cited in the bibliography. All references to *The War of the Rebellion: A Compilation of the Official Records of the Union and Confederate Armies*, are to
Series 1, unless otherwise noted.

Prologue

1. Frassanito, *Early Photography at Gettysburg*, 243–246.

2. The larger hill may have been known as "Round Top" before the battle, and
a handful of official reports written shortly after the battle by Union officers
make plain reference to Round Top Hill, although it is not always clear whether
these officers were referring to the larger hill or the smaller one or possibly both
of the hills together, despite the lack of plurals. See, for example, Treichler
Account: "Invasion of Maryland and Pennsylvania," n.d., in the possession of
Randy Treichler, Three Springs, Penn.

3. *Southern Literary Messenger*, 37 (June 1863), 373.

4. *O.R.*, 25, Pt. 2, 793.

5. Henry Heth to J. William Jones, June 1877, *SHSP*, 4 (1877), 154–154, quoting Major John Seddon's account of a conversation with Lee.

6. Three stars on the collar was also the insignia for a U.S. lieutenant general, the rank held by George Washington, Winfield Scott, and later in the war, Ulysses S. Grant. See Campbell, "Fabric of Command," 261–290.

7. Gallagher, ed., *Lee the Soldier*, xviii.

8. *O.R.*, 25, Pt. 2, 840, 842. For Lee's letter to Davis of May 30, see ibid., 832–833. For useful discussions of how the Gettysburg campaign was planned, see Jones, "Gettysburg Decision Reassessed," 64–66; Coddington, *Gettysburg Campaign*, 7.

9. Longstreet to Wigfall, May 13, 1863, Wigfall Papers, LC.

10. Allan, "Memoranda of Conversations," April 15, 1868, in Gallagher, ed., *Lee the Soldier*, 15; Longstreet to Lafayette McLaws, July 25, 1873, McLaws Papers, SHC. On the Lee cult and the endless controversy over the role Longstreet played in the Gettysburg campaign, see Piston, *Lee's Tarnished Lieutenant*; LaFantasie, "Considering Longstreet's Legacy," 60–69.

11. Longstreet to McLaws, July 25, 1873, McLaws Papers, SHC; *O.R.*, 27, Pt. 2, 305; Allan, "Memoranda of Conversations," April 15, 1868, in Gallagher, ed., *Lee the Soldier*, 13–15; Heth to Jones, June 1877, *SHSP*, 4 (1877), 154–154.

12. *O.R.*, 27, Pt. 3, 868.

13. Franklin, *Emancipation Proclamation*, 93; Donald, *Lincoln*, 407.

14. Sears, *Chancellorsville*, 82, 120.

15. Basler, ed., *Collected Works*, 7:273.

16. Ibid., 7:249, 257.

17. *O.R.*, 27, Pt. 1, 59–60.

18. Bradford, "Portrait," 322, 326; Sandburg, *Abraham Lincoln*, 408.

19. Pfanz, *Gettysburg—The First Day*, 42.

20. Calef, "Gettysburg Notes," 48.

21. Fairfield, "Capture at the Railroad Cut," *NT*, Sept. 1, 1910.

22. Culp, "Gettysburg: Reminiscences of the Great Fight by a Participant," *NT*, Mar. 19, 1885; Gordon, *Reminiscences*, 151.

23. Southard, "The 119th N.Y. at Gettysburg," *NT*, Aug. 19, 1897.

24. Broadhead, *Diary of a Lady*, 12; Stewart, "Recollections of the Battle of Gettysburg," *Philadelphia North American*, July 7, 1900.

25. Taylor, *Four Years*, 94–96.

1. Midnight to Morning

1. Long, *Memoirs of Robert E. Lee*, 277; *O.R.*, 27, Pt. 2, 446.

2. Longstreet, "Causes of Lee's Defeat at Gettysburg," 60–61. Longstreet published at least three different versions of this conversation with Lee, all with minor variations. I have relied on the earliest of these accounts.

3. Cutrer, ed., *Longstreet's Aide*, 26.

4. Owen, *In Camp and Battle*, 157.

5. Cleaves, *Meade of Gettysburg*, 140.

6. Polley, *Letters to Charming Nellie*, 129; West, *Texan in Search of a Fight*, 84.

7. West, *Texan in Search of a Fight*, 8.

8. Ibid., 53.

9. Ibid., 72.

10. Ibid., 85.

11. Spear had been promoted to major in June, although his commission would not be in his hands until August 1863. Spear et al., eds., *Civil War Recollections*, 213; CSR (Spear).

12. Spear et al., eds., *Civil War Recollections*, 7.

13. Spear, "Story of the Raising," 4; CSR (Spear).

14. Clark Diary, June 21, 1863, MSA; Spear et al., eds., *Civil War Recollections*, 30, 203.

15. Engert, ed., *Maine to the Wilderness*, 70; Spear et al., eds., *Civil War Recollections*, 32.

16. Chamberlain, "Through Blood and Fire," 896; Spear et al., eds., *Civil War Recollections*, 32.

17. Spear et al., eds., *Civil War Recollections*, 32, 311.

18. Johnston to Fitzhugh Lee, Feb. 11, 1878; Johnston to Lafayette McLaws, June 27, 1892—both Freeman Papers, LC.

19. Lawley, "The Battles of Gettysburg," *The Times* (London), Aug. 18, 1863.

20. Hood to Longstreet, June 28, 1875, in *SHSP*, 4 (Oct. 1877), 147–148.

21. Johnston to Peterkin, December 26, [after 1878], Freeman Papers, LC.

22. McLaws to Longstreet, June 12, 1873, McLaws Papers, SHC; McLaws, "Gettysburg," 68; McLaws, "The Battle of Gettysburg," *Philadelphia Weekly Press*, Apr. 21, 1886.

23. Meade, *With Meade at Gettysburg*, 101.

24. Swanberg, *Sickles the Incredible*, 54.

2. Patchwork Plans

1. Quoted in Davis, *Lincoln's Men*, 100.

2. Douglass, *Life and Times*, 269.

3. Bennett, "Truth Without Exaggeration," 52.

4. Baker, ed., *Works of William Seward*, 4:292.

5. Bennett, "Truth Without Exaggeration," 52.

6. Farley, "Reminiscences," No. IX, in Norton, *Attack and Defense*, 127–128.

7. Ibid., 128.

8. Jordan, *Some Events and Incidents*, 9.

9. Ibid., 13.

10. Ibid., 11.

11. Sterkx, "William C. Jordan," 66. On the complexities and nuances of Southern paternalism, see Stampp, *Peculiar Institution*, 162–163, 322–330; Genovese, *Roll, Jordan, Roll*, 3–25, 133–149, 661–665.

12. Sterkx, "William C. Jordan," 66.

13. Jordan, *Some Events and Incidents*, 14.

14. Ibid., 14–15.

15. Ibid., 18.

16. Ibid., 4, 24.

17. Ibid., 33, 36–37.

18. Ibid., 40.

19. Ibid., 41.

20. Oates, *War*, 206.

21. Scheibert, "Letter," 90.

22. Long, *Memoirs*, 281.

23. Hood, "Letter," 148; Longstreet, "Lee in Pennsylvania," 422.

24. Chamberlain, "Through Blood and Fire," 896.

25. Ibid., 896–897.

26. Spear et al., eds., *Civil War Recollections*, 191, 305.

27. Chamberlain, *Passing of the Armies*, 386.

28. Trulock, *In the Hands of Providence*, 121.

29. Spear to Amos Allen, Dec. 4, 1899, Chamberlain Papers, BC; Spear to Oliver W. Norton, Jan. 18, 1916, NP.

30. *CCW*, 331.

31. Meade, *Life and Letters*, 2:71.

32. *O.R.*, 27, Pt. 3, 487–488.

3. March, Countermarch

1. Sorrel, *Recollections*, 157; McLaws to Wife, July 7, 1863, SHC.

2. Longstreet, "Lee in Pennsylvania," 422.

3. *O.R.*, 27, Pt. 3, 488.

4. Johnston to McLaws, June 27, 1892; Johnston to Fitzhugh Lee, Feb. 11, 1878—both Freeman Papers, LC.

5. Abernathy, *Our Mess*, 31.

6. Kershaw, "Kershaw's Brigade at Gettysburg," 331; Wert, *General James Longstreet*, 269.

7. Longstreet, "Lee in Pennsylvania," 424.

8. McLaws, "Gettysburg," 69.

9. Ward, "Incidents and Personal Experiences," 346.

10. Oates Autobiography, Chapter 5, OFP.

11. Burnett, ed., "Letters," 292; Houghton and Houghton, *Two Boys*, 54.

12. Hunt, "Second Day," 301–302.

13. Hunt, "Second Day," 302; *CCW*, 450.

14. *CCW*, 298.

15. Taylor, *Gouverneur Kemble Warren*, 122; Miers, ed., *Wash Roebling's War*, 21. There is some dispute as to whether Meade sent Warren to Little Round Top or

whether Warren asked Meade to be sent. Warren himself maintained that "at my suggestion, General Meade sent me to the left to examine the condition of affairs, and I continued on till I reached Little Round Top." Norton, *Attack and Defense*, 309. Roebling insisted, however, that he had remembered Meade's words to Warren verbatim.

16. Meade, *With Meade at Gettysburg*, 114.

17. Brainard, *Campaigns*, 111.

18. Leeper, "Gettysburg," *NT*, Apr. 30, 1885; Porter, ed., *Under the Maltese Cross*, 165.

19. Bennett, *Beau Ideal*, 33; Norton, *Attack and Defense*, 320.

20. Bennett, *Beau Ideal*, 62; Fisher, "Born in Ireland," 234.

21. *Rochester Evening Express*, May 9, 1863; Bennett, *Beau Ideal*, 74.

22. West, *Texan in Search of a Fight*, 93.

23. Everett, ed., *Chaplain Davis*, 57; Jordan, *Some Events and Incidents*, 36.

24. *O.R.*, 27, Pt. 2, 318.

25. McLaws, "Gettysburg," 69–70.

26. Speech of Congressman Alexander White Gregg, 1906, Pinckney Papers, Brake Coll., USAMHI; Hood, "Letter," 148.

27. Longstreet, "Lee's Right Wing," 341; Wert, *General James Longstreet*, 272.

4. On Warfield Ridge

1. *Adams Sentinel*, July 26, 1864; *Gettysburg Star and Sentinel*, Aug. 19, 1875.

2. Hood, "Letter," 149.

3. Law, "Struggle for 'Round Top,'" 321; Houghton and Houghton, *Two Boys in the Civil War*, 53.

4. Law, "Struggle for 'Round Top,'" 321–322.

5. Hood, "Letter," 149–150; Law, "Struggle for 'Round Top,'" 322.

6. West, *Texan in Search of a Fight*, 85; Jordan, *Some Events and Incidents*, 42.

7. Barziza, *Adventures*, 44.

8. West, *Texan in Search of a Fight*, 183; Jordan, *Some Events and Incidents*, 47.

9. Quoted in McPherson, *What They Fought For*, 10.

10. Quoted in McPherson, *Battle Cry of Freedom*, 244.

11. *O.R.*, 18, 772–773.

12. West, *Texan in Search of a Fight*, 176, 177.

13. Nevins, ed., *A Diary of Battle*, 338–339.

14. Quoted in Longacre, "Gouverneur K. Warren," 16.

15. Warren to Emily Warren, June 22, 1863, Warren Letters, NYSL.

16. Norton, *Attack and Defense*, 309.

17. Ibid. Warren's account of the events that led him to realize that the Confederates were about to attack Little Round Top in force has been challenged by some historians. For one thing, Smith never mentioned the request by Warren to throw a shell in the direction of Warfield Ridge. For another, the sunlight

reflecting on the enemy's gun barrels seems just a little too contrived to be authentic. And for still another, the commander of the signal detachment claimed that he tried in vain to point out the approaching Confederates to Warren. I have used Warren's story with caution, realizing how flimsy his account appears to be.

18. Smith, *A Famous Battery*, 102–103.

19. Hood, "Letter," 150; Barziza, *Adventures*, 46.

20. Chilton, *Unveiling and Dedication*, 339, 350; West, *Texan in Search of a Fight*, 94; Polk, *North and South*, 27.

21. Oates, *War*, 226.

22. Powell, "With Hood at Gettysburg," *PWT*, Dec. 13, 1884; Ward, "Incidents," 348.

23. Oates, *War*, 212, 207.

24. Robertson to Bachelder, May 11, 1882, Ladd and Ladd, eds., *Bachelder Papers*, 2:860.

25. Spear and Spear, *20th Maine at Fredericksburg*, 45; Spear, "Story," 3.

26. Spear, Memorial Day Address, May 30, 1888, SP.

27. Spear et al., eds., *Civil War Recollections*, 50, 178.

28. Spear, Memorial Day Address, May 30, 1888, SP.

29. Chamberlain, "Through Blood and Fire," 898; Livermore Diary, July 2, 1863, UMO.

30. Spear et al., *Civil War Recollections*, 32.

31. Alleman, *At Gettysburg*, 41–42.

32. Ibid., 43–44.

33. Freeman, *Lee's Lieutenants*, 3:139.

34. *O.R.*, 27, Pt. 2, 309; Fremantle, *Three Months*, 268.

5. A Wild Rush

1. J. W. Jackson to Wife, July 7, 1863, 47th Alabama File, GNMP.

2. *O.R.*, 27, Pt. 2, 404.

3. Robertson to Bachelder, Apr. 20, 1876, in *BP*, 1:477.

4. Powell, "With Hood at Gettysburg," *PWT*, Dec. 13, 1884.

5. West, *Texan in Search of a Fight*, 86, 94; Barziza, *Adventures*, 45.

6. Lasswell, ed., *Rags and Hope*, 179.

7. M. J. Bulger to E. M. Law, July 9, 1896, Bulger File, ADAH.

8. Work to Thomas Langley, May 28, 1908, 1st Texas File, GNMP; Hood, "Letter," 150.

9. *O.R.*, 27, Pt. 1, 138.

10. White, *Civil War Diary*, 164.

11. Ibid.

12. Ibid.

13. Polley, *Hood's Texas Brigade*, 169.

14. Oates to Chamberlain, Mar. 8, 1897, UM. Bulger never mentioned that he had received orders from Law to report to Oates in the event of the 15th and the 47th becoming separated from the rest of the Alabama brigade on July 2. See, for example, Bulger to Law, July 9, 1896, Bulger File, ADAH.

15. Smith, *A Famous Battery*, 104.

16. Perry, "Devil's Den," 161.

17. *O.R.*, 27, Pt. 1, 510.

18. Smither to Mother, July 29, 1863, CRC; Lasswell, ed., *Rags and Hope*, 179.

19. West, *Texan in Search of a Fight*, 87.

20. Oates, *War*, 211.

21. White, *Civil War Diary*, 165.

22. *Gettysburg, July 2, 1863*, 1; White, *Civil War Diary*, 165.

23. Oates, "Gettysburg," 174; Soldier to Editor, July 7, 1863, in *Montgomery Daily Mail*, July 26, 1863.

24. Oates, "Gettysburg," 174–175; White, *Civil War Diary*, 165.

25. Oates, *War*, 211–212.

26. Ibid., 212.

6. Up Comes Vincent

1. Farley maintained after the war that the 140th New York was the last regiment in the line of march, but credible evidence, including General Warren's own recollection, indicates that the 140th was probably the lead regiment in Weed's brigade that day. See, for example, Farley's statement in Fox, ed., *New York at Gettysburg*, 3:956; Bennett, *Sons of Old Monroe*, 230–231, and the discussion in Bennett, "Truth Without Exaggeration," 70–82.

2. Brainard, *Campaigns*, 112.

3. Farley, "Reminiscences," No. IX, in Norton, *Attack and Defense*, 129.

4. *O.R.*, 27, Pt. 2, 405.

5. Hamilton, *History of Company M*, 30; Todd, *First Texas Regiment*, 16; *O.R.*, 27, Pt. 2, 405; Smith, "Devil's Den," *NT*, Mar. 4, 1886.

6. Fox, ed., *New York at Gettysburg*, 2:876; Polk, *North and South American Review*, 28.

7. Pfanz, *Gettysburg—The Second Day*, 187; Fox, ed., *New York at Gettysburg*, 2:869–870.

8. Fox, ed., *New York at Gettysburg*, 2:870.

9. *Maine at Gettysburg*, 163–164.

10. Quoted in Pfanz, *Gettysburg—The Second Day*, 191.

11. *Maine at Gettysburg*, 163.

12. Smith, *A Famous Battery*, 104; *O.R.*, 27, Pt. 2, 426.

13. Polley, *Hood's Texas Brigade*, 169.

14. Spear et al., eds., *Civil War Recollections*, 33.

15. Chamberlain asserted that he and the 20th Maine led Vincent's column, but he was mistaken. See Bateman, "The Hero of Gettysburg," *Lewiston Journal*, Sept. 1–6, 1900; Pfanz, *Gettysburg—The Second Day*, 212.

16. Norton, *Attack and Defense*, 284–285.

17. Nevins and Styple, *What Death More Glorious*, 57; Norton, *Attack and Defense*, 285.

18. Norton, *Attack and Defense*, 264. Historians have sometimes erroneously assumed that Warren personally asked Vincent to defend Little Round Top, but Warren made clear, in a letter written in 1877, that he did not summon Vincent's brigade to the hill. See Warren to Porter Farley, Oct. 23, 1877, in ibid., 314. For more on this point, see also Oliver W. Norton to Frank Huntington, Sept. 28, 1888, NP; Norton to Joshua Lawrence Chamberlain, May 6, 1901, Chamberlain Collection 10, Maine Historical Society; Norton to Washington A. Roebling, July 24, 1915, SCWC.

19. Norton, *Attack and Defense*, 264.

20. Norton to Huntington, Sept. 28, 1888, NP; Norton, *Attack and Defense*, 265.

21. Spear, "Memorial Day Speech," May 30, 1888, SP.

22. Jacklin Recollections, Brake Coll., USAMHI; Coan Account, n.d., Coan Papers, BC; Phillips and Parsegian, eds., *Richard and Rhoda*, 30.

23. Oliver Norton thought the order of march was 44th New York, 16th Michigan, 83rd Pennsylvania, and 20th Maine, but Private Elisha Coan of the 20th Maine appears to be the more reliable source. Cf. Coan, "Reply to 'Rear Rank,'" *Lincoln County News*, May 1883; Norton, *Attack and Defense*, 265.

24. Desjardin, *Stand Firm*, 37; John to Sister, July 2, 1863, 44th New York File, GNMP; Graham, *On to Gettysburg*, 9.

25. Norton, *Letters*, 165.

26. Judson, *History*, 125; Norton, *Attack and Defense*, 265.

27. For a forcefully argued, and convincing, brief that debunks the Butterfield Twins myth, see Ryan, "Say It Ain't So," 34–39.

28. Coan Account, n.d., Coan Papers, BC.

29. *O.R.*, 27, Pt. 1, 616–617; Bates, *History of Pennsylvania Volunteers*, 2:1254; Platt, "On Little Round Top," *NT*, Apr. 11, 1907.

30. Chamberlain, "Through Blood and Fire," 899; Clark Diary, July 2, 1863, MSA; Coan Account, n.d., Coan Papers, BC.

31. Nash, *History of the Forty-Fourth*, 154; Morrill to Chamberlain, July 8, 1863, in *BP*, 2:1029.

32. Chamberlain, "Through Blood and Fire," 900.

33. Alleman, *At Gettysburg*, 49.

34. Ibid., 50–52.

35. Ibid., 53, 54.

36. Ibid., 55.

37. Quoted in Coco, *Vast Sea of Misery*, 69.

38. Daily Register of Dr. Cyrus Bacon, Jr., July 2, 1863, Brake Coll., USAMHI.

39. Alleman, *At Gettysburg*, 56.

40. Norton, *Attack and Defense*, 133.

7. Through the Valley of Death

1. Hess, *Union Soldier in Battle*, 38; Faust, "Civil War Soldier," 3–38.

2. West, *Texan in Search of a Fight*, 87.

3. Stevens, *Reminiscences*, 114; Smith, *Reminiscences*, 36.

4. Ward, "Incidents," 347.

5. Ibid.

6. West, *Texan in Search of a Fight*, 98.

7. *O.R.*, 27, Pt. 2, 411.

8. The whereabouts of the 16th Michigan skirmishers has never been accurately determined, for it seems likely that they were sent forward when Vincent first placed their regiment on the far left of his brigade line. When he redeployed the 16th Michigan to the extreme right of the line, it is not clear if he sent the regiment's skirmishers with it. Company B of the 20th Maine went out to the left of the brigade line thinking it would link up with the 16th Michigan skirmishers, but never found them. The official records are silent about where this Michigan skirmish line may have actually ended up, although one officer of the 16th Michigan thought that the regiment's skirmishers deployed on Big Round Top, by which he may have meant the low shoulder of land that connected the big hill with Devil's Den. See, for example, the 16th Michigan's battle report written by Colonel Norval E. Welch, *O.R.*, 27, Pt. 1, 628; the report of Captain Walter G. Morrill, who commanded the 20th Maine skirmish line, in *BP*, 2:1029; and Graham, *On to Gettysburg*, 10. Pfanz believes that the Michigan skirmishers moved to fill the gap between the 16th's right and the 4th Maine's position behind Devil's Den. See Pfanz, *Gettysburg—The Second Day*, 214.

9. Nash, *History*, 144–145, 154.

10. *O.R.*, 27, Pt. 2, 412.

11. Fletcher, *Rebel Private*, 79; Powell, "With Hood at Gettysburg," *PWT*, Dec. 13, 1884; Smither to Mother, July 29, 1863, Brake Coll., USAMHI.

12. West, *Texan in Search of a Fight*, 94–95; Zack Landrum to Mother, July 15, 1863, Brake Coll., USAMHI.

13. Polk, *North and South*, 28; Powell, "With Hood at Gettysburg," *PWT*, Dec. 13, 1884; Laswell, ed., *Rags and Hope*, 180; Barziza, *Adventures*, 49; Landrum to Mother, July 15, 1863, Brake Coll., USAMHI.

14. Felder to Mother, July 9, 1863, CRC; Smither to Mother, July 29, 1863, Brake Coll., USAMHI; West, *Texan in Search of a Fight*, 98.

15. Laswell, ed., *Rags and Hope*, 180; Smither to Mother, July 29, 1863, Brake Coll., USAMHI.

16. *O.R.*, 27, Pt. 2, 412.

17. *O.R.*, 27, Pt. 2, 413; Barziza, *Adventures*, 47; Barziza Diary, July 2, 1863, Cobb and Hunter Family Papers, SHC.

18. Ward, "Incidents," 347–348.

19. Ibid., 348.

20. Quoted in Linderman, *Embattled Courage*, 73.

21. McCarthy, *Detailed Minutiae*, 8–9. See also Donald, "Confederate as a Fighting Man," 178–193; Catton, "The Confederate Legend," 9–23.

22. Stevens, *Reminiscences*, 114.

23. Stocker, ed., *From Huntsville to Alabama*, 105.

24. Laswell, ed., *Rags and Hope*, 180; Fletcher, *Rebel Private*, 80.

25. *O.R.*, 27, Pt. 2, 413.

26. Laswell, ed., *Rags and Hope*, 180–181; Barziza, *Adventures*, 48–49.

8. Shouting the Battle Cry

1. Norton, *Attack and Defense*, 310.

2. Ibid.

3. Ibid., 283–284.

4. Judson, *History*, 126.

5. Salter to Isabella Duffield, July 12, 1863, DPL; Sprague, "Fourth of July, '63," unidentified newspaper clipping, 44th New York File, GNMP.

6. Norton to Frank Huntington, Sept. 28, 1888, NP; Phillips and Parsegian, *Richard and Rhoda*, 30.

7. Judson, *History*, 126.

8. Colestock, "16th Michigan at Little Round Top," *NT*, Mar. 26, 1914; *O.R.*, 27, Pt. 1, 632; Ilisevich and Helmreich, eds., *Civil War Diaries*, 103; Judson, *History*, 127.

9. Judson, *History*, 127; Platt, "On Little Round Top," *NT*, Apr. 11, 1907. Platt's account contains whole passages blatantly plagiarized from Judson's *History* of the 83rd Pennsylvania. The quoted statement, however, appears to be his own.

10. Judson, *History*, 127.

11. Dennett, ed., *Lincoln and the Civil War*, 19.

12. For the term ideology, I accept, as James M. McPherson does, Eric Foner's definition: i.e., "the system of beliefs, values, fears, prejudices, reflexes, and commitments—in sum, the social consciousness—of a social group, be it a class, a party, or a section." See Foner, *Free Soil*, 4; McPherson, *For Cause and Comrades*, 94. My conception of ideology, however, has additionally been informed by the anthropological layers of meaning found in Geertz, *Interpretation of Cultures*, 193–233.

13. Rice to Michael Jacobs, Nov. 21, 1863, in *NYT*, Nov. 28, 1863.

14. Lytle to Brother, June 28, 1863, Leigh Coll., USAMHI.

15. Porter, ed., *Under the Maltese Cross*, 105.

16. Chamberlain, *Passing of the Armies*, 19–20, 385–386.

17. Hess, *Union Soldier in Battle*, 74–75.

18. My understanding of combat motivation among Union soldiers has been greatly influenced by recent quantitative studies using data assembled for Robert W. Fogel's project on the "Aging of Veterans of the Union Army," at the University of Chicago, particularly the conclusions reached by Costa and Kahn in "Cowards and Heroes," 519–548. On the question of motivation, see also Linderman, *Embattled Courage*; Hess, *Union Soldier in Battle*; McPherson, *For Cause and Comrades*; Gallagher, *Confederate War*; and Grimsley, "In Not So Dubious Battle," 175–188.

19. Judson, *History*, 123; Brown to Brother, July 7, 1863, Brown Papers, Brown University.

20. Judson, *History*, 125; Charles Brandegee to Father, July 6, 1863, Civil War Misc. Coll., USAMHI.

21. Ilisevich and Helmreich, eds., *Civil War Diaries*, 103; Brown, "On Gettysburg Field," *PWT*, May 26, 1883.

22. Martin, "Little Round Top," *Gettysburg Compiler*, Oct. 24, 1899.

23. Ibid.

24. Rittenhouse, "Battle of Gettysburg," 521; O. W. Damon, War Diary, July 2, 1863, 5th U.S. Artillery File, GNMP.

25. Martin, "Little Round Top," *Gettysburg Compiler*, Oct. 24, 1899.

26. Warren maintained that only two Parrotts were deployed on Little Round Top, but he was mistaken. See Norton, *Attack and Defense*, 312. In his defense, he may have departed from the hill after only two guns were placed and went into action; he thus may not have been aware that two additional guns were crammed into the narrow space available on the hilltop. An artillerist's diary confirms the placement of Hazlett's four guns on the summit and reports that the remaining two guns of the battery had to be taken back down the reverse slope of the hill. See Damon, War Diary, July 2, 1863, 5th U.S. Artillery File, GNMP.

27. Quoted in Taylor, *Gouverneur Kemble Warren*, 129.

28. John P. Vincent to David McConaughy, Nov. 30, 1863, McConaughy Papers, Gettysburg College; Philo H. Conklin to Mary, July 31, 1863, Johnson Family Papers, USAMHI; Salter to Isabella Duffield, July 12, 1863, DPL.

29. Quoted in Taylor, *Gouverneur Kemble Warren*, 129.

30. Rittenhouse, "Battle of Gettysburg," 522.

9. Down This Way, Boys

1. Norton, *Army Letters*, 161.

2. Nash, *History*, 145; Ilisevich and Helmreich, eds., *Civil War Diaries*, 103–104.

3. Sprague, "Fourth of July, '63," unidentified news clipping, 44th New York File, GNMP.

4. Apted Diary, July 2, 1863, FSNMP; Charles H. Salter to Isabella Duffield, July 12, 1863, DPL.

5. Rice, "Rebel Invasion of Pennsylvania," *NYT*, Nov. 28, 1863.

6. Graham, *On to Gettysburg*, 11.

7. *O.R.*, 27, Pt. 1, 630; Hosford Diary, July 2, 1863, 44th New York File, GNMP; William H. Brown to George W. Brown, July 7, 1863, Brown Papers, Brown University.

8. Benjamin F. Partridge to John B. Bachelder, Mar. 3, 1866, *BP*, 1:244; Graham, *On to Gettysburg*, 11; *Michigan at Gettysburg*, 108–109.

9. Salter to Isabella Duffield, July 12, 1863, DPL; *Michigan at Gettysburg*, 108–109.

10. Norton, "Strong Vincent," 506; R. Turrill to Daniel Ervay, July 28, 1863, 16th Michigan File, GNMP.

11. Salter to Isabella Duffield, July 12, 1863, DPL.

12. *O.R.*, 27, Pt. 1, 628.

13. Judson, *History*, 128.

14. Farley, "Reminiscences," No. IX, in Norton, *Attack and Defense*, 130. A more extensive account of the dialogue between Warren and O'Rorke may be found in the memoirs of Sergeant Henry Cribben, but it is not evident if Cribben himself heard the exchange between Warren and O'Rorke or if he was repeating— and perhaps elaborating on—what he might have learned about the conversation afterwards. Cribben also thought that Warren was on foot when he approached the 140th New York. See Youker, ed., *Military Memoirs*, 19–20.

15. Youker, ed., *Military Memoirs*, 20; Hazen, "At Gettysburg," *NT*, Aug. 25, 1892.

16. Fox, ed., *New York at Gettysburg*, 3:956; Farley, "Reminiscences," No. IX, in Norton, *Attack and Defense*, 133–134.

17. Farley to Norton, June 24, 1911, in Norton, *Army Letters*, 371. Another source says that O'Rorke shouted, "Follow me, my brave boys" and "Here they are, men." See Hazen, "Fighting the Good Fight," *NT*, Sept. 13, 1894. It is possible O'Rorke said all of these things.

18. Leeper, "Gettysburg," *NT*, Apr. 30, 1885; True Blue to [?], July 3, 1863, in *Rochester Evening Express*, July 11, 1863.

19. A few soldiers remembered that the regiment was halted long enough to load before going into the fight. See, for example, J. R. C. to Father, July 3, 1863, in *Rochester Evening Express*, July 11, 1863. Farley, however, adamantly maintained that the 140th attacked with unloaded muskets.

20. Farley, "Reminiscences," No. IX, in Norton, *Attack and Defense*, 134; J. R. C. to Father, July 3, 1863, in *Rochester Evening Express*, July 11, 1863.

21. True Blue to [?], July 3, 1863, in *Rochester Evening Express*, July 11, 1863; Hazen, "At Gettysburg," *NT*, Aug. 25, 1892.

22. Milo L. Starks to Father, July 6, 1863, 140th New York File, GNMP.

23. Farley, "Reminiscences," No. IX, in Norton, *Attack and Defense*, 139.

24. *O.R.*, 27, Pt. 2, 446.

25. Quoted in Pfanz, *Gettysburg—Culp's Hill and Cemetery Hill*, 180.

26. Howard, "Campaign," 63; Nevins, ed., *Diary of Battle*, 243–244.

27. McLaws, "Battle of Gettysburg," 78.

28. Kershaw, "Kershaw's Brigade," 334.

29. Longstreet, *From Manassas to Appomattox*, 370; Pfanz, *Gettysburg—The Second Day*, 320.

30. Wert, *General James Longstreet*, 276.

31. Tremain, *Two Days*, 89.

32. Sickles's leg was preserved, and the bones were later mounted for display. He donated his right tibia and fibula to the Army Medical Museum in Washington, D.C., where he frequently visited them in the years following the war. The leg bones are now on display at the Armed Forces Medical Museum at Walter Reed Army Hospital in Washington.

10. A Sorry Place

1. Spear et al., eds., *Civil War Recollections*, 312.

2. Spear et al., eds., *Civil War Recollections*, 33; Gerrish, "Twentieth Maine at Gettysburg," *Portland Advertiser*, Mar. 13, 1882.

3. Miller, "Address," in Miller, ed., *Reunions*, 17; Morrill to Chamberlain, July 8, 1863, in *BP*, 2:1029.

4. Livermore Diary, July 2, 1863, UMO; *Eastern Argus*, Dec. 20, 1865; *O.R.*, 27, Pt. 1, 623.

5. O'Connell Memoir, n.d., Civil War Misc. Coll., USAMHI.

6. Potter, "Gettysburg," *NT*, Feb. 25, 1892. See also Judson, *History*, 129, who describes how the 83rd Pennsylvania fell back "some ten or fifteen paces," a movement that he claims was the result of coordination between Captain Woodward and Colonel Chamberlain.

7. Chamberlain to Bachelder, n.d., *BP*, 3:1884; Chamberlain, "Through Blood and Fire," 902.

8. Livermore Diary, July 2, 1863, UMO; Coan Account, n.d., Coan Papers, BC.

9. Oates, *War*, 214.

10. LaFantasie, ed., "William C. Oates," 61; Oates, *War*, 214.

11. Jordan, *Some Events*, 42–43.

12. Ibid., 43.

13. Chamberlain to Oates, Feb. 27, 1897, Chamberlain Papers, BC. This letter is an incomplete draft or copy of a letter of the same date that Chamberlain sent to Oates.

14. Chamberlain to George A. Herendeen (official report), July 6, 1863, MSA; Chamberlain, "Through Blood and Fire," 902.

15. Spear et al., eds., *Civil War Recollections*, 34. Chamberlain later claimed that "several officers," not just Spear, informed him of the enemy's movements to

envelop the 20th Maine. He said some of those officers were surprised that they alone did not deliver the news. To placate them, Chamberlain said in a speech dedicating the 20th Maine monument on Little Round Top: "Now, as might well be believed of such gentlemen and soldiers, they are all right; no one of them is wrong." See Chamberlain, "Address," in *DTMM*, 27. Lieutenant James H. Nichols of Company K also asserted that he had reported the flanking movement to Chamberlain. See Prince, "Address," in ibid., 18. Despite this claim, it seems fairly certain that Spear was the only officer of the 20th Maine who told Chamberlain of the Confederates' impending flanking movement. See, for instance, the reminiscences of Private Elisha Coan of the regiment's color guard in Coan Account, n.d., Coan Papers, BC.

16. Chamberlain, "Through Blood and Fire," 902; Chamberlain to Herendeen, July 6, 1863, MSA. As the years went on, Chamberlain increasingly assumed sole credit for coming up with the idea of refusing the regiment's line. See, for example, Chamberlain, "Address," in *DTMM*, 27; "How General Chamberlain with His 20th Maine Held Little Round Top," *Lewiston Journal*, May 5, 1912.

17. *O.R.*, 27, Pt. 1, 623; Chamberlain to Bachelder, n.d., *BP*, 3:1884.

18. Chamberlain to Herendeen, July 6, 1863, MSA. Some accounts say that the line was refused under fire; other accounts insist that the Confederates opened fire *after* the 20th Maine's left was bent back. One regimental historian maintained that both viewpoints were valid, for the 20th Maine's right wing had come under fire from the assaulting 47th Alabama before the left wing opened up against Oates's 15th Alabama. See Prince, "Address," in *DTMM*, 17–18. To a certain degree, his conclusion is probably correct, but it's more likely that the fog of war left the Mainers with starkly different memories of what had occurred that afternoon.

19. Chamberlain, "Through Blood and Fire," 902; Chamberlain, "Address," in *DTMM*, 27; *Maine at Gettysburg*, 255; Coan Account, n.d., Coan Papers, BC.

20. Spear et al., eds., *Civil War Recollections*, 34; Chamberlain to Herendeen, July 6, 1863, MSA.

21. Keene to Sarah Keene, July 3–5, 1863, SP. Keene was killed in 1864. Ellis Spear, whose wife Susan died in 1873, married Keene's widow, Sarah, two years later. When Captain Keene died, Spear, his closest friend, wrote: "The loss to me was a severe one. . . . He was a noble fellow, of unusual ability and culture." Spear regarded his friend as one of "the heroes of the past." Spear et al., eds., *Civil War Recollections*, 127–128.

22. Clark Diary, July 2, 1863, MSA; O'Connell Memoir, n.d., Civil War Misc. Coll., USAMHI.

23. LaFantasie, ed., "William C. Oates," 61; Oates, *War*, 218.

24. Oates, "Gettysburg," 176.

25. Bulger to E. M. Law, July 9, 1896, Bulger File, ADAH. According to Major

James Campbell, who later assumed command of the 47th Alabama and wrote the official report of the regiment's conduct at Gettysburg, Bulger did not assume immediate command of the regiment when Colonel J. W. Jackson fell with fatigue during the advance from Warfield Ridge. There was, said Campbell, some confusion over command, "owing to the fact that in the charge the lieutenant-colonel [Bulger] expected the colonel to give all the necessary commands, and the colonel remained so far behind that his presence on the field was but a trammel on the lieutenant-colonel." See *O.R.*, 27, Pt. 2, 395.

26. Bulger to E. M. Law, July 9, 1896, Bulger File, ADAH.

27. *O.R.*, 27, Pt. 2, 393; Oates, *War*, 218.

28. Coan Account, n.d., Coan Papers, BC; Beyer and Keydel, eds., *Deeds of Valor*, 1:246.

29. Spear, Memorial Day Speech, May 30, 1888, SP.

30. Oates, *War*, 612–613. On Ellison, see also ibid., 227.

31. Oates, *War*, 218; William A. Edwards to W. R. Painter, Nov. 11, 1915, unidentified news clipping, 15th Alabama Regimental File, ADAH.

32. Oates, *War*, 688.

33. Oates, *War*, 219. See also Oates to John P. Nicholson, Feb. 11, 1903, WCO Correspondence, GNMP.

34. Oates, *War*, 673–674.

35. The location of the rock behind which John Oates was dragged is not known. In 1896, William Oates told Emmor Cope, the chief engineer of the Gettysburg National Military Park when it was under the administration of the War Department, that his brother "was killed on the left of his regiment near some large rocks in the vicinity of the 20th Maine monument." See *Record of the Position of Troops on the Battlefield*, Volume I, 2 July 1896, p. 28, Engineers Department, Gettysburg Battlefield Commission, GNMP.

36. Chamberlain to Herendeen, July 6, 1863, MSA; Spear et al., eds., *Civil War Recollections* 34, 313; Spear, "The Left at Gettysburg," *NT*, June 12, 1913.

37. Chamberlain, "Address," in *DTMM*, 27–28.

38. Oates to Robbins, Sept. 4, 1904, WCO Correspondence, GNMP. See also Oates to Chamberlain, Apr. 14, 1905, ibid.

39. Spear, et al., eds., *Civil War Recollections*, 34. See also *Maine at Gettysburg*, 256–257. In 1898, Tozier was awarded a Medal of Honor for his bravery on Little Round Top. One version of the Tozier story has him firing a musket while passing the colors to another man to hold temporarily. See William T. Livermore to Joshua Lawrence Chamberlain, May 22, 1899, Chamberlain Papers, Coll. 10, Maine Historical Society.

40. Chamberlain, "Through Blood and Fire," 904.

41. Spear, "The Left at Gettysburg," *NT*, June 12, 1913; Spear et al., eds., *Civil War Recollections*, 215.

11. Everywhere Men Torn and Broken

1. Farley, "Reminiscences," No. IX, in Norton, *Attack and Defense*, 137; Farley, "Reminiscences of the 140th Regiment," 227; *Rochester Evening Express*, July 8, 1863.

2. *O.R.*, 27, Pt. 1, 617–618. None of the surviving accounts confirm that the ammunition of the 20th Maine was ever replenished during the battle, despite Rice's claim to the contrary.

3. Walter, "Personal Recollections," *GASSM*, Sept. 13, 1884.

4. Davis, "Little Round Top," *NT*, Nov. 11, 1915; Brainard, *Campaigns*, 118.

5. Davis, "Little Round Top," *NT*, Nov. 11, 1915.

6. Williamson, "Little Round Top," *NT*, Sept. 1, 1892.

7. Martin, "Little Round Top," *Gettysburg Compiler*, Oct. 24, 1899.

8. Rittenhouse, "Battle of Gettysburg," 523; McElrath, "A Soldier's Death," 665.

9. Brainard, *Campaigns*, 119; Rittenhouse, "Battle of Gettysburg," 524.

10. David Jenkins to A. P. Case, Jan. 7, 1864, in *BP*, 1:75; North, *Memorial*, 106.

11. Chamberlain to Herendeen, July 6, 1863, MSA. In a report written to General Barnes two months after the battle, Chamberlain said that the lines surged back and forth four times, not three. See Chamberlain to Barnes, Sept. 3, 1863, Barnes Papers, New-York Historical Society.

12. Oates, "Gettysburg," 177.

13. Oates, *War*, 219.

14. Spear et al., eds., *Civil War Recollections*, 314.

15. Chamberlain to Barnes, Sept. 3, 1863, Barnes Papers, New-York Historical Society.

16. *O.R.*, 27, Pt. 1, 624; Chamberlain, "Through Blood and Fire," 903–904.

17. Bateman, "The Hero of Gettysburg," *Lewiston Journal*, Sept. 1–6, 1900; Chamberlain to Bachelder, n.d., *BP*, 3:1885; "How General Chamberlain with the 20th Maine Held Little Round Top," *Lewiston Journal*, May 25, 1912.

18. Desjardin, *Stand Firm*, 64; "How General Chamberlain with the 20th Maine Held Little Round Top," *Lewiston Journal*, May 25, 1912.

19. Chamberlain, "Through Blood and Fire," 904–905.

20. O'Connell Memoir, n.d., Civil War Misc. Coll., USAMHI; Spear, "Memorial Day Speech," May 30, 1888, SP.

21. Oates, *War*, 220.

22. Ibid.

23. Ibid.

24. Chamberlain to Herendeen, July 6, 1863, MSA; "The Twentieth Maine at Gettysburg," *Eastern Argus*, Dec. 20, 1865; Beyer and Keydel, eds., *Deeds of Valor*, 1:246.

25. *O.R.*, 27, Pt. 1, 624. The quotation is taken from Chamberlain's "official report" as published in the *O.R.* series and dated July 6, 1863, but it was actually

written in 1884. When the editors of the *O.R.* informed him in that year that his original report had been lost (actually a copy exists in the Maine State Archives and has been cited herein as Chamberlain to Herendeen, July 6, 1863, MSA), Chamberlain wrote a new report from memory and sent it to Washington. It was published in 1889 among other Union reports without editorial comment or explanation. My thanks to Thomas A. Desjardin for sharing this important discovery with me. See also Hall, *Stand of the U.S. Army*, 347.

26. Chamberlain, "Address," in *DTMM*, 24; Coan Account, n.d., Coan Papers, BC.

27. Chamberlain, "Through Blood and Fire," 906; Chamberlain to Herendeen, July 6, 1863, MSA; Livermore Diary, July 2, 1863, UMO; Coan Account, n.d., Coan Papers, BC.

28. Chamberlain to Herendeen, July 6, 1863, MSA; Bates, "The Hero of Gettysburg," *Lewiston Journal*, Sept. 1–6, 1900.

29. Spear, "Memorial Day Speech," May 30, 1888, SP; Spear et al., eds., *Civil War Recollections*, 36; Spear to Bachelder, Nov. 15, 1892, Bachelder Papers, New Hampshire Historical Society.

30. Oates, *War*, 220. For the rest of his life, Oates maintained that the 20th Maine did not drive the 15th Alabama from its position, but that his regiment was in the process of retreating when the Federals came rolling down the hill. In 1897, Oates wrote to Chamberlain: "I have read in a book written by the chaplain of the 20th Maine [i.e., Theodore Gerrish] in which he claims that a charge of that regiment drove mine away. I can see how that was an honest mistake for just as your men were recoiling I took advantage of it to retreat & seeing that[,] of course[,] the 20th pursued; but my regiment was not driven out by a charge but went by my order when I had lost one half of them." See Oates to Chamberlain, Mar. 8, 1897, Schoff Civil War Coll., UM.

31. Despite Oates's firm insistence that his men encountered Union troopers on foot, most historians have doubted that Union cavalry were to be found anywhere in the vicinity of Little Round Top during the late afternoon of July 2. However, one source does indicate the possibility that the 6th New York Cavalry was in the area at the time. See Clarke, "Sixth New York Cavalry," 413–414. General Law, however, said that his scouts at no time reported the presence of Union cavalry on his right. Law, "Struggle for 'Round Top,'" 323.

32. Oates, *War*, 222; Oates to Chamberlain, Mar. 8, 1897, Schoff Civil War Coll., UM.

33. Jordan, *Some Events*, 44.

34. Spear, "Element of Accident," 103.

35. Spear, "Element of Accident," 103; Gerrish, *Army Life*, 110; Spear et al., eds., *Civil War Recollections*, 317; Spear to Mildred P. Grant, Mar. 14, 1910, in Styple, ed., *With a Flash*, 300–301; Clark Diary, July 2, 1863, MSA; Livermore Diary, July 2, 1863, UMO.

36. "The Twentieth Maine at Gettysburg," *Eastern Argus*, Dec. 20, 1865; *O.R.*, 27, Pt. 1, 617.

37. Bateman, "The Hero of Gettysburg," *Lewiston Journal*, Sept. 1–6, 1900.

12. Twilight

1. Samuel W. Crawford to Peter Rothermel, Apr. 20, 1871, Rothermel Papers, PHMC.

2. Bell Recollections, n.d., 42nd Pennsylvania (13th Pennsylvania Reserves) File, GNMP; *O.R.*, 27, Pt. 1, 653.

3. *O.R.*, 27, Pt. 2, 401–402.

4. Nicholson, ed., *Pennsylvania at Gettysburg*, 1:278; Woodward, *Our Campaigns*, 213.

5. *O.R.*, 27, Pt. 2, 400.

6. Ware Diary, July 2, 1863, Ware Papers, SHC; Jackson to Rothermel, n.d., Rothermel Papers, PHMC.

7. Crawford to Rothermel, Mar. 8, 1871, Rothermel Papers, PHMC.

8. Woodward to Bates, Feb. 7, 1876, Bates Papers, PHMC; Woodward, *Our Campaigns*, 213; *O.R.*, 27, Pt. 1, 657.

9. Bard, "The 'Old Bucktails,' 42nd Reg., P.V., at the Battle of Gettysburg," *PWP*, May 19, 1886.

10. Woodward to Bates, Feb. 7, 1876, Bates Papers, PHMC.

11. Nicholson, ed., *Pennsylvania at Gettysburg*, 1:302; Baker to Annie Taylor, July 11, 1863, 42nd Pennsylvania (13th Pennsylvania Reserves) File, GNMP.

12. Minnigh, *History of Company K*, 25.

13. *O.R.*, 27, Pt. 1, 618.

14. "General M. J. Bulger: An Alabama Hero," *Montgomery Advertiser*, Oct. 2, 1898. Chamberlain later claimed credit for taking Bulger prisoner, but the Confederate officer only ever mentioned Rice by name in his own accounts of his capture.

15. Powell, "With Hood at Gettysburg," *PWT*, Dec. 13, 1884.

16. Livermore Diary, July 2, 1863, UMO; Coan Account, n.d., Coan Papers, BC.

17. Spear et al., eds., *Civil War Recollections*, 37.

18. Jordan, *Some Events and Incidents*, 45.

19. Oates, *War*, 225–226.

20. Meade, ed., *Life and Letters*, 2:89.

21. Quoted in Pfanz, *Gettysburg—Culp's Hill and Cemetery Hill*, 259.

22. Quoted in Coco, *Vast Sea*, 69.

23. There is a great deal of confusion over whether O'Rorke was taken to the Weikert farmyard or the nearby Lewis Bushman farm, or both. Farley said that O'Rorke was taken to Bushman's farmhouse (Farley, "Reminiscences," No. IX, in Norton, *Attack and Defense*, 138), but Lieutenant Rittenhouse of Hazlett's bat-

tery reported seeing "the forms of four intimate friends . . . Weed, Vincent [still alive], O'Rorke, and Hazlett" on "the piazza of a farm house" that served as the Fifth Corps' hospital, presumably the Weikert house (Rittenhouse, "Battle of Gettysburg," 524).

24. Farley, "Reminiscences," No. IX, in Norton, *Attack and Defense*, 139–140.

25. Norton to Frank Huntington, Sept. 28, 1888, NP. In another account, Norton claimed that Vincent could speak when he saw him and asked if Norton "had just come from the front." See Norton, *Army Letters*, 162. Some reports claim that Vincent was taken to the Lewis Bushman farm; it is possible that Vincent received triage treatment at the Weikerts' and was later transferred to the Bushman place.

26. Judson, *History*, 139.

27. Alleman, *At Gettysburg*, 61–68.

13. Night of the Dead

1. West, *Texan in Search of a Fight*, 86, 88, 96.

2. *O.R.*, 27, Pt. 2, 409.

3. Lasswell, ed., *Rags and Hope*, 181, 183.

4. Polk, *North and South*, 29.

5. Barziza, *Adventures*, 51–52.

6. Fletcher, *Rebel Private*, 81–82; Smith, "Reminiscences," 38.

7. Philo H. Conklin to Mary [Johnson?], July 31, 1863, Johnson Family Papers, USAMHI; Frasier Rosenkrantz to Cousin, July 20, 1863, Civil War Misc. Coll., USAMHI.

8. Samuel T. Keene to Sarah Keene, July 3–5, 1863, SP; Harlan Bailey to Maria Bailey Wright, July 13, 1863, Bailey Letters, GNMP.

9. Philo H. Conklin to Mary [Johnson?], July 31, 1863, Johnson Family Papers, USAMHI.

10. Nash, *History*, 151, 327.

11. Brown, "On Gettysburg Field," *PWT*, May 26, 1883.

12. Walter, "Personal Recollections," *GASSM*, Sept. 13, 1884; Scott, "On Little Round Top," *NT*, Aug. 2, 1894; Rittenhouse, "Battle of Gettysburg," 524.

13. Sprague to Oliver W. Norton, Jan. 16, 1910, 44th New York File, GNMP.

14. True Blue to Editor, July [?], 1863, *Rochester Evening Express*, July 17, 1863; Daily Register of Dr. Cyrus Bacon, Jr., July 3, 1863, Brake Coll., USAMHI.

15. Henry [?] to Friends at Home, July 8, 1863, in Nash, *History*, 326.

16. John F. Huntington to William Fellows, July 28, 1863, Brake Coll., USAMHI; Fox, ed., *New York at Gettysburg*, 3:957.

17. Fox, ed., *New York at Gettysburg*, 3:957.

18. Barziza, *Adventures*, 49.

19. Ibid.

20. Taylor, *Soldier's Almanac*, 21.

21. On this point, see Nevins, "The Glorious and the Terrible," 47.

22. Mitchell, *Vacant Chair*, 142.

23. Quoted in Hess, *Union Soldier in Battle*, 143. On letters of condolence and condolence literature during the Civil War era, see Faust, "Civil War Soldier," 3–38; Barton, "Painful Duties," 123–134; Schultz, "Healing the Nation," 33–41.

24. Orsell Cook Brown to A. Dunham, July 6, 1863, in Coco, *Killed in Action*, 42–43.

25. Quoted in Fahs, *Imagined Civil War*, 95.

26. Quoted in Linderman, *Embattled Courage*, 12.

27. Nicholson, ed., *Pennsylvania at Gettysburg*, 2:776.

28. Charles Brandegee to Father, July 6, 1863, Civil War Times Illustrated Coll., USAMHI; Orsell Cook Brown to Sister, July 3, 1863, Brown Letters, NYSL; Felder to Mother, July 9, 1863, CRC.

29. J. Mark Smither to Mother, July 29, 1863, Brake Coll., USAMHI; J. R. C. to Father, July 3, 1863, *Rochester Evening Express*, July 19, 1863; Erastus L. Harris to Mrs. Rachel Smith, July 4, 1863, Aug. 10, 1863, Civil War Misc. Coll., USAMHI.

30. Frank Park to Benjamin Gardner, July 7, 1863, in *Southern Advertiser*, July 29, 1863.

31. Oates to Edmund Cody, Aug. 30, 1863, in Burnett, "Letters," 372–373.

14. Waiting for Tomorrow

1. *O.R.*, 27, Pt. 1, 72.

2. Gibbon, "Council of War," 313.

3. *O.R.*, 27, Pt. 1, 73.

4. Gibbon, "Council of War," 313. Brief notations on the replies of each of the generals are printed in *O.R.*, 27, 73–74. In 1881, Hancock asserted that the council minutes prepared by Butterfield did not accurately record his views at the time. See "A Gettysburg Incident," *NYT*, Dec. 18, 1881.

5. *O.R.*, 27, Pt. 1, 73; Gibbon, "Council of War," 314.

6. *O.R.*, 27, Pt. 1, 73.

7. *O.R.*, 27, Pt. 1, 73–74; *O.R.*, 27, Pt. 1, 126.

8. *O.R.*, 27, Pt. 1, 73–74.

9. Ibid., 127.

10. Ibid.; Gibbon, "Council of War," 314.

11. Fremantle, *Three Months*, 260.

12. Quoted in Sears, *Gettysburg*, 346.

13. *O.R.*, 27, Pt. 2, 308; Taylor, *Four Years*, 99.

14. Hoke, *Great Invasion*, 355.

15. *O.R.*, 27, Pt. 2, 320.

16. Longstreet, "Lee in Pennsylvania," 424; Ross, *Cities and Camps*, 55.

17. Gallagher, ed., *Fighting*, 244.

18. Longstreet, "Lee in Pennsylvania," 429.

19. Gallagher, ed., *Fighting for the Confederacy*, 252; Longstreet, "Lee in Pennsylvania," 430.

20. West, *Texan in Search of a Fight*, 86.

21. Jordan, *Some Events*, 45.

22. Ibid.

23. Farley, "Reminiscences," No. IX, in Norton, *Attack and Defense*, 229.

24. Spear et al., eds., *Recollections*, 38.

25. Graham, *On to Gettysburg*, 12.

26. Ibid., 13. As a postscript to this anecdote, Graham wrote: "Every visit I have since made to Little Round Top, I have seen 'old Wikerts son'—his father now dead [1893]—telling interested hearers of "the wonderful acts of heroism his father and he did in taking care of the wounded in their yard that fearful day and how kind the government was to recognize their services." Ibid., 13–14.

27. Hapstonstall, "On Little Round Top," *NT*, Aug. 19, 1909; Rittenhouse, "Battle of Gettysburg," 526.

28. E. M. Hayes to Bachelder, Feb. 6, 1883, in *BP*, 2:920–921.

29. Scott, "On Little Round Top," *NT*, Aug. 2, 1894; Rittenhouse, "Battle of Gettysburg," 526.

30. Scott, "On Little Round Top," *NT*, Aug. 2, 1894; Rittenhouse, "Battle of Gettysburg," 527.

31. Farley, "Reminiscences," No. IX, in Norton, *Attack and Defense*, 231.

32. Judson, *History*, 138.

33. Alleman, *At Gettysburg*, 71–72, 74.

34. Nash, *History*, 151; Livermore Diary, July 3, 1863 [evening], UMO.

35. Farley, "Reminiscences of the 140th Regiment," 232; Brown to George W. Brown, July 7, 1863, Brown Papers, John Hay Library; Brown, "On Gettysburg Field," *PWT*, May 26, 1883; Graham, *On to Gettysburg*, 14.

36. Spear et al., *Civil War Recollections*, 39, 318; Crennel Diary, July 4, 1863, 140th New York File, GNMP.

37. Spear et al., *Civil War Recollections*, 318.

38. Nash, *History*, 150; Ilisevich and Helmreich, eds., *Civil War Diaries*, 104–105.

39. Potter, "Gettysburg," *NT*, Feb. 25. 1892; Henry [?] to Friends at Home, July 8, 1863, in Nash, *History*, 327.

40. James R. Woodworth to Phoebe Woodworth, July 21, 1863, Hotchkiss Coll., UM.

41. Charles H. Salter to Isabella Duffield, July 12, 1863, DPL.

Epilogue

1. Hawthorne, *The House of Seven Gables*, 386.

2. Meade, ed., *Life and Letters*, 2:125.

3. Basler, ed., *Collected Works*, 6:328; *NYT*, July 2, 1869.

4. *NYT*, May 5, 1914.

5. Quoted in Sears, "Gouverneur Kemble Warren," 255.

6. Taylor, *Gouverneur Kemble Warren*, 248; Fox, ed., *New York at Gettysburg*, 3:973; Longacre, "Gouverneur K. Warren," 11.

7. On the Appomattox legend created by Gordon and Chamberlain, see William Marvel, *A Place Called Appomattox* (Chapel Hill and London, 2000), 259–262.

8. LaFantasie, "Joshua Chamberlain," 44, 55.

9. Quoted in Thompson, "Young Girl," 105.

10. West, *Texan in Search of a Fight*, 187.

11. Oates, *War*, 598; Sterkx, "William C. Jordan," 65.

12. Cutrer, ed., *Longstreet's Aide*, 167.

13. Quoted in Wert, *General James Longstreet*, 410.

14. Quoted in Piston, *Lee's Tarnished Lieutenant*, 169.

15. Fremantle, *Three Months*, 269; Imboden, "Confederate Retreat," 421.

16. Allan, "Memoranda of Conversations," Apr. 15, 1868, in Gallagher, ed., *Lee the Soldier*, 14.

17. Allan, "Memoranda of Conversations," Feb. 19, 1870, in Gallagher, ed., *Lee the Soldier*, 17–18.

18. David Wills to Lincoln, Nov. 2, 1863, Robert Todd Lincoln Papers, LC.

19. Quoted in Donald, *Lincoln*, 57.

20. Basler, ed., *Collected Works*, 7:23; Barton, *Lincoln at Gettysburg*, 121.

21. Basler, ed., *Collected Works*, 7:23.

22. Quoted in Barton, *Lincoln at Gettysburg*, 186.

23. Basler, ed., *Collected Works*, 7:23.

BIBLIOGRAPHY

Listed here are the manuscript and printed sources referenced during the writing of this book. Sources dealing with more particular topics are cited in the notes.

Manuscript Sources

Note: Dates indicate the year in which private collections of historical manuscripts were consulted.

Alabama Department of Archives and History, Montgomery, Alabama
    Michael J. Bulger File
    William C. Oates Papers
    Regimental Files
        4th Alabama
        15th Alabama
        44th Alabama
        47th Alabama
        48th Alabama
Hawthorne-Longfellow Library, Bowdoin College, Brunswick, Maine
    Joshua Lawrence Chamberlain Papers
    Elisha Coan Manuscript
John Hay Library, Brown University, Providence, Rhode Island
    William H. Brown Papers
Marion Oates Leiter Charles, Washington, D.C., Newport, Rhode Island (1995)
    Oates Family Papers
Detroit Public Library, Detroit, Michigan
    Burton Historical Collection (Charles H. Salter Letter)

Perkins Library, Duke University, Durham, North Carolina
  James Longstreet Papers
Robert G. Woodruff Library, Emory University, Atlanta, Georgia
  Park Family Papers
  Memoir of Campbell Wood
Fredericksburg and Spotsylvania National Military Park, Fredericksburg,
Virginia
  Alfred M. Apted Diary
Gettysburg College, Gettysburg, Pennsylvania
  David McConaughy Collection
  F. M. Stoke Letters
  Diary of Sergeant Allen Wall
Gettysburg National Military Park, Gettysburg, Pennsylvania
  Archival Box Collection
    Samuel P. Bates Papers
    Henry Hunt Papers
    Peter Rothermel Papers
  Civilian Accounts
  Gettysburg Newspaper Clippings
  July 2, 1863 Files
    General Information on Movements and Battle
    Hood's Division
    Devil's Den
    Little Round Top: Vincent and Weed
    Little Round Top: 20th Maine
    Pennsylvania Reserves
  William C. Oates Correspondence
  Participants' Accounts
    James Barnes
    Joshua Lawrence Chamberlain
    Samuel W. Crawford
    Elon J. Farnsworth
    Henry J. Hunt
    Samuel R. Johnston
    Robert E. Lee
    James Longstreet
    Lafayette McLaws
    George G. Meade
    James Rice
    Ellis Spear
    Strong Vincent

Gouverneur K. Warren
Property Damage Claims
  James Warfield
  Jacob Weikert
Regimental Files
  Alabama Troops: General Information
  4th Alabama Infantry
  15th Alabama Infantry
  47th Alabama Infantry
  48th Alabama Infantry
  3rd Arkansas Infantry
  15th Georgia Infantry
  20th Maine Infantry
  20th Maine Infantry: Harlan Bailey Letters
  20th Maine Infantry: Samuel Keene Diary
  16th Michigan Infantry
  44th New York Infantry
  140th New York Infantry
  145th New York Infantry
  146th New York Infantry
  83rd Pennsylvania Infantry
  91st Pennsylvania Infantry
  98th Pennsylvania Infantry
  147th Pennsylvania Infantry
  155th Pennsylvania Infantry
  Texas Troops: General Information
  1st Texas Infantry
  4th Texas Infantry
  5th Texas Infantry
  5th U.S. Artillery, Battery D
  U.S. Regulars: Sharpshooters
  U.S. Regulars: Signal Corps
Confederate Research Center, Hill Junior College, Hillsboro, Texas
  Rufus K. Felder Letters
  A. C. Sims Reminiscences
Historical Society of Pennsylvania, Philadelphia, Pennsylvania
  George Gordon Meade Collection
Library of Congress, Washington, D.C.
  Joshua L. Chamberlain Papers
  Samuel W. Crawford Papers
  Douglas Southall Freeman Papers

Henry J. Hunt Papers
Robert Todd Lincoln Papers
Louis T. Wigfall Papers
Maine Historical Society, Portland, Maine
   Joshua L. Chamberlain Papers, Collection 10
Maine State Archives, Augusta, Maine
   Civil War Correspondence
   Nathan Clark Diary
Folger Library, University of Maine, Orono, Maine
   William T. Livermore Diary
Clarke Historical Library, Central Michigan University, Mount Pleasant, Michigan
   Oliver W. Norton Papers
William L. Clements Library, University of Michigan, Ann Arbor, Michigan
   Lawrence Hotchkiss Collection
      James Woodworth Letters and Diary
   James S. Schoff Civil War Collection
      Norton Letter
      Oates Letter
Pierpont Morgan Library, New York, New York
   Gilder Lehrman Collection (Henry S. Figures Letters)
National Archives, Washington, D.C.
   RG29: Records of the Bureau of the Census
   RG94: Records of Adjutant General's Office
      Compiled Service Records
         Joshua L. Chamberlain
         Porter Farley
         Ellis Spear
      Letters Received by the Commission Branch, 1863–1870
      Joshua L. Chamberlain Military Personnel File
      Records of the War Records Office
   RG109: War Department Collection of Confederate Records
      Compiled Service Records
         William C. Jordan
         John A. Oates
         William C. Oates
         John C. West
National Civil War Museum, Harrisburg, Pennsylvania
   Joshua L. Chamberlain Letters
New Hampshire Historical Society, Concord, New Hampshire
   John B. Bachelder Papers
New-York Historical Society, New York, New York
   James Barnes Manuscripts

New York Public Library, New York, New York
    Ezra Ayers Carman Papers
New York State Library, Albany, New York
    Orville Cook Brown Letters
    Grand Army of the Republic Papers
    Gouverneur K. Warren Letters
Southern Historical Collection, University of North Carolina, Chapel Hill, North Carolina
    E. P. Alexander Papers
    Cobb and Hunter Family Papers (Decimus U. Barziza Diary)
    Lafayette McLaws Papers
    Thomas Ware Papers
Pejepscot Historical Society, Brunswick, Maine
    Joshua Lawrence Chamberlain Papers
    Arnold Fernald Diary
    John Lenfest Letters
    Alice Rains Trulock Collection
Pennsylvania Historical and Museum Commission, Harrisburg, Pennsylvania
    Samuel P. Bates Papers
    Peter Rothemel Papers
Rutgers University Library, New Brunswick, New Jersey
    Roebling Collection (Roebling Letters Typescript)
Abbott Spear, Warren, Maine (1994)
    Samuel Keene Letters
    Ellis Spear Papers
Randy Treichler, Three Springs, Pennsylvania (2003)
    James M. Treichler Accounts
University of Texas, Austin, Texas
    Thomas L. McCarty Account
U.S. Army Military History Institute, Carlisle Barracks, Pennsylvania
    Robert L. Brake Collection
        1st Texas Diary
        Daily Register of Dr. Cyrus Bacon, Jr.
        Edward Bennett Letters
        H. W. Berryman Letter
        Henry H. Curran Account
        James Henry Henrick Letter
        John F. Huntington Letter
        Rufus W. Jacklin Recollections
        Zack Landrum Letters
        Joseph A. Moore Letter
        John M. Pinckney Papers

Charles N. Smith Recollection
J. Mark Smither Letter
Unknown Diary, Company I, 1st Texas
Civil War Miscellaneous Collection
   Charles Bandegee Letter
   Erastus L. Harris Letters
   John O'Connell Memoir
Civil War Times Illustrated Collection
   John G. Berry Diary
Harrisburg Civil War Round Table Collection
   William H. Clark Memoirs
Johnson Family Collection
   Philo Conklin Letters
Lewis Leigh Collection
   Henry Lytle Letter
Murray Smith Collection
   Freeman Connor Letter
Thickstun Family Papers

Books, Pamphlets, Articles, Theses, and Internet Sources

Note: Dates in Internet citations refer to the dates the sites were consulted, not the dates the sites were created.

Abernathy, William. *Our Mess: Southern Gallantry and Privations*. McKinney, Tex., 1977.

Adelman, Garry E. "Benning's Georgia Brigade at Gettysburg." *Gettysburg Magazine*, 18 (Jan. 1998), 57–66.

———. "The Fight for and Location of the 4th New York Independent Battery at Gettysburg." *Gettysburg Magazine*, 26 (July 2002), 53–68.

———. "Hazlett's Battery at Gettysburg." *Gettysburg Magazine*, 21 (July 1999), 64–73.

Adelman, Garry E., and Timothy H. Smith. *Devil's Den: A History and Guide*. Gettysburg, Pa., 1997.

Agassiz, George R., ed. *Meade's Headquarters, 1863–1865: Letters of Colonel Theodore Lyman from the Wilderness to Appomattox*. Boston, 1922.

Alexander, Edward Porter. *Military Memoirs of a Confederate: A Critical Narrative*. New York, 1907.

Allan, William. "Memoranda of Conversations with General Robert E. Lee." In Gallagher, ed., *Lee the Soldier*, 7–24.

Alleman, Tillie (Pierce). *At Gettysburg, or, What a Girl Saw and Heard of the Battle*. New York, 1889.

Annals of the War. Philadelphia, 1879.

Ayars, Peter B. "The 99th Pennsylvania." *National Tribune*, Feb. 4, 1886.

Bachelder, John B. "General Farnsworth's Death." *Philadelphia Weekly Times*, December 30, 1882.

———. *Gettysburg: What to See, and How to See It*. Boston and New York, 1873.

Baker, George E., ed. *The Works of William H. Seward*. 5 vols. Boston, 1884.

Bandy, Ken, and Florence Freeland, eds. *The Gettysburg Papers*. 2 vols. Dayton, Ohio, 1978.

Bard, John P. "The 'Old Bucktails,' 42nd Regt. P.V., at the Battle of Gettysburg." *Philadelphia Weekly Press*, May 19, 1886.

Barnes, James. "The Battle of Gettysburg." *New York Herald*, Mar. 21, 1864.

Barton, Michael. "Painful Duties: Art, Character, and Culture in Confederate Letters of Condolence." *Southern Quarterly*, 17 (Winter 1979), 123–134.

Barton, William E. *Lincoln at Gettysburg*. Indianapolis, 1930.

Barziza, Decimus et Ultimus. *The Adventures of a Prisoner of War, 1863–1864*. Ed. R. Henderson Shuffler. Austin, 1964.

Basler, Roy P., ed. *The Collected Works of Abraham Lincoln*. 8 vols. New Brunswick, N.J., 1953.

Bateman, L. C. "The Hero of Gettysburg." *Lewiston* [Maine] *Journal*, Sept. 1–6, 1900.

Bates, Samuel P. *History of Pennsylvania Volunteers, 1861–5*, 10 vols. Harrisburg, Pa., 1869–1871.

Bennett, Brian A. *Beau Ideal of a Soldier and a Gentleman: The Life of Col. Patrick Henry O'Rorke from Ireland to Gettysburg*. Scottsville, N.Y., 1996.

———. *Sons of Old Monroe: A Regimental History of Patrick O'Rorke's 140th New York Volunteer Infantry*. Dayton, Ohio, 1992.

———. "The Supreme Event in Its Existence: The 140th New York on Little Round Top." *Gettysburg Magazine*, 3 (1990), 17–25.

———. "Truth Without Exaggeration: Porter Farley's Life-Long Study of the Events on Little Round Top." *Gettysburg Magazine*, 28 (Jan. 2003), 49–86.

Bennett, Edward. "Round Top." *National Tribune*, May 23, 1889.

———. "Gettysburg: The Battle as Seen by a Member of the 44th N.Y." *National Tribune*, May 6, 1886.

Beyer, W. F., and O. F. Keydel. *Deeds of Valor, or How American Heroes Won the Medal of Honor*. Detroit, Mich., 1907.

Blight, David W., and Brooks D. Simpson, eds. *Union and Emancipation: Essays on Politics and Race in the Civil War Era*. Kent, Ohio, and London, 1997.

Boritt, Gabor S., ed. *The Gettysburg Nobody Knows*. New York, 1997.

Botsford, Theophilus F. *A Boy in the Civil War*. 7th ed. Montgomery, Ala., 1914.

Bradfield, J. O. "At Gettysburg." *Confederate Veteran*, 30 (1922), 225, 236.

Bradford, Gamaliel. "A Portrait of General George Gordon Meade." *American Historical Review*, 20 (Jan. 1915), 314–329.

Bradley, Thomas W. "At Gettysburg: The Splendid Work Done By Smith's Battery." *National Tribune*, Feb. 4, 1886.

Brainard, Mary G. G. *Campaigns of the One Hundred and Forty-Sixth Regiment, New York State Volunteers*. New York, 1915.

Broadhead, Sarah M. *The Diary of a Lady of Gettysburg, Pennsylvania*. Hershey, Pa., 1992.

Brooks, Charles E. "The Social and Cultural Dynamics of Soldiering in Hood's Texas Brigade." *Journal of Southern History*, 67 (Aug. 2001), 535–572.

Brown, Andrew. *Geology and the Gettysburg Campaign*. Harrisburg, Pa., 1962.

Brown, J. Willard. *The Signal Corps, U.S.A., in the War of the Rebellion*. Boston, 1896.

Brown, William H. "On Gettysburg Field." *Philadelphia Weekly Times*, May 26, 1883.

Bruner, Gary D. "Up Over Big Round Top: The Forgotten 47th Alabama." *Gettysburg Magazine*, 22 (July 2000), 6–22.

Burnett, Edmund Cody, ed. "Letters of Barnett Hardeman Cody and Others, 1861–1864." *Georgia Historical Quarterly*, 23 (1939), 265–299, 362–380.

Busey, John W., and David G. Martin. *Regimental Strengths and Losses at Gettysburg*. Baltimore, 1994.

Bush, James G. *A Short History of the Fifth Regiment, U.S. Artillery*. New York, 1895.

Bryne, Frank L., and Andrew T. Weaver, eds. *Haskell of Gettysburg: His Life and Letters*. Madison, Wisc., 1970.

Cain, Marvin R. "A 'Face of Battle' Needed: An Assessment of Motives and Men in Civil War Historiography." *Civil War History*, 29 (1982), 5–27.

Calef, John H. "Gettysburg Notes: The Opening Gun." *Journal of the Military Services Institution of the United States* (Jan./Feb. 1907), 40–58.

Campbell, Edward D. C., Jr. "The Fabric of Command: R. E. Lee, Confederate Insignia, and the Perception of Rank." *Virginia Magazine of History and Biography*, 98 (April 1990), 261–290.

Campbell, John T. "Sights at Gettysburg." *National Tribune*, Sept. 17, 1908.

Cashin, Joan E., ed. *The War Was You and Me: Civilians in the American Civil War*. Princeton, N.J., 2002.

Catton, Bruce. "The Confederate Legend." In *The Confederacy* [Booklet issued by Columbia Records to accompany the recording, "The Confederacy," by Richard Bales and the National Gallery Orchestra (LS 1004)]. New York, ca. 1955, 9–23.

———. *Glory Road*. Garden City, N.Y., 1952.

———. *Never Call Retreat*. Garden City, N.Y., 1965.

Chamberlain Association of America. *Joshua Lawrence Chamberlain: A Sketch*. N.p., 1906.

Chamberlain, Joshua L. "Address." In *Dedication of the Twentieth Maine Monuments at Gettysburg, Oct. 3, 1889*. Waldoboro, Maine, 1891, 26–31.

———. "The Maine 20th at Gettysburg." *The Maine Farmer*, Dec. 28, 1865.

———. *The Passing of the Armies*. New York, 1915.

———. "The Twentieth Maine at Gettysburg." *Eastern Argus*, Dec. 20, 1865.

———. "Through Blood and Fire at Gettysburg." *Hearst's Magazine*, 23 (June 1913), 894–909.

Chilton, F. B. *Unveiling and Dedication of Monument to Hood's Texas Brigade*. Houston, Tex., 1911.

Clarke, Augustus P. "The Sixth New York Cavalry, Its Movements and Service at the Battle of Gettysburg." *United Service Magazine*, 16 (1896), 411–415.

Cleaves, Freeman. *Meade of Gettysburg*. Norman, Okla, 1960.

Coan, Elisha S. "Reply to 'Rear Rank.'" *Lincoln County* [Maine] *News*, May 1883.

———. "Round Top." *National Tribune*, June 4, 1885.

Coco, Gregory A. *Killed in Action: Eyewitness Accounts of the Last Moments of 100 Union Soldiers Who Died at Gettysburg*. Gettysburg, Pa., 1992.

———. *A Strange and Blighted Land: Gettysburg—The Aftermath of a Battle*. Gettysburg, Pa., 1995.

———. *A Vast Sea of Misery: A History and Guide to the Union and Confederate Field Hospitals at Gettysburg, July 1–November 20, 1863*. Gettysburg, Pa., 1988.

———. *Wasted Valor: The Confederate Dead at Gettysburg*. Gettysburg, Pa., 1990.

Coddington, Edwin B. *The Gettysburg Campaign: A Study in Command*. New York, 1968.

Colestock, W. W. "The 16th Michigan at Little Round Top." *National Tribune*, Mar. 26, 1914.

Collier, Colvin L. *"They'll Do to Tie To!" The Story of the Third Regiment, Arkansas Volunteers, Confederate States of America*. Little Rock, Ark., 1959.

Connor, Seldon et al. *In Memoriam: Joshua Lawrence Chamberlain*. Circular No. 5, Whole Number 328, Military Order of the Loyal Legion of the United States, Commandery of the State of Maine. Portland, Maine, 1914.

Costa, Dora L., and Matthew E. Kahn. "Cowards and Heroes: Group Loyalty in the American Civil War." *Quarterly Journal of Economics*, 118 (May 2003), 519–548.

Crawford, Samuel W. "The Pennsylvania Reserves at the Battle of Gettysburg." *Philadelphia Weekly Press*, Sept. 8, 1886.

Creighton, Margaret. "Living on the Fault Line: African American Civilians and the Gettysburg Campaign." In Cashin, ed., *The War Was You and Me*, 209–236.

Crocker, E. C. "Hazlett's Battery at Gettysburg." *National Tribune*, Mar. 8, 1906.

Culp, E. C. "Gettysburg: Reminiscences of the Great Fight by a Participant." *National Tribune*, Mar. 19, 1885.

Cutrer, Thomas W., ed. *Longstreet's Aide: The Civil War Letters of Thomas J. Goree*. Charlottesville, Va., 1995.

Davis, E. J. "Little Round Top." *National Tribune*, Nov. 11, 1915.

Dennett, Tyler, ed. *Lincoln and the Civil War in the Diaries and Letters of John Hay*. New York, 1939.

Desjardin, Thomas A. *Stand Firm Ye Boys from Maine: The 20th Maine and the Gettysburg Campaign*. Gettysburg, Pa., 1995.

Donald, David Herbert. "The Confederate as a Fighting Man." *Journal of Southern History*, 25 (May 1959), 178–193.

———. *Lincoln*. New York, 1995.

Douglass, Frederick. *Life and Times of Frederick Douglass*. Rev. 1892 ed. New York, 1962.

Dowdey, Clifford, and Lewis H. Manarin, eds. *The Wartime Papers of Robert E. Lee*. New York, 1961.

Dyer, John P. *The Gallant Hood*. Indianapolis, 1950.

E.C.C. "Battery D, 5th Artillery." *National Tribune*, Dec. 10, 1891.

Early, John Cabell. "A Southern Boy at Gettysburg." *Civil War Times Illustrated*, 9 (June 1970), 35–48.

Edwards, William A. "Letter to W. R. Painter." Unidentified news clipping, Nov. 11, 1915.

Eicher, David J. *The Longest Night: A Military History of the Civil War*. New York, 2001.

Elmore, Thomas L. "A Meteorological and Astronomical Chronology of the Gettysburg Campaign." *Gettysburg Magazine*, 13 (July 1995), 7–21.

Engert, Roderick, ed. *Maine to the Wilderness: The Civil War Letters of Pvt. William Lamson, 20th Maine Infantry*. Orange, Va., 1993.

Everett, Donald E., ed. *Chaplain Davis and Hood's Texas Brigade*. San Antonio, 1962.

Fahs, Alice. *The Imagined Civil War: Popular Literature of the North and South, 1861–1865*. Chapel Hill and London, 2001.

Fairfield, George. "The Capture at the Railroad Cut." *National Tribune*, Sept. 1, 1910.

Farley, Porter. "Reminiscences of the 140th Regiment New York State Volunteers, No. IX." *Rochester Democrat & Chronicle*, Dec. 3, 1877. Reprinted in Norton, *Attack and Defense*, 125–140.

———. "Bloody Round Top." *National Tribune*, May 3, 1883.

———. "Otis's Regiment at Gettysburg and the Wilderness." *Army and Navy Journal*, Apr. 22, 1899.

———. "Reminiscences of Gettysburg." *National Tribune*, Jan. 30, 1878.

———. "Reminiscences of the 140th Regiment, New York Volunteer Infantry." *Rochester Historical Society Publications*, 22 (1944), 199–252.

Faust, Drew Gilpin. "The Civil War Soldier and the Art of Dying." *Journal of Southern History*, 67 (2001), 3–38.

———. *"A Riddle of Death": Mortality and Meaning in the American Civil War*. 34th

Annual Fortenbaugh Memorial Lecture, Gettysburg College. Gettysburg, Pa., 1995.

Fishel, Edwin C. *The Secret War for the Union: The Untold Story of Military Intelligence in the Civil War.* Boston and New York, 1996.

Fisher, Donald M. "Born in Ireland, Killed at Gettysburg: The Life, Death, and Legacy of Patrick Henry O'Rorke." *Civil War History*, 39 (1993), 225–239.

Fleegle, John. "At Round Top." *National Tribune*, Jan. 1, 1914.

Fleming, Thomas. "A Husband's Revenge." *American Heritage*, 18 (Apr. 1967), 65–75.

Fletcher, William A. *Rebel Private: Front and Rear—Memoirs of a Confederate Soldier.* New York, 1995.

Foner, Eric. *Free Soil, Free Labor, Free Men: The Ideology of the Republican Party before the Civil War.* 2nd ed. Oxford and New York, 1995.

Foote, Shelby. *The Civil War, A Narrative: Fredericksburg to Meridian.* New York, 1963.

The Fourth Annual Gettysburg Seminar, Gettysburg National Military Park, March 4, 1995. Gettysburg, Pa., 1995.

Fox, William F., ed. *New York at Gettysburg: Final Report on the Battlefield at Gettysburg.* 3 vols. Albany, N.Y., 1900–1902.

Franklin, John Hope. *The Emancipation Proclamation.* Garden City, N.Y., 1963.

Frassanito, William A. *Early Photography of Gettysburg.* Gettysburg, Pa., 1995.

———. *Gettysburg: A Journey in Time.* New York, 1975.

Frederickson, George M. *The Inner Civil War: Northern Intellectuals and the Crisis of the Union.* New York, 1965.

Freeman, Douglas Southall. *Lee's Lieutenants: A Study in Command.* 3 vols. New York, 1942–1946.

———. *R. E. Lee: A Biography.* 4 vols. New York, 1934–1935.

Fremantle, Arthur J. L. *Three Months in the Southern States.* New York, 1864.

Furgurson, Ernest B. *Chancellorsville: The Souls of the Brave.* New York, 1992.

Gallagher, Gary W. *The Confederate War.* Cambridge, Mass., 1997.

Gallagher, Gary W., ed. *Fighting for the Confederacy: The Personal Recollections of General Edward Porter Alexander.* Chapel Hill and London, 1989.

———. *The First Day at Gettysburg: Essays on Confederate and Union Leadership.* Kent, Ohio, 1992.

———. *Lee the Soldier.* Lincoln, Neb., 1996.

———. *The Second Day at Gettysburg: Essays on Confederate and Union Leadership.* Kent, Ohio, 1993.

———. *The Third Day at Gettysburg and Beyond.* Chapel Hill, N.C., 1994.

———. *Three Days at Gettysburg: Essays on Confederate and Union Leadership.* Kent, Ohio, 1999.

Geertz, Clifford. *The Interpretation of Cultures.* New York, 1973.

"General Chamberlain in Wartime." *Portland* [Maine] *Daily Advertiser*, Mar. 21, 1903.

"General M. J. Bulger: An Alabama Hero." *Montgomery Advertiser*, Oct. 2, 1898.

Genovese, Eugene D. *Roll, Jordan, Roll: The World the Slaves Made.* New York, 1974.

Gerrish, Theodore. *Army Life: A Private's Reminiscences of the War.* Portland, Maine, 1882.

Gettysburg, July 2, 1863: Col. William C. Oates to Colonel Homer R. Stoughton. Abbeville, Ala., 1888.

Gettysburg Discussion Group Web Site, www.gdg.org, March 23, 2000.

Gettysburg National Military Park Library Web Site, www.nps.gov/gett/ library/ libmain.htm, February 10, 2000.

Gibbon, John. "The Council of War on the Second Day." In Johnson and Buel, eds., *Battles and Leaders.* Vol. 3, 313–314.

Gibney, John Michael. "A Shadow Passing: The Tragic Story of Norval Welch and the Sixteenth Michigan at Gettysburg and Beyond." *Gettysburg Magazine*, 6 (Jan. 1992), 33–42.

Glover, Edwin A. *Bucktailed Wildcats.* New York, 1960.

Golay, Michael. *To Gettysburg and Beyond: The Parallel Lives of Joshua Lawrence Chamberlain and Edward Porter Alexander.* New York, 1994.

Gordon, John B. *Reminiscences of the Civil War.* New York, 1904.

Graham, Ziba B. *On to Gettysburg: Ten Days from My Diary of 1863.* A Paper Read Before the Commandery of the State of Michigan, Military Order of the Loyal Legion of the U.S., Detroit, Mich., 1893.

Grindlay, James G. "The 146th New York at Little Round Top." In Johnson and Buel, eds., *Battles and Leaders.* Vol. 3, 315.

Hackett, J. P. "The Fifth Corps at Gettysburg." *National Tribune*, July 29, 1915.

Hall, Jeffrey C. *The Stand of the U.S. Army at Gettysburg.* Bloomington, Ind., 2003.

Hardin, Martin D. *History of the Twelfth Regiment, Pennsylvania Reserves Volunteer Corps.* New York, 1890.

Hamilton, D. H. *History of Company M, First Texas Volunteer Infantry, Hood's Brigade, Longstreet's Corps, Army of Northern Virginia.* Groveton, Tex., 1925.

Harris, Erastus L. "Little Round Top." *National Tribune*, Aug. 2, 1888.

Harris, J. C. "Gettysburg: The Rebel Repulse at Round Top." *National Tribune*, Jan. 8, 1885.

Harrison, Kathleen Georg. "'Our Principal Loss Was in This Place': Action at the Slaughter Pen and at the South End of Houck's Ridge." *Gettysburg Magazine*, 1 (1989), 45–69.

Hapstonstall, S. W. "On Little Round Top." *National Tribune*, Aug. 19, 1909.

Hassler, Warren W., Jr. *Crisis at the Crossroads: The First Day at Gettysburg.* Montgomery, Ala., 1970.

Hawthorne, Nathaniel. *The House of Seven Gables* (1851). In *Hawthorne: Novels.* Ed. Millicent Bell. Library of America edition. New York, 1983.

Hazen, Samuel R. "At Gettysburg." *National Tribune*, Aug. 25, 1892.

———. "'Fighting the Good Fight': The 140th New York and Its Work on Little Round Top." *National Tribune*, Sept. 13, 1894.

Hess, Earl J. *The Union Soldier in Battle: Enduring the Ordeal of Combat.* Lawrence, Kan., 1997.

Heth, Henry. "Letter to J. William Jones." *Southern Historical Society Papers*, 4 (1877), 151–160.

Hillyer, George. *Battle of Gettysburg: Address Before the Walton County, Georgia, Confederate Veterans, August 2d, 1904.* Walton County, Ga., 1904.

Hoke, Jacob. *The Great Invasion of 1863.* Dayton, Ohio, 1887.

Hood, John Bell. *Advance and Retreat.* New Orleans, 1880.

———. "Letter from John Bell Hood." *Southern Historical Society Papers*, 4 (1877), 145–150.

Hoole, William Stanley, ed. *Historical Sketches of the Forty-Seventh Alabama Infantry Regiment, C.S.A.* University, Ala., 1982.

Houghton, W. R., and M. B. Houghton. *Two Boys in the Civil War and After.* Montgomery, Ala., 1912.

"How General Chamberlain with the 20th Maine Held Little Round Top." *Lewiston* [Maine] *Journal*, May 25, 1912.

"How the War Affects Americans." *Continental Monthly*, 3 (Apr. 1863), 411–420.

Howard, Oliver O. "Campaign and Battle of Gettysburg." *Atlantic Monthly*, 38 (July 1876), 48–71.

Huber, A. H. "Little Round Top." *National Tribune*, Sept. 1, 1892.

Hunt, Henry J. "The Second Day at Gettysburg." In Johnson and Buel, eds., *Battles and Leaders.* Vol. 3, 290–313.

Hyde, Thomas W. *Following the Greek Cross or Memories of the Sixth Army Corps.* Cambridge, Mass., 1894.

———. "Recollections of the Battle of Gettysburg." Military Order of the Loyal Legion of the United States, Maine Commandery, *War Papers*, 1 (1898), 189–206.

Ide, Harry, comp. "The 91st Pennsylvania Volunteer Infantry." freepages.military. rootsweb.com/~pa91/index.html, Nov. 25, 2003.

Ilisevich, Robert, and Jonathan Helmreich, eds. *The Civil War Diaries of Seth Waid III.* Meadville, Pa., 1993.

Imboden, John D. "The Confederate Retreat from Gettysburg." In Johnson and Buel, eds., *Battles and Leaders.* Vol. 3, 420–429.

Jacklin, Rufus W. "The Famous Old Third Brigade." Military Order of the Loyal Legion of the United States, Commandery of Michigan, *War Papers* (1898), 2:39–50.

———. "The 16th Michigan: The Work It Helped to Do in Saving Little Round Top." *National Tribune*, Dec. 19, 1895.

Jacobs, Michael. "The Battle of Gettysburg." *Evangelical Quarterly Review*, 15 (1864), 225–245.

———. *Notes on the Rebel Invasion of Maryland and Pennsylvania and the Battle of Gettysburg*. Gettysburg, 1909.

Johnson, Charles F. "The Short, Heroic Life of Strong Vincent." *Journal of Erie Studies*, 17 (Spring 1988), 27–39.

Johnson, Robert U., and Clarence C. Buel, eds. *Battles and Leaders of the Civil War*. 4 vols. New York, 1884–1889.

Jones, Archer. "The Gettysburg Decision." *Virginia Magazine of History and Biography*, 68 (1960), 331–343.

———. "The Gettysburg Decision Reassessed." *Virginia Magazine of History and Biography*, 76 (1968), 64–66.

Jones, Kenneth W., comp. "Muster Rolls: 15th Alabama Infantry Regiment." http:www. tarleton.edu/~kjones/15muster.html, March 19, 2000.

———. "The 15th Alabama Volunteer Infantry Regiment." www.tarleton .edu/activities/pages/facultypages/jones/#4, December 28, 1996.

Jordan, David M. *"Happiness Is Not My Companion": The Life of General G. K. Warren*. Bloomington, Ind., 2001.

Jordan, William C. *Some Events and Incidents During the Civil War*. Montgomery, Ala., 1909.

Joslyn, Mauriel P. "'For Ninety Nine Years or the War': The Story of the 3rd Arkansas at Gettysburg." *Gettysburg Magazine*, 14 (Jan. 1996), 52–63.

Judson, Amos M. *A History of the Eighty-Third Regiment, Pennsylvania Volunteers*. Erie, Pa., 1865.

Keegan, John. *The Face of Battle*. London, 1976.

Keneally, Thomas. *American Scoundrel: The Life of the Notorious Civil War General Dan Sickles*. New York, 2002.

Kershaw, Joseph B. "Kershaw's Brigade at Gettysburg." In Johnson and Buel, eds., *Battle and Leaders*. Vol. 3, 331–338.

Kilmer, George L. "Crisis on Round-Top." *Gettysburg Compiler*, Sept. 15, 1896.

Kinsel, Amy J. "'From These Honored Dead': Gettysburg in American Culture, 1863–1930." Ph.D. Dissertation, Cornell University, 1992.

Knupfer, Peter. "Aging Statesmen and the Statesmanship of an Earlier Age: The Generational Roots of the Constitutional Union Party." In Blight and Simpson, eds., *Union and Emancipation*, 57–78.

Kolchin, Peter. *American Slavery: 1619–1877*. New York, 1993.

Krick, Robert K. "'If Longstreet . . . Says So, It Is Most Likely Not True': James Longstreet and the Second Day at Gettysburg." In Gallagher, ed., *Second Day at Gettysburg*, 57–86.

———. "Three Confederate Disasters on Oak Ridge: Failures of Brigade Leadership on the First Day at Gettysburg." In Gallagher, ed., *First Day at Gettysburg*, 92–139.

Ladd, David L., and Audrey J. Ladd, eds. *The Bachelder Papers*. 3 vols. Dayton, Ohio, 1994–1995.

LaFantasie, Glenn W. "Becoming Joshua Lawrence Chamberlain." *North & South*, 5 (Feb. 2002), 29–38.

———. "Conflicting Memories of Little Round Top." *Columbiad*, 3 (Spring 1999), 106–130.

———. "Considering Longstreet's Legacy." *MHQ: The Quarterly Journal of Military History*, 11 (Winter 1999), 60–69.

———. "Joshua Chamberlain and the American Dream." In Gabor S. Boritt, ed., *The Gettysburg Nobody Knows*. New York, 1997, 31–55.

———. "Lincoln and the Gettysburg Awakening." *Journal of the Abraham Lincoln Association*, 16 (Winter 1995), 73–89.

———. "The Other Man [on Little Round Top]." *MHQ: The Quarterly Journal of Military History* (Summer 1993), 69–75.

LaFantasie, Glenn W., ed. *Gettysburg: Colonel William C. Oates and Lieutenant Frank A. Haskell*. New York, 1992.

———. "William C. Oates Remembers Little Round Top." *Gettysburg Magazine*, 21 (July 1999), 57–63.

Laine, J. Gary, and Morris M. Penny. *Law's Alabama Brigade in the War Between the Union and the Confederacy*. Shippensburg, Pa., 1996.

Laney, Daniel M. "Wasted Gallantry: Hood's Texas Brigade at Gettysburg." *Gettysburg Magazine*, 16 (1997), 27–45.

Lasswell, Mary, ed. *Rags and Hope: The Recollections of Val C. Giles, Four Years with Hood's Brigade, Fourth Texas Infantry, 1861–1865*. New York, 1961.

Law, Evander M. "The Struggle for 'Round Top.'" In Johnson and Buel, eds., *Battles and Leaders*. Vol. 3, 318–330.

Lawley, Francis. "The Battles of Gettysburg." *The Times* (London), Aug. 18, 1863.

Lee, Fitzhugh. *General Lee: A Biography of Robert E. Lee*. New York, 1894.

Leeper, Joseph W. "Gettysburg: The Part Taken in the Battle by the Fifth Corps." *National Tribune*, Apr. 30, 1885.

Linderman, Gerald. *Embattled Courage: The Experience of Combat in the American Civil War*. New York, 1987.

Long, A. L. *Memoirs of Robert E. Lee*. New York, 1887.

Longacre, Edward G. *The Cavalry at Gettysburg: A Tactical Study of Mounted Operations During the Civil War's Pivotal Campaign, 9 June–14 July 1863*. Rutherford, N.J., 1986.

———. "Gouverneur K. Warren—A Personality Profile." *Civil War Times Illustrated*, 10 (Jan. 1972), 11–20.

———. *Joshua Chamberlain: The Soldier and the Man*. Conshohocken, Pa., 1999.

Longstreet, James. *From Manassas to Appomattox*. Philadelphia, 1896.

———. "Causes of Lee's Defeat at Gettysburg." *Southern Historical Society Papers*, 5 (1878), 54–85.

———. "Lee in Pennsylvania." In *Annals of the War*, 414–446.

———. "Lee's Invasion of Pennsylvania." In Johnson and Buel, eds., *Battle and Leaders*. Vol. 3, 244–251.

———. "Lee's Right Wing at Gettysburg." In Johnson and Buel, eds., *Battles and Leaders*. Vol. 3, 339–354.

———. "Letter from General Longstreet." *Southern Historical Society Papers*, 5 (1878), 52–53.

———. "The Mistakes of Gettysburg." *Philadelphia Weekly Times*, Feb. 23, 1878.

McCarthy, Carlton. *Detailed Minutiae of Soldier Life in the Army of Northern Virginia, 1861–1865*. Richmond, 1882.

McClendon, William A. *Recollections of War Times By An Old Veteran While Under Stonewall Jackson and Lieutenant General James Longstreet*. Montgomery, Ala., 1909.

McElfresh, Earl B. *Gettysburg Battlefield: The First Day's Battlefield—Gettysburg, Pennsylvania, 1863*. A Civil War Watercolor Map Series. Olean, New York, 1994.

———. *Gettysburg Battlefield: The Second and Third Days' Battlefield—Gettysburg, Pennsylvania, 1863*. A Civil War Watercolor Map Series. Olean, New York, 1994.

———. *A Theater Map of the Gettysburg Campaign 1863*. A Civil War Watercolor Map Series. Olean, New York, 2003.

McElrath, T. P. "A Soldier's Death." *Army and Navy Journal*, Mar. 13, 1886.

McElroy, John. "The Battle of Gettysburg." *National Tribune*, July 29, 1915.

McKelvey, Blake. "Rochester's Part in the Civil War." *Rochester History*, 23 (Jan. 1961), 1–24.

McLaws, Lafayette. "The Battle of Gettysburg." Address Read Before the Confederate Veterans Association, Apr. 27, 1896. N.p., n.d.

———. "The Battle of Gettysburg." *Philadelphia Weekly Press*, Apr. 21, 1886.

———. "The Federal Disaster on the Left." *Philadelphia Weekly Press*, Aug. 4, 1886.

———. "Gettysburg." *Southern Historical Society Papers*, 7 (1879), 64–90.

———. "McLaws' Division and the Pennsylvania Reserves." *Philadelphia Weekly Press*, Oct. 20, 1886.

McLean, James L. Jr., and Judy W. McLean, eds. *Gettysburg Sources*. 3 vols. Baltimore, 1986–1990.

McMurry, Richard M. *John Bell Hood and the War for Southern Independence*. Lexington, Ky., 1982.

McPherson, James M. *Battle Cry of Freedom: The Civil War Era*. New York and Oxford, 1988.

———. *For Cause and Comrades: Why Men Fought in the Civil War.* New York and Oxford, 1997.

———. *Ordeal by Fire: The Civil War and Reconstruction.* 2nd ed. New York, 1992.

———. *What They Fought For, 1861–1865.* Baton Rouge and London, 1994.

Maihafer, Harry J. "The Decision of Paddy O'Rorke." *Military Review,* 46 (1966), 68–76.

Maine at Gettysburg: Report of the Maine Commissioners. Portland, Maine, 1898.

Marcot, Roy. "Berdan Sharpshooters at Gettysburg." *Gettysburg Magazine,* 1 (July 1989), 35–40.

Mark, Penrose G. *Red, White, and Blue Badge.* Harrisburg, Pa., 1911.

Martin, Augustus P. "Little Round Top." *Gettysburg Compiler,* Oct. 24, 1899.

Maurice, Frederick, ed. *An Aide-de-Camp of Lee: Being the Papers of Colonel Charles Marshall.* Boston, 1927.

Meade, George Gordon [Jr.], ed. *The Life and Letters of George Gordon Meade.* 2 vols. New York, 1913.

———. *With Meade at Gettysburg.* Philadelphia, 1930.

Melcher, H. S. "Little Round Top." *National Tribune,* Mar. 5, 1885.

———. "The Twentieth Maine at Gettysburg." *Lincoln County* [Maine] *News,* March 13, 1885.

———. "The 20th Maine at Little Round Top." In Johnson and Buel, eds., *Battles and Leaders.* Vol. 3, 314–315.

Mehney, Paul D. "Cowardice or Confusion? Norval Welch and the Sixteenth Michigan at Little Round Top." *Michigan History Magazine,* 82 (1998), 60–65.

Michigan at Gettysburg: July 1st, 2nd and 3rd, 1863. Proceedings Incident to the Dedication of the Michigan Monuments upon the Battlefield of Gettysburg, June 12th, 1889. Detroit, 1889.

Miers, Earl Schenck, ed. *Wash Roebling's War.* Newark, Del., 1961.

Miller, Samuel L. "Address." In *Dedication of the Twentieth Maine Monuments at Gettysburg, Oct. 3, 1889.* Waldoboro, Maine, 1891, 31–35.

———. "Address." In Miller, ed., *Reunions,* 10–29.

Miller, Samuel L., ed. *Dedication of the Twentieth Maine Monuments at Gettysburg, October 3, 1889.* Waldoboro, Maine, 1891.

———. *Reunions of the Twentieth Maine Regiment Association at Portland.* Waldoboro, Maine, 1881.

Minnigh, H. N. *History of Company K, 1st (Inft.) Penn'a Reserves,"The Boys Who Fought at Home."* Duncansville, Pa., 1891.

Mitchell, Reid. *Civil War Soldiers.* New York, 1988.

———. "The Infantryman in Combat." *North & South,* 4 (Aug. 2001), 12–21.

———. *The Vacant Chair: The Northern Soldier Leaves Home.* New York, 1993.

Moore, Frank, ed. *Rebellion Record: A Diary of American Events.* 12 vols. New York, 1861–1868.

Moore, Joseph Addison. *Address on the Three Days' Operations of the 147th P.V.V.I. at Gettysburg, July 1, 2, and 3, 1863*. Harrisburg, Pa., 1889.

Morgan, James. "Who Saved Little Round Top?" www.gdg.org/flash.html, Jan. 16, 2003.

Morris, Roy, Jr. *The Better Angel: Walt Whitman in the Civil War*. New York and Oxford, 2000.

Muffly, Joseph W. ed. *The Story of One Regiment: A History of the 148th Pennsylvania Vols*. Des Moines, 1904.

Nash, Eugene A. *A History of the Forty-Fourth Regiment New York Volunteer Infantry in the Civil War, 1861–1865*. Chicago, 1911.

Nevins, Allan. "The Glorious and the Terrible." *Saturday Review*, 44 (Sept. 2, 1961), 9–11, 46–48.

Nevins, Allan, ed. *A Diary of Battle: The Personal Journals of Colonel Charles S. Wainwright, 1861–1865*. New York, 1962.

Nevins, James H., and William B. Styple. *What Death More Glorious: A Biography of Strong Vincent*. Kearny, N.J., 1997.

Nichols, James H. "Letter to Theodore Gerrish." *Lincoln County* [Maine] *News*, Apr. 1882.

Nicholson, John P., et al., eds. *Pennsylvania at Gettysburg*. 4 vols. Harrisburg, Pa., 1893–1939.

North, Edward. *A Memorial of Henry Hastings Curran*. N.d., n.p.

Norton, Oliver W. *Army Letters, 1861–1865*. Chicago, 1903.

———. *The Attack and Defense of Little Round Top*. New York, 1913.

———. "Strong Vincent and His Brigade at Gettysburg." In Bandy and Freeland, eds., *Gettysburg Papers*. Vol. 2, 499–516.

Oates, William C. "Gettysburg—The Battle on the Right." *Southern Historical Society Papers*, 6 (1878), 172–182.

———. *The War Between the Union and the Confederacy and Its Lost Opportunities*. New York and Washington, D.C., 1905.

O'Brien, Kevin. "Col. Strong Vincent and the Eighty-third Pennsylvania Infantry at Little Round Top." *Gettysburg Magazine*, 7 (July 1992), 41–50.

———. "'Stubborn Bravery': The Forgotten 44th New York at Little Round Top." *Gettysburg Magazine*, 15 (July 1996), 31–44.

Oeffinger, John C., ed. *A Soldier's General: The Civil War Letters of Major General Lafayette McLaws*. Chapel Hill and London, 2002.

Owen, William Miller. *In Camp and Battle with the Washington Artillery of New Orleans*. Boston, 1885.

P. M. F. "A Visit to Gettysburg." *Maine Farmer*, Nov. 2, 1882.

Paludan, Phillip Shaw. *"A People's Contest": The Union and the Civil War, 1861–1865*. New York, 1988.

Pardoe, George. "Capture of Little Round Top." *National Tribune*, Apr. 2, 1914.

Pardoe, Rosemary. "John A. Oates: 'No Brothers Loved Each Other Better.'" www.users.globalnet.co.uk/~pardos/JohnOates.html, Mar. 17, 2000.

Paris, Comte de (Louis Philippe Albert d'Orleans), Oliver O. Howard, Henry W. Slocum, and Abner Doubleday. "Gettysburg After Thirty Years." *North American Review*, 152 (1891), 129–147.

Paver, John M. *What I Saw from 1861 to 1864*. Indianapolis, 1906.

Penny, Morris M., and J. Gary Laine. *Struggle for the Round Tops: Law's Alabama Brigade at the Battle of Gettysburg, July 2–3, 1863*. Shippensburg, Pa., 1999.

Perry, W. F. "The Devil's Den." *Confederate Veteran*, 9 (Apr. 1901), 161–163.

Pfanz, Harry W. *Gettysburg—Culp's Hill and Cemetery Hill*. Chapel Hill and London, 1993.

———. *Gettysburg—The First Day*. Chapel Hill, N.C., 2001.

———. *Gettysburg: The Second Day*. Chapel Hill, N.C., 1987.

Phillips, Marion G., and Valerie Phillips Parsegian, eds. *Richard and Rhoda: Letters from the Civil War*. Washington, D.C., 1981.

Phisterer, Frederick. *New York in the War of the Rebellion, 1861 to 1865*. 5 vols. Albany, N.Y., 1912.

Pierrepont, Alice V. D. *Reuben Vaughan Kidd: Soldier of the Confederacy*. Petersburg, Va., 1947.

Piston, William Garrett. "Cross Purposes: Longstreet, Lee, and Confederate Attack Plans for July 3 at Gettysburg." In Gallagher, ed., *Third Day at Gettysburg*, 31–55.

———. *Lee's Tarnished Lieutenant: James Longstreet and His Place in Southern History*. Athens, Ga., 1987.

Platt, Philander. "The Defense of Little Round Top." *National Tribune*, Aug. 5, 1915.

———. "On Little Round Top." *National Tribune*, Apr. 11, 1907.

Polk, J. M. *The North and South American Review*. Austin, 1914.

Polley, J. B. *Hood's Texas Brigade: Its Marches, Its Battles, Its Achievements*. New York, 1910.

———. *A Soldier's Letters to Charming Nellie*. New York and Washington, D.C., 1908.

Porter, John T., ed. *Under the Maltese Cross: Antietam to Appomattox*. Pittsburgh, 1910.

Potter, David M. *The Impending Crisis, 1848–1861*. New York, 1976.

Powell, David A. "A Reconnaissance Gone Awry: Capt. Samuel R. Johnston's Fateful Trip to Little Round Top." *Gettysburg Magazine*, 23 (July 2000), 88–99.

Powell, Robert M. *Recollections of a Texas Colonel at Gettysburg*. Edited by Gregory A. Coco. Gettysburg, Pa., 1990.

———. "With Hood at Gettysburg." *Philadelphia Weekly Times*, December 13, 1884.

Powell, William H. *The Fifth Army Corps (Army of the Potomac)*. New York, 1896.

Prince, Howard L. "Address." In *Dedication of the Twentieth Maine Monuments at Gettysburg, Oct. 3, 1889*. Waldoboro, Maine, 1891, 7–26.

Private, Company H, Fifth Texas Regiment. "Pickett's and Hood's Charges at Gettysburg." *Southern Bivouac*, 3 (1884), 75–78.

Pullen, John J. "Effects of Marksmanship: A Lesson from Gettysburg." *Gettysburg Magazine*, 2 (Jan. 1990), 55–60.

———. "The Gordon-Barlow Story, with Sequel." *Gettysburg Magazine*, 8 (Jan. 1993), 5–8.

———. *Joshua Chamberlain: A Hero's Life and Legacy*. Mechanicsburg, Pa., 1999.

———. *The Twentieth Maine: A Volunteer Regiment in the Civil War*. Philadelphia, 1957.

R.T. "On the Second Day." *National Tribune*, Mar. 22, 1894.

Reardon, Carol. "'I Think the Union Army Had Something to Do With It': The Pickett's Charge Nobody Knows." In Boritt, ed., *The Gettysburg Nobody Knows*, 122–143.

Reiff, W. C. "Coffee on Little Round Top." *National Tribune*, May 19, 1904.

———. "Trials of a Boy in the Gettysburg Campaign." *National Tribune*, Aug. 6, Aug. 13, 1896.

Revised Report of the Select Committee Relative to the Soldiers' National Cemetery, Together with the Accompanying Documents, as Reported to the House of Representatives of the Commonwealth of Pennsylvania. Harrisburg, 1865.

Rice, Edmond Lee, comp. *Civil War Letters of James McDonald Campbell of the 47th Alabama Infantry Regiment*. Waynesville, N.C., n.d.

Rice, James R. "The Rebel Invasion of Pennsylvania: The Truth Regarding Some Important Historical Facts." *New York Times*, Nov. 28, 1863.

Rice, Larry H. "The Role of Colonel Strong Vincent in Determining the Outcome of the Battle of Little Round Top." *Journal of Erie Studies*, 1 (Jan. 1973), 37–56.

Rittenhouse, Benjamin F. "The Battle of Gettysburg as Seen from Little Round Top." In Bandy and Freeland, eds., *Gettysburg Papers*, 2:517–531.

Robertson, Jerome B. *Touched with Valor: Civil War Papers and Casualty Reports of Hood's Texas Brigade*. Ed. Harold B. Simpson. Hillsboro, Tex., 1964.

Robertson, John, ed. *Michigan in the War*. Lansing, Mich., 1882.

Rollins, Richard. "Robert E. Lee and the Hand of God." *North & South*, 6 (Feb. 2003), 13–25.

Ross, Fitzgerald. *Cities and Camps of the Confederate States*. Ed. Richard B. Harwell. Urbana, Ill., 1958.

Royster, Charles. *The Destructive War: William Tecumseh Sherman, Stonewall Jackson, and the Americans*. New York, 1991.

Ryan, James G. "Say It Ain't So." *Blue & Gray*, 13 (June 1996), 34–39.

Sanborn, Lucius. "Through Gettysburg." *National Tribune*, Oct. 22, 1908.

Sandburg, Carl. *Abraham Lincoln: The Prairie Years and the War Years*. One-volume ed. New York, 1954.

Sanderson, W. H. "Repulse of the Rebels from Little Round Top." *National Tribune*, Apr. 2, 1891.

Sauers, Richard A. *A Caspian Sea of Ink: The Meade–Sickles Controversy*. Baltimore, 1989.

Sauers, Richard A., ed. *The Gettysburg Campaign, June 3–August 1, 1863: A Comprehensive, Selectively Annotated Bibliography*. Westport, Conn., 1982.

Scheibert, Justus. "Letter from Major Scheibert, of the Prussian Royal Engineers." *Southern Historical Society Papers*, 5 (1878), 90–93.

———. *Seven Months in Rebel States during the North American War, 1863*. Ed. William Stanley Hoole. Tuscaloosa, Ala., 1958.

Schmidt, Lewis G. *A Civil War History of the 147th Pennsylvania Regiment*. Allentown, Pa., 2000.

Schultz, Jane E. "Healing the Nation: Condolence and Correspondence in Civil War Hospitals." *Proteus*, 17 (Fall 2000), 33–41.

Scott, John O. "The Texans at Gettysburg." *Sherman Register*, Mar. 31, 1897.

Scott, Thomas. "On Little Round Top: A Batteryman's Reminiscences of Gettysburg." *National Tribune*, Aug. 2, 1894.

Sears, Stephen W. *Chancellorsville*. Boston and New York, 1996.

———. *Controversies and Commanders: Dispatches from the Army of the Potomac*. Boston and New York, 1999.

———. "Dan Sickles, Political General." In *Controversies & Commanders*, 197–224.

———. *Gettysburg*. Boston and New York, 2003.

———. "Gouverneur Kemble Warren and Little Phil." In *Controversies & Commanders*, 255–287.

Seiser, Augustus Friedrich. "August Seiser's Civil War Diary." *Rochester Historical Society Publications*, 22 (1944), 174–198.

Sherry, Jeffrey F. " 'The Terrible Impetuosity': The Pennsylvania Reserves at Gettysburg." *Gettysburg Magazine*, 16 (Jan. 1997), 68–80.

Sickles, Daniel E., David McM. Gregg, John Newton, and Daniel Butterfield. "Further Reflections of Gettysburg." *North American Review*, 412 (Mar. 1891), 257–286.

Silliker, Ruth L., ed. *The Rebel Yell and the Yankee Hurrah: The Civil War Journal of a Maine Volunteer*. Camden, Maine, 1985.

Simpson, Harold B. *Hood's Texas Brigade: Lee's Grenadier Guard*. Waco, Tex., 1970.

Smith, James E. "The Devil's Den." *National Tribune*, Mar. 4, 1886.

———. *A Famous Battery and Its Campaigns*. Washington, D.C., 1892.

Smith, Karlton. "Captain Samuel R. Johnston and the Art of Reconnaissance." www.nps.gov/gett/getttour/sidebar/johnston.htm, Oct. 19, 2001.

Smith, M. V. *Reminiscences of the Civil War.* N.d., n.p.

Sorrell, G. Moxley. *Recollections of a Confederate Staff Officer.* New York, 1905.

Southard, Edwin. "The 119th N.Y. at Gettysburg." *National Tribune,* Aug. 19, 1897.

Spear, Abbott, and Ellis Spear. *The 20th Maine at Fredericksburg: The Conflicting Accounts of General Joshua L. Chamberlain and General Ellis Spear.* Union, Maine, 1989.

Spear, Abbott, et al., eds. *The Civil War Recollections of General Ellis Spear.* Orono, Maine, 1997.

Spear, Ellis. "The Element of Accident in War." In Spear and Spear, *20th Maine at Fredericksburg,* 96–103.

———. "The Hoe Cake of Appomattox." Military Order of the Loyal Legion of the United States, Commandery of the District of Columbia, *War Papers* (1913), 387–396.

———. "The Left at Gettysburg." *National Tribune,* June 12, 1913.

———. "The Story of the Raising and Organization of a Regiment of Volunteers in 1862." Military Order of the Loyal Legion of the United States, Commandery of the District of Columbia, *War Papers* (1903), 441–453.

———. "A Visit to Gettysburg." *Lincoln County* [Maine] *News,* June 9, 1882.

Stampp, Kenneth M. *The Peculiar Institution: Slavery in the Ante-Bellum South.* New York, 1956.

Stannard, David E., ed. *Death in America.* Philadelphia, 1975.

Sterkx, H. E. "William C. Jordan and Reconstruction in Bullock County, Alabama." *Alabama Review,* 15 (Jan. 1962), 61–75.

Stevens, C. A. *Berdan's United States Sharpshooters in the Army of the Potomac, 1861–1865.* St. Paul, Minn., 1892.

Stevens, John W. *Reminiscences of the Civil War.* Hillsboro, Tex., 1902.

Stewart, Salome Myers. "Recollections of the Battle of Gettysburg." *Philadelphia North American,* July 7, 1900.

Stocker, Jeffrey D., ed. *From Huntsville to Appomattox: R. T. Coles's History of 4th Regiment, Alabama Volunteer Infantry, C.S.A., Army of Northern Virginia.* Knoxville, 1996.

Storrick, W. C. *Gettysburg: The Place, the Battles, the Outcome.* Harrisburg, Pa., 1932.

Styple, William B., ed. *With a Flash of His Sword: The Writings of Major Holman S. Melcher, 20th Maine Infantry.* Kearny, N.J., 1994.

Swanberg, W. A. *Sickles the Incredible.* New York, 1956.

Swinton, William. *Campaigns of the Army of the Potomac.* New York, 1866.

Sypher, Josiah R. *History of the Pennsylvania Reserve Corps.* Lancaster, Pa., 1864.

Taylor, Emerson Gifford. *Gouverneur Kemble Warren: The Life and Letters of an American Soldier.* Boston, 1932.

Taylor, George B. *The Soldiers' Almanac for 1863*. Staunton, Va., 1863.

Taylor, John Dykes. *History of the 48th Alabama Volunteer Infantry Regiment, C.S.A.* University, Ala., 1985.

Taylor, Walter H. *Four Years with General Lee*. New York, 1877.

Thomas, Emory M. *Bold Dragoon: The Life of J. E. B. Stuart*. New York, 1986.

———. *Robert E. Lee*. New York, 1995.

Thompson, O. R. Howard, and William H. Rauch. *History of the "Bucktails."* Philadelphia, 1906.

Tibbetts, Elsie Dorothea. *From Maine to Gettysburg, 1863–1913*. Bangor, Maine, 1913.

Tilney, Robert. *My Life in the Army: Three Years and a Half with the Fifth Army Corps, Army of the Potomac, 1862–1865*. Philadelphia, 1912.

Todd, George T. *First Texas Regiment*. Waco, Tex., 1963.

———. "Recollections of Gettysburg." *Confederate Veteran*, 8 (1900), 240.

Tremain, Henry Edwin. *Two Days of War: A Gettysburg Narrative and Other Excursions*. New York, 1905.

Trowbridge, L. S. *Michigan Troops in the Battle of Gettysburg*. N.p., 1889.

Trudeau, Noah Andre. *Gettysburg: A Testing of Courage*. New York, 2002.

Trulock, Alice Rains. *In the Hands of Providence: Joshua L. Chamberlain and the American Civil War*. Chapel Hill and London, 1992.

Tucker, A. W. "From Comrade Tucker." *National Tribune*, Feb. 4, 1886.

———. "Orange Blossoms." *National Tribune*, Jan. 21, 1886.

Tucker, Glenn. *High Tide at Gettysburg: The Campaign in Pennsylvania*. Indianapolis, 1958.

———. *Lee and Longstreet at Gettysburg*. Indianapolis, 1968.

Tucker, Phillip Thomas. *Storming Little Round Top: The 15th Alabama and Their Fight for the High Ground, July 2, 1863*. Cambridge, Mass., 2002.

Tuffs, R. W. "First on Little Round Top." *National Tribune*, Sept. 1, 1910.

U.S. Congress. *Report of the Joint Committee on the Conduct of the War at the Second Session, Thirty-Eighth Congress, Army of the Potomac, General Meade*. Washington, D.C., 1865.

U.S. War Department. *The War of the Rebellion: A Compilation of the Official Records of the Union and Confederate Armies*. 70 vols. in 128 parts, index, and atlas. Washington, D.C., 1880–1901.

Vaughan, Turner. "Diary of Turner Vaughan, Co. 'C,' 4th Alabama Regiment, C.S.A." *Alabama Historical Quarterly*, 18 (1956), 573–604.

Vincent, Boyd. "The Attack and Defense of Little Round Top." In Bandy and Freeland, eds., *Gettysburg Papers*. Vol. 2, 485–498.

Walker, Elijah. "The 4th Maine at Gettysburg." *National Tribune*, Apr. 8, 1886.

Wallace, Willard. *Soul of the Lion: A Biography of Joshua L. Chamberlain*. New York, 1960.

Walter, Thomas F. "Personal Recollections and Experiences of an Obscure Soldier." *Grand Army Scout and Soldiers' Mail*, Sept. 13, 1884.

Ward, W. C. "Incidents and Personal Experiences on the Battlefield at Gettysburg." *Confederate Veteran*, 8 (1900), 345–349.

Warner, Ezra J. *Generals in Blue*. Baton Rouge, 1964.

———. *Generals in Gray*. Baton Rouge, 1959.

Warren, Emily F. "General Warren on Little Round Top." *Century*, 33 (Mar. 1887), 803–804.

Wert, Jeffry D. *General James Longstreet: The Confederacy's Most Controversial Soldier—A Biography*. New York, 1993.

West, John C. *A Texan in Search of a Fight*. Waco, Tex., 1901. Reprint, 1969.

West, Oscar W. "On Little Round Top." *National Tribune*, Nov. 22, 1906.

White, Russell C., ed. *The Civil War Diary of Wyman S. White, First Sergeant of Company F, 2nd United States Sharpshooter Regiment, 1861–1865*. Baltimore, 1991.

White, W. T. "First Texas at Gettysburg." *Confederate Veteran*, 30 (1922), 185, 197.

Whittelsey, E. L. "Vincent's Brigade on Little Round Top." *National Tribune*, Nov. 5, 1908.

Williams, George F. *Bullet and Shell*. New York, 1883.

Williams, T. Harry. *Lincoln and His Generals*. New York, 1952.

Williamson, R. L. "At Gettysburg: Another of Weed's Brigade Tells What They Did on Round Top." *National Tribune*, Sept. 1, 1892.

Wills, Garry. *Lincoln at Gettysburg: The Words That Remade America*. New York, 1992.

Winslow, George B. "On Little Round Top." In McLean and McLean, eds., *Gettysburg Sources*. Vol. 3, 150–155.

Wittenberg, Eric J. "John Buford and the Gettysburg Campaign." *Gettysburg Magazine*, 11 (July 1994), 19–55.

Woods, James A. "Defending Watson's Battery." *Gettysburg Magazine*, 9 (July 1993), 40–47.

———. "Humphreys' Division's Flank March to Little Round Top." *Gettysburg Magazine*, 6 (Jan. 1991), 59–61.

Woodward, Evan Morrison. *Our Campaigns: The Second Pennsylvania Reserve Volunteers*. Philadelphia, 1865.

Wright, James R. "'I Will Take the Responsibility': Strong Vincent Moves to Little Round Top—Fact or Fiction?" *Gettysburg Magazine*, 25 (Jan. 2002), 48–60.

———. "Time on Little Round Top." *Gettysburg Magazine*, 2 (Jan. 1990), 51–54.

———. "Vincent's Brigade on Little Round Top." *Gettysburg Magazine*, 1 (July 1989), 41–44.

Wright, James R., ed. "A Letter of Oliver W. Norton." *Gettysburg Magazine*, 1 (July 1989), 41–44.

Yeary, Mamie, comp. *Reminiscences of the Boys in Gray, 1866–1865*. Dallas, Tex., 1912.

Youker, J. Clayton, ed. *The Military Memoirs of Captain Henry Cribben of the 140th New York Volunteers*. N.p., 1911.

Youngblood, William. "Personal Observations at Gettysburg." *Confederate Veteran*, 19 (1911), 286–287.

———. "Unwritten History of the Gettysburg Campaign." *Southern Historical Society Papers*, 38 (1910), 312–318.

INDEX

Page numbers in *italics* refer to illustrations. Numbered regiments are listed in alphabetical order according to the spelled-out form of their numerals (i.e., 15th Alabama is alphabetized as Fifteenth Alabama).